ABRIDGMENT OF THE OQUAL CYCLE

THE 84-YEAR RHYTHM OF HUMAN CIVILIZATION

FIRST EDITION | 2023

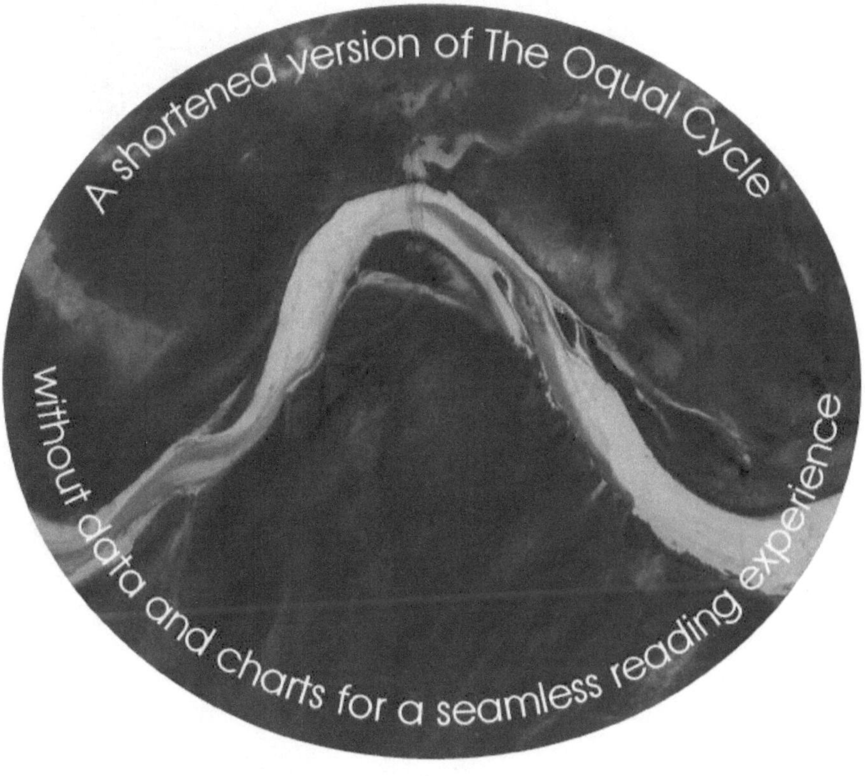

A shortened version of The Oqual Cycle without data and charts for a seamless reading experience

OQUANNIUM XPRESS

AMJAD FAROOQ

www.oqualcycle.com

ABRIDGMENT OF THE OQUAL CYCLE

THE 84-YEAR RHYTHM OF HUMAN CIVILIZATION

FIRST EDITION | 2023

www.oqualcycle.com

Copyright © 2023 by Amjad Farooq | All rights reserved

The content of this book is for informational and educational purposes only. It is not intended to provide medical, legal, financial, or any other advice or consultation. The author declares no conflict of interest nor was this work financially supported by any private or public organization. The author declares no affiliation to any religious, social, economic, political, or any other organization. The author is providing this book and its contents on an "as-is" basis. The author makes no representations or warranties of any kind. No part of this book may be reproduced, recorded, or transmitted in any form without express written permission of the author. Although the author has made every effort to ensure that the information provided in this book is accurate, he does not assume and hereby disclaims liability for any loss, damage, or disruption caused by errors, or any other inconsistencies—whether they result as a consequence of the use and application of any of the contents of this book, or from negligence, accident, or due to any other cause.

Book Essentials

Final Version on 2023-08-18
First Published on 2023-04-23
Published by Oquannium Xpress
Dimensions: 6"W x 9"H x 1"D
Length: 390 pages (142 kilowords)
Approximate Reading Time: 18 hours

Book Formats

ISBN 978-1-960887-04-7 | Ebook (EPUB)
ISBN 978-1-960887-08-5 | Digitalbook (PDF)
ISBN 978-1-960887-06-1 | Audiobook (MP3)
ISBN 978-1-960887-05-4 | Paperback (B&W)

Book Page

www.oqualcycle.com

OQUANNIUM XPRESS
Miami • Florida • USA
www.oquannium.com

CONTENTS

Preface	....	6
Prologue	....	9
Epilogue	....	381
Literature	....	387

|1|	Essential Principles	....	28
|1.1|	Physical Basis	....	31
|1.2|	Central Dogma	....	47
|1.3|	Generational Impact	....	71
|2|	Political Waves	....	79
|2.1|	Global Hegemony	....	82
|2.2|	Global Politics	....	128
|2.3|	Global Reset	....	144
|3|	Cultural Waves	....	160
|3.1|	Demographic Trends	....	162
|3.2|	Cultural Dysphoria	....	182
|3.3|	Consumption Mania	....	200
|3.4|	Institutional Fraud	....	213
|4|	Xenophobic Waves	....	241
|4.1|	White Supremacy	....	245
|4.2|	Global Anti-Semitism	....	262
|4.3|	Hindu-Muslim Conflict	....	283
|5|	Economic Waves	....	302
|5.1|	National Income	....	305
|5.2|	National Debt	....	309
|5.3|	Money Printing	....	318
|5.4|	Stock Market	....	324
|6|	Climate Waves	....	333
|6.1|	Temperature	....	337
|6.2|	Droughts	....	342
|6.3|	Floods	....	350
|6.4|	Storms	....	357
|6.5|	Climateganda	....	360

PREFACE

Today, almost every nation-on-earth is teetering on the brink of a societal meltdown as it finds itself in the midst of a sociopolitical upheaval, the like of which has not hitherto been witnessed in our lifetime.

Yet, hardly anyone realizes that like a winter that returns every year, such a concerted turmoil across the globe is also periodic due to what I have dubbed the "oqual cycle"—with the adjective "oqual" coined from Latin and literally meaning "84-year" with the oqual cycle therefore essentially being the "84-year cycle".

Admittedly, most public institutions around the world not only seem to have lost credibility but they have also seemingly become irrelevant.

Such a once-in-a-lifetime synchronization of dire sociopolitical straits across much of the globe is no coincidence but rather written in the stars thanks to the mysterious spell of oqual cycle on human civilization.

Not only here at home in America but friends and frenemies from every corner of the world also confide in me:

> "What happened to our civil liberties that we once had taken for granted during much of our earlier lives?"
>
> "What happened to what were once our rock-solid institutions that provided stability and direction in the face of adversity?"
>
> "What happened to the good old institution of marriage and our moral compass that once defined who we were?"
>
> "What happened to the rather upbeat zeitgeist of our earlier lives?"

Well, they have all been temporarily oqualled (or silenced) rather than being forever quelled due to the dire spell of oqual cycle that began a quarter-of-a-century ago almost at the outset of 21st century.

However, the good old days are just round the corner and inching ever closer so as to herald the beginning of a new dawn of hope and prosperity after the dust from the looming World War III has settled in about a decade or so as the oqual cycle draws to a close.

What in the world is oqual cycle?

On the basis of scientific reasoning and mathematical modeling of history over the past 600 years, the oqual cycle posits that human civilization seemingly undergoes a sweeping global reset once every 84 years on average in order to purge itself of a plethora of wrongdoings from the societal ills through excesses and imbalances to transgressions amassed over that multidecadal period.

Unfortunately, there is no free music as one must pay the piper.

Indeed, such a societal reboot (or revitalization) is typically accomplished through a global conflict with the potential to not only wreak havoc but also strike fear into the hearts and minds of people on an apocalyptic scale so that they can put their sociopolitical differences aside and come together for the common good of the world at large.

The oqual cycle therefore lends human society a subtle albeit deadly mechanism to break ties with its dysfunctional past in order to begin anew rather than being held hostage from moving forward under its own weight, or even worse, continue down the rabbit hole in perpetuity with the potential for self-destruction.

More specifically, the oqual cycle posits that the sociopolitical progress of human civilization does not follow a linear course but rather it waxes and wanes in a cyclical manner over a period of 84 years due to what appears to be its coupling with the orbiting of the second outermost planet Uranus around the Sun.

Put another way, the overall human progress waxes and wanes in a sinusoidal manner over the course of oqual cycle in a similar fashion to the waxing and waning of the Moon over the course of a lunar month.

In fact, almost every facet of human civilization from politics through economy to climate appears to be beholden to an 84-year rhythm that propagates in sync with the oqual cycle in a manner reminiscent of our daily and annual rituals.

The oqual cycle is thus essentially a lower-order harmonic of the daily and annual cycles in that the trio seemingly act in a concerted fashion to orchestrate the full gamut of our extraordinary and complex lives.

Of particular note is the salient observation that Uranus appears to exert a subtle control over human civilization by virtue of its ability to modulate the terrestrial climate in a sinusoidal fashion in sync with the oqual cycle in a manner akin to the annual climate cycle dictated by the orbiting of Earth around the Sun.

Admittedly, the unprecedented rise in global temperature witnessed over the past quarter-of-a-century is in no small part due to the Uranian spell on our planet and, as such, global warming is expected to not only plateau out but also head south as the current oqual cycle draws to a close over the next decade or so.

Likewise, the wrath of natural disasters from droughts through flooding to storms with an increasing frequency and intensity seen over the past quarter-of-a-century also seems to be largely due to the cyclical flux of our planet undergoing a self-cleansing process under the watchful eye of oqual cycle rather than a direct consequence of human activities.

While the drummed-up specter of global warming seems to be nothing more than a hyperbole hatched by devious actors around the globe in order to advance their propaganda, there appears to be nevertheless a seemingly upward trend in global temperature over the long run though far from being anywhere near as apocalyptic as that forecast by climate scientists.

Importantly, the oqual cycle not only serves as a model par excellence for making sense of the rapid climate change swamping our planet but also the ongoing sociopolitical trials-and-tribulations of our own times that in no small part elicit a wistful yearning for the rather sweet memories of our recent past from the second half of the 20th century.

To say that the oqual cycle represents a Rosetta stone of human civilization that should help us navigate our future with rational wisdom in lieu of blissful ignorance would be to put it mildly.

Taken together, The Oqual Cycle is a must-read for everyone in that it not only transcends national, ethnic, political, religious, and demographic boundaries but it will also become your most-trusted companion to guide you as you navigate uncharted landscape of your life—the younger you are, the more relevant the oqual cycle is to your life.

PROLOGUE

In 1971, I took my first breath in a nondescript abode planted in the middle of nowhere and shrouded in utter wilderness in rural Mirpur—a city located in the foothills of Himalayas in the northeastern region of Azad Kashmir in Pakistan.

Since my early childhood, I have been awestruck by stories of uncannily-similar upheavals paying us homage time and again.

My beloved grandmother often used to share anecdotal accounts of her forefathers and their belief that every century was like a revolving year with many shared features but on an extended timescale.

While attending university in England during the 1990s, I would become familiar with the oft-repeated cliché: "History repeats itself!"

After moving to America as a postdoctoral scholar a couple of years before the 21st century rolled in, I would learn that while history does not repeat, it nevertheless rhymes and chimes as if it were an integral part of our DNA.

More recently, I would learn that the rise and fall of great powers typically occurs over a cyclical pattern of roughly between 80-120 years as theorized by the Polish-American political scientist George Modelski in his 1987 book titled "Long Cycles in World Politics" [1]—though Modelski's model is based on some questionable data and misinterpretation of historical facts, not to mention that the author is obsessed with the notion of each new century ushering in the rise of a new hegemonic power at odds with reality and, in doing so, he completely dehegemonizes the towering roles that the likes of Spain and France played in shaping the world during much of the 16th and 18th centuries, respectively.

Next, I would stumble upon the work of American historians William Strauss and Neil Howe published in their 1997 book titled "The Fourth Turning" [2]—although difficult to read particularly with regard to its biblical approach rather than a scientific one, I was nevertheless able to curate the central premise of Strauss-Howe model that can be summed up as human civilization cycling through a long human life that spans a period of between 80-100 years with each cycle ending in a crisis of epic proportions.

However, according to the mathematically-driven work of Russian-American ecologist-turned-anthropologist Peter Turchin published in his 2016 book titled "Ages of Discord" [3], such cycles of human civilization are envisioned to last between 150-200 years—though Turchin's model is based on historical records that barely stretch back three centuries and it is therefore not clear how the author can make such outlandish claims against the backdrop of a rather limited timespan of data at his fingertips.

Tellingly, the aforementioned books paint a very confusing picture that leaves one wandering whether the cycles of human civilization last 80, 100, 120, 150, or 200 years—or, perhaps, they occur randomly without a fixed periodicity in which case the whole thing becomes somewhat murky stripping a logical mind of any real enthusiasm of paying heed to such doctrine.

Being a logically-driven mind to the quartic power coupled with an analytical and perfectionist approach to life thanks to my Virgoan cosmotype, I was understandably dumbstruck by the lack of a methodical strategy adopted by the authors in the aforementioned triad of models proposed for the cyclical nature of human civilization.

Admittedly, genuine cycles such as our daily and annual rhythms operate over a predefined timespan, and cycles without a fixed periodicity represent nothing more than a conjecture rather than a serious scientific framework.

That line of reasoning coupled with a nagging curiosity would lead me to launch my own investigation to look into what is arguably the single most important aspect of understanding our society, and through this highly-rewarding process, I was finally able to connect the dots between time and space as I developed the theory of oqual cycle using mathematical modeling and scientific reasoning to account for the cyclical nature of human civilization in a succinct and logical manner on the basis of tons of historical data both at qualitative and quantitative level.

In order to fully comprehend the recurring spell of oqual cycle on our lives, this book therefore delves deep into the causes that bring about eerily-similar revolutions in human civilization every 84 years on average.

Nevertheless, the book provides a logical rather than an exhaustive treatment of history and how it continues to shape human civilization with particular emphasis on connecting the dots between archetypal (or quintessential) events and trends that seem to repeat at remarkably regular intervals of 84 years on average.

In other words, the major historical events represent constituent elements of a larger multi-tier 84-year cascade rather than isolated cases.

Unlike the rise and decline of human civilizations over the course of millennia as documented by the works of European scholars such as Oswald Spengler [4] and Arnold Toynbee [5], the oqual cycle directly impacts our own lives due to the fact that its periodicity equates to an average human lifespan.

Needless to say, the oqual cycle bears huge implications for us at an individual level and how we view the world at large.

In a manner that our understanding of the cyclical nature of a day or a year helps us plan our lives accordingly, the oqual cycle likewise unpacks our own successes and failures in life in that they very much happen to be an intricate function of the ups and downs in our society over which we have little or no control.

Why certain generations for example consistently view the world through rose-colored glasses while others are flabbergasted at their naivete also becomes crystal clear due to the differential spell of oqual cycle on our lives—it matters a lot not only where we are born but also when we are born.

In light of the ongoing sociopolitical bedlam across the globe showing no signs of easing, The Oqual Cycle bears the potential to become our best companion in its ability to guide us through our worst insecurities yet lend a comfort with the promise of a new dawn of optimism and prosperity in the not-too-distant-future.

The Oqual Cycle is indeed indispensable for the sociopolitical health of nations.

It should serve as a reminder to the-powers-that-be to avoid falling into economic quagmires such as debt trap and money printing at the wrong time lest they take the whole nation down with them into a deep canyon between a rock and a hard place with self-destruction all but guaranteed.

Should great powers pay heed to The Oqual Cycle, the quasi-apocalyptic wars that have hitherto paid us homage at least once in a lifetime could altogether be averted.

The Oqual Cycle is also a godsend for the well-being of our planet in that it identifies the disruptive forces that must be kept at bay lest their cooperative action leaves our world on the precipice of a mental collapse.

A once-in-a-millennium book, The Oqual Cycle will not only lead to a paradigm shift in our perception of human civilization but it is also a must-read for an intellectual and curious mind craving for an answer to what in the world is going on, why it is going on, and when they can expect to see the back of hard times that somehow appear to have become endemic to our society since the outset of 21st century.

On a personal note, I wish I had been cognizant of such a phenomenal aspect of our society from an early age so that I had been well-prepared in advance of the trials-and-tribulations of my prime years rather than making sense of them now in a retrospective manner.

In all, the book is divided into six chapters.

The first chapter serves as a primer for understanding the essential principles of oqual cycle.

Once this prerequisite has been met, the readers are fully equipped to browse other chapters in any sequence they so wish in order to gain an in-depth understanding of oqual cycle with respect to key facets of human civilization such as politics, culture, xenophobia, economy, and climate.

All told, the book walks the reader through the current sociopolitical upheavals unfolding across the globe and what potentially lies on the other side of the bedlam after all the nuclear dust has settled and humanity once again begins to rise from the ashes over the next decade or so courtesy of the mysterious spell of Uranus on our planet.

What has Uranus got to do with all this?

CONCURRENCE BETWEEN URANIAN SOLSTICES AND GLOBAL RESETS

Once every 84 years, Uranus enters its southern winter solstice—the southern midwinter point when the southern pole of Uranus is minimally exposed to direct sunlight over the course of its one full turn around the Sun.

In line with what humanity has endured over the past five centuries, the year during which such a solstice occurs appears to be the annus horribilis due to the fact that it typically coincides with the oqual cycle reaching its crescendo and unleashing the worst of its destructive rage upon our civilization.

Since the birth of Modern Age in 1451, the annus horribilis of oqual cycle has befallen humanity in 1524, 1608, 1692, 1776, 1860, and 1944.

Spaced apart by exactly 84 years, those were really-really horrible times that amounted to nothing short of a hell-on-earth and the like of which is encountered only once-in-a-lifetime.

Not only was each annus horribilis noted above flanked by a synchronized-and-synergized wave of deadly conflicts unfolding across the globe but also bore witness to civil wars breaking out across many nations and culminating with the establishment of a nouveau sociopolitical system under a new world order.

For example, 1944 was sandwiched between the destructive World War II (1939-1945) coupled with the dreadful Holocaust (1941-1945) on one side, and the bloody Indian Partition (1947) along with the chaotic births of the State of Israel (1948) and People's Republic of China (1949) on the other—America would emerge as the new hegemon taking up the reins from Britain.

Likewise, 1860 was flanked by the deadly Crimean War (1853-1856) between Russia and Turkiye coupled with the Indian Mutiny (1857) against the British colonialists on one side, and the American Civil War (1861-1865) along with the Franco-Mexican War (1861-1867) on the other—Britain would hold onto its global dominance though closely checked by the rapid rise of America just as the 19th century bid farewell.

On the same token, 1776 was preceded by the Russo-Turkish War (1768-1774) and followed by the American Independence War (1775-1783) coupled with the Anglo-French War (1778-1783)—America would become a sovereign nation and Britain emerged as the new hegemon taking up the baton from France.

Prior to that, 1692 was straddled with the deadly Nine Years War (1688-1697) between France and Netherlands with the latter supported by various European powers including England due to its own existential crisis of the Glorious Revolution (1688-1689)—France would emerge as the new hegemon taking up the mantle from Netherlands.

Before that, 1608 was marred by the consequential sixth phase of the Eighty Years War (1599-1609) between Spain and Netherlands with each supported by various European powers—Netherlands would emerge as the new hegemon taking the helm from Spain.

Finally, 1524 was underscored by the 1529 Treaty of Cambrai in the midst of the fifth phase of the so-called Italian Wars (1521-1530) pitting Spain against France for the control of Italian peninsula as well as global dominance with each side supported by various European powers—Spain would emerge as the new hegemon and Portugal having passed on the torch.

Why should I care about our checkered past?

OUR SOCIOPOLITICAL TITANIC HAS ALREADY HIT THE ICEBERG WITH OUR LEADERS SCRAMBLING TO AVERT THE UTTER CARNAGE WAITING AHEAD

Once every 84 years on average, human society reaches a nadir when it becomes boxed-cornered-and-trapped under its own weight of a plethora of wrongdoings from the societal ills through excesses and imbalances to transgressions amassed over the course of oqual cycle.

This self-inflicted trauma is further exacerbated by Mother Nature which seemingly reserves the worst of its scourge on humanity by virtue of its ability to unleash a barrage of natural disasters just when we are at our worst and least prepared.

Such synergism between Mother Nature and humanity's unraveling plunge the society into an even deeper sociopolitical crisis.

Today, that is exactly the status quo around much of the globe as sociopolitical quandary of virtually every nation has turned into an insoluble Rubik's cube.

Not only that but many nations even believe that they are being battered by Mother Nature for their excesses and imbalances though they understand not that such retribution is nothing more than a stroll in the park compared to what awaits them ahead over the next decade or so.

Arguably, our sociopolitical system has been hitting a new low with each passing year with no signs of troughing out since the outset of 21st century.

In metaphorical terms, our sociopolitical Titanic hit the iceberg nearly a quarter-of-a-century ago and since then it has only continued to sink with no sign of lifeboats anywhere in plain sight.

Ironically, every sociopolitical step taken by our leaders to fix the leak has only served to exacerbate the plight of our sinking Titanic due to the fact that such a Band-Aid has always been a slippery slope.

Instead of sending out an SOS call to the masses to come forward and make sacrifices during what have been rather difficult times over the past quarter-of-a-century, the-powers-that-be have been going out of their towers to make life even easier for hoi polloi in an attempt to remain politically popular rather than what was best for their nation.

For example, over the past couple of decades, the global financial system has been flooded with decatrillions-of-dollars of printed money coupled with virtually every nation taking on ever more debt to purportedly address the dire economic straits of the masses.

Yet, such generous handouts have been akin to an addict being given a license to continue to overdose on heroin in that they only served to fuel the reckless lifestyle of hoi polloi having become accustomed to living beyond their means and becoming an ever-rising burden on society.

Just as the addict encounters their rendezvous with destiny once-in-a-lifetime, so does humanity as a whole so as to purge and cleanse our society of its reckless violations of the laws of nature in lieu of continuing down the rabbit hole in perpetuity with the potential for self-destruction.

Such a proofreading mechanism, which can also be viewed as a reality check or quality control, revitalizes human civilization by enabling it to break ties with its dysfunctional past so as to begin anew just as the oqual cycle moves past its annus horribilis.

When is the next annus horribilis due?

THE NEXT ANNUS HORRIBILIS IS LURKING ON THE HORIZON

While the oqual cycle is not set in stone, it nevertheless begins and ends with each full turn of Uranus around the Sun once every 84 years—a timespan dubbed "oquannium" that is to oqual cycle what annum is to an annual cycle.

In particular, the oqual cycle can be viewed as a tale of two diametrically-antagonistic halves: a constructive phase of relative peace followed by a destructive spell of sociopolitical upheaval, with each lasting some 42 years.

Having nominally begun in 1955 and set to bid farewell in 2038, the current oqual cycle is in the latter stages of its destructive spell with the year 2028 in line to become the next annus horribilis—the year during which Uranus is poised to enter its next southern winter solstice.

If 2028 is the annus horribilis of the current oqual cycle, then 2039 will be the annus mirabilis of the next one in a manner similar to 1955, 1871, 1787, 1703, 1619, 1535, and 1451 since the outset of Modern Age.

While annus horribilis is indicative of the fact that the worst of the fallout from our wrongdoings amassed over the course of oqual cycle is already upon us or approaching its crescendo, annus mirabilis all but guarantees the beginning of good times if they have not already arrived on our shores years earlier than anticipated.

Taken together, the ongoing sociopolitical crisis will soon morph into a global conflict of epic proportions that will end no earlier than annus horribilis (2028) of the current oquannium (1955-2038) but by no later than annus mirabilis (2039) of the next cycle (2039-2122) so as to acquiesce to a new dawn of hope and prosperity—such a forecast is deduced with a high degree of confidence in line with the recurring spell of oqual cycle on our civilization.

As the saying goes, no pain no gain.

Indeed, a large-scale global conflict with the potential to not only wreak havoc on an astronomical scale but also strike fear into the hearts and minds of people appears to be a prerequisite for breaking ties with our past and old traditions so as to revitalize human society and usher in a brighter tomorrow under a new world order spearheaded by a nation that has proved itself as the manufacturing powerhouse head-and-shoulders above its competitors.

Without such a real-life horror show a la hell-on-earth, people on opposite sides of the sociopolitical spectrum refuse to see eye-to-eye in order to come to a consensus necessary to rid the society of its wrongdoings amassed over the course of oqual cycle.

In particular, when a society has gone astray and lost its moral compass as is the case across much of the globe today, havoc combined with fear appear to be blessings-in-disguise in that they serve to jumpstart a new beginning so as to reset our sociopolitical system.

On the one hand, fear appears to be an incredibly-effective therapy for deranged individuals to come to their senses and exercise humility after having lost the moral compass or having become accustomed to living beyond their means and a burden on society over the course of oqual cycle.

On the other hand, havoc seems to facilitate the removal of old traditions so as to usher in new technologies coupled with creating megatons of highly-rewarding jobs that motivate otherwise discouraged individuals to get back to work just as the human society sets about rebuilding from scratch.

As for the loss of human life on a humongous scale, it seems that biology is also in on the act collaborating closely with the oqual cycle to pull off its own magic of pitting humanity against a deadly audit so as to proofread its own product before continuing further afield and, in doing so, ensuring the survival of the fittest at the expense of the weak.

No matter how advanced and progressive our civilization may come to be viewed as, it seems that humanity simply cannot shake off the oversight of biology and the wrath of nature.

While it pains me a great deal to deliver such a dire forecast of what lies ahead in the near future, I am only a messenger who is reverberating echoes from the past that seem to be repetitive and unavoidable at remarkably regular intervals of 84 years on average.

Still, a new dawn of good-old-shiny-happy days is on the horizon and will likely arrive some time during the 2030s in a manner akin to the beginning of relatively prosperous times during the 1950s, 1870s, and 1790s savored on American soil and across much of the globe.

However, the ongoing sociopolitical upheaval will get multiples worse over the next decade or so before we see the light at the end of the oqual tunnel.

In other words, the human society not only finds itself in a bind but has also been rolling downhill since the outset of 21st century and it will continue to do so for at least another decade before it reverses course and begins to climb uphill once again with a renewed vigor just as it did some 84 years ago during the 1950s.

In particular, the decade centered on annus horribilis (2028) of the current oquannium (1955-2038) does not bear good omens as it will not only be paralyzed by deadly conflicts and civil wars unfolding across the globe but the odds of a nuclear war breaking out over that period are also statistically high.

With that ominous decade roughly stretching from 2023-2033 having just kicked off, we can already see the tip of the nuclear iceberg threatening to capsize our civilization like never before.

While the countdown has already begun, many are quick to dismiss the utter bedlam waiting ahead as nothing more than fear-mongering on the pretense that none of such doom and gloom has ever borne fruition in their lives except that it only occurs once-in-a-lifetime.

Admittedly, hardly any adult who faced the scourge of World War II (1939-1945) is alive today nor any adult today will be alive some 84 years from now when annus horribilis (2112) of the next oquannium (2039-2122) rolls in.

What is however indisputable is the fact that when one makes a deal with the devil, they cannot expect to have an angel waiting for them on the other side.

Why is a nuclear war all but a mathematical certainty?

TRILLIONS WERE NOT INVESTED IN NUKES JUST SO THAT THEY WOULD BE FOR THE SHOWROOM

As the oqual cycle draws to a close, with the current one poised to do so in 2038, the battle for determining the new world order gets under way across the globe so as to usher in a new dawn under a nouveau sociopolitical system.

Not only does such a global conflict straddling the annus horribilis outshine its predecessor due to the emergence of ever more destructive killing machines over the course of oqual cycle but the world leaders also do not shy away from using the most lethal arsenal at their disposal as they lock horns to settle the contest for the control of the world and its resources.

Since the dawn of the current oquannium (1955-2038), global powers have hitherto funneled trillions-of-dollars toward developing a paraphernalia of nukes in order to gain a military edge over their rivals.

To believe that such apocalyptic weapons are only for the showroom would be to sweep history under the rug.

Paradoxically, that ought to be a huge credit to humanity for being so resourceful in that it does not invest in something it will never use.

Still, when the specter of a nuclear war is contemplated, it is often viewed as nothing more than a razzmatazz better suited for science fiction than becoming a real-life documentary.

Yet, the same audience would put the probability of a nuclear war befalling humanity at 10% in any given year—little they realize that such odds amount to a mathematical certainty of a nuclear war breaking out over the next decade.

Importantly, the hope that the most destructive weapon at one's disposal will not be unleashed is nothing more than a folly that has come back to haunt humanity time and again.

Nevertheless, the looming nuclear war will in all likelihood be a tactical one with the potential to turn a few cities into ghost towns rather than an all-out apocalypse for humans have a built-in evolutionary mechanism to exercise restraint and tamp down collateral damage when faced with utter annihilation.

The notion that humanity could one day nuke itself into extinction is nothing more than a hyperbole.

Still, the looming threat of a societal collapse is not lost on those with means—while they are yet to learn about the dire spell of oqual cycle on human civilization, many uber-wealthy individuals have already begun to shop for either giant bunkers or citizenships in far-flung safe-havens in preparation for all hell breaking lose on earth over the next decade or so.

Although such wealthy fools and their entourage of financial advisors are drawing parallels between today and the zeitgeist of 1980s, we are in fact currently traveling through a similar time and space as we did some 84 years ago vis-à-vis our sociopolitical system in line with the oqual theory supported by a barrage of eye-popping data rather than opinion.

Thus, the next decade or so will be very much akin to the 1940s in a manner reminiscent of recurring annual seasons.

Just as the annual winter does not necessarily have to replicate its predecessor, the same also holds true for the oqual cycle as it draws to a close.

While the looming global conflict is unavoidable, it is hard to conclude if it will be a shadow of World War II (1939-1945) or whether it will make its predecessor look like a dress rehearsal.

Still, given the 800-pound gorilla of our wrongdoings amassed over the past several decades, it is hard to imagine anything other than the latter outcome for the magnitude and intensity of the global conflict befalling humanity at the dusk of oqual cycle appear to be proportional to the extent of our deviations from the laws of nature as evidenced through the unfolding of one crisis after another with each plunging us ever deeper into a canyon without a rescue over the past quarter-of-a-century.

Will the ongoing Russia-Ukraine War turn into a full-fledged World War III?

NATO HAS ALREADY STARTED FIGHTING RUSSIA THROUGH A PROXY WAR

While the seeds for the ongoing dire sociopolitical straits were planted nearly quarter-of-a-century ago by America and its European lapdogs via a double whammy of first through the expansion of NATO and then closely dogged by the decades-long self-destructive 9/11 Wars, they have finally begun to sprout around the globe with a vengeance.

In 2022, after decades of provocation by NATO, Russia's full-fledged invasion of Ukraine came hot on the toes of the 84th anniversary of Poland's annexation by Nazi Germany as the previous oquannium (1871-1954) neared its end.

In 1939, few at the time believed that such a preemptive action by the Nazis against Poland was the beginning of a global conflict as World War II (1939-1945) came home more than two years later with the Japanese attack on Pearl Harbor in 1941 and, in doing so, drawing the then rising global power of United States into the war.

Unsurprisingly, the echoes of 1939 have once again begun to reverberate with the 2022 Ukraine-Russia conflict showing no signs of abating.

Just as Nazi Germany and Soviet Union signed a pact to divide Poland between them in 1939, so did Russia and China some 84 years later in 2022 to go about their territorial business with a mutual understanding and cooperation in their attempt to reclaim what they believe to be their destiny in Ukraine and Taiwan, respectively.

With a 20/20 hindsight in a decade from now, the ongoing Ukraine-Russia conflict will come to be viewed as the start of World War III though it is yet to come home just like its predecessor some 84 years earlier.

In fact, more than a year into the conflict, the 2022 Ukraine-Russia tussle has not only gained enormous inertia but it has already turned into a NATO-Russia war in that without the overpowering military support from the West, the Siberian Tiger would have long toppled its much smaller Western neighbor.

To add salt to Russian wounds, NATO has refused to engage in diplomacy as it ups the ante in order to escalate the conflict already threatening to spiral out of control.

Bluntly put, NATO has already started fighting Russia through a proxy war in what is essentially an unequal contest in that the latter's conventional military power is no match for the West's paraphernalia of hi-tech arsenal and spurs.

Nevertheless, Russia's nuclear capability is something to be reckoned with as the deployment of nukes will not only level the battlefield but also take the NATO bully by the horns without even breaking a sweat.

Sooner or later, the Siberian Tiger will indeed be forced to heavily rely upon its nukes as the NATO-Russia war chugs along in that facing the prospect of a crushing defeat at the hands of its immortal enemy would be simply unfathomable for Russian leaders for whom a world without Russia ought to be no world at all.

It is indeed rare that the opposing sides in a global conflict are equally balanced in terms of their military might.

Accordingly, when one warring party feels frustrated or is facing defeat with conventional firepower as Russia is poised to do so over the next couple of years, it will have no choice but to resort to the deployment of its nukes as a last resort to salvage something out of nothing.

In what I call "Oquandra", the power of oqual cycle to forecast sociopolitical future is personified as the modern-day equivalent of Cassandra.

> "Only fools would call Russia's nuclear saber-rattling a bluff", Oquandra says.

> "Russia can no longer get out of the mess it has trapped itself into without the use of nukes", Oquandra adds.

> "The Siberian Tiger with a barrage of nukes at its disposal will soon begin to feel like a Cornered Tiger and you know what happens next", Oquandra goes onto lament as she breaks the rather bad omens.

Admittedly, given its gigantic landmass and sparsely-populated cities unlike many Western nations with densely-crowded metropolises, Russia would clearly enjoy a strategic advantage when a nuclear war does finally break out.

In a nutshell, the probability of World War III becoming a nuclear one is all but unity.

Nukes not playing even a tactical role in such a looming conflict flanking 2028 would be at odds with a time-tested human tradition, particularly when they are already on the bench warming up to be introduced at a short notice in the deadly game of thrones that is all but upon us.

To argue against such a highly probable outcome would be like saying that one can go through the whole winter without a snowstorm.

That is possible but not a realistic outcome.

How does America benefit from the outbreak of World War III?

WORLD WAR III LENDS AN UNCOMFORTABLE SOLUTION TO AMERICA'S SOCIOPOLITICAL UPHEAVAL

World War III would be a boon for America in that it will provide a perfect smokescreen (or camouflage) for a barrage of nation's Ponzis from social security through national debt to dollar hegemony teetering on the precipice of going up in smoke any day, not to mention that the looming global conflict will also create tons of opportunities to reboot the nation's old-and-degenerate economic engine from scratch just as World War II did some 84 years earlier.

Not only will World War III put an end to decades-long economic stagnation in America and across much of the globe but it also appears to be the only mechanism to return to those good old days of economic prosperity enjoyed by the masses in line with the oqual theory.

This is due to the fact that the thermodynamic bottleneck holding the socioeconomic system hostage can only be overcome through the release of free energy via a large-scale global conflict.

While those in the upper echelons of global powers understand this thermodynamic rule very well, they are however not quite sure when to get such a transformation underway though their job is made all the more easier given that such timing is largely determined by annus horribilis of oqual cycle.

Toward this goal, America has turned Ukraine into a battleground with monetary and military aid having already exceeded the $100B mark within the first year alone of what is likely to be a long and protracted Russia-Ukraine War undergoing a slow and painful metamorphosis into World War III.

To put that into perspective, Ukraine's economic output runs at $200B annually.

Thus, the $100B windfall for Ukraine would be equivalent to God showering America with a lotto of at least $12T annually—while an unlikely scenario to bear fruition, one cannot imagine how such a godsend could make every American so rich that they could all retire at 18 and never have to work ever again.

Till then, Americans must continue to work if only to pay their bills and fund wars.

Indeed, it is mind-boggling to say the least as to why Americans cannot see the World War III in the making and being bankrolled by their tax dollars.

To add to their incognizance, Western media have already taken victory laps on behalf of Ukraine without even realizing that the Siberian Tiger has not even been awoken yet and what they have so far witnessed is nothing more than a mouse playing with the big cat's tail.

Slumbering it may very well be but Russia is fully aware of the fact that it is fighting America not Ukraine and, when two superpowers lock horns, there can be no peaceful solution.

Rather, utter annihilation of our world is on the cards over the next decade or so as exquisitely forecast by the dire spell of oqual cycle on human civilization.

Has World War III not been debated ad nauseam throughout our lives?

So why should it happen now when it has never happened before?

Had the ongoing Ukraine crisis between two global powers pitting Russia directly against America occurred a couple of decades earlier, it would not in-and-of-itself be a recipe for World War III to break out.

Today, however, the ever-bloating sociopolitical upheaval serves as a catalyst to turn such a crisis into a full-fledged global conflict.

Indeed, the 1962 Cuban Missile Crisis did not lead to a war between the two global powers, much less a global conflict, due to the fact that it transpired against a backdrop of relatively prosperous times that would make the sociopolitical dilemmas of that era look like a stroll in the park compared to what the world is facing today.

Ever wondered why chemists are darn good at solving problems?

Because they have all the solutions!

Not only that but a chemist would also tell you that one can have all the reactants they desire in a test tube but, without a catalyst, they are not going to attack each other nuclearphilically or otherwise.

Today, the sociopolitical upheaval is nothing short of a potent catalyst on the verge of being unleashed to turn the ongoing Ukraine Crisis into World War III.

Add to that the fact that the fools who have been debating World War III since the 1960s are utterly ignorant of history in that the odds of a global conflict dwindle as human society walks past annus horribilis of oqual cycle as it did some 84 years earlier in 1944 but then they begin to swindle as it cycles back to that horrible year as is the case today with the next annus horribilis (2028) barely years away.

With the writing already on the wall without hors d'oeuvres in the hall, one can only disregard the dire spell of oqual cycle at their own peril as it inches ever closer to our day of reckoning.

Given the perpetuity of a plethora of crimes from having normalized a culture of living beyond means through institutional fraud run amok to the hilt to debilitating economic stagnation that continue to bloat by the day, one would be naïve to think that such calamities will somehow disappear and a better tomorrow will emerge by itself.

Heck no!

Such a societal reboot does not occur spontaneously but rather it happens to be an endothermic process.

In a manner that an endothermic reaction requires the input of heat so as to lower the activation energy of the transition state to generate a product, a destructive mechanism with the potential to strike fear and chaos into the hearts and minds of people on an apocalyptic scale seems to be a prerequisite to rid our society of such a baggage of evils so as to make way for a fresh start.

Just as World War II (1939-1945) accomplished that goal some 84 years ago so will World War III over the next decade or so as utter fear and chaos engulf our society and, in doing so, purge humanity of mischief so as to enable it to come to its senses once more.

A brighter tomorrow is indeed on the cards but only after humanity has been handed due retribution for having gone bonkers over the past several decades.

Once a few cities have been nuked into the ground, hardly anyone would indeed be left with the urge to continue a reckless lifestyle of self-indulgence and hedonism nor would anyone dare to put up a Ponzi over the several decades that follow until people's memories of hard times begin to fade away once more.

Unfortunately, such deadly punishment seems to be the only mechanism to put human society back on its track after it has not only lost its moral compass but also moral protractor—one could of course pick them up at WHSmith but why bother learning geometry when bots can do everything for you these days:

> Bot > You: Hey bot!
> Bot > Me: Hello!
> Bot > You: How many angles does the pentagon have?
> Bot > Me: Right now, the Pentagon has only one angle! World War III!

Admittedly, the Pentagon is gung-ho on turning the Russia-Ukraine War into a global conflict without even realizing the scale of utter carnage waiting ahead.

Can American leaders not see where such escalation could lead to?

After having been on cocaine for decades through running excesses and imbalances at every societal level, America's parable today is akin to an addict who has simply lost control of their life in that every new step that they take in the misguided belief that it will turn their poor state of affairs around only serves to exacerbate their dilemma.

And when everything goes up in smoke at home, they also set the world on fire.

Indeed, the US government is led to believe that a global conflict offers a perfect solution to its sociopolitical upheaval at home and to once again regain global preeminence just as it did some 84 years earlier in the wake of World War II.

After all, what kind of an American capitalist would not want another global conflict where Europe and Asia get razed to the ground and US companies earn trillion-dollar contracts to rebuild them.

That ploy seems quite plausible except that unlike World War II, America will not come out of World War III unscathed as today's world is very different from what it was some 84 years earlier.

With the likes of Russia and China not only vying to hold their own with their hypersonic technology having made the globe look like a small village but, in many ways, the Eurasian nations are militarily far more advanced than the United States would like to believe due to greed and hubris in an echo of Nazi Germany.

And we know how that panned out for Nazi Germany.

Unfortunately, a similar fate awaits America as the time to pass on the baton of global leadership is inching ever closer with the ominous-and-defining decade centered on annus horribilis (2028) of the current oquannium (1955-2038) having already begun.

A contributing factor to America's foxy ploy turning roxy is the fact that the morale within the US Armed Forces (USAF) is at an historic low in an echo of the American society at large.

With United States having bankrupted itself morally and financially through the decades-long 9/11 Wars waged under the guise of freedom and democracy yet driven by the capitalist interests of the wealthy, the rank-and-file of USAF are much more cognizant of America's true intentions today than they have ever been in the nation's 250-year history.

With America's hidden war propaganda having been laid bare, the odds of United States achieving its capitalist goals and goods through World War III therefore do not bode well.

Nor do they bode well for America's whipping boys across the Atlantic.

Unlike some 84 years earlier when they were the belligerents on steroids and precipitated their own self-destruction through World War II, European nations today are completely oblivious to being fooled and tricked into Siberian Tiger's den with dire consequences of being badly mauled and left bruised once again.

It seems that Europe has learned nothing from history.

As the saying goes, those who fail to learn from history are doomed to repeat it.

It is indeed highly probable that Europe will be caught in the deadly crossfire between Eurasia and America for a battle for the control of world's resources as World War III begins-in-earnest over the next couple of years or so.

How will China benefit from the looming World War III?

CHINA IS RUBBING ITS HANDS WITH SIBERIAN GLEE AND FEET WITH INDIAN GHEE AS IT MANOEUVERS TO TAKE UP THE BATON OF GLOBAL LEADERSHIP

On the other side of the looming conflict, China is aptly and deservedly positioned to emerge as the new hegemon taking up the baton of global leadership from America some time between annus horribilis (2028) of the current oquannium (1955-2038) and annus mirabilis (2039) of the next cycle (2039-2122).

However, such a transfer of global power is unlikely to happen without a showdown between the two superpowers in a manner akin to the fact that the alpha male in a lion pride does not get dethroned by a younger and more hungrier competitor without putting up a fight of his life.

In that sense, the looming World War III can also be viewed as a rite of passage for the newly-minted hegemon to take up the mantle from its predecessor.

But, for China, such a rite of passage goes through Taiwan for without its soul the Asian Giant cannot claim to be whole, much less a leader of the world.

Being fully aware of such a deadly confrontation and coronation waiting on the horizon, China is working round the clock to beef up its military paraphernalia with the Chinese navy today being the largest in the world and rapidly dwarfing its US counterpart—a truly daunting feat that should not be lost on anyone given that the wars are won and lost at sea.

And when it comes to battling it out at sea, preponderance reigns supreme over all else in guaranteeing the triumph as attested by history time and again.

In fact, history shows that the hegemon is often dethroned not because it is no longer powerful enough to knock out its rival but because it lacks the stamina to go the full round due to the low morale within its ranks echoing the rather poor state of the nation as a whole having fallen prey to moral disintegration as a result of self-indulgence and waning zest for life.

When China and America finally square up against each other over the next decade or so, it is quite clear which nation would be fighting tooth-and-nail and which one would be grappling with a low morale—or rather which one of them would be fighting to the death and which one fighting for life.

Top that up with the fact that China has also begun to salivate at the prospect of shepherding the world in accordance with its national interests as it rapidly expands its radius of geopolitical influence around the globe.

That is all the more damning for the Western powers given that the center of economic gravity is set to shift to Asia over the next decade or so after a hiatus of some 500 years.

Those who have not already booked a Mandarin class for their golden child, it would pay to move fast while supplies last.

Without keeping you further on tenterhooks, ladies and gentlemen, please fasten your seat belt as you brace yourself to indulge in a brain-stretching roller-coaster of a chef-d'oeuvre untold in a blunt-and-brutal yet entertaining-and-captivating language punctuated with bucketloads of finger-licking humor so as to periodically mellow out the rather difficult conversation.

As the 16th century English monarch Henry VIII used to say to each one of his six wives, I will not keep you long!

1 | ESSENTIAL PRINCIPLES

From our daily lives through monthly rituals to annual traditions, we are surrounded by a perpetual stream of never-ending cycles.

In a manner akin to our universe, such cycles are also infinite in that we do not only experience them on a daily, monthly, or yearly basis but human civilization is also governed by them on an ever-increasing timescale over decades, centuries, millennia, and so forth, such that the latter essentially represent lower-order harmonics of our more familiar cycles though we cannot directly experience them within the rather limited bounds of our lifetime.

Nevertheless, a logical interpretation of historical data lends a powerful insight into one such harmonic of human civilization with a periodicity of 84 years.

How does this new harmonic fit into our lives?

A new day begins every 24 hours in what is referred to as the "daily cycle" or "circadian rhythm"—it is governed by the spinning of the Earth on its polar axis in relation to the Sun.

A new moon appears roughly every 30 days in what is called the "lunar cycle" or "monthly cycle"—it is dictated by the rotation of the moon around the Earth.

A new year begins every 365 days in what is termed the "annual cycle"—it is orchestrated by the orbiting of the Earth around the Sun.

A new sociopolitical order begins every 84 years in what is introduced (or debuted) herein as the "oqual cycle"—a lower-order harmonic of the daily and annual rhythms that appears to be coupled to the orbiting of the second outermost planet Uranus around the Sun.

However, unlike the daily and annual cycles, the rhythm of oqual cycle is somewhat subtle and intricately nuanced in that it occurs only once in our lifetime, thereby rendering it rather more difficult to understand its impact on our lives—a scenario made all the more challenging due to the lack of quantitative historical records stretching back more than a couple of centuries at best.

Nevertheless, that makes deciphering the oqual cycle all the more exciting unlike working with a low-hanging fruit.

To be clear, the oqual cycle envisions human progress occurring in a highly ordered-and-cyclical manner rather than in a random-and-linear fashion to which the world-over subscribes to, albeit with much ignorance and hubris.

Admittedly, every form of matter and energy in the universe is governed by a rhythm from the femtosecond vibrations of chemical bonds through the daily-and-annual rituals of humans to the repetitive centennial-millennial-and-megannial patterns of climate change—with "megannial" being the adjective form of "megannium" meaning a period of one millions years.

The question therefore is not whether human progress is also rhythmic but rather over what timescale.

The oqual cycle posits that such a rhythm occurs once every 84 years, which coincidentally also happens to be equivalent to the average human lifespan.

Indeed, the oqual rhythm parallels our own lives in that our perspective on life undergoes a drastic change (or assessment) as we hit our fifth decade in the midst of our career highs only to never touch those heights again—it is as if we take an irreversible 180-degree turn as we approach our midlife and begin to reap the fruits (or thorns) of our actions during our earlier years.

However, unlike our life's rhythm, the oqual rhythm embodies the sociopolitical progress and decline of nations, or even human society as a whole.

In mathematical terms, the oqual rhythm could be viewed as the overall output of the summation of billions of our individual rhythms—after all, the oqual rhythm does not fall from the sky but rather it is the net result of our combined actions at any given point in time and space.

Accordingly, the oqual cycle lends a powerful model for not only making sense of the ongoing sociopolitical trials-and-tribulations of our own times but it should also help us navigate our future with rational wisdom in lieu of blissful ignorance.

Importantly, the oqual cycle views the study of our past as a marriage between history and science, or historioscience, rather than merely an art involved with documentation of the past events without an interplay between them.

In particular, historioscience heavily draws from other disciplines such as social and physical sciences though it primarily relies on mathematical analysis of past data and events rather than setting up new experiments.

Without further digression, let us delve deeper into the intricacies of oqual cycle.

Toward that goal, this chapter is subdivided into the following sections:

          1.1 Physical Basis
          1.2 Central Dogma
          1.3 Generational Impact

| 1.1 | PHYSICAL BASIS

With a knack for logical and quantitative approach to understanding whatever I stumble upon, my curiosity rarely kills the cat.

On the contrary, it occasionally leads me to have a moment of epiphany.

Not only did I recently encounter one such moment of epiphany but also a moment of inertia when I serendipitously came upon the rather ominous but hitherto an undiscovered connective tissue between A and B, where:

- A = The year during which the second outermost planet Uranus enters its southern winter solstice once every 84 years.

- B = The decade centered on that recurring year being accompanied by really-really horrible times to have befallen humanity in that they have hitherto amounted to nothing short of a quasi-apocalypse over the past five centuries.

Add to this the finding that tons of centuries-old historical data both at qualitative and quantitative level not only happen to best fit a periodicity of exactly 84 terrestrial years but they also happen to be synchronized with the corresponding Uranian year (which is equivalent to 84 terrestrial years)—while correlation does not necessarily imply causation, it is nevertheless the first step toward developing a theory that appears to be orchestrated by celestial bodies.

Of particular note is the observation that altering such periodicity even by one terrestrial year dramatically throws archetypal events and repetitive patterns into a disarray such that they begin to lack a discernible cyclical trend.

Given that one terrestrial year is to a Uranian year what a 5-day week is roughly to a terrestrial year, one can immediately see how shortening our year to 360 days or lengthening it to 370 days would palpably screw up the cyclicity of our annual rituals within a matter of a decade, if not sooner.

That is exactly what happens to oqual cycle as it goes haywire if one were to alter its periodicity even by one terrestrial year.

So far so good but what exactly is a solstice, you might ask?

Solstice is the timepoint at which the northern (or southern) pole of a planet is minimally or maximally exposed to sunlight during the course of its one full turn around the Sun.

For example, the Earth experiences two such solstices around June 21st and December 21st each year—which respectively mark the summer solstice (the longest day of the year) and the winter solstice (the shortest day of the year) with respect to the northern pole and vice versa relative to the southern pole.

In the context of Uranus, the southern winter solstice denotes the southern midwinter point when the southern pole of Uranus is minimally exposed to direct sunlight over the course of its one full turn around the Sun.

Why do Uranus's solstices mark the midpoint in Uranian winters?

Is such a scenario not at odds with what the Earth experiences?

URANUS EXHIBITS A REMARKABLE IDIOSYNCRASY IN OUR SOLAR SYSTEM

If it were not for our Earth's obliquity (or axial tilt), the sunlight would hit the equator all year round in an equal measure such that there would be no seasonal variations in light or temperature.

One cannot imagine life without seasons on Earth.

However, things are not so rosy on Uranus.

In a manner that the orbital period of Earth around the Sun defines the length of a terrestrial year, the orbital period of Uranus circumscribes one Uranian year—which is equivalent to 84 terrestrial years.

In other words, the Earth completes 84 orbital rotations around the Sun for every round that the Uranus does.

Likewise, the oqual cycle is to a Uranian year what the annual cycle is to a terrestrial year.

And the oquannium is to an oqual cycle what the annum is to an annual cycle.

That is pretty much where similarities between the two planets end and differences begin to emerge when one takes a closer look at the ice giant.

Unlike the rather small axial tilt of 23° for the Earth's polar (or spin) axis with respect to a line perpendicular to its orbital plane around the Sun, the Uranus's polar axis is tilted by a whopping 98°.

Thus, unlike the Earth and the other six planets that orbit the Sun with a quasi-upright tilt like a spinning top, Uranus does so practically on its side a la rolling ball (or water wheel) with its spin axis being almost parallel to the orbital plane as if its poles have no qualms about staring directly at the mighty star of our solar system.

Given such an idiosyncratic orientation of Uranus, the Sun continuously shines almost directly on each of its poles during their respective summer solstices—the time point at which each pole reaches its maximal exposure to sunlight during the orbital cycle.

On the other hand, each pole of Uranus is continuously bathed in complete darkness during its winter solstice—the time point at which each pole reaches its minimal exposure to sunlight during the orbital cycle.

Accordingly, such solstices mark the midpoint of a 21-year-long summer (which is essentially one long uninterrupted day without dark) or the midpoint of a 21-year-long winter (which is akin to one long uninterrupted night without light).

It is noteworthy that such a framework is in sharp contrast to the Earth's solstices which for their part mark the beginning of a winter or summer due to the rather differential inclination of the Earth's polar axis relative to the Sun—the Earth orbits the Sun with its polar axis being roughly perpendicular to the orbital plane as if its poles are somewhat shy of looking directly at the heart of our solar system.

In addition to its idiosyncratic axial tilt that produces extreme 21-year seasons, Uranus also exhibits many other distinguishing quirks.

While Earth's magnetic field is more or less aligned with its spin axis, it is tilted by a staggering 59° relative to the spin axis of Uranus (vide supra).

Such a lopsided (or off-centered) configuration produces a multipolar rather than a dipolar effect such that Uranus experiences a rather non-uniform magnetic field with its strength being much greater in the northern hemisphere relative to the southern half.

Importantly, a sturdy and uniform magnetic field, as is the case on Earth, is critical to shielding a planet against the constant scourge of solar wind—a moving mass of ionized particles that flies outward at supersonic velocity from the outer surface of the Sun toward other planets including our own.

However, such a shielding against solar wind does not appear to be much of a big deal on Uranus where the poorly-configured setup of magnetic field is further compromised by its flipping on and off like a light switch such that the ice giant gets whipped by the solar wind on a daily basis.

When does Uranus encounter its next southern winter solstice?

On the basis of astronomical data courtesy of Voyager-2 launched by NASA in 1977 to probe the outer space [6], the south pole of Uranus was imaged looking directly and maximally at the Sun in 1986.

In 1986, the ice giant therefore must have been in the midst of its southern summer solstice with the southern hemisphere continuously bathing in sunlight and the northern hemisphere being plunged into darkness.

In 2007, 21 years later, Uranus reached its southern autumn equinox when the planet's equator bore the brunt of the Sun's radiation.

In 2028, another 21 years later, Uranus is poised to enter its next southern winter solstice.

Thus, the current oqual cycle is poised to end in 2038 with the next one beginning in 2039—assuming that 2028 marks the midwinter point on the southern pole of Uranus and each Uranian year begins with the start of southern spring from the perspective of earthlings.

How many oqual cycles has humanity encountered since the birth of Modern Age in the 15th century?

Circa 1451, the advent of a fast-moving printing press by the German inventor Johannes Gutenberg revolutionized European civilization in that it allowed mass-production of information that could then be quickly circulated among intellectuals, thereby opening up collaborations and driving technological advances as well as enabling masses to read and write.

Given such a paradigm shift that tilted the balance of philosophical power from Asia to Europe some 500 years ago as Gutenberg's printing press could only print modular letters in lieu of cursive text that formed the bedrock of Asian languages, the year 1451 is used as a reference point to mark the birth of Modern Age.

Equally remarkable is the fact that the Italian explorers Christopher Columbus and Amerigo Vespucci, who together discovered the New World and laid much of the groundwork for the early maritime technology that enabled humanity to map the world as we know it today, both took their first breath in 1451.

Add to that the fact that the fall of the Byzantine Empire representing the last remaining vestiges of the Roman Empire in 1453, when the Ottomans marched into Constantinople (the modern-day Istanbul), also occurred almost in parallel with the birth of Modern Age (1451-date).

Coincidentally, the year 1451 also happens to be the start of a new Uranian year beginning with the southern spring.

The ice giant must therefore have been onto something as it heralded a new Uranian year with a bang of its own to match so many groundbreaking events unfolding here on Earth in 1451 or thereabout.

Notably, humanity will have experienced seven full bouts (or spells) of oqual cycle between the birth of Modern Age in 1451 and the start of the next cycle in 2039, or arithmetically put: $(2039-1451)/84 = 7$.

With the first oqual cycle (OC1) beginning in 1451 since the birth of Modern Age, the second oqual cycle (OC2) began in 1535 (1451+84=1535) with each new one emerging every 84 years thereafter.

The current and seventh oqual cycle nominally began in 1955 and is poised to end in 2038, or arithmetically put: $1450+(7\times84) = 2038$.

Importantly, the synchronization of oqual cycle with the Uranian year starting with southern spring and ending with southern winter is corroborated by tons of historical data on human civilization undergoing ebbs and flows over the past five centuries or so.

In particular, a new dawn of sociopolitical order appears to have taken hold on our lonely planet every 84 years on average starting nominally in 1451.

Although it serves as a prerequisite to break ties with our dysfunctional past in order to begin anew, such a global reset is far from being a free lunch but rather occurs only after the piper is paid for our transgressions amassed over the course of oqual cycle.

In line with what humanity has endured over the past five centuries, the year during which Uranus enters its southern winter solstice is what I have dubbed "annus horribilis" in that it typically coincides with the oqual cycle reaching its crescendo and unleashing the worst of its destructive rage upon our civilization.

Since the outset of Modern Age in 1451, the annus horribilis of oqual cycle has befallen humanity in 1524, 1608, 1692, 1776, 1860, and 1944.

Spaced apart by exactly 84 years, those were really-really horrible times that amounted to nothing short of a hell-on-earth and the like of which is encountered only once-in-a-lifetime.

Not only was each annus horribilis noted above flanked by a synchronized-and-synergized wave of deadly conflicts (or hegemonic wars) unfolding across the globe but also bore witness to civil wars breaking out across many nations and culminating with the establishment of a nouveau sociopolitical system under a new world order.

For example, 1944 was sandwiched between the destructive World War II (1939-1945) coupled with the dreadful Holocaust (1941-1945) on one side, and the bloody Indian Partition (1947) along with the chaotic births of the State of Israel (1948) and People's Republic of China (1949) on the other—America would emerge as the new hegemon taking up the reins from Britain.

Likewise, 1860 was flanked by the deadly Crimean War (1853-1856) between Russia and Turkiye coupled with the Indian Mutiny (1857) against the British colonialists on one side, and the American Civil War (1861-1865) along with the Franco-Mexican War (1861-1867) on the other—Britain would hold onto its global dominance though closely checked by the rapid rise of America just as the 19th century bid farewell.

On the same token, 1776 was preceded by the Russo-Turkish War (1768-1774) and followed by the American Independence War (1775-1783) coupled with the Anglo-French War (1778-1783)—America would become a sovereign nation and Britain emerged as the new hegemon taking up the baton from France.

Prior to that, 1692 was straddled with the deadly Nine Years War (1688-1697) between France and Netherlands with the latter supported by various European powers including England due to its own existential crisis of the Glorious Revolution (1688-1689)—France would emerge as the new hegemon taking up the mantle from Netherlands.

Before that, 1608 was marred by the consequential sixth phase of the Eighty Years War (1599-1609) between Spain and Netherlands with each supported by various European powers—Netherlands would emerge as the new hegemon taking the helm from Spain.

Finally, 1524 was underscored by the 1529 Treaty of Cambrai in the midst of the fifth phase of the so-called Italian Wars (1521-1530) pitting Spain against France for the control of Italian peninsula as well as global dominance with each side supported by various European powers—Spain would emerge as the new hegemon and Portugal having passed on the torch.

Other than the quartet of 21-year seasons from spring through summer and autumn to winter, there are also three critical junctures that underscore the oqual cycle as described below:

1) **Annus mirabilis**—The 1st year of oqual cycle that all but guarantees the beginning of good times if they have not already arrived on our shores years earlier than anticipated after the dust from the sociopolitical fallout from the previous cycle has settled. In particular, the decade centered on annus mirabilis marks the beginning of several decades of relative peace and prosperity ahead. For example, good times began across much of the globe around annus mirabilis (1955) of the current oquannium (1955-2038) as fondly remembered through the Golden Age in America (1950-1970), Swinging Sixties in Britain (1960s), and Les Trente Glorieuses in France (1945-1975). Likewise, some 84 years before, annus mirabilis (1871) of the previous oquannium (1871-1954) also heralded decades of relatively happy times as epitomized by the Gilded Age in America (1870-1900), the Late Victorian Era in Britain (1870-1901), and La Belle Époque in France (1870-1914).

2) **Annus turnilis**—The 43rd year of oqual cycle that marks its midpoint (or turning point) when sociopolitical progress of human society begins to turn south and ushers in decades of chaos ahead until they morph into an insoluble maze as the oqual rhythm nears its end. Notably, the turning point is marked by an archetypal crisis during the decade centered upon annus turnilis though none has ever paid heed to such a harbinger of things to come over the decades that followed. For example, the decades-long 9/11 Wars (2001-2021) followed shortly after the arrival of annus turnilis (1997) of the current oquannium (1955-2038). Likewise, some 84 years earlier, World War I (1914-1918) sprang out immediately after annus turnilis (1913) of the previous oquannium (1871-1954). While run-of-the-mill conflicts break out throughout the oqual cycle, large-scale protracted wars such as World War I and the 9/11 Wars not only befall humanity once-in-a-lifetime but they also serve as a primer (or precursor) to plunge the human society into an even greater sociopolitical chaos that ultimately leads to hegemonic wars such as World War II (1939-1945) and the looming World War III as the oqual cycle draws to a close.

3) **Annus horribilis**—The 74th year of oqual cycle during which Uranus enters its southern winter solstice, the midwinter point indicative of the

fact that the worst of the sociopolitical fallout from our wrongdoings amassed over the course of oqual cycle is either already upon us or approaching its crescendo. Such a hell-on-earth usually occurs during the decade centered on annus horribilis. For example, annus horribilis (2028) of the current oquannium (1955-2038) is all but set to witness the looming World War III on an epic scale so as to bring about a global reset and usher in a new dawn of hope and prosperity. Likewise, some 84 years before, annus horribilis (1944) of the previous oquannium (1871-1954) was sandwiched between the destructive World War II (1939-1945) coupled with the dreadful Holocaust (1941-1945) on one side, and the bloody Indian Partition (1947) along with the chaotic births of the State of Israel (1948) and People's Republic of China (1949) on the other.

Of particular note here is the fact that the annus horribilis of each oqual cycle is flanked by hegemonic wars—a series of global conflicts that are all but obligatory for breaking ties with our dysfunctional past in order to begin anew under a new world order spearheaded by a nation that has proved itself as the manufacturing powerhouse head-and-shoulders above its competitors.

It is also noteworthy that the outbreak of World War I (1914-1918) almost in parallel with the onset of the second half (1913-1954) in lieu of erupting closer to the end of previous oquannium (1871-1954) must not be assumed as being an anomaly.

Rather, World War I marked the archetypal midcycle conflict in a manner similar to the 9/11 Wars that breaks out as the oqual cycle reaches its midpoint and plants the seeds for the decades-long sociopolitical upheaval that is subsequently resolved by an even bigger global conflict.

That it came to be referred to as a world war at all is nothing more than a case of semantics thanks to illogical historians, not to mention that it was renamed from being a Great War to World War I in hindsight in the wake of the outbreak of World War II (1939-1945) a couple of decades later.

From a logical perspective and for the sake of consistency, the honor of the first-ever world war taking place across all corners of the globe in fact belongs to the so-called Nine Years War (1688-1697) fought between the then rising power of France and the decaying empire of Netherlands with the latter closely supported by England and other European nations as the third oquannium (1619-1702) drew to a close with what were once mighty Dutch forced to pass on the baton of global hegemony to Les Gaules.

It should also be emphasized that while the decade centered on annus horribilis of oqual cycle is typically accompanied by really-really horrible times a la hell-on-earth, humanity is in fact mired in a sociopolitical chaos during much of the second half (over the course of autumn and winter) of oqual cycle in stark contrast to a period of relative harmony enjoyed by the masses during the first half (over the course of spring and summer).

In particular, the fallout from our wrongdoings amassed over the course of oqual cycle reaches a tipping point around annus horribilis in the midst of oqual winter, which for the current oquannium (1955-2038) arrived in 2018 and will last until 2038.

With that in mind, the winter is therefore not coming but it is already upon us.

Needless to say, the next decade or so will be a time of extreme trials and tribulations for humanity-writ-large.

Nevertheless, a new dawn of hope and prosperity awaits us all on the other side of the looming World War III just as the next oqual cycle begins to breathe down our neck with the arrival of 2030s.

How does a planet as far away in outer space as Uranus orchestrate human civilization on Earth?

Do other celestial bodies also have a say in the affairs of earthlings?

THE PHYSICAL BASIS OF URANIAN SPELL ON OUR LIVES REMAINS MYSTERIOUS

Few would doubt the impact of the planet Earth on human civilization from how the daily cycle controls our circadian rhythm to how the annual cycle powers our lives from harvesting crops to breeding.

If the Earth seems so central to our activities, one wonders whether other celestial bodies could also play a similar role in dictating our lives—albeit to a lesser extent as they become more and more distant from our planet.

Indeed, the rotation of the Moon around the Earth dictates the monthly (or lunar) cycle characterized by the ebb-and-flow of ocean tides, migration and breeding of many animals, and even menstruation in humans.

Thus, it would be quite ingenuous to rule out the possibility that the other planets in our solar system somehow modulate terrestrial life.

This school of thought is indeed corroborated by a recent study indicating that the gravitational tug (or coupling) between Jupiter and Venus modulates terrestrial climate over hundreds of millennia [7].

In fact, life on Earth would not even be possible without the other planets escorting and providing a convoy of sorts for the jewel in the crown of our solar system.

It should therefore be hardly surprising that being the planetary elephant in our solar system with an orbital period of around 12 years and a magnetosphere that even dwarfs that of the Sun itself, Jupiter likely unleashes its spell on human behavior in a subtle manner.

According to the 2008 book titled "Life Cycles" by the Australian psychologist Neil Killion [8], human beings start a new chapter in their lives every 12 years or so.

In other words, a notable transition occurs in our lives around ages 12, 24, 36, 48, 60, 72, and 84—the latter being the magic number that appears to define the average length of human lifespan.

In many ways, Killion's theory appears to be very familiar to us.

For example, the onset of puberty in humans occurs around the age of 12.

Around the age of 24, most athletes reach their physical peak while many others get married, become parents, or graduate from university to begin a new phase in their lives.

Around the age of 36, most of us peak mentally and intellectually, and for many academic scientists, they either land their first autonomous appointment as an investigator or their first major grant.

Around the age of 48, many of us are either promoted to the rank of grandparents, managers, or executives, while others begin to see the best of their career achievements in the rearview mirror as they begin to wind down and accept the hard reality that they no longer boast the same energy or enthusiasm that they did a decade earlier.

Around the age of 60, many of us ride off into the sunset wherein we either begin to reap the fruits of our decades-long labor or we face the music for having lived a reckless life.

Around the age of 72, humans usually become fearless as they have nothing to lose careerwise or otherwise, and many begin to speak their mind for the first time ever in their lives—however, in my case, that moment arrived at 12 and has stuck with me ever since even though sailing against the wind would cost me more than an arm and a leg at every stage in my life.

Rest assured, I still have two arms and two legs.

I guess I must have been born with lots of arms and legs. Allahu akbar!

Finally, around the age of 84, most of us bid farewell to Mother Earth.

While Killion's theory is indeed supported by the periodic 12-year transitions in the lives of numerous movers and shakers to have set foot on earth over the past century or so, there are nevertheless going to be many individuals who stand out as an exception to this life pattern though such anomalies should in no way pour cold water over what is arguably an eye-popping model governing our lives.

What impact does Jupiter have on the oqual cycle?

Together with Jupiter and Uranus, Saturn and Neptune make up the quartet of outer planets in our solar system—they are also called Jovian planets for their rather gigantic size due to their predominantly gaseous composition.

The Jovian planets are far from being solitary creatures unaware of each other's footprint in space but rather they are conjoined in a celestial marriage of sorts.

In particular, Uranus appears to be more or less gravitationally coupled with its three neighbors on an 84-year timescale, or a multiple thereof.

For example, with an orbital period of 12 years, Jupiter makes 7 turns around the Sun for every turn of Uranus such that the two planets realign in space with respect to Earth once every 84 years (12x7=84).

Likewise, with an orbital period of 29 years, Saturn would also more or less realign in space with Uranus once every 84 years or so (29x3=87).

With an orbital period of 165 years, the outermost planet Neptune roughly aligns with Uranus once every other Uranian year (165/2=83).

Given that the combined orbital period of Uranus with its Jovian neighbors is roughly 84 years or a multiple thereof, it implies that the three other outer planets are also likely to have a say in governing the oqual cycle.

In particular, such gravitational coupling between the quartet of outer planets likely renders Uranus as an orchestrator of sorts with respect to its ability to modulate terrestrial activities with the trio of Jupiter-Saturn-and-Neptune acting as improvisers, chaperones, or even celestial mirrors to transmit astronomical effects instigated by the ice giant via electromagnetic radiation or gravitational tuning.

It could well be that Uranus is not only in a gravitational tug with its three Jovian neighbors but that their magnetic fields are also coupled such that they act in concert to attune solar wind as it heads toward Earth.

Additionally, the gravitational tug between the Jovian planets could also modulate the axial tilt of Earth such that the total amount of solar irradiance striking our planet oscillates over a period of 84 years.

To be clear, solar irradiance is the total solar energy reaching the Earth via the full gamut of electromagnetic radiation from the high-energy γ-rays and x-rays through ultraviolet-light-and-infrared to microwaves and radiowaves though the latter have negligible impact on heating our planet.

In attuning solar wind and solar irradiance, Uranus along with its Jovian partners could therefore directly modulate terrestrial climate, which may very well be the missing link between the oqual cycle and its celestial origin.

Admittedly, as discussed later in §6.1, that is exactly what seems to be the case—the terrestrial climate indeed appears to oscillate more or less in sync with the progression of oqual cycle.

Not only that but the Earth appears to alternate between a COOLING period and a WARMING spell, with each stage lasting some 42 years, over the course of oqual cycle.

Strikingly, the COOLING period correlates with a zeitgeist of relative peace and harmony over the first half of oqual cycle whereas the WARMING spell occurs during the second half when our society plunges into decades of utter madness as is the case across much of the globe today.

I should also add that while Uranus may be located in outer space more than a billion miles from Earth, electromagnetic radiation such as x-rays from the ice giant have not only been detected on our planet but they can also reach us faster than a flight from Miami to Gran Manzana.

Thus, the impact of Uranus on our lives is not completely out of the physical realm even though the exact mechanism by which the ice giant orchestrates terrestrial life and climate in sync with its orbital rotation around the Sun unequivocally remains mysterious.

That should hardly be surprising given that our current understanding of the universe is primitive at best and the onus lies squarely on the future generations of astronomers to shed new light on how exactly celestial bodies impact the affairs of earthlings.

Long story short, the lack of a physical basis for the oqual cycle should in no way undermine what otherwise appears to be a Rosetta stone of human civilization.

What exactly is oqual cycle in mathematical terms?

HUMAN PROGRESS PROPAGATES ALONG A HELICAL PATH

In a manner akin to the daily and annual cycles that govern our lives, the oqual cycle dictates the waxing and waning of human civilization albeit over a much longer timespan than its higher-frequency counterparts.

The oqual cycle can therefore be envisioned as being a lower-order harmonic of the daily and annual cycles with which it seems to share many features.

For example, as discussed later in §6.1, the Earth's surface temperature appears to oscillate over a period of 84 years in a manner reminiscent of its dynamics over the course of a day or a year.

On the other hand, the ebbs and flows in our daily and annual rhythms seem to parallel the ups and downs in human civilization over the course of oqual cycle.

Another way to look at the relationship between the oqual rhythm and its higher-order harmonics is through a series of concentric circles with their increasing radii being indicative of the longer period of the corresponding harmonic over which it completes one full oscillation.

Admittedly, the central premise of oqual cycle is that the progress of human civilization is akin to a circular ride in a theme park, wherein one gets to see the same view time and again albeit in an uncanny way, rather than propagating along a railway track without any reference to its past.

Needless to say, the oqual cycle puts human progress on the same footing as most natural phenomena wherein things are circling back and forth, or cycling, rather than moving along a linear track.

Think how the darkness-of-the-night follows the light-of-the-day and vice versa in a perpetual daily cycle.

Think how the winter follows the summer and vice versa in a perpetual annual cycle.

Think how the planets orbit the Sun in a cyclical manner, with each completing one full rotation over a fixed period of time.

Add to that a spate of solar cycles driven by the cyclical variation in the number of sunspots on the Sun's surface that modulate terrestrial climate over decadal, centennial, and millennial timespans.

Likewise, as embodied in the so-called Milankovitch Cycles, terrestrial climate is also regulated by cyclical variation in the Earth's movements with respect to its orbital dynamics such as:

1) **Orbital Eccentricity**—The extent to which a planet's orbit around the Sun deviates from a perfect circle. In the case of Earth, such orbital eccentricity varies between a near-circle to a semi-ellipse over a period of roughly 100 kiloyears.
2) **Axial Tilt**—The angle between a line perpendicular to the orbital plane of a planet and its spin axis (also called axial obliquity). Although the current axial tilt of Earth is around 23°, it can fluctuate by at least one degree in either direction over a period of around 41 kiloyears.
3) **Axial Precession**—The wobbling of a planet as it rotates about its spin axis in a manner akin to a top spinning slightly off-center. The Earth takes nearly 26 kiloyears to complete one full axial precession.

It is not only our physical world but cyclical phenomena are also a hallmark of biology as one could not imagine life without the likes of:

1) **Kreb's cycle**—Powers virtually all living cells;
2) **Calvin cycle**—Turns atmospheric carbon dioxide into glucose in plants with the aid of solar energy and water; and
3) **Urea cycle**—Transforms the rather toxic ammonia byproduct in our body into urine.

Simply put, cycles are essential to fuel our physical and biological worlds and keep them self-sufficient without the need for an external driver.

In fact, everything in nature is on the move but it is essentially spinning along a circle rather than moving along a line.

That is the reason why our ancestors never found the "edge" of the earth nor we will ever find the "edge" of the universe as neither traces out linearity but rather each curves back onto itself conforming to an infinite circle or a sphere in three-dimensional space.

One therefore does not have to be a rocket scientist to realize that the progress of human civilization must also be circular rather than linear without any relationship to its past.

However, like other natural phenomena, human progress does not merely circle back onto itself—if it did, no progress would be made at all in stark contradiction to our everyday experiences.

Rather, such a spinning motion occurs along a dynamic circle that is constantly on the move in time and space.

For example, although the Earth rotates around the Sun, its orbit is not fixed in space but rather carves out a helical path with one helical turn completed each year—we are essentially getting a free ride in space courtesy of Earthship traveling a distance of nearly 600M miles each year.

Like Earth, other planets also trace out a similar helical trajectory as they orbit the Sun.

For its part, the Sun itself is not stationary but rather it is also on the move tracing out a helical path as it orbits the Milky Way—the galaxy of which our solar system is a part of.

In a similar fashion, the circle of human progress can also be envisioned to be traveling along a helical path in a manner akin to climbing a spiral staircase—such that each helical turn represents one complete circle.

In a nutshell, the oqual cycle posits that the progress of human civilization does not follow a linear course but rather it spirals (or spins) along an infinite helical path at a reciprocal velocity of 84 years per helical turn in sync with Uranus tracing out a helical path as it orbits the Sun.

In mathematical terms, such a helix of radius r and pitch p within the framework of three-dimensional space (x,y,z) at time t can be described by the following set of parametric equations:

$$x[t] = r.\cos(t)$$
$$y[t] = r.\sin(t)$$
$$z[t] = (p/2\pi).t$$

wherein r can be envisioned as the radius of Uranus's orbit around the Sun, and p would then be the lateral distance that Uranus moves forward in space once every 84 years.

However, things begin to head south during the second half of the ride along the helical turn—being equivalent to traveling from one maximum (or the top of a mountain) to the next minimum (or the bottom of a valley) along a sinusoidal wave.

Put another way, the helix of human civilization may also be viewed as being amphipathic such that one side of the helix is the polar opposite of the other.

Thus, when traveling along the helix, humans find themselves at two extremes every 42 years as they switch their odyssey from the hydrophobic side of the helix to the hydrophilic or vice versa.

Such a mathematical model not only accounts for the waxing and waning of human civilization over the course of oqual cycle but also its overall progress in time and space a la movement of Uranus and other celestial bodies.

|1.2| CENTRAL DOGMA

Ever since United States came into being as a nation in 1776, its leaders have been telling Americans that they are riding an express train supercharged with a double dose of capitalism-and-democracy and that their next stop is the idyllic land of nirvana (or utopia).

Yet, almost 250 years later, that dream of a utopian society run amok to the nth degree remains a fantasy at best.

American leaders have not been alone in spewing out such an asinine rhetoric over the past couple of centuries but they have also been joined by many leaders elsewhere around the world whose experiment to end bad times once-and-forever only exacerbated the pain and suffering of their people.

How can one oqualize (or rationalize) such razzmatazz that promised so much jazz but delivered little shazz?

Well, our past is the foundation upon which our present and future are built—the past acts rather like a rug under our feet which if pulled out not only makes us lose our balance but also our nuance.

In other words, the world leaders failed to pay heed to history.

They did not seem to realize that not only are we connected to our past via our DNA but also through our sociopolitical wave that has continued to ebb and flow since the beginning of times.

That is not only due to their own ignorance and hubris but, perhaps, more so from the ineptitude of seasoned historians—who for the most part have continued to deliver lessons of history as if it were a one-way train speeding along a linear track with no relation to its past.

Alas, it ain't.

Regrettably, it is not only the world leaders but even pundits-and-gurus remain ignorant of the cyclical nature of history and how it governs our lives due to their optimism bias—the misguided belief that tomorrow must necessarily be better than today and that bad times have long been put to the sword so as to never return again.

In particular, such idiocy runs deep in the media tail that wags the societal dog and therefore serves as a perpetual pill to keep the masses indoctrinated with their warped worldview rather than hard facts.

Being an optimist is a great virtue but being a realist is multiples greater.

Although many of my fellow Americans are renowned for seeing the glass half full, their ignorance and hubris also see no bounds.

While the embers of the decades-long self-destructive 9/11 Wars continue to rage to this day with the nation teetering on the brink of a looming bankruptcy coupled with social-and-moral decadence at home from soaring public debts through shrinking middle class to faltering infrastructure, so many Americans nevertheless do not shy away from prophesizing that the United States is destined for a utopian era waiting on the horizon with the promise of making its past look tame by comparison.

Little do they realize that the best days of America long took a trip down memory lane and what awaits them ahead is a rendezvous with destiny to pay for their excesses and imbalances amassed over the course of so many decades.

While one may be able to evade the scourge of courts due to what has essentially become an anarchic society wherein serial criminals are not only handsomely bred but also richly rewarded for their wicked acts, no one can keep the full force of the laws of nature at bay.

Nor does irrational optimism end well.

With World War III all but having begun with Russia's invasion of Ukraine in 2022, almost every form of frothy investment from bonds through stocks to real estate is set to plunge to ground zero over the next decade and, in doing so, leaving tens-of-millions of Americans poor and destitute.

Yet, so many fools continue to live in lalaland rather than face the hard reality as they plow ever more money into such bogus investments in the misguided belief that the worst is behind them and out of fear-of-missing-out (FOMO) the financial train ingenuously believed to be destined for Shangrila.

Nothing could be further from the truth.

In actuality, the financial train is headed to the fool's paradise and it is already too late for many to get off and avoid a terrible fate awaiting them ahead.

So what gives?

HUMAN PROGRESS WAXES AND WANES IN A CYCLICAL MANNER

On the basis of scientific reasoning and mathematical modeling of history over the past 600 years, the oqual cycle posits that human civilization seemingly undergoes a sweeping global reset once every 84 years on average in order to purge itself of a plethora of wrongdoings from the societal ills through excesses and imbalances to transgressions amassed over that multidecadal period.

Unfortunately, there is no free music as one must pay the piper.

Indeed, such a societal reboot (or revitalization) is typically accomplished through a global conflict with the potential to not only wreak havoc but also strike fear into the hearts and minds of people on an apocalyptic scale so that they can put their sociopolitical differences aside and come together for the common good of the world at large.

The oqual cycle therefore lends human society a subtle albeit deadly mechanism to break ties with its dysfunctional past in order to begin anew rather than being held hostage from moving forward under its own weight, or even worse, continue down the rabbit hole in perpetuity with the potential for self-destruction.

More specifically, the oqual cycle posits that the sociopolitical progress of human civilization does not follow a linear course but rather it waxes and wanes in a cyclical manner over a period of 84 years due to what appears to be its coupling with the orbiting of the second outermost planet Uranus around the Sun.

In an analogy with a pendulum, the progress of human civilization appears to swing (or oscillate) forth from one extreme to the other and then back again over a period of 84 years.

In an analogy with the trials and tribulations of a mouse with an average lifespan of one year, the oqual cycle is to humans what the annual cycle is to mice.

Just as mice remain clueless about annual seasonal changes affecting their lives so do humans with respect to the spell of Uranian seasons.

The ignorance of mice does not change the fact that the annual cycle substantially impacts their lives nor does our own ignorance about the dire spell of oqual cycle on our own lives.

How does the oqual cycle fit in with the Uranian seasons?

In sync with the changes in Uranian climate with respect to its southern pole, the oqual cycle is subdivided into a quartet of 21-year seasons chronologically dubbed spring, summer, autumn, and winter.

Simply put, the oqual cycle on Earth is perfectly synchronized with the Uranian year in that it begins with the southern spring and ends with the southern winter.

In terms of cyclical progress of human civilization over a period of 84 years, such a quartet of seasons can also be viewed as dawn (spring), sunrise (summer), sunset (autumn), and dusk (winter).

Needless to say, a 21-year timespan of oqual cycle equates to an oqual quarter and a 7-year period represents one oqual month.

In an alternative but a mutually-inclusive framework, the oqual cycle is envisioned as a doublet of two symmetrical (or antagonistic) halves: a constructive period marked by a rather upbeat zeitgeist (over the course of spring and summer) followed by a destructive spell during which the societal zeitgeist turns on its head (over the course of autumn and winter), with each lasting for some 42 years on average.

In other words, human progress waxes over the first half of oqual cycle to reach a zenith and then wanes during the second half to hit a nadir in a sinusoidal manner reminiscent of the waxing and waning of the Moon over the course of a lunar month.

Why does human progress wax and wane over the course of oqual cycle?

When human society hits a nadir (or crisis-of-a-lifetime) in the face of sociopolitical upheaval having reached a climax as the oqual cycle draws to a close, it becomes boxed-cornered-and-trapped with no way out.

Paradoxically, such a checkmate serves as a blessing-in-disguise to revitalize human society and provide it with a renewed vigor to rebuild a just sociopolitical system that seemingly works for most people as it reaches its zenith during the first half of oqual cycle before it turns on its head.

For example, during the first half (1955-1996) of the current oquannium (1955-2038), the sociopolitical temperature was by-and-large relatively healthy across much of the globe with occasional bouts of sociopolitical crisis that were largely contained within the national or regional borders rather than becoming sticky so as to draw the whole world into a quandary.

Today, long gone are those good old days as we find ourselves in the midst of what appears to be not only a concerted and synchronized sociopolitical upheaval unfolding across the globe but that has also continued to plunge humanity into an ever-deepening canyon with the passing of each year since the onset of the second half (1997-2038) of the current oquannium (1955-2038).

In a manner similar to the good old days of our own lives during the first half (1955-1996) of the current and seventh oquannium (1955-2038), a similar zeitgeist of relative calm and prosperity also panned out during the first half (1871-1912) of the previous and sixth oquannium (1871-1954), yet the second half (1913-1954) was mired in utter sociopolitical crises and deadly conflicts as epitomized by the quartet of World War I (1914-1918), Influenza Pandemic (1918-1920), Great Depression (1929-1939), and World War II (1939-1945).

Likewise, the first half (1787-1828) of the fifth oquannium (1787-1870) bore witness to a period of relative harmony, whereas the second half (1829-1870) saw the world hit a low yet again through sociopolitical upheavals and conflicts such as the Mexican-American War (1846-1848), the European Revolutions (1848-1849), the Crimean War (1853-1856) between Russia and Turkiye, the Indian Mutiny (1857) against the British colonialists, the American Civil War (1861-1865), and the Franco-Mexican War (1861-1867).

Long story short, humanity has consistently faced a multidecadal period of trials and tribulations during the second half of every qual cycle since the birth of Modern Age in 1451.

On the other hand, the first half of oqual cycle has by and large equated to a period of relative peace and prosperity.

What sociopolitical forces cooperate to produce the rather happy times during the first half of oqual cycle?

The relatively calm and prosperous 42-year period over the course of the first half of oqual cycle is powered by the steady rise of a myriad of progressive sociopolitical forces such as morality, peace, collectivism, globalism, entrepreneurship, moderation, transparency, nonpartisanship, ethnic harmony, baby boom, economic well-being, and institutional trust.

To add icing on the cake, such progressive forces act in a positively-cooperative (or synergistic) manner in that their combined output is much more productive than the sum of their individual parts—their concerted action engineers a sociopolitical system spearheaded by a relatively healthy dose of prosperity enjoyed by the masses rather than restricted to a small minority of wealthy.

In particular, the deluge of such sociopolitical tailwinds descending upon our civilization during the first half of oqual cycle is further inundated with groundbreaking scientific discoveries and technological advances that are often viewed in hindsight as among the greatest of all time.

For example, what came to be known as the Golden Age in America—an era that bore witness to the discoveries of DNA double-helix (1953) and protein structure (1957) coupled with NASA's moon landing (1969), the development of internet's precursor Arpanet (1969), and Alto's launch of first-ever GUI-based personal computer (1973)—largely overlapped with the oqual spring (1955-1975) of the current and seventh oquannium (1955-2038).

Likewise, the oqual spring (1871-1891) of the previous and sixth oquannium (1871-1954) coincided with the so-called Gilded Age in America, the Late Victorian Era in Britain, and La Belle Époque in France—an era that attested to the development of typewriter (1868), the discovery of DNA (1869), and the opening of Suez Canal (1869) to add to the launch of telephone (1876), light bulb (1879), gasoline car (1886), movie camera (1891), and air conditioner (1902).

On the same token, the oqual spring (1787-1807) of the fifth oquannium (1787-1870) would usher in a new economic system on American soil termed Market Economy wherein production of goods and services were to be solely driven by the supply-demand equilibria buttressed by corporate competition without interference from any external forces—it is indeed no coincidence that the engine of modern capitalism in the form of New York Stock Exchange came into being in 1792 at the dawn of the fifth oqual cycle to add to a number of other ground-breaking innovations such as the launch of the optical telegraph (1792), the development of maiden vaccine against the smallpox virus (1796), the birth of steam train (1812), and the debut of photographic camera (1816).

While scientific discoveries and technological advances are also aplenty during the second half of oqual cycle, their predominantly applied-and-commercial nature pales in comparison to the largely fundamental-and-seminal breakthroughs made during the first half.

However, all good things eventually come to an end due to what appears to be a universal rhythm that apparently transcends the underpinnings of every form of matter and energy in nature.

Admittedly, the rather favorable sociopolitical forces essential for the maintenance and integrity of overall prosperity of a society begin to wane and head south as the oqual cycle approaches its summit (or turning point) after what is often viewed in the rearview mirror as a nostalgic period of some 42 years.

Why do the rather good times of the first half of oqual cycle eventually come to an end?

Over the rather long 42-year constructive phase of relative peace and harmony enjoyed over the course of the first half of oqual cycle, people's memories of hard times endured during the nadir at the dusk of previous oqual cycle largely become erased, or rather, they brush aside lessons of history in the tainted belief that it would never repeat.

Such a toxic combo of ignorance and hubris coupled with prosperity not only plants a false sense of complacency but also democratizes a culture of living beyond means, and in doing so, it makes younger generations become self-indulgent and hedonistic such that they feel that good times will perhaps never end but they always do.

One indeed cannot have the cake and eat it too!

The resulting triumph of hedonism over collectivism fuels the resurgence of a plethora of regressive sociopolitical forces such as immorality, conflict, individualism, populism, fraud, debt, corruption, partisanship, xenophobia, baby bust, wealth polarization, and institutional distrust.

To add gasoline to fire, such regressive forces act in a negatively-cooperative (or counter-synergistic) manner in that their combined output is much more toxic than the sum of their individual parts—their concerted action produces a sociopolitical system that is heavily rigged in favor of a small minority of wealthy wherein the masses become exploited rather than being justly rewarded for their proportional contributions to the society.

While the first half of oqual cycle is underscored by a bucketload of progressive forces acting in a concerted fashion to outweigh the malaise of regressive forces, the balance of power turns on its head during the second half when the regressive forces conspire to not only neutralize but also override the overpowering weight of their better counterparts.

Indeed, during the second half of oqual cycle, greed mongers and wicked souls within the human society act in a concerted fashion to not only hijack the system so as to funnel resources away from the masses toward a small minority of wealthy and elite but they also set about pulverizing moral values that had served as the bedrock of our civilization during the first half.

In other words, our sociopolitical system is pushed to its limit with all levers of control being turned to full throttle with self-destruction all but guaranteed.

For example, much of the globe has been bedeviled by an ever-deepening canyon of sociopolitical upheaval with each passing year since the outset of the second half (1997-2038) of the current oquannium (1955-2038) as summed up below in a chronological order:

1) NATO Expansion (1999-date)
2) Consumption Mania (2000-date)
3) 9/11 Wars (2001-2021)
4) Climate Propaganda (2006-date)
5) Global Financial Crisis (2007-2008)
6) Money Printing (2008-date)
7) Debt Mania (2008-date)
8) Cultural Dysphoria (2008-date)
9) Arab Spring (2010-2012)
10) Libyan Civil War (2011-date)
11) Syrian Civil War (2011-date)
12) Coronavirus Pandemic (2019-2023)
13) Consumer Price Inflation (2021-date)
14) Russia-Ukraine War (2022-date)

Add to such sociopolitical crises the fact that our society is also being peppered by disruptive forces from both the far-left and the far-right as the current oqual cycle nears its end.

On the far-left, the leaders and their herd muddy the societal waters through what has come to be dubbed "Wokeism"—a deeply-polarizing and disruptive ideology that claims to be aware of what it perceives to be sociopolitical prejudices, injustices, and inequalities endemic to human society as embodied in the so-called "critical race theory".

On the far-right, the leaders up the ante by gaslighting the majority into believing that they are the victims of the minority in order to win their votes rather than addressing real-life problems—such a divisive ideology powered in no uncertain terms by demagoguery is further exacerbated by right-wing politics emerging across the globe.

As if such a confluence of rightwing polarizing politics and leftwing propaganda does not spark a crisis vying to hold its own, Mother Nature also gets in on the act as it appears to reserve the worst of its scourge on humanity by virtue of its ability to unleash a barrage of natural disasters just when we are at our worst and least prepared during the second half of oqual cycle.

Such synergism between Mother Nature and humanity's unspectacular unraveling plunge the society into an even deeper sociopolitical crisis.

For example, the second half (1997-2038) of the current oquannium (1955-2038) has hitherto witnessed some of the most crippling natural calamities of our lifetime such as the 2004 Indian Ocean Tsunami, the 2005 Kashmir Earthquake, the 2008 Sichuan Earthquake, the 2010 Haiti Earthquake, the 2011 Japanese Tsunami, the 2019 Coronavirus Pandemic, and the 2023 Turkiye Earthquake.

In a similar manner, the second half (1913-1954) of the previous and sixth oquannium (1871-1954) was marred by the 1918 Influenza Pandemic across the globe, the 1920 Haiyuan Earthquake in China, the 1923 Kanto Earthquake in Japan, the 1934 Dust Bowl over North America, the 1935 Quetta Earthquake in Pakistan, and the 1948 Ashgabat Earthquake in Turkmenistan.

Likewise, during the second half (1829-1870) of the fifth oquannium (1787-1870), the world was plagued by some of the worst natural disasters recorded in recent memory such as the 1833 Sumatra Tsunami in Indonesia, the 1846 Third Cholera Pandemic across the globe, and the 1868 Arica Earthquake in Chile.

Against the backdrop of such natural calamities coupled with sociopolitical upheaval showing no signs of easing, it is therefore hardly surprising that the second half of oqual cycle spanning a 42-year destructive phase culminates with an utterly dysfunctional society marred by systemic corruption and incompetence at all levels.

The resulting dire societal straits trigger a crisis-of-a-lifetime that paves the way for the dismantling of the old-and-degenerate system through a global conflict of epic proportions so as to usher in a nouveau sociopolitical order.

Henceforth, the oqual cycle begins all over again after having experienced two consecutive bouts of construction followed by destruction, with each lasting for some 42 years on average.

With each essentially mirroring the other, such a pair of constructive-destructive stages can also be viewed as an 84-year symmetrical dyad of peace-crisis, growth-decay, boom-bust, upturn-downturn, uphill-downhill, ascendance-descendance, integration-disintegration, progression-regression, winding-unwinding, folding-unfolding, coupling-uncoupling, bonding-unbonding, fusion-fission, nucleation-atomization, and so forth.

Is oqual cycle akin to climbing and descending a mountain then?

HUMAN PROGRESS IS AKIN TO TRAVERSING THROUGH A SERIES OF MOUNTAINS AND VALLEYS

When viewed through the prism of oqual cycle, it seems that human progress is akin to climbing and descending a mountain over a period of 84 years, and then repeating the whole process all over again.

Over the course of an oqual cycle, we seemingly climb uphill to reach the summit during the first 42 years followed by rolling downhill to reach the valley beneath over the next 42 years.

However, it is important to keep in mind that neither climbing uphill during the first half of oqual cycle nor rolling downhill during the second half encounters a smooth journey.

Rather, each stage is punctuated with a rough (or rugged) landscape that temporarily involves falling into a spate of local minima (or gorges) followed by rising up the local maxima (or ridges) as the oqual cycle continues the journey either uphill or downhill.

In other words, even during what is overall a time of sustained growth and prosperity for the masses while climbing uphill, human civilization nevertheless encounters occasional setbacks and crises though they rarely metastasize beyond national or regional borders.

In a similar manner, during what is overall a time of stagnation and regression while rolling downhill, human civilization nonetheless experiences short bursts of rapid growth and innovation though their benefits rarely trickle down to the masses.

Do we plant our own downfall after reaching the summit?

When viewing the sphere of our civilization from a wider angle, it seems that humans are in fact the victims of their own success—the fallout from the very forces that catapult them to the summit of the oqual mountain during the first half seemingly comes back to haunt them or becomes somewhat of a drag on their checkered progress during the second half.

Put another way, the seeds of our downfall in the second half of oqual cycle are actually planted during the first half—the first half is essentially a double-edged sword in that the very forces that conspire to produce a relatively calm and prosperous period do so with a sizeable amount of undesirable secondary effects that only come into play as we enter the second half.

Thus, the hard times encountered during the second half could also be viewed as a by-product of our earlier actions during the first half.

For example, new technologies such as phone, television, refrigerator, car, and air conditioner which had been an exclusive domain of the wealthy and elite prior to World War II (1939-1945) became democratized by leaps-and-bounds across much of the Western world just as the first half (1955-1996) of the current oquannium (1955-2038) kicked off.

Such a paradigm shift in the sociopolitical order during the second half of the 20th century was made possible due to the redirection of mass production from military arsenal to consumer goods and services as World War II drew to a close—thereby fueling an unprecedented economic boom that created high-paying jobs en masse and brought prosperity to virtually every corner of America in what would come to be called America's Golden Age (1950-1970).

However, such an economic boom also created a consumer culture as a by-product that would not only make the younger generations adopt a reckless lifestyle of living beyond their means but would also put their health and that of their environment in peril.

Admittedly, the unprecedented rise in ailments from diabetes through cancer to cardiovascular disease over the past half-a-century-or-so is largely a making of our own despicable behavior from abusing carcinogen-laden cosmetics through consuming processed foods to a sedentary lifestyle befitting a couch potato.

Likewise, the scientific and technological breakthroughs during the first half (1955-1996) of the current oquannium (1955-2038) also laid the foundations for the manufacturing of synthetic drugs en masse with the result that the perpetual use of such toxins has left our precarious bodies on the brink of collapse—thanks to modern-day profit-driven bogus medical practices that seem to have a nasty drug for every cure from children to the elderly without properly warning the public of their long-term devastating effects, thereby sucking them into a vicious cycle of drug dependency.

Dirven by the capitalist propaganda to make money by any means possible, there is now a drug for everything to decimate the health of the unsuspecting hoi polloi.

There is a drug to stimulate your appetite, another one to suppress it, yet another one to push your stools out, and then the magic pill that puts you to sleep, and then there is another silver bullet at your disposal to wake you up.

And that is before even mentioning a plethora of nasty compounds being marketed to help the masses focus on their studies, boost intelligence, avoid procrastination, keep anxiety at bay, and even make them happy.

Yet, drugs do far more harm to our bodies in that for every bodily function that they purportedly resolve, they create another ten problems.

Notably, a quantum leap in the chemical synthesis of drugs during the second half of the 20th century has also led to mass production of all sorts of recreational drugs today—the widespread abuse of such harmful substances not only causes addiction but also continues to destroy the lives of addicts and their families on an unprecedented scale.

Today, the opioid crisis worldwide may represent the tip of the iceberg of young generations having lost zest for life but the seeds of their downfall were planted many decades earlier during a time of relative peace and harmony.

It is not just the intoxication of our bodies that is the disorder of the day but our despicable behaviors have also left our environment on the brink of collapse thanks in large part to today's consumer culture that in no small part has been powered by the scientific and technological breakthroughs made during the first half (1955-1996) of the current oquannium (1955-2038).

SOCIOPOLITICAL UPHEAVAL IS A HALLMARK OF THE SECOND HALF OF OQUAL CYCLE

According to Murphy's law, anything that can go wrong will go wrong. While that law remains deeply controversial, its validity is best demonstrated during times of sociopolitical crisis that befalls humanity during the second half of oqual cycle.

Indeed, being in the midst of the second half (1997-2038) of the current oquannium (1955-2038), most of us would wholeheartedly bear testimony to such a bedlam firsthand.

What were once relatively good old days during the second half of the 20th century came to an abrupt end at the outset of 21st century across much of the globe just as the current oquannium (1955-2038) entered its second half—a 42-year period that nominally kicked off in 1997 though the sparks did not go off until the hijacked planes struck America on 2001/09/11.

To put this into the context of the annual cycle, the beginning-in-earnest of the second half of the current oqual cycle in 2001 in lieu of 1997 would be akin to a storm arriving about a fortnight later than expected.

Witnessed firsthand as I saw unprecedented plumes of smoke billowing over Downtown Manhattan along with the rising sun from the rather comfort of a high-rise building in Midtown, that fateful day on 9/11 marked a watershed that signaled the arrival-in-earnest of a 42-year tumultuous period across the globe as it brought virtually every nation-on-earth to conform to a new normal that has stuck with us ever since.

Yet, each one of the four American presidents to have been at the helm since 9/11 did not shy away from reassuring the faithful at home and abroad with a rather absurd message that America's best days were yet to come—even when the naked truth has been the diametric opposite all along.

Worse yet, in the aftermath of 9/11 attacks, many worshippers of capitalism across America rekindled the fairytale of a utopian era waiting on the horizon with the promise of making America's past look tame by comparison—even if that came at the expense of preemptively annihilating millions of innocent souls across the globe and destroying other nations with impunity.

To the contrary, America has been steadily rolling downhill ever since 9/11 though still quite a distance away from reaching a deep canyon with a rock and a hard place anxiously waiting below for the catch-of-a-lifetime.

Tellingly, America's spectacular fall from grace has also wrapped virtually every other nation-of-the-world into a sociopolitical quagmire from where all roads lead to a deep canyon.

Although widely-touted as a leader of the free world during much of the 20th century, America has been acting more like a ringleader of the mafia since 9/11.

While the list of America's crimes over the past several decades is exhaustive, it can be summed up under the following two major points:
- 1) Using 9/11 attacks as a pretense and under the false guise of weapons of mass destruction being developed by Iraq, America and its NATO poodles not only razed to ground but also created chaos and power vacuum across much of the Middle East through waging unethical-illegal-and-immoral decades-long wars in the name of democracy and freedom even though the hidden propaganda was to exercise America's might

and subdue weaker nations harboring natural resources, strategic importance, or posing threat to the petrodollar; and

2) Robbing the economic prosperity of future generations of Americans through printing trillions of dollars in a reckless manner and borrowing to the hilt to finance the unnecessary 9/11 Wars as well as to promote an irresponsible and immoral culture of living beyond means that has not only left the American society teetering on the ropes but also the planet earth—overconsumption is largely a making of America and its brand of sick capitalism that has infected virtually every other nation-on-earth with no signs of cresting.

What used to be the good-old-shiny-happy days for much of the second half of the 20th century indeed appear to have evaporated forever in the aftermath of 9/11 just as they did some 84 years earlier with the onset of World War I in 1914.

In line with the dire spell of oqual cycle, that despicable period coincided with the second half (1913-1954) of the previous and sixth oquannium (1871-1954).

Admittedly, those earlier times witnessed two world wars, an economic depression, extreme poverty, resurgence of xenophobia, soaring public debts, widening wealth gap, shrinking middle class, growing sociopolitical partisanship, rise of populism, metastasis of Ponzism, and plummeting trust of governments in America and across much of the globe.

That period also witnessed the borders of so many nations redrawn as well as the birth of new nations on an unprecedented scale from Gandhi's India (1947) and Jinnah's Pakistan (1947) to Ben-Gurion's Israel (1948) and Mao's China (1949).

On the other hand, the 1920s saw an exponential rise and spread of Ponzism—the widespread emergence of a paraphernalia of get-rich-quick and pump-and-dump schemes unleashed by the likes of fraudsters, swindlers, and con-artists whose concerted actions planted the seeds for the 1929 historic crash of the stock market that would subsequently lead to the Great Depression (1929-1939) followed by World War II (1939-1945).

Some 84 years later, Ponzism has once again grown into an 800-pound gorilla since the onset of the second half (1997-2038) of the current and seventh oquannium (1955-2038)—such a fraudulent culture has hitherto caused the popping of the 2000 Dotcom Bubble and the 2007 Housing Bubble.

In the wake of the 2019 Coronavirus Pandemic, Ponzism has been run amok to the quartic power in the form of cryptos, non-fungible tokens (NFTs), special purpose acquisition companies (SPACs), and meme stocks—the stocks of virtually bankrupt and zombie companies heavily traded on the market and catapulted to the sky, merely due to their popularity on social media rather than their corporate fundamentals, only for them to come back crashing to earth and leaving fools holding the bag.

Indeed, such Ponzi schemes not only propelled the stock markets but also the housing markets around the globe to become extremely frothy and bubblicious in 2021—a crash-of-a-lifetime is thus once again on the cards, and like the 1929 crash, it will also leave millions of fools-and-horses without clothes.

Regrettably, such reckless behavior on the part of humanity is nothing short of signs of terrible times on the horizon threatening to upend the very fabric of society to which we have become accustomed to in our lives.

Of course, such a familiar movie has been playing out during the second half of every oqual cycle since the beginning of times.

One notable case from these earlier times is the launch of railway transport during the early 19th century.

While the first half (1787-1828) of the fifth oquannium (1787-1870) saw the launch of railway transport across many parts of Europe and North America, the second half (1829-1870) provided an opportunity for the Ponzi schemes to capitalize on its growing popularity in the United Kingdom in what came to be known as the 1846 Railway Mania—fraudsters scammed millions of people of their life-savings through selling shares of bogus companies that would claim to build new railway lines even though they only existed on paper a la SPACs of today.

Being in the midst of the second half (1997-2038) of the current oquannium (1955-2038), no one should therefore be surprised that a similar drama of Ponzi schemes and sociopolitical chaos is being played out once again in plain sight.

In disguise of the Oracle of Omaha Warren Buffett, only when the tide goes out does one get to see those who are skinny-dipping (or swimming naked).

As the oqual cycle draws to a close, the tide does indeed go out on such fraudsters and their accomplices leaving them not only embarrassed and humiliated but also behind bars for good.

Such a dire fate does not only await individuals with a bad karma but also nations that have continued to transgress unabated over the course of oqual cycle.

While America has been by far the largest perpetrator of transgressions over the past several decades, its allies in Asia and Europe have also closely followed in its dirty footsteps.

The likes of Japan, United Kingdom, and the European Union have practically destroyed their economies—and hence sociopolitical homeostasis—through aggressive money printing that began almost in concurrence with the onset of the second half (1997-2038) of the current oquannium (1955-2038).

While the currencies of other nations by-and-large carry little value outside their borders, their respective leaders have nevertheless been tearing down their rather healthy sociopolitical strata over the past couple of decades through taking on excessive debt so as to fuel the addiction of their people rapidly becoming accustomed to being provided for rather than being able to stand on their own feet a la their parents and grandparents before them.

Today, it is therefore no coincidence that virtually every nation-of-the-world has hit an abyss—the like of which we have not seen in a lifetime—as viewed through virtually every angle from economic well-being to sociopolitical stability.

With the ongoing sociopolitical upheaval around the world having reached a tipping point and rapidly approaching a deep canyon, there is simply going to be no soft landing.

Rather, when push comes to shove, the only viable solution is to completely do away with the old system and begin anew.

Tellingly, a new dawn of good-old-shiny-happy days is on the horizon and will likely arrive some time during the 2030s in a manner akin to the beginning of relatively prosperous times during the 1950s, 1870s, and 1790s savored on American soil and across much of the globe.

However, the ongoing sociopolitical upheaval will get multiples worse over the next decade or so before we see the light at the end of the oqual tunnel.

In other words, the human society not only finds itself in a bind but has also been rolling downhill since the outset of 21st century and it will continue to do so for at least another decade before it reverses course and begins to climb uphill once again with a renewed vigor just as it did some 84 years ago during the 1950s.

In particular, the decade centered on annus horribilis (2028) of the current oquannium (1955-2038) does not bear good omens as it will be paralyzed by a global conflict of epic proportions due to the convergence and resurgence of so many regressive sociopolitical forces such as debt, populism, corruption, xenophobia, partisanship, wealth gap, and dysfunctional governments.

While a global conflict is not absolutely necessary to bringing about such a reset every 84 years, it is all but obligatory.

WHY A GLOBAL CONFLICT IS A PREREQUISITE TO BRING THE ONGOING SOCIOPOLITICAL UPHEAVAL AROUND THE GLOBE TO AN END

Few would disagree that the current sociopolitical system around the globe has hit a nadir like never before in our lives.

Not only has it become inundated with swamp from left-and-right but it is also broken down to bare bones such that it cannot be fixed but rather it needs to be wholly replaced by a new system with the mandate to begin anew at the expense of dismantling corrupt and dysfunctional institutions.

In other words, when the sociopolitical system hits such a low, it is time to drain the swamp.

In particular, such a swamp spearheaded by deep societal rifts serves as a thermodynamic bottleneck making it energetically unfavorable for people on opposite sides of the sociopolitical spectrum to come to a consensus and agree to work together.

That is until they fall into an abyss-of-a-lifetime.

Simply put, when people hit their lowest point, only then are they open to working together so as to usher in the greatest change (or revolution) in their sociopolitical system.

History has shown time and again that such a nadir on average occurs once in a lifetime, or once every 84 years, as the sociopolitical upheaval that takes hold during the second half of oqual cycle reaches a tipping point and, in doing so, triggers a global conflict of epic proportions so as to acquiesce to a new dawn of hope and prosperity.

As the saying goes, there is no rose without a thorn.

Admittedly, a large-scale global conflict with the potential to not only wreak havoc on an astronomical scale but also strike terror into the hearts and minds of people appears to be a prerequisite for breaking ties with our past and old traditions so as to revitalize human society and usher in a brighter tomorrow.

Without such a real-life horror show, people on opposite sides of the sociopolitical spectrum refuse to see eye-to-eye in order to come to a consensus necessary to rid the society of its wrongdoings amassed over the course of oqual cycle.

In other words, only under such an apocalyptic scenario, people put their differences aside and come together for a common cause that involves rebooting their society and beginning anew.

More specifically, a global conflict revitalizes the human society by leaps and bounds via a three-pronged mechanism as follows:

1) **Constructive fear**—The global conflict strikes fear into the hearts and minds of people so that they can put their differences aside and come to a consensus necessary to dismantle old-and-dysfunctional institutions and replace them with new ones better suited for new times. For example, social security benefits to take care of people from the cradle to the grave irrespective of their contributions to the society in America and across much of the Western world began on either side of World War II (1939-1945). In fact, revolutionary institutions such as America's Social Security Administration (1935), United Nations (1945), UK National Insurance Act (1946), UK National Assistance Act (1948), UK National Health Service (1948), and North Atlantic Treaty Organization (1949) only came into being during the crisis-of-a-lifetime as the previous oquannium (1871-1954) headed for the exit. Others such as European Union (1957), Federal Aviation Administration (1958), National Aeronautics and Space Administration (1958) would follow hot on the heels of the nominal start of the current oquannium (1955-2038). Needless to say, a similar roster of revolutionary institutions also took hold at the cusp of previous oqual cycles. Likewise, the looming World War III will provide a perfect backdrop to dismantle so many failed experiments such as social-welfare programs across much of the Western world that have brought it down to its knees. Only under the veneer of such an apocalyptic-esque scenario will the Western governments become emboldened to axe such free handouts that have contributed to their downfall.

2) **Technological renaissance**—The global conflict causes a large-scale destruction of infrastructure with the potential to turn cities renowned for their hustle-and-bustle into ghost towns. While this may seem like a setback at first sight, it actually serves to create new opportunities for

mass employment, widespread entrepreneurship, and modernization of industry as rebuilding from ashes gets underway. Thus, new technologies waiting on the fringes of the society quickly move to the center of our civilization and become the toast of the town. It seems as if the global conflict helps to quickly clear out old technologies and traditions lest they strangulate human civilization through their ability to hold us hostage from moving forward to a new experiment. In the aftermath of World War II (1939-1945), the US government enacted the so-called Marshall Plan (1948) so as to provide war-torn Europe with a massive financial aid to help it not only get back on its feet once more but also do so with a vengeance. At home on American soil, a quantum leap in the production of goods and services due to the availability of new technologies catapulted the US economy to the moon in the post-WWII era though with the false perception that the good times were perhaps never going to end. Notably, new technologies such as phone, television, refrigerator, car, and air conditioner, which had been an exclusive domain of the wealthy and elite prior to World War II quickly became democratized across much of the Western world as the previous oquannium (1871-1954) reached its climax. Likewise, similar economic booms and rapid democratization of new technologies have also been witnessed at the transition of previous oqual cycles. With the threat of World War III looming large over our head and shoulders, old technologies are already being cleared out and making way for new ones to take their place from how we work, how we socialize, how we conduct business, and so forth. Expect new technologies such as digital currencies, autonomous cars, and delivery robots to become a-dime-a-dozen in about a decade or so on the other side of World War III.

3) **Survival of the fittest**—As cruel as the laws of nature may seem, they are nevertheless unavoidable due to biology's inherent drive for the survival of the fittest at the expense of the weak. It seems that not only a global conflict but even regional and civil wars are a product of biology designed to weed out the weak so as to concentrate limited resources for the betterment of the fittest. It may come as a surprise to witness the murder of the weaker cub by their stronger sibling while the mother lioness not only sits by quietly but also makes no attempt to intervene so as to strike a truce between her two warring offspring unless one understands the ruthless power of biology. Unfortunately, a global conflict appears to be a biological mechanism that keeps human population in check through staging a large-scale destruction of human life every 84 years on average either through a direct hit or indirectly via

destroying essential supply lines necessary for survival. Since such a mass execution disproportionately affects the weak who in the eyes of biology are unnecessarily sucking resources away from the more competitive individuals and becoming a burden on the society, it exquisitely serves its purpose in ensuring the survival of the fittest. By a conservative estimate, the three major calamities of the second half (1913-1954) of the previous oquannium (1871-1954) in the form of World War I (1914-1918), the Influenza Pandemic (1918-1920), and World War II (1939-1945) together reduced the then global population of around 2000M by at least 10%. Given that the global population has exponentially exploded since the end of WWII to 8000M today, the looming WWIII bears the potential to make its predecessor look like a dress rehearsal as we approach the interface of the current (1954-2038) and next (2039-2122) oquannia.

OQUAL CYCLE REPRESENTS A ROSETTA STONE OF HUMAN CIVILIZATION

History tells us that humans boast a dubious reputation of burning themselves down and then rising from the ashes to start all over again.

The oqual cycle argues that such a process of purification (or regeneration) does not occur randomly but rather in an orderly and cyclical manner over a period of 84 years on average.

While the cyclical nature of human civilization is hardy a breaking news, a number of characteristics nevertheless set the oqual cycle apart from the previous models as summarized below:
1) It has a fixed periodicity of exactly 84 years.
2) It is globally synchronized in that the trials and tribulations of human society across the globe occur in lockstep with each other.
3) It is universal in that it envisions almost every facet of human civilization from politics through economy to climate to oscillate in a synchronized manner over a period of 84 years.
4) It is based on a systematic calendar synchronized with the Uranian year beginning with the southern spring and ending with the southern winter.

Simply put, the oqual cycle not only supersedes the previous models but it also appears to be a lower-order harmonic of the daily and annual cycles.

Nevertheless, credit must be given where credit is due for it is the painstaking work of previous authors whose provocative models laid the foundation for the development of the theory of oqual cycle.

Notably, the oqual cycle is not set in stone in a manner akin to the annual cycle but rather its dynamics are highly fluid and malleable with respect to the recurrence of eerily-similar events spaced apart by some 84 years.

For example, the worst storm of an annual winter does not necessarily arrive in January or February in the northern hemisphere but it may also stop us in our tracks as early as December in one year or as late as March in the following year.

In a similar manner, the archetypal (or quintessential) events within an oqual cycle may also occur at the beginning of a season or toward the end.

Just as the worst winter storms of two consecutive years may be bifurcated by as little as 9 months to as much as 15 months (12 ± 3 months), the global conflicts (or hegemonic wars) preceding the reset of sociopolitical order (or other archetypal events) may also be separated by as little as 63 years to as much as 105 years (84 ± 21 years) between two consecutive oqual cycles—though they usually occur within a much narrower window of between 77 to 91 years (84 ± 7 years).

However, just as the annual cycle on average occurs over 365 days, the oqual cycle does so over an average period of 84 years.

Likewise, just as some annual winters are relatively mild and pass by quietly, the dusk (or winter) of one oqual cycle may seamlessly blend into the dawn (or spring) of the next without too much drama and chaos on display.

Like annual winters which can be relatively mild or extremely severe, not all oqual cycles are created equal either—some end with an apocalyptic-esque bang while others seamlessly transition from one cycle to the next depending on the magnitude and intensity (or amplitude) of wrongdoings amassed over the course of the cycle.

The fact that the oqual cycle may end with a quasi-apocalypse or transition from one cycle to the next in a somewhat subtle manner could explain why our sociopolitical system is proposed to undergo a global reset over a period roughly spanning the length of almost two oqual cycles according to the 2016 book titled "Ages of Discord" by Peter Turchin [3].

Notwithstanding such an alternative school of thought, the odds of the current oqual cycle transitioning into the next one without much noise are however extremely low.

In fact, oqual cycles typically end with a crescendo rather than a whimper.

On the basis of our ongoing dire sociopolitical straits having continued to hit a new low with each passing year since the outset of the 21st century with no signs of reversing the trend, the current oqual cycle indeed appears to be heading for a quasi-apocalyptic end rather than checking out with a relatively mild snowstorm.

Thus, although the doctrine of oqual cycle may suggest that our lives are governed by determinism, it is ultimately our own actions that in fact dictate the severity of the fallout from such a rendezvous with destiny.

While human beings do have the free will to change the course of their rendezvous with destiny so as to eliminate crises and wars (or at least tone them down), their egos almost always get the better of them such that they keep spinning through alternating stages of rebuilding and destruction over what appears to be a period of 84 years.

Long story short, the spell of oqual cycle on human civilization is stochastic (or probabilistic) rather than deterministic in a manner similar to the spell of daily and annual cycles on our lives.

For example, the daily cycle dictates our sleeping and working habits but, ultimately, we can choose not to wake up in the morning or go about our lives.

Likewise, the seasonal changes during the annual cycle provide us with an ample opportunity to make changes to our lives through activities such as planting or harvesting crops but, once again, it is up to us to take advantage of nature's bounties as idle hands reap nothing.

What is the biological significance of oqual cycle?

The oqual cycle lends human society a subtle mechanism to cleanse itself of its wrongdoings (or rectify its errors) lest they snowball into an insoluble labyrinth.

Thus, the oqual cycle essentially serves as a quality control in the progress of human civilization which parallels mechanisms such as backtracking (or proofreading) in cellular polymerases to ensure the fidelity of the product before continuing upstream or further afield.

Ecology also lends a fitting parallel to the importance of oqual cycle.

Just as forest fires eliminate the weed and dead vegetation on the floor so as to clean up and refuel the soil with new nutrients, the oqual cycle is equally necessary to revitalize human society after it reaches its lowest point once in a lifetime, or every 84 years on average.

In analogy with technology, human civilization appears to behave like a desktop computer that begins to slow down after running for some time as it becomes increasingly corrupted due to a myriad of what could be envisaged as unnecessary-and-bureaucratic processes holding its RAM hostage, thereby making it choppy and less productive.

Like a computer, human civilization thus requires a reboot to rid itself of such background noise in order to remain productive and competitive.

Absent an oversight of oqual cycle, humans would be at a disproportional risk of burning themselves out or driving themselves into oblivion due to the buildup of errors in perpetuity and lack of checkpoints in the progress of their civilization.

One cannot imagine life without there being no darkness of the night.

Nor can one imagine life without seasons that shower us with surprises and challenges all year round.

Why one should therefore imagine life without the oqual cycle that seemingly provides an intricately-nuanced mechanism to help us purge our society of all the baggage at periodic intervals, spaced apart by 84 years, so as to ensure that we can continue to plod along with a renewed vigor and energy rather than take the risk of crumbling under its weight.

In a nutshell, the oqual cycle is ultimately a product of evolution in that our biology appears to have gone to great lengths to ensure the long-term survival of its most advanced creation.

Why understanding the oqual cycle is so important?

As the saying goes, those who fail to learn from history are doomed to repeat it.

Admittedly, humans have a notorious reputation for failing to learn from their past mistakes and seemingly indulge in repetitive wrongdoings that plunge our society into a period of extreme trials-and-tribulations once in our lifetime, or once every 84 years on average.

For example, the status quo around the globe marred by dysfunctional and corrupt governments is not only the result of wrong choices made by the-powers-that-be over the past several decades but it has also propelled our society into a sociopolitical upheaval, the like of which we have not witnessed in our lifetime since World War II (1939-1945).

That global conflict all but marked the end of the previous oquannium (1871-1954) and laid the foundations for the beginning of the next cycle (1955-2038) that we are currently navigating.

A corollary of oqual cycle is that, once every 84 years on average, human civilization on the whole:
1) Hits an abyss-of-a-lifetime after its sociopolitical order becomes utterly dysfunctional turning into an insoluble Rubik's cube due to persistent violation of the laws of nature over several decades;
2) Pays the piper or faces a severe retribution in order to redeem and cleanse itself of its malpractices and wrongdoings; and
3) Experiences a sense of rebirth (or renaissance) as it sets about remaking itself in an image that is diametric opposite of its dysfunctional past.

Importantly, such a societal reboot does not occur randomly but rather appears to be more or less synchronized with the orbiting of Uranus around the Sun once every 84 years.

Of particular note is the fact that most nations simultaneously experience a deluge of favorable tailwinds over the course of the first half of oqual cycle followed by a barrage of unfavorable headwinds during the second half in a more or less synchronized manner.

This in-and-of-itself is evidence that the ups and downs in human civilization are not random but rather under the thumb of celestial bodies with Uranus leading the charge.

With an understanding and appreciation of the dire spell of oqual cycle on our lives, not only do we stand to understand ourselves better but the future generations also stand to benefit for they will be handsomely equipped with much knowledge and wisdom so as to minimize the fallout from such calamities that befall humanity once-in-a-lifetime, if not completely bypass them altogether.

|1.3| GENERATIONAL IMPACT

In sync with the changes in Uranian climate with respect to its southern pole, the oqual cycle is subdivided into a quartet of 21-year seasons chronologically dubbed spring, summer, autumn, and winter.

On average, each one of these four seasons begets a new generational cohort such that one can also view the progression of oqual cycle through the lens of successive generations.

Such a quartet of oqual generations is designated Generation 1 to Generation 4 (G1-G4), which respectively correspond to the four seasons from Spring to Winter.

HOW ONE CAN VIEW THE WAXING AND WANING OF OQUAL CYCLE THROUGH THE LENS OF SUCCESSIVE GENERATIONS

While cascading through a set of four distinct generations (G1-G4), the oqual cycle begins with a honeymoon in spring, undergoes a sense of awakening during summer, begins to unravel with the arrival of autumn, and ends in a cataclysmic crisis in winter in order to cleanse out the old system and herald a new dawn.

Simply put, during times of crisis in the midst of oqual winter particularly circa annus horribilis, people not only gel together to overcome shared agonies and sufferings but also agree to come to a consensus in a non-partisan manner after having navigated to a sociopolitical abyss.

The post-crisis First Generation (G1) born during oqual spring, under the clout of renewed cultural growth and a heightened sense of community coupled with institutional trust, has it much easier because their parents bore the brunt of the woes so that their children would be spared the throes.

As G1 comes of age during oqual summer, the Second Generation (G2) begins to take hold against the backdrop of the society undergoing a period of awakening so as to challenge the authority of elders and the status quo.

Having forgotten to learn the lessons from the trials-and-tribulations that their parents and grandparents had to endure during the preceding oqual winter marred by a crisis of epic proportions, G1 and G2 begin to unravel and break away from the greater good of the society in order to pursue selfish individualism during oqual autumn as the Third Generation (G3) crops up.

The resulting societal entropy (or disorder) ushers in a crisis-of-a lifetime as the final and Fourth Generation (G4) of oqual cycle emerges during a period of sociopolitical bedlam in the midst of oqual winter.

Notably, such a generational model parallels the open secret that the wealth rarely lasts beyond four generations in that the riches of one generation become diluted with each successive generation through the extravaganza and reckless squandering of the wealth by their children and grandchildren such that the great-grandchildren are unlikely to shower in the fruits of the intense labor of their great-grandparents.

Yet, in many ways, the seeds of such wealth destruction were planted in parallel with the accumulation of wealth by the first generation in that its hard work made life easy for their children who in turn made it even easier for their own children such that these subsequent generations not only ended up losing zest for life but also their trove of treasure handed down to them.

Consistent with this notion, one can then also view the waxing and waning of human progress over the course of oqual cycle due to differential challenges placed upon successive generations as follows:

1) During oqual winter, hard times carve out a commendable generation of strong people on the back of hard lessons.
2) During the following oqual spring, strong people bring about good times thanks to their selflessness, hard work, and high moral compass.
3) As the oqual summer sets in, good times inevitably beget a despicable generation of weak people with the urge for hedonistic pleasure aplenty but the will for making sacrifices as rare as diamonds—this is due to the lack of challenging times in their lives as a result of the hard work of their parents and grandparents having made life so easy such that it is being taken for granted.
4) Upon the arrival of oqual autumn, weak people begin to dismantle the very values that made their parents and grandparents so successful in life—such unavoidable violation of the basic laws of nature unsurprisingly returns the human society back to square one, or the crisis-of-a-lifetime, during the oqual winter.

Long story short, a rendezvous-with-destiny is therefore not only inevitable but it also seems to be a prerequisite for bringing about a reset (or revolution) in our sociopolitical order so as to break ties with the past and purge the society of a plethora of wrongdoings—from the societal ills through excesses and imbalances to transgressions—amassed over the course of oqual cycle in an attempt to herald a new dawn of hope and prosperity.

OQUAL CYCLE DIFFERENTIALLY SHAPES GENERATIONAL COHORTS

Most of us are familiar with the so-called "cultural generations" such as the Boomers and the Millennials in America as fed to the masses by media pundits and further espoused by the work of Strauss and Howe in their 1991 book titled "Generations" [9].

Not only do such cultural generations vary from one nation to another but they also stretch over a differential timespan of as little as a decade to as much as three decades.

To add insult to injury, such groupings of individuals are predicated on the personal viewpoint of none other than the tail that wags the dog.

In marked contrast, the oqual generations are based on a scientific and logical approach in that each generation is:
1) Named First through Fourth in a sequential order;
2) Universal in that it is applicable to every nation across the globe;
3) Fixed in length spanning a period of exactly 21 years;
4) Coincident with an oqual (or Uranian) season; and
5) A recurring archetype that remerges with each spell of oqual cycle.

In a nutshell, not only do oqual generations span a fixed timespan but they also form a constellation with their respective archetypes (or predecessors) from previous oqual cycles.

For example, the First Generation (G1) of every oqual cycle can be grouped (or clustered) together into a unique constellation that shares a similar societal outlook on life, albeit to a varying degree for each one of its archetypes, just as one annual winter is different from another but nevertheless all winters share the same core structure.

Simply put, one can group together oqual generations across all oqual cycles into four constellations (A-D) with each housing one of the four generations (G1-G4)—thus, all G1 generations belong to one unique constellation, ditto for G2 generations, and so forth.

How does the oqual cycle create such generational constellations?

During the course of oqual cycle, progressive sociopolitical forces—such as morality, peace, collectivism, globalism, entrepreneurship, moderation, transparency, nonpartisanship, ethnic harmony, baby boom, economic well-being, and institutional trust—steadily rise over the first half followed by a more-or-less symmetrical drop during the second half.

On the other hand, regressive sociopolitical forces—such as immorality, conflict, individualism, populism, fraud, debt, corruption, partisanship, xenophobia, baby bust, wealth polarization, and institutional distrust—decline over the first half of oqual cycle but rear their ugly head as they begin to precipitously surge during the second half.

Such an asymmetrical contribution of various sociopolitical headwinds and tailwinds across the two halves differentially shapes the characteristics or perception of the worldview of various generations that emerge during the course of oqual cycle.

For example, individuals born during the winter (G4) of an oqual cycle by-and-large hold a positive view of the society since much of their adult lives coincide with the first half, inundated with plenty of optimism and prosperity, of the next cycle.

Admittedly, most individuals born during the winter (1934-1954) of the previous oquannium (1871-1954) have held the society and institutions in a rather high esteem till quite recently since the sociopolitical system largely worked for the masses throughout much of their adult lives coincident with the first half (1955-1996) of the current oquannium (1955-2038)—and many of such individuals still continue to subscribe to that view even in the face of utter sociopolitical chaos unfolding before their eyes.

In marked contrast, individuals born during the summer (G2) of an oqual cycle by-and-large hold a negative view of the society since much of their adult lives coincide with the second half, mired in utter chaos and sociopolitical upheaval, of the same cycle.

Indeed, most individuals born during the summer (1976-1996) of the current oquannium (1955-2038) view the society as largely a collection of oppressive institutions whose goal is to enslave and exploit the masses in that the sociopolitical system has been rigged in favor of a small minority of wealthy and elite throughout what has hitherto been much of their adult lives during the second half (1997-2038).

On the other hand, individuals born during the spring (G1) and the autumn (G3) of an oqual cycle by-and-large hold a rather mixed perception of the society between the two extremes noted above.

Thus, individuals born during the spring (1955-1975) of the current oquannium (1955-2038) generally view the society as so-so since much of their adult lives have straddled across both the first half and the second.

Likewise, individuals born during the autumn (1997-2017) of the current oquannium (1955-2038) are also poised to view the society as so-so since much of their adult lives will be straddling across the second half of the current cycle and the first half of the next one.

Importantly, like the ducklings of the winter (1934-1954) of the previous oquannium (1871-1954), the sucklings born during the winter (2018-2038) of the current oquannium (1955-2038) will also see the world through rose-colored glasses as they come of age.

In fact, today's infants and toddlers along with the babies born over the next decade or so will be the luckiest-in-a-lifetime as they will come out of their shells into a world full of optimism and prosperity under the clout of renewed cultural growth and a heightened sense of community coupled with institutional trust and a functional government that will once again deliver for the masses.

I should add that those planning to have a baby in the near future must do so by no later than annus mirabilis (2039) of the next oquannium (2039-2122) lest they come of age in a world where a pair of rose-colored glasses once again begins to break their bank as it has been doing so over the past several decades.

Notwithstanding this rationale, the birth rate however typically spikes during the oqual spring rather than oqual winter after all the dust from the fallout of sociopolitical upheaval has settled.

Admittedly, the oqual spring (1955-1975) of the current oquannium (1955-2038) witnessed an unprecedented upsurge in baby boom across the globe with the world population having skyrocketed by almost 50% against the backdrop of relatively prosperous times.

While that scenario is unlikely to pan out during the oqual spring (2039-2059) of the next oquannium (2039-2122) due to the planet already being overpopulated, a baby boom is nevertheless on the cards as the curtain is raised over the next cycle in about a decade or so, thereby putting an end to the rather measly birth rate being witnessed today.

On a personal note, having been born in 1971 on the cusp of spring-summer of the current oquannium (1955-2038), I had been baffled all my life as to why my mentors and seniors born a generation or two before me during the winter (1934-1954) of the previous oquannium (1871-1954) always saw the world through rose-colored glasses when my own experiences were the diametric opposite.

Not only did I begin to lose trust in almost every institution, particularly in the wake of the self-destructive 9/11 Wars waged to merely bloat the pockets of the ruling elite at the expense of killing and uprooting millions, but it even provoked my literary mind to coin catchphrases in order to capture a rising wave of corrupt and fraudulent behavior in our society that I have witnessed over the past quarter-of-a-century as idiomatically expressed below:

> "The doctors have their best interests at your carte (or card) rather than your best interests at their heart!"
>
> "Beware of lawyers! The only law they practice is how to rip one off and then get away with it in broad daylight!"
>
> "Be mindful of big enchiladas promoting a financial product! The odds of it being a fraud are all but unity!"
>
> "While taking a stroll down the street, one should be more mindful of getting shot by the cops at point-blank range rather than getting mugged!"

Guided by the oqual theory, no longer do I remain baffled about my past experiences nor do I continue to hold the misguided view that perhaps my mentors and seniors were simply naïve and ingenuous but rather our experiences are shaped by the differential spell of oqual cycle on our lives.

It matters a lot not only where we are born but also when we are born.

Though we still remain clueless as to how we are born and why we are born.

Nevertheless, such is the power of oqual cycle as it not only arms one to improve their optics through a circular prism like never before but it also equips them to decode almost every human behavior and societal phenomenon that befalls us.

In short, the oqual theory argues that we are not only connected to our past via our genotype (or DNA) but also through our phenotype (or characteristics) due to the cyclical nature of our civilization.

HOW CAN OQUAL CYCLE HELP ME RATIONALIZE MY OWN SUCCESSES AND FAILURES IN LIFE

The readers should note how successes and failures in their own lives waxed and waned in parallel with the rhythm of oqual cycle.

This is due to the fact that the prevailing sociopolitical atmosphere at each stage of one's life intricately determines their fate.

For example, as a university professor in the field of biomedical research who began to apply his trade at the outset of the 21st century just as the current oquannium

(1955-2038) had taken a turn for the worst, I should have been mindful of the dire spell of its ugly second half (1997-2038) that has hitherto spared few in academia.

Tellingly, among a wide array of academic scientists of my generation, I have only once-in-a-blue-moon come across someone who is even barely satisfied with how things have turned out for what they had perceived to be a rather prestigious and fruituous (or fructuous) career choice during their college years against the backdrop of then relatively prosperous and upbeat times—though such happy times were on their last leg as most of us would be left stranded in the middle of nowhere rather than being given a ride off into the sunset.

Little any of us would have known during our good old college years that we would come of age during times of a rising wave of sociopolitical upheaval that would accompany us from our heydays till well into our old age—and that we will never see good times in spite of having sacrificed our lives for a career that we took to heart with all our passion and zest abound.

Rather than being rewarded for our ingenuity and dedication to a career that only the brightest in the society stand a chance of pursuing, the-powers-that-be made us feel like "criminals" and put us through so much "interrogation" that it almost became impossible to do the science that we had dreamed of during our college years.

Indeed, most of us would wholeheartedly attest to the fact that such a bureaucratic red tape made us squander most of our precious time and resources that we ought to have devoted to what we loved most.

To add salt to our proverbial wounds, an overwhelming majority of us would even switch fields to pursue the utter garbage that had become politically "popular" and easily "fundable" rather than what would set our pulse racing every morning.

Necessity may be the mother of invention but the ground-breaking scientific discoveries are the product of pure serendipity—a transition state of nirvana that can only be achieved when scientists are unshackled so as to enable them to pursue the craziest ideas without a bureaucratic oversight for they should not need to justify to anyone why they do what they do for their passion alone is the best metric of their productivity and promise of what they stand to deliver for the society-writ-large.

Admittedly, it is therefore hardly surprising that scientific discoveries by-and-large appear to have hit a roadblock during the second half (1997-2038) of the current oquannium (1955-2038) and arguably pale in comparison to what the generations before us unearthed during the first half (1955-1996)—that was made possible in no small part due to there being relatively prosperous times when bureaucracy took the backseat and allowed scientists to unleash their full potential without becoming entangled in the sociopolitical drama.

That is all the more damning given that the rather paltry bucket-load of dollars allocated toward scientific research during the second half of the 20th century pale in comparison to the humongous ocean-load of funds that have already been squandered during the first quarter of the 21st century alone—thanks to the bureaucratic and wasteful practice of today's corrupt and fraudulent institutions having adopted and normalized a culture of ever-diminishing returns on research dollars.

Against the backdrop of such a pandemonium and powered by their deadly motto of "Fake it till you make it!", the second half (1997-2038) of the current oquannium (1955-2038) has unsurprisingly bred a growing generation of fraudsters and charlatans who have exploited the equally-fraudulent institutional system to steal most of the resources away from bona-fide scientists bereft of projecting such a misleading caricature.

In nature, the opposites attract.

But, it is the "likes" that have attracted the "likes" vis-à-vis the funding of scientific research over the past quarter-of-a-century—a fraudulent institutional system only stands to resonate with fraudsters and their shenanigans.

Even Nobel prizes have become so politicized that they are now being handed out to devious actors a la Gore (2007), Obama (2009), and Bernanke (2022) who have blood on their hands respectively through promoting the climate propaganda so as to divert attention away from pressing issues affecting the well-being of our planet, waging immoral wars to annihilate humanity out of the devilish urge to control and subjugate the weak, and wrecking the financial system so as to ravage the livelihoods of billions around the globe.

These are all signs of the times when nature wages a war of its own to push back against the self-proclaimed Gog and Magog and, in doing so, it purges the society of utter evil so as to give humanity a fresh start.

However, the honeymoon period barely lasts more than a few decades before the likes of Gog and Magog take root once more and bring the society into utter disrepute every 84 years on average as exquisitely embodied in the oqual cycle.

2 | POLITICAL WAVES

Not long ago, the American spaceship was comfortably cruising at a sky-high altitude as the 21st century rolled in over two decades ago.

Even the distant stars appeared to be aligned for the then sole superpower to continue to call the shots in its quest to dominate the universe at large.

Add to that the euphoria of American Dream run amok to the nth degree.

Many Americans even believed that unlike the British Empire upon which the sun never set, the American hegemony was rising with the sun and that America's best days were yet to come.

To others, it seemed like a utopian era waiting on the horizon with the promise of making America's past look tame by comparison.

Bluntly put, there was no limit to what United States could and would not conquer so as long it remained not only head-and-shoulders but also chest-and-waist above other nations even if that required dismantling any competitor who dared to challenge the American supremacy.

It would simply continue to be the American Way or the Highway.

However, with the new century having barely gotten its feet wet, the nation would be struck by the 9/11 attacks in 2001 and, in a split second of horror, America's horoscope turned upside down.

Quel dommage! What a pity!

Alas, the 9/11 attacks did not fall out of the sky.

Indeed, rather than merely relying on the stars to do the heavy lifting, the US government would take matters into its own hands so as to guarantee America's destiny through turning the 9/11 attacks into a pretext so as to finish off the unsettled business.

What followed next were a series of decades-long perpetual wars across the Middle East propagandized in the name of democracy and freedom but with the hidden objective of changing the world order so as to extend the branches of America's hegemonic tree farther than ever before.

However, such a criminal and reckless grand plan that would kill and uproot millions of innocent lives would not only backfire but would also come back to haunt America for generations to come.

Admittedly, more than two decades later, the embers of the wars waged in the aftermath of 9/11 continue to rage to this day.

While the 9/11 Wars kept seething overseas, America continued to decay at home from soaring public debts through shrinking middle class to faltering infrastructure.

The continued failure of the US government to address such shortcomings coupled with the loss of public trust ultimately morphed into a rage that led one half of America to elect Donald Trump to the nation's highest office in 2016.

Yet, the other half of America continues to be petrified by the humiliating aspect of not only having had a conman run their country but with him being the odds-on favorite to make a comeback and take the helm once more in 2024.

Perhaps, what this other half of America does not get is that Trump is not the cause of the status quo but rather the effect and symptom of his predecessors having not only failed Americans but also having sold America to the wealthy at the expense of the poor.

If Trump's rise to power was a canary-in-the-coalmine, then his ability to govern with an iron fist with no regard for the rule of law marked the beginning of the end of unraveling of America before its very own eyes.

In the context of oqual cycle, Trump's inauguration to the nation's highest office in 2017 could not have been more fitting or rather preordained.

Exactly 84 years earlier in 1933, Adolf Hitler came to power in what came to be known as Nazi Germany.

Like Trump, Hitler also avowed to make Germany great again.

Not only did Hitler terribly fail but he also left an indelible stain on humanity.

Like the Nazi madman, Trump is on an irreversible mission to hollow out what little remains of America's global prestige and leave behind a lasting impact of his bigotry for generations to come.

On a brighter note, just as a more peaceful and prosperous Germany emerged from the clutches of Hitler, a similar fate also awaits America—albeit in the shadow of China that is all but set to take up the mantle of global leadership over the next decade or so.

Indeed, America is not the first hegemon to fall from grace but rather it is merely following in the footsteps of its predecessors whose hegemony for the most part lasted no more than a period of around 84 years.

In the context of oqual cycle, the precipitous decay of the American hegemony over the past quarter-of-a-century should be hardly surprising given that such a contrasting change in fortunes befalls every nation, hegemonic or not.

However, in the case of hegemons, they face the dire prospect of having to pass on the baton of hegemony to one of their competitors—a fate that America is set to exercise as it prepares to relinquish its role to the new sheriff in town.

Nevertheless, during the decade beginning with annus horribilis (2028) of the current oquannium (1955-2038) and ending with annus mirabilis (2039) of the next cycle (2039-2122), Americans on both sides of the political aisle will finally cluster together and put their differences aside so that America can once again rise from the ashes—yet in a triumph of free will over determinism.

In order to appreciate the full gamut of political waves that seemingly oscillate in sync with the progression of oqual cycle, let us dissect our discussion further into the following sections:

    2.1 Global Hegemony
    2.2 Global Politics
    2.3 Global Reset

| 2.1 | GLOBAL HEGEMONY

In a way that human lifespan runs about 84 years on average, it seems that this also holds true for the hegemon's shelf-life—the length of time over which a global power exercises absolute hegemony (or dominance) over other nations.

That should be hardly surprising in that both lifespans are under the thumb of oqual cycle and, as such, they share features beyond just their lengths.

Just as human life is occasionally cut short or extends well beyond the average length, so does the hegemony of a global power—the age of neither is set in stone but nevertheless it gyrates around 84 years.

In a manner that humans typically reach their overall peak at the age of 42 beyond which their star begins to dim and then eventually bows out at around 84, the global dominance of a power also appears to reach a crescendo over the first 42 years before unwinding over the following 42 years as it enters the wilderness but before passing the torch onto to a newly-crowned hegemon.

Not only are hegemons mortal with an average lifespan of 84 years but their rise and fall also appears to occur in parallel with the waxing and waning of human civilization over the course of oqual cycle in what is dubbed the "hegemony oquacycle".

Nevertheless, due to a combination of atypical sociopolitical forces at play coupled with right choices made, some global powers may be able to extend their lifespan and exert their hegemony across two consecutive rounds of oqual cycle as was the case for the British Empire over much of the combined course of the fifth (1787-1870) and sixth (1871-1954) oquannia.

Notably, the hegemon's global dominance over rival powers typically peaks at around the midpoint of oqual cycle before it becomes embroiled in excesses and imbalances that subsequently plant its downfall from grace.

For example, America's hegemony peaked just prior to the outbreak of 9/11 Wars almost in parallel with the onset of the second half (1997-2038) of the current and seventh oquannium (1955-2038).

Indeed, America was widely believed to be the sole superpower during much of the 1990s after the apoptosis of its closest rival the Soviet Union in 1991.

However, such exorbitant hubris of being the sole superpower was exactly what led the capitalist cabal to dig the nation's grave through waging decades-long and self-destructive 9/11 Wars.

That America's precipitous fall from grace would begin almost in sync with the onset of such an asinine self-defeating pursuit to the delight of its rivals should therefore be hardly surprising.

In fact, barely a decade later, America's sole superpowerness would be challenged by the rapid rise of China just as the Teenies (2010s) kicked off.

It should be noted that the hegemonic peak of a global power is not necessarily coincident with the peak of its imperial inertia—a global power may for example continue to bloat and add new colonies to its imperial crown well past its hegemonic peak but it may no longer be the most powerful entity relative to its rivals, with one of them usually being the hegemon.

What is the difference between a global power and imperial power?

A global power exerts its geopolitical influence outside its comfort zone in far-flung regions, typically located on the other side of a large body of water rather than solely connected via land.

A global power is therefore inherently an imperial power but the converse may not necessarily be true.

For example, prior to the birth of Modern Age in 1451, the Ottoman Empire and the Chinese Empire were two of the greatest imperial powers of their time but neither was a global power in the sense that their sphere of geopolitical influence was largely restricted over large body of contiguous landmass rather than stretching across vast oceans.

In that sense, Portugal became the first true global power at the outset of Modern Age in that it was able to conquer oceans and colonize unfamiliar territories, which no other nation had ever done before in the history of humanity.

Simply put, Portugal was the first nation to break through the glass ceiling of global hegemony as it pioneered maritime navigation across vast oceans and paved the way for European colonization of regions outside the comfort zone of Afro-Eurasia centered around the Mediterranean Sea.

What causes the rise and fall of hegemons?

While previous works such as the 1987 book titled "Long Cycles in World Politics" by the Polish-American political scientist George Modelski [1] and the 2021 book titled "Principles for Dealing with the Changing World Order" by the American financier Ray Dalio [10] lend deep insights into the rise and fall of great powers, such a change in political fortunes however appears to be synchronized with the waxing and waning of the broader human civilization over the course of oqual cycle—implying that a similar set of forces are at play in triggering the rise and fall of hegemons as well as human society as a whole as discussed under §1.2.

In particular, the hegemon's rise and fall from grace over the course of oqual cycle is marked by a cascade of four distinct steps, each of which occurs in tandem with the corresponding 21-year Uranian season as chronologically outlined below:

1) **Spring -> Hegemon rises to global dominance**—Hegemon's rise to global dominance causes the standard of living at home to precipitously rise due to the fact that it controls the world's resources and therefore gets to have the first bite before letting others munch on leftovers and substandard products. Not only that but it also turns into Mecca for immigrants as new riches attract people from unskilled workers to undertake dirty and low-paid jobs through highly-skilled professionals to geniuses from all over the world. In particular, being in charge of the world's reserve currency implies that the hegemon simply prints its way to glory through luring top minds from across the globe to its shores at the expense of other nations having to grapple with not only a massive brain drain but also having footed the bill for their education only to lose their best on a "free" transfer. One only has to look at how the fortunes of America bloated overnight in the aftermath of World War II almost in parallel with the start of spring (1955-1975) of the current oquannium (1955-2038). For its part, Britain experienced such a virtue across much of both the fifth (1787-1870) and sixth (1871-1954) oquannia. However, the increase in standard of living results in wages skyrocketing such that the cost of manufacturing goes through the roof at home and it is only a matter of time before the hegemon loses its manufacturing competitiveness to other nations.

2) **Summer -> Hegemon loses manufacturing prowess**—As manufacturing costs surge at home, the hegemon begins to heavily rely on imported goods and services, which is made all the more easier given that they are essentially "free" in that they are being paid for with "worthless"

notes of junk paper due to monetary hegemony that comes with global dominance—the hegemon's national currency effectively serves as the world currency with a lion's share of global trade. In other words, the hegemon becomes a consumer nation on steroids as its populace begins to indulge in the fruits of others' labor without having to break its own sweat in stark violation of the unforgiving laws of nature. Against the backdrop of virtually free goods and services being imported from poorer nations, manufacturing jobs for the masses at home become increasingly few and far between due in no small part to hegemon's big manufacturers having moved their headquarters overseas due to dirt cheap labor and taking the technological know-how with them. In particular, one of these poorer countries usually serves as a feeder nation in that it provides a lion's share of goods and services to the hegemon, thereby not only rapidly improving its own standard of living but also beginning to salivate at the prospect of dethroning its master once it has stolen its technological know-how. Today, one only has to look at how China has been stealing America's technological know-how in return for being its feeder ever since its revolutionary leader Deng Xiaopeng signed an historic trade pact with the then 39th POTUS Jimmy Carter in 1979 almost in parallel with the start of summer (1976-1996) of the current oquannium (1955-2038). Prior to China, America stole Britain's technological know-how during the 19th century in return for being its feeder and, in doing so, knocked Britain off its hegemonic perch. For its part, Britain stole much of French technology during the 18th century, and France did it to Netherlands during the 17th century, and so forth.

3) **Autumn -> Hegemon begins to unravel**—With little to do at home, the hegemon starts creating bogus service-oriented jobs aplenty and additionally ratchets up unnecessary bureaucracy to keep the masses occupied lest their idle hands erupt into a sociopolitical upheaval not that they will never do so but such a fool's errand nonetheless helps to buy time, all the while furnishing big fat handouts to others who have no drive for work and have become accustomed to an easy life under the guise of social welfare. Top that up with the fact that the hegemon is now largely powered by low-paid immigrants in that they feed the masses, raise their kids, do their dirty laundry, and even build their homes and offices. Due to the lack of challenging and rewarding work in the service industry and even at home thanks to immigrants taking care of everything, the masses begin to unravel through self-indulgence and hedonistic pleasure, while others start to suffer from addiction and

mental disease. In parallel with the woes of the masses, what has now become the 800-pound gorilla of bureaucratic oversight puts the intellectuals and creative minds in the pincer hold, thereby kissing innovation and entrepreneurship goodbye to add to a faltering infrastructure at home due to its negligence for decades. To make up for the loss in productivity and innovation at home, the hegemon prints ever more money and borrows to the hilt so as to make up for all else having failed and keeping the masses addicted to living beyond their means as well as to fund unnecessary self-destructive wars against nations with potential resources in a last-ditch effort to flex its muscles in the hope that perhaps something can be salvaged out of others' misfortunes. One only has to look at America's unraveling beginning almost in parallel with the start of autumn (1997-2017) of the current oquannium (1955-2038) to see that the proof of such proclamation lies in the pudding from pursuing self-destructive gambits such as the 9/11 Wars to printing and borrowing money to the hilt. Likewise, Britain also faced a similar fate just as the autumn (1913-1933) of the previous oquannium (1871-1954) kicked off as it immediately got embroiled in World War I (1914-1918) driven by the conviction that it would be a boon to turn its sinking Titanic around yet it ended up sinking even faster than it would have had it not been a party to precipitating that global conflict. In the face of the moral fabric of the society having been decimated, the hegemon begins to crumble under its own weight of a plethora of wrongdoings from societal ills through excesses and imbalances to transgressions. The resulting sociopolitical upheaval quickly turns into an insoluble Rubik's cube that can only be resolved through a global conflict.

4) **Winter -> Hegemon falls from grace**—The fall from grace of hegemon is all but complete against the backdrop of typically the feeder nation vying to hold its own and challenging for global dominance. The resulting standoff and the contest for the control of world's resources is often resolved through a global conflict with the hegemon being given a bloody nose if refusing to bow out peacefully as the oqual cycle nears its end. While Britain bowed out gracefully in the face of rising American dominance during the winter (1934-1954) of the previous oquannium (1871-1954) though in large part due to having been fixated on the rising threat of Germany and therefore not having seen America as a potential threat to its hegemony, it is unlikely that the United States will be willing to make way for China peacefully as the winter (2018-2038) of

the current oquannium (1955-2038) draws to a close. What would be a bloody World War III is all but set to provide the stage over the next decade or so as it oversees the coronation of China to take up the baton of global hegemony from America.

Taken together, the hegemon essentially digs its own grave after having become globally dominant.

In particular, global hegemony serves as a curse-in-disguise in that it turns a respectable and honorable nation into a society of parasites who become accustomed to sucking blood of weaker nations and then they pay a hefty price for their transgressions.

The plight of the hegemon is very much akin to a wealthy family whose riches can easily make or break the offspring depending on how they are raised.

In order to get a glimpse of how the hegemony of various global powers has been foxtrotting with each spell of oqual cycle since the birth of Modern Age, let us take a look at each one of them in a chronological order beginning with Portugal and then followed by Spain before we move onto the trio of Netherlands-France-and-Britain and, then finally, round off our journey with America against the backdrop of China rubbing its hands with Siberian glee and feet with Indian ghee as it prepares to take up the baton of global leadership over the next decade or so as the current oquannium (1955-2038) draws to a close.

Enter Portugal!

PORTUGAL WAS THE FIRST BONA-FIDE GLOBAL POWER WHOSE HEGEMONY LARGELY COINCIDED WITH THE FIRST OQUANNIUM (1451-1534)

Although its birth can be traced back to 1415 with the conquest of Ceuta, a city located at the northernmost tip of Morocco but ceded to Spain in 1668, it was not until the development of a more advanced maritime technology almost in parallel with the emergence of a printing press by German inventor Johannes Gutenberg circa 1451 that the Portuguese Empire truly came of age and quickly began to dwarf other rival powers by leaps and bounds.

While other imperial powers of its time and those that came before had primarily relied on land to expand their sphere of power such that their influence was largely restricted to the comfort zone of Afro-Eurasia centered around the Mediterranean

Sea, Portugal would colonize regions in far-flung corners of the world due to being the first nation to have developed long-distance maritime capabilities.

Powered by what were then their avant-garde naval carracks (or ships), the Portuguese were the first among humanity to step outside their comfort zone and set up trade links elsewhere around the globe beginning almost in tandem with the start of the first oquannium (1451-1534).

What were the groundbreaking naval milestones of the Portuguese explorers?

In 1456, led by Alvaro Fernandes, the Portuguese were likely the first humans to land on what was then the uninhabited archipelago of Cape Verde located in the Atlantic Ocean off the coast of western Africa—the archipelago would begin to receive its first permanent human settlers in 1462 and remained under the control of Portugal until 1975 when it became an independent nation.

In 1471, led by Fernao Gomes, the Portuguese would expand their imperial radius along the coast of southern Africa as they set foot on what is today Elmina—a city located on the south coast of Ghana—and would set up a trading post in 1478 to manage the lucrative trade of commodities such as gold and ivory.

In 1482, led by Diogo Cao, the Portuguese would become the first Europeans to cross the equator along the western coast of southern Africa as they explored what are modern-day nations of Congo, Angola, and Namibia.

In 1488, led by Bartolomeu Dias, the Portuguese became the first Europeans to reach what is today the Cape of Good Hope in South Africa as they continued to expand their monopoly of trade along the western coast of Africa.

Once the Portuguese explorers had conquered the daunting equator driven by the angst that perhaps they would simply fall over the "edge" under the force of gravity and may never return home, there was simply no stopping the Lusitanians in their long-stated goal of linking Europe to Asia via a maritime route in order to capitalize on the spice trade—which up till then had only been possible via overland routes across Eurasia and Africa—as well as to spread Christianity in an effort to counter the growing influence of Islam to which the Portuguese were hardly strangers as Muslim rule over the Iberian peninsula had existed in one form or another for almost 800 years (0711-1492).

Why did the Portuguese make linking Europe to Asia via a maritime route the holy grail of their explorations on their carracks?

There were three reasons for establishing such a maritime link:

1) **Security**—Traveling by sea was much safer than overland routes which were fraught with danger and required careful maneuvering through war zones as well as to avoid being ambushed and looted.
2) **Efficiency**—The carracks could carry much more cargo than a cumbersome caravan of camels, thereby increasing efficiency and reducing shipping costs.
3) **Speed**—While the carracks barely sailed a little faster than the camels could stride on their feet, they nevertheless had an advantage in being kept on the move nonstop unlike a caravan that must be fed and rested at night.

So when did the Portuguese reach Asia?

In 1498, led by Vasco de Gama, the Portuguese would become the first Europeans and finally realize their dream of reaching resource-rich Asia as their carracks docked at what is today Calicut, a city located along the Malabar Coast in the southwestern state of Kerala in India.

A truly momentous feat that would have been equivalent to humanity's landing on the Moon in 1969, the Portuguese Empire had arguably touched the peak of its global dominance after having reached India and returning home with bucketloads of goodies to the delight of their royals.

So contagious was the aroma of Indian spices that it would quickly infect other European royals from the French through the Dutch to the British for whom reaching India would become the benchmark to gauge the success of their own imperial ambitions.

But, not so much for Spain.

In what came to be called the 1494 Treaty of Tordesillas, Portugal and Spain signed an agreement to steer clear of each other in their exploratory endeavors with the former given a monopoly roughly stretching over the Eastern Atlantic Ocean and the latter over the Western Atlantic Ocean.

For this reason, Spain would never reach India but rather focus its maritime efforts on the New World.

As for Portugal, its love affair with India would deepen fast and furious and, unlike the short-lived teenage infatuation, it would soon turn into "Hasta la muerte, baby!"—"Till death us do part, baby!"

In 1500, the Portuguese would establish their first ever trading post on Indian soil at Calicut against the backdrop of their archrival Spain vying to hold its own.

In 1505, the construction of several forts along the southwestern coast of India to protect its trading interests would effectively mark the beginning of Portuguese colonial rule on Indian soil that would last until the handover of what is today the southwestern coastal state of Goa to India in 1961.

In order to expand their spice trade beyond India, the Portuguese would soon thereafter conquer key coastal regions across southeast Asia including the likes of what are today the Malaysian state of Malacca (1511) and the Chinese region of Macau (1557).

However, what would become the eternal and most palpable legacy of the Portuguese Empire would not be planted in Asia but rather in South America.

In 1500, led by Pedro Alvares Cabral, the Portuguese first set foot on what is today the Brazilian city of Porto Seguro.

Subsequent colonization of what is modern-day Brazil would not only bring more riches to the Portuguese through the highly profitable trade of precious commodities such as gold, diamond, sugar, and brazilwood, but it would also conceive what is today the fifth largest country by landmass and seventh most-populous nation in the world.

However, Portuguese success also planted its own downfall as colonial riches soon began to weigh on its ruling elite that had become accustomed to biting off more than it could chew.

With Spain lurking in its shadow, it would only be a matter of time before Portugal would begin to look to its past for unrivaled glory.

Indeed, Spain had been quietly luring Portuguese explorers and their technological know-how into its own ranks with ever more lucrative contracts including the legendary Christopher Columbus who had gained all his maritime training on Portuguese ships.

However, the pivotal moment for the shift of hegemonic power would come during the fifth phase of the so-called Italian Wars (1521-1530)—straddling the annus horribilis (1524) of the first oquannium (1451-1534)—which pitted Spain against France for the control of Italian peninsula as well as global dominance with each side supported by various European powers.

In the aftermath of what came to be called the 1529 Treaty of Cambrai, Spain would emerge as the dominant global power ousting Portugal that had up till then been the trailblazer in establishing maritime trade and colonization of far-flung continents.

Although its imperial links in one way or another would stretch across almost six centuries beginning with the conquest of Ceuta in 1415 and ending with the handover of Macau to China in 1999, the global dominance of the Portuguese Empire (1415-1999) over other rival powers and hence its Golden Age was largely restricted over the course of the first oquannium (1451-1534) before the Spanish Empire would take up the baton of global hegemony.

Nevertheless, Portugal can take pride in its imperial legacy in that not only Portuguese culture is celebrated across many corners of the world today but Portuguese language also serves as lingua franca of nations much larger than itself such as Brazil, Angola, and Mozambique.

Adios Portugal! Bienvenida España!

SPAIN STOLE THE SHOW DURING THE SECOND OQUANNIUM (1535-1618)

In 1492, exactly midway through the first oquannium (1451-1534) since the birth of Modern Age in 1451, the maiden journey made by the Italian explorer Cristoforo Colombo—better known by his Anglicized alias Christopher Columbus—through the Atlantic Ocean to reach India in search of spices accidentally ended up in the New World.

What would later come to be called the "Americas", the 1492 Voyage by Columbus marked a tipping point in the fortunes of the Portuguese Empire that up till then had been calling the shots as it had been the dominant global power for many decades and would continue to be so for several more.

Why did that mark a tipping point for Portugal?

Rather than Portugal, the serendipitous exploration of the Americas by Columbus was being funded by its archrival Spain and it signaled a harbinger of things to come—or rather the beginning of a change of guards for the global dominance from one power to another.

This was particularly poignant given that Columbus had received his exploratory know-how with the Portuguese ships and his defection to Portugal's archrival was nothing short of having bitten the hand that once used to feed him.

Although it traces its roots to the conquest of the Canary Islands off the coast of Morocco that first began in 1402, it would not be until the 1492 Voyage of Columbus to the New World that the Spanish Empire would truly begin to flex its muscles and put a grin on its face.

That ocean-shattering year at the closing of the 15th century would also mark another turning point in the rapidly bloating fortunes of the Spanish Empire with what came to be called the "1492 Reconquista"—when the last Muslim stronghold over Granada fell to Spain and Muslim rule over the Iberian peninsula since 0711 finally came to an abrupt end after nearly 800 years.

How did the New World come to be called the Americas?

Soon after the 1492 Voyage of Columbus, another Italian explorer Amerigo Vespucci would follow in his compatriot's footsteps to the New World on behalf of the Spanish Empire.

Notwithstanding his multiple trips to the New World over the next decade or so, Columbus however continued to argue that the landmass that he had discovered was a contiguous part of Asia rather than a new continent.

However, Vespucci broke ranks with Columbus as he claimed the New World to be a separate entity and, quite rightly, the new continent would be named "America" in his honor—a Latinized form of his first name Amerigo.

The division of Vespucci's America into two Americas is quite recent and largely gained traction as European colonization came to a grinding halt during the 19th century and paved the way for the development of distinct cultural identities between what are today North America and South America.

The discovery of tectonic plates during the 20th century further reaffirmed the notion that North America and South America were two distinct continents.

When did the Spanish begin to colonize the Americas?

Soon after the 1492 Voyage by Columbus, the Spanish would begin to explore and colonize much of Central and South America—a pursuit that was largely driven by the mouthwatering prospect of trading precious commodities such as gold, silver, and sugar.

However, the Spanish explorations of the New World were also motivated by their desire to preach Christianity and proselytize the native tribes though they ended up killing most of them through the introduction of deadly pathogens such as smallpox and measles to which the indigenous people had no immunity and many of those who survived would be butchered to make way for Europeans.

With the exception of the Portuguese colonization of eastern coast of South America that would later become what is modern-day Brazil, the Spanish pretty much had a free reign over the New World as granted by the 1494 Treaty of Tordesillas, which had required the only other major maritime power of the time Portugal to limit its explorations over the Eastern Atlantic Ocean while letting Spain have the monopoly over what lay on the other side of Western Atlantic Ocean.

In 1503, the Spanish would build the fist sugar mill on the island of Hispaniola—home to modern-day nations of Dominican Republic and Haiti.

In 1511, the Spanish colonized what is the modern-day island nation of Cuba and, soon thereafter, discovered huge gold deposits that would subsequently spark off the so-called "1512 Cuban Gold Rush".

In 1513, the Spanish discovered what is the modern-day US state of Florida.

In 1516, back on European soil, the fortunes of the Spanish Empire would bloat with the inheritance of a handful of other European crowns courtesy of royal marriages through the so-called Habsburg Dynasty of Germanic origin that ruled during much of the second millennium over Central Europe under the political entity called the "Holy Roman Empire" with the modern-day Austria being its nucleus—through such dynastic union, Spain would extend its suzerainty over parts of what are modern-day France, Italia, Germany, Austria, Belgium, and Netherlands.

In 1521, the Spanish would continue their steadfast march in the Americas virtually unchallenged as they began colonizing what is modern-day nation of Mexico after defeating the native Aztec Empire.

In 1530, after having been emboldened by their emergence as the dominant power on the European continent in the wake of the fifth phase of the so-called Italian Wars (1521-1530) almost in parallel with the start of the second oquannium (1535-1618), the Spanish would up the ante on their colonial ambitions as they began to put down the marker in the Americas.

In 1532, the Spanish would take on the native Inca Empire stretching across much of what are modern-day nations of Ecuador, Peru, and Chile along the western coast of South America.

In 1536, the Spanish landed on what is modern-day Argentinian capital of Buenos Aires.

In 1539, the Spanish inaugurated the first printing press in what is modern-day Mexico City.

In 1551, the Spanish laid the foundation of what is the modern-day Universidad Nacional Autónoma de México.

In 1580, after having colonized much of Central and South America, the Spanish Empire would reach the peak of its global dominance over other rival powers, particularly after the unification of the kingdoms and imperial possessions of Portugal and Spain into a single political entity called the "Iberian Union"—when Spain invaded Portugal after it fell into an existential crisis in the wake of the death of its king without an heir apparent.

Given their ever-expanding empire stretching from Eurasia through Africa to the Americas coupled with bountiful resources being imported en masse from the New World, the Spanish must have felt reassured that the Almighty's blessings would perhaps never put an end to their riches, particularly having the Holy Roman Empire in bed with them.

Alas, with riches comes corruption and moral disintegration of human society, and the Spanish would be no exception to this unforgiving law of nature.

This should have been hardly surprising given that the best days of the Spanish Empire were already in the rearview mirror with the annus turnilis (1577) of the second oquannium (1535-1618) having already rubbed shoulders with Los Toros even before the Iberian Union came into being in 1580.

Indeed, the constant stream of precious metals such as gold and silver pouring in from the New World without the production of new goods and services to have gone with them would only fuel consumer price inflation at home against the backdrop of Spanish having become heavily dependent upon the import of raw materials and manufactured goods from other countries in an echo of the plight of today's America.

Given such excesses and imbalances that would lead to heavy taxation and a heavy-handed approach against other Europeans under their imperial authority through the Habsburg Dynasty, it would only be a matter of time before the Spanish Empire would begin to unravel and face revolts.

With the ominous second half (1577-1618) of the second oquannium (1535-1618) having already arrived, the writing had indeed been on the wall for some time.

In 1581, what is modern-day Protestant nation of Netherlands would declare independence from the Catholic monarchs of the Spanish Empire after decades of oppression and persecution against the backdrop of what came to be known as the Eighty Years War (1568-1648)—a sluggish and drawn-out multidecadal conflict that pitted the rising Dutch Empire against the decaying Spanish Empire with each supported by various European powers.

Although Netherlands would not clear the final hurdles against the deeply-rooted Spanish Empire until after the final phase of the Eighty Years War (1618-1648), it nevertheless had gained an upper hand and dethroned Spain several decades earlier as the dominant global power in the wake of the sixth and consequential phase of the Eighty Years War (1599-1609)—when the Dutch forces not only scored land and naval victories against their former masters but the heavy cost of the war also left Spain with no choice but to declare state bankruptcy, though that was also triggered in no small part due to the rather overstretched Spanish Empire across the globe having turned into a bogeyman usurping ever more resources but delivering fewer and fewer rewards.

In fact, against the backdrop of gargantuan excesses and imbalances as the 16th century closed out, the Spanish morale had fallen so low in that they could not even hold their own against the then English rookies during a naval face off in the English Channel in what is widely referred to as the "1588 Spanish Armada".

Taking on the mighty Dutch a decade later would therefore prove to be a whole different ball game against men rather than boys.

That the sixth phase of the Eighty Years War (1599-1609)—straddling the annus horribilis (1608) of the second oquannium (1535-1618)—would catapult the mighty Dutch to global preeminence just in time for the arrival of the third oquannium (1619-1702) speaks volumes about the dire spell of oqual cycle on the incumbent hegemon mired in self-indulgence, corruption, and exploitation of other nations.

It was not just on the European soil that the fearless Dutch would put one up against the Spanish but they would also begin to seize Iberian colonies across the globe almost in parallel with the beginning of an auspicious spell of the first half (1619-1660) of the third oquannium (1619-1702).

As for Spain, the Dutch insult would soon turn into Portuguese injury with the breakup of the Iberian Union in 1640.

If being given a bloody nose by the Dutch had not served as a signal that Los Toros no longer possessed the Midas touch in the wake of the sixth phase of the Eighty Years War (1599-1609), the quasi-velvet divorce with Portugal most certainly marked the end of global dominance of the Spanish Empire in 1640.

That would follow the Catalan Revolt (1640-1659) which would keep Spain bogged down at home for another couple of decades, all the while the fortunes of the Dutch Empire would continue to swell as it took up the baton of global dominance against the backdrop of rapid disintegration of its former master.

Although its imperial links in one way or another would stretch across almost six centuries beginning with the maiden albeit failed conquest of Canary Islands in 1402 and ending with its withdrawal from Western Sahara in 1975, the global dominance of the Spanish Empire (1402-1975) over other rival powers and hence its Golden Age was largely restricted over the course of the second oquannium (1535-1618) before the Dutch Empire would take up the baton of global hegemony.

Nevertheless, Spain can take heart from its imperial legacy in that not only Spanish culture is celebrated across much of the Americas today but Spanish language also serves as lingua franca of almost two-dozen nations, ranking only second to the English language in terms of its global impact.

And, of course, the globe's love affair with Spain will forever remain as strong as a bull through Encierro and El Clasico.

Que sera sera España! Enter Netherlands!

DUTCH DOMINATE THE GLOBE DURING THE THIRD OQUANNIUM (1619-1702)

With imperial ambitions of their own, the dynastic union of the Spanish Empire with the Habsburg Dynasty in 1516 was a blessing-in-disguise for the Dutch in that they would get to hone their exploratory skills firsthand around the globe with the big boys who had already made the conquest of the New World look like a cakewalk.

What appears to be a customary feature of the transition of power, it seems that the hegemon digs its own grave by nurturing its rival on milk and meat without even realizing that the hand being used to feed would be bitten sooner or later.

And so the Dutch working in the service of the Spanish stood to benefit from their avant-garde maritime know-how not to mention that they would also steal much of the proprietary technology of navigation in deep oceans just as their masters had done it to the Portuguese before them.

Add to that the millennia-old history of the Dutch having mastered the art of how to tame wind and water due to their low-lying and flood-prone terrain and you get the best of both worlds.

Indeed, the Dutch ingenuity would take their maritime know-how acquired under the tutelage of their masters to a new level such that their own ships would soon overshadow the Spanish fleet and begin to rule the ocean waves as the 17th century rolled in.

When did the Dutch Empire come into being?

The roots of the Dutch Empire can be traced back to 1581 with their maiden albeit failed attempt to establish a colony in what is today the Pomeroon-Supenaam region of Guyana located on the northern coast of South America—a truly bold effort given that the Dutch had yet to break free from the shackles of the Spanish Empire.

Nevertheless, the fledgling Dutch Empire would taste its first colonial success in 1595 when the Dutch ships reached the Indonesian island of Java and, in doing so, signed their first ever contract to trade spices from Asia to Europe to the ire of the Portuguese who up till then had a complete monopoly over that lucrative market for almost a century.

Soon thereafter, a head-to-head clash of the titans would break out and last more than 60 years through what came to be called the Dutch-Portuguese War (1602-1663)—a long and protracted conflict across the globe during which the Dutch would significantly weaken the remaining vestiges of the Portuguese Empire, primarily through capturing their colonial possessions, all the while the demoralized Spanish would leave their Iberian partner all by itself to fend and defend in the face of adversity.

In 1603, the Dutch fleet attacked and blockaded but failed to capture Goa, the headquarter of the then Portuguese India, and the modern-day southwestern Indian state.

In 1605, the Dutch opened their first ever trading post on Indian soil in what is modern-day coastal city of Machilipatnam in the southeastern Indian state of Andhra Pradesh.

However, it was not until their triumph over the Spanish during the sixth phase of the Eighty Years War (1599-1609) that the Dutch Empire would truly come of age and begin to put down its colonial marker across the globe, particularly in light of having emerged as the dominant global power over its European rivals.

Buoyed by their status as the new sheriff in town earned almost in parallel with the arrival of the third oquannium (1619-1702), there was no stopping the plucky Dutch from what they could and would not achieve over the next 84 years or so.

In 1614, on the western front, the Dutch began to colonize much of northeastern coast of what is modern-day United States that they would name "New Netherland".

In 1623, on the western front, the Dutch would seize what is today the southeastern Brazilian state of Bahia from the Portuguese and, soon thereafter, would also colonize much of the northeastern coast of Brazil.

In 1625, on the eastern front, the Dutch would exercise complete monopoly over the lucrative spice trade from the Indonesian archipelago of Maluku Islands at the expense of the Portuguese.

In 1626, on the western front, the Dutch purchased what is today the borough of Manhattan from the native tribes and named it New Amsterdam—which would be later renamed to New York by the British in 1666.

In 1634, on the western front, the Dutch seized from the Spanish what is today the Caribbean nation of Curaçao off the northern coast of South America.

In 1641, on the eastern front, the Dutch captured the trading posts from the Portuguese in what is the modern-day Malaysian state of Malacca.

In 1642, on the eastern front, the Dutch captured what is modern-day Taiwan from the Spanish to further exert their supremacy.

In 1650, on the western front, the Dutch colonized what is modern-day nation of Suriname on the northern shores of South America.

In 1652, on the eastern front, the Dutch established a settlement on the Cape of Good Hope in South Africa.

By 1658, on the eastern front, the Dutch would have all trading posts on the island nation of Sri Lanka under their thumb after years of having laid siege to the Portuguese who were sent packing home.

By 1663, on the eastern front, the Dutch had amassed an equally impressive array of colonial posts dotted across all corners of irresistible India—stretching from what are modern-day Indian states of Gujarat on the northwestern coast through the Malabar Coast and Tamil Nadu on the southern coast to Andhra Pradesh and West Bengal on the eastern coast—to add to the ever-growing woes of the Portuguese who nevertheless kept renewing their vows and praying for divine intervention to never have to be separated from their most spicy colony till death in the face of Dutch onslaught showing no signs of easing.

Before too long, the Portuguese prayers would indeed be answered in no uncertain terms with the onset of the second half (1661-1702) of the third oquannium (1619-1702) as it would bear bad omens for the Dutch in line with the dire spell of the second half of oqual cycle on the hegemon.

Enter the British and French spoilers (or rather the saviors).

While the rise of the British Empire in its shadows had always been a thorn in the flesh of the Dutch hegemony ever since their first sparring encounter in what came to be called the First Anglo-Dutch War (1652-1654)—during which the British Navy attacked the Dutch merchant ships in the English Channel so as to ward them off from trading with Britain in an effort to exercise complete monopoly over its own maritime borders—the hostilities between the emerging British power and the dominant Dutch power would however grow much deeper than the ocean with the onset of the second half (1661-1702) of the third oquannium (1619-1702).

In what came to be known as the Second Anglo-Dutch War (1665-1667)—during which the Dutch would cede their rule in entirety over New Netherland including the handover of Manhattan—the British would not only significantly weaken Dutch hegemony over global trade but the Achilles' heel of Netherlands would also be laid bare to the delight of its European rivals, particularly France with its own aspirations of becoming a dominant global player.

Buoyed by such a mouthwatering prospect and driven by their motto "Battre le fer quand il est chaud!"—"Pound the iron when it is hot!"—the French with the blessings of the British would open up their own front against the decadent Netherlands through the so-called Franco-Dutch War (1672-1678).

During that conflict, much of Netherlands would be initially overrun but the Dutch regrouped and beat back the French forcing them to bury the hatchet in what was essentially a war of attrition but it nevertheless signaled that the days of Dutch hegemony were numbered.

As for the Portuguese, they could not have been more thankful to Virgencita de Lisboa against the backdrop of a concerted effort by the British and the French to keep the Dutch hegemony in check lest it decimated what little remained of Portugal's imperial legacy—not to mention that the Lusitanians were also relieved to see the back of being stalked and pursued around the globe by the Dutch a la lovers from hell.

What caused the rapid decline of the Dutch masters?

With a vast network of colonial outposts scattered across the globe, the Dutch literally became filthy rich during the 17th century through trading a vast array of commodities from nutmeg and opium through sugar and rice to cotton and silk.

In sync with their global hegemony during much of the 17th century, the Dutch also developed what was arguably the world's first global currency in the guilder and a banking system that would serve as the kernel upon which rests today's modern financial system.

However, it is an open secret that the wealth kills the health and the greed buries the creed of a society.

Indeed, the jinx of the colonial riches would soon begin to engulf the Dutch society as epitomized by the self-indulgence of younger generations and their waning zest for life against the backdrop of endemic corruption as the 17th century closed in.

To say that the fall of Netherlands from grace was just as quick as its rise would be to put it Dutchly.

With the annus horribilis (1692) of the third oquannium (1619-1702) lurking on the horizon, the time to pass on the baton of global hegemony had all but arrived.

With its own ambitions of rising to global hegemony brewing fast, France would begin to feverishly salivate at the prospect of now-or-never in the wake of witnessing the rapid decline of the Dutch and its European allies being in utter disarray as underscored by their internal conflicts coupled with the existential crisis having befallen England through the so-called Glorious Revolution (1688-1689)—a sociopolitical uprising triggered by the alienization of what was then a largely Protestant nation by the newly-crowned Catholic monarch James II followed by his deposition and subsequent accession to the throne of his Protestant daughter Mary II and her Dutch husband William III, who also happened to be the de-facto leader of Netherlands, as co-monarchs of England (as well as Wales, Scotland and Ireland due to the dynastic union of the quad since 1603).

Even the quasi-dynastic union facilitated by the Glorious Revolution with England would not save Dutch hegemony from the onslaught of indomitable French determined to rewrite history.

Driven by what had arguably grown into the most powerful military against the backdrop of its European rivals facing one crisis after another, the mighty French would indeed waste no time and move in for the kill in order to rise to their own glory as well as motivated by the urgency to prevent the dynastic union of England and Netherlands through what came to be called the Nine Years War (1688-1697)—a contest for global hegemony that erupted just before the outbreak of Glorious Revolution pitting the rising power of France all by itself against the Grand Alliance spearheaded by the Dutch and closely supported by much of what are modern-day England, Spain, Portugal, Germany, Austria, Switzerland, Belgium, and Italy.

Although the main theatre lay in Europe, the bloody Nine Years War was the first-ever large-scale global conflict that would be fought on the shores of every major continent from the Americas through Eurasia to Africa.

In North America, France would lock horns with the then emerging power of England for the control of colonial outposts.

In the Caribbeans, France would take on the combined naval forces of Spain and England.

In Asia, France would go on the offensive against the combined naval forces of Netherlands and England.

In spite of so many European powers acting in concert across all corners of the world to tame the alpha male, France nevertheless held its own and single-handedly gave them all a heck of a run for their money, all the while decimating the Dutch economic engine and effectively putting an end to its hegemony.

In what came to be called the "1697 Treaty of Rijswijk", all parties would finally agree to end the costly conflict that barely moved a needle in anyone's direction in terms of strategic gains or losses though the French aggression had undoubtedly dethroned the Dutch making way for France to emerge as the new dominant global power on the back of a powerful army, the most advanced naval force, and a far-reaching maritime trade network just as the third oquannium (1619-1702) drew to a close.

Although its imperial links in one way or another would stretch across almost four centuries beginning with the maiden albeit failed conquest of Guyana in 1581 and ending with Suriname being granted independence in 1975, the global dominance of the Dutch Empire (1581-1975) over other rival powers and hence its Golden Age was largely restricted over the course of the third oquannium (1619-1702) before the French Empire would take up the baton of global hegemony.

Still, Netherlands can take delight in its imperial legacy in that not only much of today's financial system traces its roots to the Dutch Golden Age but the Dutch language also continues to command a sizeable following across all four major continents.

Tot ziens Netherlands! Bienvenue France!

FRANCE FASHIONS THE WORLD DURING THE FOURTH OQUANNIUM (1703-1786)

The roots of the French Empire can be traced to 1534 with the exploration of what is modern-day Gulf of Saint Lawrence sandwiched between the Canadian provinces of Quebec and Newfoundland as it empties into the Atlantic Ocean.

A few decades later, that maiden excursion by the French explorers would be followed by multiple attempts to colonize warmer regions in the New World such as the modern-day Brazilian city of Rio de Janeiro (1555) and the US state of Florida (1562) but to no avail due to the then strong colonial oversight of the Spanish and Portuguese who between them had already laid claims to the strategic points across the globe as they were the first to settle where no other European had ever dared to do so.

However, the rapid decline of the Spanish and Portuguese colonial might as the 17th century rolled in would open up the door for other Europeans and only then would French colonization gain traction in earnest.

In particular, the French explorers capitalized on the maritime know-how of what were now the trio of pace setters in the Portuguese-Spanish-and-Dutch ships, and by the end of 17th century, France itself would become a leading maritime power eclipsing its European rivals.

But, first came the baby steps, one at a time.

In 1608, the French would establish a settlement in what is modern-day Canadian province of Quebec to begin fur trade.

In 1625, the French would begin their settlement on the island of Tortuga off the northern coast of modern-day Caribbean nation of Haiti.

In 1630, France colonized what is the modern-day French overseas territory of Guyane (or French Guiana) located on the northern coast of South America.

In 1635, France colonized what is the modern-day French overseas territory of Martinique in the Caribbeans, and over the next couple of decades, it would also control many other Caribbean islands.

In 1668, the French established their first ever trading post on Indian soil in the modern-day northwestern state of Gujarat, and over the next several decades, they would open up additional fortified factories dotted across both the western and eastern coasts of India with Puducherry becoming their headquarter.

In 1682, the French explored the Mississippi River and laid claim to what is modern-day US state of Louisiana.

In 1697, in the aftermath of the Nine Years War (1688-1697) that cemented the supremacy of France over its European colonial rivals, the Western half of Hispaniola corresponding to the modern-day nation of Haiti would be ceded by the Spanish to the French.

Once having emerged as the most dominant global power almost in parallel with the arrival of the fourth oquannium (1703-1786), the French supremacy would be put to the test right away through what came to known as the Spanish Succession War (1701-1714) in the midst of a new dawn renowned for heralding the emergence of new institutions at the expense of old ones.

What was the Spanish Succession War about?

Triggered by the death of childless Spanish monarch Charles II in 1700, the Spanish Empire was plunged into a crisis of epic proportions.

Without an heir apparent, the appointment of Charles II's successor to the Spanish throne was now a matter of dispute between his blood relatives in the rival dynasties of German Habsburg and French Bourbon with each respectively reigning over and beyond what are modern-day Austria and France.

Given that Charles II had named his great-nephew Prince Philip born to the French Bourbons as his heir presumptive in his will, the accession to the Spanish throne by decree of the young French prince was however not welcome by the German Habsburgs and other Europeans in that they feared that a potential dynastic union between Spain and France would threaten the balance of power.

This was particularly alarming given that France had not only emerged as the dominant global power in the wake of the Nine Years War (1688-1697) but that it now also stood to inherit a large Spanish Empire scattered across the globe were that dynastic union to go through.

Without a diplomatic solution, much of Western Europe would burst into another conflict of Spanish Succession War (1701-1714) with the wounds from the Nine Years War (1688-1697) having yet to heal and pretty much along similar warring factions with France once again taking on the Grand Alliance made up much of what are modern-day Austria, Germany, Switzerland, Belgium, Italy, Netherlands, Britain, Portugal, and Spain—though the latter was split along Habsburg and Bourbon loyalties.

After a decade of futile exercise of having battered each other with each side becoming exhausted in a war of attrition, France nevertheless emerged as the kingmaker with the young French prince now being recognized as King Philip V of Spain by all parties on the condition that there would be no dynastic union between Los Toros and Les Gaules.

Being the new sheriff in town, France would not only call the shots and pull the levers of international politics over the next several decades but it would also richly benefit from its colonies across the globe serving as hubs of lucrative trade from fur-sugar-and-coffee in the Americas to spices-cotton-and-silk from India.

Notably, in line with its national interests, France would play a central role in dictating a favorable outcome of the accession to the throne of new monarchs through first the Polish Succession War (1733-1738) and then closely followed by the Austrian Succession War (1740-1748)—the latter conflict would also turn centuries-old Habsburg-Bourbon rivalry into a strategic alliance.

With France being obsessed with exerting its omnipotent authority over Europe a la new Russian bride who could not be trusted running household affairs, it was inevitable that its overseas empire would remain vulnerable to its eternal enemy Britain—which, for its part, was not only rising fast and furious with its own hegemonic ambitions to shepherd the world but had also prioritized its colonial empire over the never-ending family politics across the European continent.

And so France's lax foreign policy would prove disastrous particularly with the ominous annus turnilis (1745) of the fourth oquannium (1703-1786) having already entered the rearview mirror.

In what came to be known as the Carnatic Wars (1744-1763), Britain would significantly weaken the French colonial grip on its Indian possessions and emerge as the dominant colonial power on the Asian Diamond.

That is all the more troubling given that France entered the Carnatic Wars as the odds-on favorite to gain an upper hand on the Indian peninsula with the capture of what was then Madras (Chennai today), the headquarter of the British Empire on Indian soil, but would soon lose the advantage due to prioritizing its hegemony in Europe rather than squander limited resources on overseas adventures with an unpredictable future as they were a high-risk investment unlike Britain which had no choice but to only funnel its investments into its overseas empire.

Against the backdrop of the Carnatic Wars (1744-1763), France and Britain would also lock horns in Europe and across the globe wherever their colonial possessions crisscrossed in what came to be called the Seven Years War (1756-1763).

With each supported by their European allies, the British would significantly weaken the French hegemony across the globe with Les Gaules forced to cede to The Lions a handful of their North American territories as the Seven Years War drew to a close.

It is noteworthy that such territorial cession was not driven due to Les Gaules being unable to hold their own against The Lions but rather due to the fact that whereas France always had its coeur in Europe, Britain's heart was everywhere but in Europe for the reasons that would become clearer later on in this section.

Although France would flex its muscles and show that it still had the teeth through the capture of what is today the French Island of Corsica directly off the northern coast of the Italian island of Sardinia in 1769, the days of French hegemony were all but over.

With the annus horribilis (1776) of the fourth oquannium (1703-1786) now also lurking on the horizon, few would have bet that the French hegemony would defy the odds and keep the dire spell of oqual cycle at bay.

With trouble brewing within its own Thirteen Colonies in North America, few would have also bet that it would be The Lions that would ultimately knock Les Gaules off their hegemonic perch.

In what is referred to as the American Independence War (1775-1783), France would indeed conspire with American colonists largely out of its own grievances against its eternal enemy and tip the balance of power in favor of what was then a tiny and fledgling nation without even a proper military gear running along the eastern coast of what is modern-day United States.

In addition to providing American colonists with much-needed military know-how, wherewithal, troops, and its powerful navy, the French would also directly engage the British through the so-called Anglo-French War (1778-1783) in Europe as well as on North American shores.

In doing so, the French would not only make American victory against what were now the mighty British on ascendance look like a cakewalk but Les Gaules would also give The Lions a bloody nose through their own direct conflict.

In the aftermath of America's push for independence clearing its final hurdles in 1783, one might have been led to believe that the French hegemony had been resurrected after the British were sent packing home in the wake of their North American Empire having been chopped in half.

Rather, as is the case with all decadent hegemons being on their last leg due to overspending and being overleveraged with debt as the oqual cycle draws to a close, France's myopic decision to spearhead the American Independence War (1775-1783) against the British only exacerbated its financial woes as it served to empty out what little remained in its coffers and, before too long, Les Gaules would be bankrupt and their empire left in tatters.

That the curtain over French hegemony had finally been drawn just as the fourth oquannium (1702-1786) closed out was further underscored by the so-called French Revolution (1789-1799)—a bloody insurrection led by the peasants against the state in the face of dire financial straits sparked by the overindulgence of the ruling elite coupled with poor economic policies to add to the heavy cost of participation in the American Independence War (1775-1783).

In particular, the French Revolution was the result of centuries-old grievances and injustices amassed due to feudal practices such as the monarchy and aristocracy continuing to exploit the masses for their self-enrichment.

The French Revolution heralded a new dawn on French soil in that it would lead to the creation of a constitutional monarchy coupled with democratic rights for the masses as embodied in the motto "liberté, égalité, fraternité" at the expense of doing away with ancient practices of feudalism and absolute monarchy as epitomized by the execution of the French King Louis XVI by guillotine in 1793 and the rise of Napoleon Bonaparte as France's new statesman in 1799.

While the American Independence War (1775-1783) turned out to be a shot in the foot for the French in the face of what amounted to be nothing more than a pyrrhic victory, it would be a godsend for the British.

In fact, what appeared to be a loss for the British turned out to be a huge gain in the face of its archrival left to lick its wounds and being unable to take care of itself, much less continue to be a leader of the world.

Additionally, a loss can sometimes be a win in that it can help one to concentrate their energy where it matters most rather than spewing it out in all directions.

For the ascendant British Empire with its own ambitions of global hegemony, the Thirteen Colonies in North America were no longer profitable from an entrepreneurial angle in a manner akin to an adult child sticking around without a job and becoming a burden on the family.

Given that the Thirteen Colonies had grown up to fend for themselves, letting them go their own way would therefore have been the right thing to do anyway.

While their liberation from the imperial crown may have been perceived to tarnish the prestige of the British Empire, it nevertheless paved the way for Britain to look elsewhere for its ultimate glory and riches to topple what little remained of French hegemony.

With Britain having outmaneuvered its colonial rivals on the Indian peninsula prior to the outbreak of the American Independence War (1775-1783), it was now time to channel its energy and time on the Holy Cow with milk and meat aplenty.

The British must have wondered: "Why waste energy milking the last drop out of an old cow when we can get bucketloads at a fraction of the cost only if we are willing to go the extra mile!"

In hindsight, the American Independence War (1775-1783) marked a new era of riches for the British Empire in that it was finally able to add the jewel to its crown with India knocking on the door and, in doing so, it would effectively dethrone France and emerge as the undisputed heavy-weight hegemon almost beginning in parallel with the arrival of the fifth oquannium (1787-1870).

As for the French, they would put up one last fight to salvage something out of nothing through the so-called Napoleonic Wars (1803-1815) but it would be to no avail as Britain had already gone from strength to strength thanks to its timely divorce from the Thirteen Colonies a couple of decades earlier that would not only put a stop to its bleeding but also open the door to a highly-profitable marriage with its Indian bride.

Fast forward by some 200 years and today's France has nevertheless every raison d'etre joyeux—reason to be joyful.

Although its imperial links in one way or another would stretch across more than four centuries beginning with reaching Montreal in 1534 and ending with its withdrawal from the island nation of Vanuatu in 1980, the global dominance of the French Empire (1534-1980) over other rival powers and hence its Golden Age was largely restricted over the course of the fourth oquannium (1703-1786) before the British Empire would take up the baton of global hegemony.

While France would undoubtedly dominate affairs head-and-shoulders above its rivals on the European continent during much of the fourth oquannium (1703-1786), its global hegemony however left much to be desired as it was often kept in check by Britain and sometimes even eclipsed.

That was largely due to the fact that France's overseas policy was spasmodic at best as it failed to heavily fortify its colonial outposts across the globe due to the following three reasons:

1) Sandwiched between an array of hostile European neighbors, France had to heavily invest in fortifying long stretches of its land borders to keep the adversaries out at home at the expense of fortifying its overseas territories to expand its empire.
2) Located at the heart of Europe, France became ambivalent about whether it should prioritize the expansion of its empire across large swathes of the European continent or whether it ought to devote more resources to its overseas territories.
3) Being a Catholic nation, the French had for centuries believed even before their rise to global hegemony that they were the true standard-bearers of Catholicism and, as such, they wasted far too much energy locking horns with their European rivals in an effort to call the shots and reign over much of what was then a predominantly Catholic Europe in lieu of channeling their energy into their overseas territories.

Had France been an island and a Protestant nation, the alpha male on testosterone would have easily pipped its archrival Britain to the title of the largest empire to have ever existed and la langue française would have easily been lingua franca of the world today though the French would argue: "On s'en fiche!"—"We do not care!"

Quel dommage! What a pity!

Nevertheless, France can take heart from its imperial legacy in that not only French culture is celebrated across the globe today but the French language also serves as lingua franca of at least a dozen nations, ranking only behind English and Spanish in terms of its global impact.

And, of course, the French not only invented testosterone but also gave the world the alpha male.

Au revoir France! Enter Gran Britannia!

BRITAIN BATTERS THE GLOBE OVER TWO CONSECUTIVE OQUANNIA BEGINNING WITH FIFTH (1787-1870) AND ENDING WITH SIXTH (1871-1954)

The roots of the British Empire can be traced as far back as 1497 when English explorers led by their Italian talisman Giovanni Caboto accidentally landed on what is today the Canadian province of Newfoundland in lieu of their planned mission to reach Asia in search of spices.

That costly debacle would put the then England's colonial ambitions on hold for almost a century during which it would sharpen its tools on improving its maritime know-how, primarily through privateering Portuguese and Spanish ships.

So, like the French and the Dutch, the British were also late to both the cisatlantic and transatlantic party.

Nevertheless, after the political unification of the kingdoms of England and Wales into a single nation in 1535 (with the duo having already been in a dynastic union since 1284), the British would get off their colonial mark in earnest as the 16th century neared its end.

In 1585, the British would establish a temporary settlement in Roanoke Island off the coast of what is modern-day US state of North Carolina.

In 1607, the British would establish their first permanent colony in the New World on what is today a historic site of Jamestown in the US state of Virginia and, over the following decades, they would begin to colonize other regions along the northeastern coast of what is modern-day United States and often encroaching on Dutch settlements.

In 1608, the British would set foot on Indian soil on what is today the coastal city of Surat in the western state of Gujarat and, over the following decades, they would begin to establish trading posts across both the western and eastern coasts alongside and often encroaching on Portuguese territories which had been established there since 1500.

In 1623, the British would colonize what is the modern-day Caribbean nation of Saint Kitts and, over the following decades, other Caribbean islands such as Barbados and Jamaica were also added to the imperial crown.

In 1630, the British established a colony in what is the modern-day nation of Guyana located on the northern coast of South America.

In what came to be known as the Second Anglo-Dutch War (1665-1667), the British would annex from the Dutch the so-called New Netherland running along the northeastern coast of what is modern-day United States.

With that morale-boosting victory and after having emerged unscathed in the wake of the Glorious Revolution (1688-1689), the British would up the ante and stamp their authority over their ever-expanding colonial outposts stretching across the globe from Asia to the Americas as the 17th century closed out.

In 1707, the political unification of the duo of England-and-Wales with Scotland created what we know today as "Great Britain" and, only from this point onward, what was up till then the English-and-Welsh Empire would truly become the British Empire whose global might would now rank only second to that of France but ahead of its other European rivals.

By 1752, Britain had amassed what came to be called the Thirteen Colonies running contiguously along the eastern coast of what are modern-day US states of Massachusetts in the north to Georgia in the south.

In 1770, Britain colonized what is the modern-day Australian state of New South Wales and, over the next several decades, the rest of the island would also fall under the British control.

In 1795, Britain seized what is the modern-day Cape of Good Hope in South Africa from the Dutch and, over the next several decades, the British would also expand their colonial footprint across other strategic regions in Africa.

Buoyed by its ever-bloating empire across the globe, it would now only be a matter of time before Britain would dislodge France from its hegemonic perch.

In what came to be known as the Carnatic Wars (1744-1763), Britain would significantly weaken the French colonial grip on its Indian possessions and emerge as the dominant colonial power on the Asian Diamond.

Against the backdrop of the Carnatic Wars (1744-1763), Britain would also lock horns with France in Europe and across the globe in what came to be called the Seven Years War (1756-1763).

On the Indian peninsula, the British victory in the 1757 Battle of Plassey against the Mughal vestiges supported by the French military in what is modern-day eastern state of West Bengal would mark the birth of British Raj (1757-1947)—though it was in no small part masterminded by The Lions to force the coup of the Mughal leadership by its own military chief Mir Jafar in return for a stake in the power.

For his betrayal of his duty to his motherland, Mir Jaffer continues to be reviled and derided even to this day across much of the Indian peninsula.

On the North American shores, the British would significantly weaken the French hegemony with Les Gaules forced to cede to The Lions a handful of their colonial territories as the Seven Years War (1756-1763) drew to a close.

Nevertheless, the British triumph in the Seven Years War (1756-1763) came at a heavy cost, particularly on North American shores.

With the nation's debt rising fast and coffers running dry, Britain would move swiftly to impose a direct tax on its Thirteen Colonies through what came to be known as the 1765 Stamp Act.

However, the plan would backfire with a vengeance as it would not only be opposed by the colonists but their grievances would also quickly shift what was up till then a fringe movement demanding independence from Britain to the front-and-center of the then fledgling American society.

With Britain refusing to back down, the rapidly-bloating American tinderbox was set alight through the so-called American Independence War (1775-1783).

With the Thirteen Colonies being wholeheartedly supported by Britain's archrivals unable to fathom its rapid rise and led by France with the blessings of Spain and Netherlands, The Lions would bow out gracefully to the demands of American colonists without becoming scarred and left to lick their wounds.

In fact, what appeared to be a loss for Britain turned out to be a blessing-in-disguise in that the Thirteen Colonies were no longer profitable and would have only been a drain on the precious resources of an empire on ascendancy.

Ironically, the American Independence War (1775-1783) would propel Britain to global hegemony at the expense of France beginning almost in parallel with the arrival of the fifth oquannium (1787-1870).

The rise of Britain to global dominance was to a large extent facilitated by France's botched-and-bungled attempt to financially and materially support the American colonists during the American Independence War (1775-1783)—a myopic gambit that would leave Les Gaules demoralized and bankrupt with The Lions left to rub their paws with French glee and claws with Indian ghee.

With Britain having outmaneuvered its colonial rivals on the Indian peninsula prior to the outbreak of the American Independence War (1775-1783), it was now time to project its unparalleled power from another corner of the world.

Admittedly, the American Independence War (1775-1783) marked a new era of riches for the British Empire not only through its rapid rise on the Indian peninsula but also across Africa and Australia.

In particular, Britain would plunder the Indian peninsula over the next couple of centuries through exploiting the masses to produce a wide array of commodities from grain through spices to textiles and then exporting them across the globe for hefty profits—the resulting wealth would be used to upgrade infrastructure and industry at home and across its vast global empire, thereby quickly bloating into an 800-pound gorilla that its rivals feared would be impossible to dethrone.

It is indeed no coincidence that Britain's 18th Century Industrial Revolution began almost in parallel with its global hegemony and, in particular, after the birth of its colonial rule on the Indian peninsula in 1757.

The colonial riches would soon turn Britain into the toast of the town among its European admirers and many of them would have had no qualms about entering into a marriage of convenience with The Lions.

But, Britain espoused the idea of not only "Love thy neighbor!" but also "Marry thy neighbor!".

In 1801, driven by such conviction, the political marriage of Great Britain with Ireland would create what we know today as the "United Kingdom" and, with that master stroke, the British Empire would begin to not only rule the ocean waves like never before but it would also come home in earnest.

However, being the leader of the world also comes with a lot of headaches, particularly when one is left to deal with an alpha male on testosterone.

Unaware or perhaps refusing to accept the fact that there was a new sheriff in town, a resurgent France led by Napoleon would make one last-ditch effort to regain its supremacy in Europe and across the globe through the so-called Napoleonic Wars (1803-1815).

Without even flinching, Britain would quickly rise to the challenge and put one final nail in the coffin of what little remained of French hegemony on the back of a massive bankruptcy and a reign of terror that had unfolded during the French Revolution (1789-1799).

Only after the British had delivered the coup-de-grâce would it dawn upon France that it no longer possessed the Midas touch that it once did and that it was time to take the back seat and let The Lions run the global show.

With the alpha male having been finally tranquilized, Europe would take a sigh of relief against the backdrop of relative peace over the several decades that followed but in the misguided belief that the happy times would perhaps never end but they always do thanks to the perpetual spell of oqual cycle.

With the annus horribilis (1860) of the fifth oquannium (1787-1870) lurking on the horizon, much of the globe would be plunged into utter chaos and bloodshed once more beginning with the Crimean War (1853-1856) pitting the rising power of Russia against the ailing Ottoman Empire with the latter supported by various European powers with Britain and France leading the charge to maintain a balance of power.

Although triggered by the dispute over the rights of Orthodox Christians in what is modern-day Israel-Palestine then under the control of the Ottoman Empire but with Russia demanding that the Ottoman's Orthodox subjects be placed under its direct protection, the Crimean War (1853-1856) was also in no small part due to the Siberian Tiger flexing its muscles and trying to boost its hegemony across the Eurasian continent.

Backed by the vast network of its global empire in terms of both manpower and resources, Britain would crack down on Russian dissent through its unwavering backing of the Ottomans with little at their disposal to challenge the British supremacy.

However, the Crimean War (1853-1856) also exposed numerous shortcomings of the British military in terms of its logistical and tactical failures.

That should have hardly raised eyebrows given that hegemons fall prey to endemic corruption and self-indulgence as the oqual cycle draws to a close.

To add insult to injury, the Crimean War (1853-1856) would be followed by the 1857 Indian Mutiny—a sociopolitical uprising and revolt by the Indian masses due to their own grievances after having been oppressed and exploited for almost a century at the hands of their British overlords.

Nevertheless, the Indian rebellion would be put down quickly and the British colonial rule would reach new heights with India now falling under the direct rule of the British

Crown during the then Queen Victoria's reign (1837-1901) through what came to be known as the 1858 Government of India Act.

Long story short, Britain largely survived being dethroned as the fifth oquannium (1787-1870) neared its end due to the fact that there was simply no other rival big enough to topple its global hegemony as elaborated below:

1) Russia was never a serious threat to Britain's hegemony due to largely being concerned with maintaining its gargantuan imperial footprint in Eurasia rather than having global ambitions.
2) Other potential rivals such as Italia (1861), Japan (1868), and Germany (1871) only came into being more or less at the outset of the sixth oquannium (1871-1954) after the unification of a plethora of their respective weak and divided kingdoms.
3) For its part, the modern-day America (1865) also came into being almost at the outset of the sixth oquannium (1871-1954) after the Mexican cession of what is today much of American Southwest from Texas to California in the aftermath of the Mexican-American War (1846-1848) and, before too long, the fledgling nation would plunge into the so-called American Civil War (1861-1865) right away rather than challenge Britain for global hegemony.

Notably, the birth of what are modern-day nations of Italia (1861), America (1865), Japan (1868), and Germany (1871) almost in parallel with the arrival of sixth oquannium (1871-1954) was no coincidence but exactly in line with the fact that new systems and institutions are born at the expense of old ones with the start of a new oqual cycle.

As for Britain, it would defy the oquannia-old traditions of stepping aside and making way for a new sheriff in town and instead go onto reach the peak of its global dominance just as the sixth oquannium (1871-1954) kicked off.

However, before too long, Britain's global hegemony would come to be kept in check by the rapid rise of Germany and America on either side of the Atlantic as the 19th century bid farewell.

While Britain had dodged the oqual bullet in having been able to retain its hegemony and being extended a new lease on life as the fifth oquannium (1787-1870) closed out, its luck to evade the scourge of another oqual cycle would nonetheless run out with the passing of the next and sixth oquannium (1871-1954).

In particular, fearing the meteoric ascent of what was then the young and restless nation of Imperial Germany (1871-1918) that had been carved out of the merger of numerous German states with a shared language and culture just as the sixth oquannium (1871-1954) kicked off, Britain would take extreme measures to counter the rising threat of The Eagles running The Lions ragged on the European continent and thereby challenging its global hegemony.

The outbreak of World War I (1914-1918) almost in tandem with the annus turnilis (1913) of the sixth oquannium (1871-1954) would thus be a godsend for Britain to do exactly that.

While there is no doubt that Germany started World War I to pursue its hegemonic goals, Britain's lukewarm diplomacy leading up to that conflict suggests that the then leader of the world saw a golden opportunity to advance its own strategic goals through wrecking its potential rival.

Although the 1919 Treaty of Versailles would bring World War I to an end, its humiliating and draconian treatment of Germany as being the sole aggressor who would be forced to bear the full cost of the war and make territorial concessions was in no uncertain terms driven by the propaganda to cripple Deutschland so much so that it would never be able to stand on its feet again, much less challenge anyone's hegemony ever again.

While that propaganda headed by Britain undoubtedly neutralized Germany's threat to its hegemony, it somehow never dawned upon The Lions that it would not only come back to haunt them but that another rising power from across the Atlantic was also salivating with its own ambitions of rising to global supremacy.

Indeed, the 1919 Treaty of Versailles served no purpose but to only provoke The Eagles to propel a madman to the their nation's highest office filled with hate and revenge for the humiliation of his country at the hands of its enemies.

Before too long, Germany would once again square up against Britain and its allies with the outbreak of World War II (1939-1945).

The heavy cost of World War II both in terms of human life and monetary terms would literally bankrupt Britain as it would be forced to rapidly roll back its colonial empire and hand over the baton of global hegemony to America just as the sixth oquannium (1871-1954) drew to a close.

Although its imperial links in one way or another would stretch across more than five centuries beginning with reaching Newfoundland in 1497 and ending with the handover of Hong Kong to China in 1997, the global dominance of the British Empire (1497-1997) over other rival powers and hence its Golden Age was largely restricted over the course of the fifth (1787-1870) and sixth (1871-1954) oquannia before America would emerge as the new hegemon.

Why did the British hegemony buck the trend in that it lasted two consecutive oquannia when all of its predecessors fizzled away after just one oquannium and its successor is also on track to follow that trend?

In addition to the fact that there was no potential rival well-positioned to topple Britain from its hegemonic perch as it completed the first of two oquannia in 1870, there were three other cooperative forces that bore good omens for The Lions:

1) Being an island nation with no land borders to share with hostile neighbors, Britain had a naturally impregnable hypermoat that not only required little TLC to keep its defense in pristine shape at home but it would also free up precious resources for the fortification of its overseas territories unlike its European rivals.
2) With no contiguous neighbors to conquer or distract, Britain's fate was sealed as it could only look out to the Atlantic rather than over continental Europe for expanding its empire.
3) Being a Protestant nation, Britain's job of concentrating its energy and resources on colonizing far-flung regions across the globe was made all the easier given that it would have been a fool's errand to even contemplate ruling over what was then a largely Catholic Europe.

Had Britain lacked even one of these virtues, it is quite unlikely that The Lions would have been able to Anglicize the world as much as they did.

Indeed, Britain can take heart from its imperial legacy in that not only has British culture become deeply endemic to most nations of the world today but the English language also serves as lingua franca of the globe in almost every domain of human civilization from trade through arts to sciences.

In fact, such has been the impact of the British legacy that anyone who can read and write today is expected to possess at least a basic command of the English language.

Although Britain may no longer be calling the shots and pulling the levers of international politics as it once did, its impact on shaping global civilization will surely live on till eternity not to mention that it still continues to punch well above its weight with The Oqual Cycle being its latest gift to the world at large.

Goodbye Britannia! Bienvenidos Estados Unidos!

AMERICA AXES THE GLOBE DURING THE SEVENTH OQUANNIUM (1955-2038) AS IT PREPARES TO HANDOVER THE BATON TO CHINA

Unlike its predecessors having risen to global hegemony on the back of millennia-old history, America not only had very humble beginnings but also surprised other nations with its meteoric rise after its independence from Britain in 1776 in the wake of the American Independence War (1775-1783) just in time to welcome the arrival of the fifth oquannium (1787-1870) with a bang of its own.

Barely after having learned to walk on its own feet, the newly-born nation would begin to expand its territory westward from what was then a narrow strip of land running contiguously along the eastern coast of what are modern-day US states of Massachusetts in the north to Georgia in the south.

In 1803, the then tiny United States purchased France's colonial possessions roughly stretching across the north-south corridor in what are the modern-day US states of Louisiana in the south cutting through Nebraska to Montana in the north.

In 1812, after years of being choked by Britain in terms of its desire to continue expanding its territorial radius westward over Native lands and its ability to freely trade with Europe, the then fledgling America would declare war on what was then the mighty British Empire in what can be referred to as the British-American War (1812-1815) in the hope that it could strike a blow to The Lions already showing signs of exhaustion due to having been bogged down for years in the Napoleonic Wars (1803-1815) across the globe.

However, partly driven by the urge to annex much of what is modern-day Canada, that gamble would backfire in no uncertain terms in that not only did it not help to resolve any of the nation's grievances but it also severely damaged its honor and dignity.

In 1814, in the midst of British-American War (1812-1815), America would suffer a huge setback after the British troops burned down numerous capitol buildings in was then and still is the US capital city of Washington—though it was in no small part a retaliation for the destruction and looting of what was then the capital of Canada in modern-day Toronto by American troops a year earlier.

Notwithstanding the British blow, America's resolve to expand its territory would nevertheless march along before too long—albeit only westward and southward.

In what is known as the First Seminole War (1816-1819), America invaded what was then the Spanish Florida on the pretext that the Native tribe of Seminoles was complicit in helping to free the Black slaves from their White owners.

In 1821, in the aftermath of that conflict, the Sunshine State would join the Union after Spain agreed to its cession through what came to be called the 1819 Adams-Onis Treaty.

However, the Seminoles refused to accept White rule over what they considered to be their homeland for centuries and millennia.

In 1835, the resulting standoff would usher in the Second Seminole War (1835-1842) during which the US military upped the ante as it went about relocating Seminoles out of Florida to federal territories in the American Southwest specifically earmarked for the Native tribes.

In 1845, what was then the Republic of Texas decided to become integrated into the United States in spite of Mexico laying claim to what is today the Lone Star State.

In 1846, America would lock horns with Mexico in an effort to further push its territorial orbit westward through what came to be called the Mexican-American War (1846-1848)—a bloody armed conflict during which the United States annexed from Mexico what is today much of American Southwest from Texas to California and, in doing so, literally laid the groundwork for the massive territory to be whitewashed through prioritizing White settlements at the expense of ravaging the livelihoods of Native tribes and driving them into all but extinction.

In 1848, in the aftermath of the Mexican-American War (1846-1848), American sovereignty would stretch from the Pacific Ocean in the west to the Atlantic Ocean in the east in what is today called the US Mainland.

Would Canada be the next target after America's territorial expansion southward and westward were effectively complete?

As for Canadians, they had never forgotten the destruction of their capital city in 1813 and, quite understandably, they not only had their heart in their mouth but were also convinced that America would soon pay them another visit even with the mighty British Empire at their disposal.

In 1857, out of an abundance of caution, Canada would move its capital city from Toronto to Ottawa, which was not only further out from the American border but was also better fortified.

However, America would soon become embroiled in a sociopolitical upheaval unfolding at home and would have to put its territorial ambitions on hold to the much delight of fearful Canadians.

Indeed, cracks would soon begin to appear among Whites over the inhumane treatment of Black people, particularly with regard to the expansion of slavery into newly conquered territories in the American West.

While much of the American North espoused the idea of emancipation of slaves, the American South felt that this was a nothing-burger due to what it believed to be the superiority of Whites over Blacks.

And the political stakes of the American South would be further boosted through the intervention of the US Supreme Court.

In 1857, the US Supreme Court ruled that the Black people were not entitled to citizenship because they hailed from an inferior race and therefore they could not be granted the same privilege as White people.

In 1860, Abraham Lincoln was propelled to the nation's highest office as the 16th POTUS even though he failed to win in any one of more than a dozen slave states in the American South.

Being vehemently opposed to slavery, Lincoln's victory appeared to be the final nail in the Union's coffin as it not only irked the slave states but also sparked the secession of South Carolina a little more than a month after the 1860 election.

In 1861, another six slave states—namely Mississippi, Florida, Alabama, Georgia, Louisiana, and Texas in the order of their secession—would join South Carolina and, together, they would form the Confederate States of America as the nation erupted into what arguably remains the bloodiest conflict on American soil in what is called the American Civil War (1861-1865).

Although four more slave states—namely Virginia, Arkansas, North Carolina, and Tennessee—joined the Confederacy soon after the outbreak of civil war in 1861, the Union army would ultimately emerge victorious and keep the nation united as we know it today.

In 1863, Lincoln issued the executive order called Emancipation Proclamation in the midst of the ongoing civil war to abolish slavery, thereby setting millions of Black people free.

With the arrival of the sixth oquannium (1871-1954), the American society had indeed been remade for all intents and purposes to add to a roster of new institutions having been erected at the expense of old ones in line with the recurring spell of oqual cycle.

The births of many more nations across the globe including the likes of what are modern-day nations of Italia (1861), Japan (1868), and Germany (1871) would also join the ranks of what was now a heavy-weight America with the arrival of a new oquannium.

Before too long, driven by the then rapidly-expanding railroad economy, America would become a manufacturing powerhouse and the largest global economy surpassing that of Britain just as the 19th century closed out.

Admittedly, as promised by an auspicious spell of oqual cycle, America was not alone but would also be joined by most other nations of the world in savoring those happy times during much of the first half (1871-1912) of the sixth oquannium (1871-1954) as evidenced by:

- The Gilded Age in America (1870-1900)
- The Late Victorian Era in Britain (1870-1901)
- La Belle Époque (The Beautiful Epoch) in France (1870-1914)
- Gründerzeit (Founding Period) in Germany (1871-1900)

During the early 20th century, America was relishing its rapid rise to having become a global power on the back of what was now a powerful military, the largest economy, and a nation feeding the world in that its exports of goods and services far exceeded its imports.

However, the outbreak of World War I (1914-1918) would put a prompt end to happy times across much of the globe and serve as a harbinger of terrible times to engulf humanity over the next several decades that followed.

Nevertheless, the World War I also offered America an opportunity to rub shoulders with the big European boys and test the waters for its own hegemonic ambitions of patrolling the world and controlling its precious resources with the then dominant British Empire looking increasingly vulnerable to falling apart under its own wright.

In particular, witnessing Germany as a rising power threatening to knock Britain off its hegemonic perch, the World War I served as nothing short of a godsend for America to press home its own claim to rising to global hegemony.

To achieve that goal, America would play a leading role in crafting the draconian 1919 Treaty of Versailles that would make sure that Germany would never be able to stand on its feet again, thereby leaving the United States as the sole heir to what was then Britain's hegemonic throne.

In the event that the 1919 Treaty of Versailles failed to crush Germany, America would also draft during the 1920s and 1930s what came to be called the "War Plan Red"—a backup plan to directly attack many strategic territories of the British Empire in an effort to knock it off its hegemonic perch should it become necessary.

However, the War Plan Red became moot after the 1919 Treaty of Versailles handsomely delivered goods in having planted a much-anticipated rematch between a resurgent Germany and decadent Britain already on its last leg through World War II (1939-1945).

And with that self-destructive conflict unfolding across Eurasia kilomiles away from American shores, the United States had finally hit a home run without even breaking a sweat.

Indeed, the heavy cost of World War II not only reduced much of Europe and the world to ashes but it also fired up America's economic engine at home to new heights.

To say that America fiddled while the globe burned would be a huge understatement.

Inevitably, World War II would also bankrupt Britain as it would be forced to rapidly roll back its colonial empire and hand over the baton of global hegemony to America just as the sixth oquannium (1871-1954) drew to a close.

That there was a new sheriff in town was further underscored by the 1944 Bretton-Woods Agreement that propelled the American dollar to become the world's new reserve currency at the expense of the British pound just as the annus horribilis (1944) of the sixth oquannium (1871-1954) rolled around.

However, the onset of dollar hegemony in 1944 did not quite hit home as Britain dared to exercise its hegemonic will once more through what came to be called the 1956 Suez Crisis—when the empire upon which the sun never set tried to regain control of the Suez Canal after it had been nationalized by Egypt but being left to lick its wounds and having lost its imperial mojo forever due to the intervention of what was now mighty America.

Not only did America stand shoulder-to-shoulder with Egypt during the 1956 Suez Crisis but it also threatened to offload its bond holdings in sterling with the potential to exacerbate the collapse of the British pound which had already begun in the aftermath of the 1944 Bretton-Woods Agreement.

Such a stab-in-the-back would come as a bombshell for Britons leaving many of them holding their head in their hands as they pondered: "With friends like America, who needs enemies!"

If the 1944 Bretton-Woods Agreement had not signaled the end of British hegemony, the 1956 Suez Crisis surely marked the beginning of America's role as the dominant global power that was now single-handedly calling the shots and pulling the levers of geopolitics just as the current and seventh oquannium (1955-2038) had kicked off.

Buoyed by such a hegemonic virtue at its disposal, America would quickly up the ante on imposing what we now know is a dehumanizing, morally-corrupted, and environmentally-destructive worldview upon the rest of the world beginning with what came to be known as the Vietnam War (1955-1975).

Although that decades-long asinine ploy left America deeply wounded at home and away, its capitalist urge to control and enslave the world never waivered.

With the money printer at one's disposal, who would indeed back off from doing exactly that.

After taking the dollar off the gold standard in 1971, America would predictably bring its money printer to the fore and simply print its way to self-indulgence, excesses, and imbalances under the guise of capitalism.

While other nations worked off their back and by the sweat of their brow, America would enjoy the fruits of their labor in exchange for what one could call nothing more than junk pieces of paper.

However, those who exploit and enslave others face the music sooner or later as every one of America's predecessors did.

America would therefore be no exception to following in their footsteps.

As the saying goes, those who fail to learn from history are doomed to repeat it.

As the oqual cycle goes, those who pay no heed to the dire spell of its second half are destined to self-destruct themselves as it reaches its crescendo around annus horribilis.

With the onset of the ominous second half (1997-2038) of the current oquannium (1955-2038), America would indeed reignite its wounds as it once again began decades-long 9/11 Wars (2001-2021) to exert its might over the world and its resources driven by its capitalist propaganda.

Alas, the oqual cycle will have none of that and leave America deeply wounded for its aggression and continuing violation of the laws of nature.

Not only did that gambit backfire but it would also come back to haunt America in that the embers of the 9/11 Wars continue to rage to this day with the nation teetering on the brink of a looming bankruptcy with the US dollar edging ever closer to losing its global luster a la British pound in 1944 over the next decade or so coupled with social-and-moral decadence at home from soaring public debts through shrinking middle class to faltering infrastructure.

In what I call the "9/11 Curse", America literally dug its own grave in lieu of using the tragedy to undertake a moment of self-reflection so as to channel much-needed resources toward addressing what were then already becoming a growing plethora of domestic issues rather than funneling every dollar of US taxpayer overseas to smash the world into pieces with the sole intention of bloating the coffers of its ruling elite and the wealthy at the expense of the pain and suffering of the masses that we can all see in plain sight today.

In fact, the onset of 9/11 Wars marked the beginning of the end of American hegemony in the footsteps of its predecessors just as they also happened to cross the annus turnilis of oqual cycle.

Notably, self-destructive gambits such as the 9/11 Wars unfolding around annus turnilis (1997) of the current and seventh oquannium (1955-2038) are renowned for plunging hegemons into an irreparable and irreversible turmoil from which they never seem to recover.

Some 84 years before the 9/11 Wars, the World War I (1914-1918) marked the beginning of the end of the then hegemon Britain just as the previous and sixth oquannium (1871-1954) moved past its annus turnilis (1913).

Rewind the clock back by another 84 years, the outbreak of so-called Anglo-Khasi War (1829-1833) in sync with the onset of annus turnilis (1829) of fifth oquannium (1787-1870) between the Khasi kingdom in what is modern-day northeastern Indian state of Meghalaya and Britain marked the beginning of decades-long hostilities between the colonialists and natives that would ultimately boil over into the 1857 Indian Mutiny—though largely suppressed, that widespread and violent rebellion nevertheless bore the potential to topple British hegemony.

Some 84 years earlier, the outbreak of so-called Carnatic Wars (1744-1763) between the then dominant power of France and the rising power of Britain almost in tandem with the onset of annus turnilis (1745) of the fourth oquannium (1703-1786) signaled the beginning of the end of French hegemony.

Take the clock back by another 84 years, the outbreaks of the duo of Anglo-Dutch War (1665-1667) and Franco-Dutch War (1672-1678) barely years after the onset of annus turnilis (1661) of the third oquannium (1619-1702) was a reminder that the Dutch hegemony had already peaked and the decades that followed would indeed send the Netherlands into bewildering wilderness.

Some 84 years earlier, the 1581 Declaration of Independence by Netherlands from the shackles of the then hegemon Spain came just after the onset of annus turnilis (1577) of second oquannium (1535-1618) against the backdrop of the ongoing Eighty Years War (1566-1648) and marked the beginning of the end of Spanish hegemony.

Rewind back by another 84 years, the 1492 Voyage by Christopher Columbus to the New World on behalf of the then rising power of Spain almost in parallel with the onset of annus turnilis (1493) of the first oquannium (1451-1534) signaled that the Golden Age of the Portuguese Empire was on its last leg.

To say that America is on the road to becoming a shadow of its past over the next decade or so would be to put it mildly.

It is noteworthy that the world's principal currency also follows the hegemon in a phenomenon referred to as "monetary hegemony"—the hegemon is endowed with the privilege of being the de-facto head of the international monetary system such that its currency commands a lion's share of international trade and foreign exchange reserves.

Just as GBP was dethroned by USD during annus horribilis (1944) of the previous oquannium (1871-1954), CNY is likewise set to oust the latter some time between annus horribilis (2028) of the current oquannium (1955-2038) and annus mirabilis (2039) of the next cycle (2039-2122).

Yet, so many fools naively believe that USD will continue to be the king in spite of having no clue as to what it takes to continue to be the monetary hegemon.

In order to land the privilege of becoming the monetary hegemon and continue to hold that status, a nation must satisfy the following three criteria:

1) Be a manufacturing powerhouse not only head-and-shoulders but also chest-and-waist above all other nations such that the world becomes dependent upon the export of that nation's goods and services. Today, that nation is unarguably China. Some 84 years earlier, America was where China is today. In other words, once the world becomes dependent upon your merchandize, it is only a matter of time before you begin to demand that the payment be made in your own currency in lieu of the reserve currency of another nation. Indeed, China is already on that path and CNY will heavily cut into the dollar's share of international trade over the next decade or so.

2) Boast a powerful military that can match or surpass that of any other rivals vying to compete with your desire to become the monetary hegemon. A powerful military is de rigueur to defending your currency

lest the nation gets bulldozed by a more powerful force. Some 84 years earlier, it was American military that caught up with the British military and emerged as the dominant force in the aftermath of World War II (1939-1945). Today, it is Chinese military that is not only becoming a headache for America but it is also set to overtake the US Armed Forces over the next decade.

3) Stockpile as much gold as possible so that it can be used as a collateral to lure the world into adopting your currency with the promise of being able to swap the paper notes with a set amount of gold anytime one so desires. Pegging the currency to gold is an old bait-and-switch scheme that has been used time and again to kill rival currencies throughout history but once everyone gets hooked, the process of taking the paper notes off the gold standard begins in no uncertain terms so as to allow the money printer to go brrr without any checks and balances. Some 84 years earlier, it was America that began to hoard the yellow metal like an Indian bride with its gold reserves reaching 20 kilotonnes by 1940 and overshadowing those of Britain. It was indeed on the back of such massive heaps of gold reserves coupled with America's military might and its manufacturing prowess that the dollar became the king in 1944. While America's gold reserves today amount to no more than 10 kilotonnes, China likely holds at least five-fold as much and possibly even more given that the Asian Giant has not only been the largest miner of the yellow metal but also the largest gold importer from every corner of the world over the past couple of decades.

Not only is China the only nation today that satisfies all three conditions noted above but America has also made passing the baton of monetary hegemony to the Asian Giant all the more easier through weaponizing the dollar in the wake of the ongoing Russia-Ukraine War that began in 2022.

In fact, trade sanctions against Russia have jumpstarted the demand for a new international currency at the expense of the dollar with CNY likely to emerge as the winner for the reasons stated above.

Add to that the fact that America has not only been consistently running a trade deficit since the outset of 21st century but is also rapidly becoming buried under heaps of debt and printed money.

Together with a deeply-divided and decadent American society having lost its moral compass, these represent signs of a hegemon rapidly collapsing under its own weight and unfit to lead the world.

With China being the exact mirror image of the sociopolitical upheaval facing America today, the time to pass on the baton of global hegemony is indeed inching ever closer with the passing of each year.

Pass or not, China only has to showcase its humongous gold vaults to kill the dollar overnight.

There is no doubt that the Asian Giant is looking to do exactly that when push comes to shove due for example to reclaiming its long-lost soul Taiwan over the next decade or so.

In fact, Chinese bilateral trade with most nations of the world today is already being conducted in CNY while many other countries are beginning to pivot toward the yuan out of fear of their increasing reliance on USD with an unpredictable future against the backdrop of Uncle Sam having been diagnosed with an untreatable and a rare form of schizophrenia.

Additionally, a growing list of countries such as Russia and Iran have not only started using CNY in international trade—wherein yuan as a form of payment is accepted between any two trading partners outside China—but they are also leading the charge toward de-dollarization through negotiating with other nations to pay in CNY for their commodities and to accept it in return for their exports.

That CNY is on an ascending trajectory is further underscored by the fact that its share of global trade has precipitously risen to almost 10% over the past decade, all the while a growing number of central banks around the globe are beginning to empty out their dollar reserves in exchange for yuan.

With yuan rising fast in international trade, China is aptly and deservedly positioned to emerge as the new hegemon taking up the baton of global leadership from America some time between annus horribilis (2028) of the current oquannium (1955-2038) and annus mirabilis (2039) of the next cycle (2039-2122).

However, such a transfer of global power is unlikely to happen without a showdown between the two superpowers in a manner akin to the fact that the alpha male in a lion pride does not get dethroned by a younger and more hungrier competitor without putting up a fight of his life.

In that sense, the looming World War III can also be viewed as a rite of passage for the newly-minted hegemon to take up the mantle from its predecessor.

But, for China, such a rite of passage goes through Taiwan for without its soul the Asian Giant cannot claim to be whole, much less a leader of the world.

Being fully aware of such a deadly confrontation and coronation waiting on the horizon, China is working round the clock to beef up its military paraphernalia with the Chinese navy today being the largest in the world and rapidly dwarfing its US counterpart—a truly daunting feat that should not be lost on anyone given that the wars are won and lost at sea.

And when it comes to battling it out at sea, preponderance reigns supreme over all else in guaranteeing the triumph as attested by history time and again.

In fact, history shows that the hegemon is often dethroned not because it is no longer powerful enough to knock out its rival but because it lacks the stamina to go the full round due to the low morale within its ranks echoing the rather poor state of the nation as a whole having fallen prey to moral disintegration as a result of self-indulgence and waning zest for life.

When China and America finally square up against each other over the next decade or so, it is quite clear which nation would be fighting tooth-and-nail and which one would be grappling with a low morale—or rather which one of them would be fighting to the death and which one fighting for life.

Top that up with the fact that China has also begun to salivate at the prospect of shepherding the world in accordance with its national interests as it rapidly expands its radius of geopolitical influence around the globe.

That is all the more damning for the Western powers given that the center of economic gravity is set to shift to Asia over the next decade or so after a hiatus of some 500 years.

Those who have not already booked a Mandarin class for their golden child, it would pay to move fast while supplies last.

And as Americans prepare to kiss their Casino Dream goodbye, the Sino Dream is finally coming home for the Chinese.

|2.2| GLOBAL POLITICS

Political forces such as globalism, pluralism, populism, nationalism, and fascism do not crop up randomly but rather appear to be closely intertwined with the spell of oqual cycle.

While positive forces such as globalism and pluralism reign supreme during the first half of oqual cycle, negative forces powered by nationalism and populism rear their ugly head during the second half.

For example, leaders considered to be on the extreme fringes of politics and being viewed as unelectable or unfit for office such that they become the butt of jokes during the first half of oqual cycle steadily gain popularity with the onset of second half and then often go onto rewrite a nation's history.

Admittedly, the second half (1997-2038) of the current and seventh oquannium (1955-2038) has already witnessed a rising wave of divisive-and-nationalist leaders gaining foothold in countries such as:

- Russia → Vladmir Putin (since 2000)
- Turkiye → Recep Erdogan (since 2003)
- Britain → Nigel Farage (since 2006)
- France → Marine Le Pen (since 2011)
- China → Xi Jinping (since 2012)
- Pakistan → Imran Khan (since 2013)
- India → Narendra Modi (since 2014)
- America → Donald Trump (since 2016)
- Brazil → Jair Bolsonaro (since 2019)
- Italia → Giorgia Meloni (since 2022)

A similar scenario of far-right nationalist leaders springing out across the globe also panned out during the second half (1913-1954) of the previous and sixth oquannium (1871-1954) in nations as far-flung as:

- British India → Muhammad Ali Jinnah (1913-1948)
- Soviet Union → Joseph Stalin (1922-1952)
- Italia → Benito Mussolini (1922-1943)
- Turkiye → Mustafa Kemal Atatürk (1923-1938)
- China → Chiang Kai-Shek (1928-1949)
- Germany → Adolf Hitler (1933-1945)

And, you bet, nor were far-right and divisive leaders in short supply during the second half (1829-1870) of the fifth oquannium (1787-1870):
- Turkiye → Sultan Abdulmejid I (1839-1861)
- France → Emperor Napolean III (1848-1870)
- Italia → Giuseppe Garibaldi (1849-1882)
- America → Jefferson Davis (1853-1865)
- Russia → Tsar Alexander II (1855--1881)
- British India → Syed Ahmed Khan (1857-1898)
- Germany → Otto Von Bismarck (1862-1890)

Long story short, the rightwing nationalist (or populist) tide seemingly oscillates in tandem with the progression of oqual cycle such that it ebbs during the first half and then begins to flow during the second half in what is dubbed the "politics oquacycle".

On the other hand, globalism is a mirror image of populism in that it rises during the first half of oqual cycle and then decays during the second half.

What causes the rise of far-right nationalist politics with the onset of the second half of oqual cycle?

The factors driving such divisive propaganda are often a by-product of grievances and injustices in the society either driven by the ruling elite at home or due to geopolitics or unfair trade policies imposed by other nations.

For their part, the nationalist leaders quickly latch onto such societal shortcomings and exploit them for their own political gains.

For example, the draconian treatment of Germany in the aftermath of World War I (1914-1918)—as stipulated in the 1919 Treaty of Versailles crafted by the likes of Britain, France, and America—began almost in tandem with the onset of second half (1913-1954) of the previous oquannium (1871-1954)—not only would it lead to the rapid rise and popularity of nationalist politics across Deutschland but it would also provoke the masses to propel a madman to their nation's highest office filled with hate and revenge for the humiliation of his country at the hands of its enemies.

Simply put, the cruel and disproportionate punishment handed out to Germany—largely driven by the propaganda to cripple the then fast-rising global power so much so that it would never be able to stand on its feet again, much less challenge anyone's hegemony ever again—only served to plunge the world into an even deeper crisis with the outbreak of World War II (1939-1945) exactly two decades later.

Shamefully, those who call the shots and pull the levers of international politics somehow always seem to sweep history under the rug due to their own greed and hubris.

It should therefore hardly raise eyebrows to learn that the world has once again begun to navigate similar waters to those it encountered some 84 years earlier with today's sociopolitical upheaval bearing stunning echoes of the past.

In 1999, in an echo of the poor treatment of Germany by the 1919 Treaty of Versailles some 84 years earlier, provocation of Russia by NATO—a close-knit military alliance among 32 Western nations led by the United States—was officially undertaken almost in parallel with the onset of second half (1997-2038) of the current oquannium (1955-2038) that in hindsight appears to have been the trigger for the looming World War III.

In 2000, NATO's provocation would be met by the rise to power in Russia of Vladimir Putin—a nationalist leader who would make sure that the Siberian Tiger would live up to its billing and take the NATO bully by the horns.

In fact, NATO has doubled its inertia in an attempt to rub shoulders with Russia's borders since the breakup of USSR in 1991.

In so doing, NATO provoked Russia to not only annex Crimea in 2014 but also provided it with fresh tinder to restart the war in Ukraine in 2022.

In Einstein's disguise, insanity is doing the same thing over-and-over again but expecting a different outcome.

If not kept in check, insanity can often lead to self-destruction in a manner akin to a malignant tumor.

In the Western world, that should set off alarm bells given that the US foreign policy not only runs on insanity but also hubris-on-steroids.

It has not only been misfiring on all cylinders for decades but it will also come back to haunt the West, particularly in the wake of the ongoing Russia-Ukraine War showing no signs of easing.

Let us take a deeper look into the mindset of NATO driven by the monetary urge to control and subjugate the non-Western world.

NATO IS THE ANTITHESIS OF PEACE

In 1949, NATO was created as a counterweight to keep the imperial ambitions of the former USSR in check during what came to be known as the "Cold War" between the self-proclaimed "free-and-capitalist" America and the West-declared "evil-and-communist" Soviet Union.

In 1991, the USSR underwent political apoptosis yielding 15 independent nations such as the likes of modern-day Russia, Ukraine, and Belarus.

With the perceived threat of communism all but having perished in the aftermath of the dissolution of USSR, one would have noted that the days of NATO would also be numbered as it would quickly become irrelevant and obsolete in a post-Soviet world.

Alas, the exact opposite transpired.

Rather than welcoming Russia into the fold of Western world, the US and its European vassals doubled-down and set about making an enemy out of the Siberian Tiger for a world without a declared enemy would be too peaceful for America in its quest to extend its hegemony over every corner of the world, not to mention that the US military is nothing short of being an industrial complex that generates huge profits for its stakeholders.

Like a corporation, the military industrial complex of the United States (MICOTUS) must continue to grow in order to generate ever more profits and the bigger the enemy, the greater the profits.

Toward this propaganda, America pushed for the expansion of NATO's European footprint eastward during the 1990s even when the perceived threat of communism was no longer on the menu.

By 2004, NATO would end up swallowing not only an array of Eastern-European states such as Poland and Hungary that provided a buffer zone between the West and the former USSR but also three former Soviet republics—namely Estonia, Latvia, and Lithuania—precariously sitting within breathing distance of Moscow.

This was all the more alarming given that George Kennan—an architect of the US policy toward the Soviet Union in the post-WWII era that ensured that the Cold War (1947-1991) would never turn hot—had warned against the expansion of NATO nearly a decade earlier.

In 1997, in an op-ed on NATO's decision to march into Eastern Europe [11], Kennan observed:

> "The view, bluntly stated, is that expanding NATO would be the most fateful error of American policy in the entire post-cold-war era. Such a decision may be expected to inflame the nationalistic, anti-Western and militaristic tendencies in Russian opinion; to have an adverse effect on the development of Russian democracy; to restore the atmosphere of the cold war to East-West relations, and to impel Russian foreign policy in directions decidedly not to our liking."

In 1998, in an op-ed by Thomas Friedman on NATO's appetite for a meteoric expansion [12], Kennan foretold:

> "I think it is the beginning of a new cold war. I think the Russians will gradually react quite adversely and it will affect their policies. I think it is a tragic mistake. There was no reason for this whatsoever. No one was threatening anybody else. This expansion would make the Founding Fathers of this country turn over in their graves."

In that same 1998 op-ed [12], Kennan went onto add:

> "I was particularly bothered by the references to Russia as a country dying to attack Western Europe. Don't people understand? Our differences in the cold war were with the Soviet Communist regime. And now we are turning our backs on the very people who mounted the greatest bloodless revolution in history to remove that Soviet regime. And Russia's democracy is as far advanced, if not farther, as any of these countries we've just signed up to defend from Russia. It shows so little understanding of Russian history and Soviet history. Of course there is going to be a bad reaction from Russia, and then [the West] will say that we always told you that is how the Russians are but this is just wrong."

How ironic then that the West is behaving toward Russia today exactly along the lines foreseen by Kennan a quarter-of-a-century earlier.

How come the West-Russia relations have hit a nadir despite the fact that the USSR is no more?

What triggered the collapse of USSR?

Other than the dire economic straits that befell the USSR in the aftermath of the decade-long Soviet-Afghan War (1979–1989), one of the major catalysts for the dissolution of USSR was the assurance given to Russians by the West that NATO would not move an inch eastward in the post-Soviet era.

Alas, the naïve Russians should have known better that the West never keeps promises nor did they pay heed to the adage that if you yield an inch, they will take a mile.

In 1991, before the collapse of USSR, a distance of at least 1000 miles separated the NATO frontline in Denmark to Russia's northwestern border with Latvia.

In 2004, just over a decade after the breakup of USSR, NATO had moved its goalposts eastward all the way to Russia's northwestern border when it struck military alliance with the trio of former Soviet republics of Estonia, Latvia, and Lithuania.

Add to this the fact that the number of NATO states has doubled to 32 since the breakup of USSR in 1991.

In particular, against the backdrop of the then nascent Ukraine-Russia War barely months after it broke out in early 2022, NATO upped the ante by extending invitation to Finland and Sweden to join its ranks—while the former Scandinavian nation sitting at the northwestern corner of Siberian Tiger has already been added, the latter is all but ratified.

In adding these new outfits to its ranks, NATO has today more than doubled its border with Russia to 1600 miles.

Such an unprecedented provocation and exponential growth of the most powerful military killing machine ever created in the history of mankind is not only an attempt to continue to subjugate the non-Western nations but it also runs counter to the righteous segment of humanity vying for peace on earth.

To say that NATO's metastasis in the post-Soviet era is reminiscent of a malignant tumor threatening to wreak havoc on the body fast and furious would be to put it mildly.

Admittedly, Russia is not the only target of NATO but it also poses threat to every other non-Western nation harboring natural resources such as the Middle-Eastern countries, being strategically important such as the likes of Afghanistan and Pakistan, or with the potential to challenge Western supremacy such as the likes of China and India—each one of the latter two nations accounts for nearly 18% of humanity on earth compared to a hair above 10% for the Western world with America accounting for a meager 4%.

That NATO is out to get you is overwhelmingly supported by earth-shattering data over the past several decades.

One only has to look at how NATO bombing decimated Soviet-aligned federation of Yugoslavia (1999) into pieces barely after the curtain had been lowered onto the Soviet Union.

Not only did Yugoslavs adopt communism but they also shared close cultural and ethnic ties with the Soviets through their Slavic consanguinity.

In a manner akin to the dissolution of USSR, the breakup of Yugoslavia into the likes of modern-day Serbia and Croatia therefore served as the final nail in the coffin of communism in NATO's view even if it came at a huge cost of butchering humanity.

The NATO bombing of Yugoslavia was followed by the utter carnage of the likes of Afghanistan (2001-2021) and Iraq (2003-2011) by NATO-in-disguise-of-America using the 9/11 attacks as a pretext.

More recently, the shameful annihilation of Libya (2011) and Syria (2018)—after they began to grow a spine rather than submit to the will of Western powers—speaks volumes of evil acts committed on the part of NATO.

As the Holy Quran asserts:
> "Wa itha qeela lahum la tufsidu fil-ardh, qaalu innama nahnu muslihoon!"— "When they are told not to fight on earth, they claim that they are in fact the peacemakers!"

Like the Quranic parable, a seasoned criminal would often claim that their actions are pious and that they never intend to harm anyone when interrogated about their inner motives.

When grilled about its hidden propaganda, NATO-à-la-criminal claims that its only purpose is self-defense and maintenance of peace on earth.

Simply put, when other nations go to a war, it is because they have evil intentions but when NATO wages a war, it is for peaceful purposes!

Ironically, by its very own admission albeit in a surreptitious manner, NATO is a criminal enterprise whose goals run counter to peace.

Indeed, bombing weaker nations and tearing them apart does not help bring about peace—not to mention that they pose no threat to anyone, much less to the West.

Rather, the only threat such weaker nations pose is their failure to put Western interests before their own.

In other words, NATO is essentially a state-sponsored mafia that uses force to subjugate the weak and vulnerable so that the West can have the first bite on their precious resources and commodities with the producers left with the "leftovers".

As the saying goes, actions speak louder than words.

Judging by its actions, the West is far from satisfied with NATO being the sole killing machine at its disposal.

Toward that deplorable goal, an offshoot of NATO named AUKUS—a trilateral nuclear security pact signed between Australia, UK, and US in 2021—has already emerged to specifically deal with the rise of China as it readies to free itself in earnest from the shackles of slavery that it has been subjected to at the hands of Western overlords over the past couple of centuries or so.

In West's defense, however, one could understand the rising fear of non-Western world that together makes up almost 90% of humanity on earth—yet its resources and commodities being central to Western appetite of a reckless standard of living that it enjoys at the expense of poor and destitute.

Accordingly, the Western thinktank likely subscribes to the notion that the best way to deal with such fear is to go on the offensive and enslave those whom you can lest they enslave you.

That school of thought might have held water in the past but, in today's world, we can do a lot better than use our might to suppress the weak and vulnerable.

To say that NATO is nothing short of being a deadly fox vying to guard the henhouse would be to put it lightly.

Indeed, the Russian chickens are not out of the woods yet as the NATO fox appears to be moving ever closer for what it believes will be the kill of the century.

Alas, the NATO fox knows not that it is rather being tricked into the Siberian Tiger's den and that it will soon be fighting for its life.

NATO IS BREATHING DOWN RUSSIA'S NECK

Today, NATO sits cunningly so close to Moscow that every time it sneezes, the Russians reportedly catch flu.

If such a reckless behavior and utter disregard for Russians does not constitute an act of aggression, then there ain't such a thing as aggression by any stretch of the imagination.

In spite of vociferous opposition from Russia in the face of ever-rapidly expanding NATO posing serious security challenges for the successor to the former USSR, America and its European poodles would be far from satisfied with their hidden propaganda of cornering Russia such that it could be easily balkanized—or broken up into smaller states.

To that end, America and its European allies began to set their sights on wooing Ukraine since as early as 2002.

In so doing, Ukraine would be showered with undivided attention and material aid so as to compel it to tie the knot with NATO for it would mark the death knell for the territorial integrity and survival of Russia.

In 2007, the Russian President Putin would tellingly push back on NATO's aggression toward Russia and the world-writ-large during his address to the annual 43rd Munich Security Conference [13].

In that 2007 speech, Putin noted:
> "Today we are witnessing an almost uncontained hyper use of force—military force—in international relations, force that is plunging the world into an abyss of permanent conflicts. As a result we do not have sufficient strength to find a comprehensive solution to any one of these conflicts. Finding a political settlement also becomes impossible. We are seeing a greater and greater disdain for the basic principles of international law. And independent legal norms are, as a matter of fact, coming increasingly closer to one state's legal system. One state and, of course, first and foremost the United States, has overstepped its national borders in every way. This is visible in the economic, political, cultural and educational policies it imposes on other nations. Well, who likes this? Who is happy about this? And of course this is extremely dangerous. It results in the fact that no one feels safe. I want to emphasize this—no one feels safe! Because no one can feel that international law is like a stone wall that will protect them. Of course such a policy stimulates an arms race. The force's dominance inevitably encourages a number of countries to acquire weapons of mass destruction. Moreover, significantly new threats—though they were also well-known before—have appeared, and today threats such as terrorism have taken on a global character."

In a reference to NATO in that same 2007 speech, Putin observed:
> "It turns out that NATO has put its frontline forces on our borders, and we continue to strictly fulfill the treaty obligations and do not react to these actions at all. I think it is obvious that NATO expansion does not have any relation with the modernization of the Alliance itself or with ensuring security in Europe. On the contrary, it represents a serious provocation that reduces the level of mutual trust. And we have the right to ask: against

whom is this expansion intended? And what happened to the assurances our western partners made after the dissolution of the Warsaw Pact? Where are those declarations today? No one even remembers them. But I will allow myself to remind this audience what was said. I would like to quote the speech of NATO General Secretary Mr Woerner in Brussels on 1990/05/17. He said at the time that 'the fact that we are ready not to place a NATO army outside of German territory gives the Soviet Union a firm security guarantee'. Where are these guarantees?"

In spite of Putin's ominous warning that NATO having moved its frontline right up to Russia's borders and America's perpetual violation of international law was unacceptable some 15 years ago, the West would nevertheless continue to march along the path of provocation at full throttle as if it were on cocaine with misguided euphoria showing no signs of abating.

In fact, West's crush on Ukraine would become so obsessive that it would even go as far as supporting a coup d'état to overthrow a democratically-elected government of Ukraine in 2014—after its pro-Russian President Viktor Yanukovych rejected an offer of economic aid from the European Union in favor of a deal with Russia—and help pro-Western puppet Petro Poroshenko to come to power so that NATO could finally add Ukraine to its ranks.

Alas, led by their talismanic leader Putin, Russia would have none of that as any attempt by NATO to phagocytose Ukraine and turn it into a bulwark would mark a red line and patience no more for the Russians.

Given the threat of humongous NATO looming large over its head and shoulders with the potential for nuclear missiles to be stationed on Ukrainian soil minutes away from Russian territory, Russia would understandably begin to fight back and go on the offensive for the first time since the breakup of former USSR in 1991.

In 2014, within days of pro-Russian Ukrainian President Viktor Yanukovych having been deposed by the US-led coup, Russia would annex the Crimean peninsula from Ukraine not only out of its concerns for its own security but also to show that it had teeth to bite back should anyone dare to stare at Ukraine—a nation that not only shares more than a thousand-mile border but also close cultural and historic ties with Russia.

Add to this the fact that Eastern Ukraine, bordering Russia, is dominated by ethnic Russians who have overwhelmingly continued to favor Ukraine remaining a part of the Russian sphere of influence rather than move in bed with the alien and unpredictable West.

Unsurprisingly then, Ukraine has been far from being a united and monolithic nation since emerging as a sovereign state in the aftermath of the collapse of USSR in 1991.

Indeed, Ukraine has hitherto largely existed as a deeply-divided and fractured nation—a feat further exacerbated by the poor treatment of its minorities, including in particular the ethnic Russians.

Still, despite Russia flexing its muscles vis-à-vis the annexation of Crimea in 2014, NATO would nevertheless continue to cajole Ukraine out of not only utter disregard for its much larger eastern neighbor but also posing existential threat to its very existence.

In response, Russia began to threaten to go all into Ukraine out of its concerns for its own security unless NATO backed off from its propaganda.

Yet, NATO upped-the-ante and kept doubling down on its goal to extend its military hegemony over Ukraine.

In 2021, Russia would offer a befitting riposte to NATO knocking on its doorstep as it began to amass troops along its Western border with Ukraine.

With a bargaining chip in one hand and from a position of strength, Russia would now not only require NATO to back off from its backyard but it would also demand that the following four conditions be honored:

1) Ukraine should remain militarily neutral and bury its ambitions of ever becoming a pawn in NATO's dirty game of chess.

2) NATO membership to the trio of former Soviet republics of Estonia, Latvia, and Lithuania should be rescinded. Ditto for formerly militarily-neutral Eastern-European nations—such as Poland, Czech Republic, Slovakia, Hungary, Romania, Slovenia, Croatia, Montenegro, Albania, North Macedonia, and Bulgaria—that joined NATO after 1997.

3) Although abandoned unilaterally by America in 2019, the 1987 Intermediate-Range Nuclear Forces Treaty should be reinstated. That treaty required the former USSR and USA to eliminate all of their missiles with a striking range between 500km to 5500km.

4) Signed in 2015, the Minsk agreements that required Ukraine to grant autonomy to Donbas region in Eastern Ukraine should be implemented.

While Russia clearly played hard ball against the West, it is unlikely that satisfying all of these conditions would have been necessary to offset Putin's appetite for an aggression toward Ukraine.

Yet, the West refused to yield an inch to Russia's demands for it may not only keep a much-needed World War III at bay but it could also invite a long-lasting peace on earth.

Alas, peace is to NATO what sunlight is to a vampire!

Admittedly, while the ongoing Russia-Ukraine War may be viewed as an act of aggression on the part of Putin as drummed up by the Western media due to their personal biases, it is in essence a brainchild of NATO either directly or as a by-product of its perpetual war-mongering behavior toward Russia even in a post-Soviet era.

However, NATO's pivot to take such an aggressive step toward Russia will backfire with a vengeance as it has all but invited World War III onto its doorstep.

That does not bode well for humanity-writ-large.

Nor does it conceal the throttle-bottom that the Ukrainian leader Volodymyr Zelensky has turned out to be since his rise to power in 2019.

Either poorly-informed, or perhaps merely driven by the greed for the perceived albeit tainted riches that the Western nations enjoy, Zelensky would have been well-advised that smaller nations live at the mercy of their giant neighbors who set the political tone and order around them.

Thus, Zelensky's push to have Ukraine join NATO would have been equivalent to Canada or Mexico striking a military alliance with the likes of superpowers such as Russia or China.

Can one imagine Chinese missiles arriving on Canadian or Mexican soil?

What would America's response be?

If one believes, it would be anything other than US military launching an outright invasion of Canada or Mexico, then they are advised to review a quick primer on the 1962 Cuban Missile Crisis.

If America would not allow Russian missiles in Cuba, then why Russia should be okay with a potential for NATO's missiles to be stationed in Ukraine in the not too distant future.

As for Zelensky having turned himself into a Western puppet and being exploited to do the bidding on behalf of NATO, he should have paid heed to the adage: "what is good for the goose is good for the gander!".

NATO IS THE GOOSE THAT LAYS THE GOLDEN EGGS

Like the proverbial goose that lays the golden eggs, killing NATO would be equivalent to killing MICOTUS—a hugely profitable enterprise for its stakeholders.

With a 20/20 hindsight, one wonders what if NATO had been dismantled in parallel with the dissolution of the former USSR in 1991.

Under that scenario, few would doubt that Ukraine would be enjoying warm relations with both the West and Russia today rather than fighting tooth-and-nail for its survival.

In fact, the breakup of NATO would have also brought Russia closer to the West on both economic and military fronts—thereby altogether eliminating the risk of any geopolitical chasm developing between the two superpowers with the potential to turn our planet into ashes like never before.

Instead, NATO would march along unhindered in its quest to becoming an 800-pound gorilla so as to kill and annihilate anyone who would dare challenge the Western supremacy over other nations of the world.

Did I not proclaim earlier that NATO was a goose?

How then does NATO all-of-a-sudden become a gorilla?

Like Einstein's theory of wave-particle duality, NATO also exhibits goose-gorilla duality depending on the context.

For its stakeholders and friends, NATO is the goose that lays the golden eggs.

For its foes and enemies, NATO is the gorilla that sets about crushing them to pieces.

As the saying goes: if you cannot beat them, join them.

With that in mind, the young Putin would indeed express his interest in having Russia join NATO as soon as he took the helm in 2000 [14]—a truly humble undertaking for an alpha-squared male.

In 2000, when asked about his views on NATO being a friend or foe in a BBC interview [15], Putin reflected:

> "Russia is part of the European culture. And I cannot imagine my own country in isolation from Europe and what we often call the civilized world. So it is hard for me to visualize NATO as an enemy. I think even posing the question this way will not do any good to Russia or the world. The very

> question is capable of causing damage. Russia strives for equitable and candid relations with its partners. The main problem here lies in attempts to discard previously agreed common instruments—mainly in resolving issues of international security. We are open to equitable co-operation, to partnership. We believe we can talk about more profound integration with NATO but only if Russia is regarded as being an equal partner. You are aware we have been constantly voicing our opposition to NATO's eastward expansion."

In that same BBC interview [15], when quizzed whether Russia could possibly join NATO, Putin added:

> "I don't see why not. I would not rule out such a possibility—but I repeat—if and when Russia's views are taken into account as those of an equal partner. I want to stress this again and again. The situation that was laid down in the founding principles of the United Nations—that was the situation that was agreed upon in the world at the end of World War II. All right, the situation may have changed. Let's assume there is a desire on the part of those who perceive the change to install new mechanisms of ensuring international security. But pretending—or proceeding from the assumption—that Russia has nothing to do with it and trying to exclude it from this process is hardly feasible. And when we talk about our opposition to NATO's expansion—mind you, we have never ever declared any region of the world a zone of our special interests. I prefer to talk about strategic partnership. Its attempts to exclude us from the process is what causes opposition and concern on our part. But that does not mean we are going to shut ourselves off from the rest of the world. Isolationism is not an option."

However, Putin's apparently-sincere intentions for peace coupled with his desire to have Russia become fully integrated into Europe were not only ridiculed but also swept under the rug by Western leaders.

After all, peace is bad for those with vested interests in developing ever more destructive killing machines and with the urge to shepherd the world according to what they see fit.

Ironically, such jingoistic propaganda of NATO has pushed Russia into China's orbit—thereby gifting the latter a strategic partner in its quest to challenge the Western supremacy.

Simply put, the China-Russia alliance has not only been fueled by the West but it also represents a self-inflicted wound.

Perhaps, MICOTUS would beg to disagree as it would reassure its stakeholders that the bigger the enemy, the greater the financial reward.

Indeed, the rapidly-growing China-Russia alliance is a boon for MICOTUS.

Without such a powerful foe to lock horns with, MICOTUS would struggle to metastasize at a breakneck pace—in awe of leukemia—to the tune of an ever-increasing budget rapidly approaching the one-trillion-dollars-a-year milestone.

In his farewell address to the nation in 1961, the then 34th POTUS Dwight Eisenhower prophesized that without proper checks and balances, MICOTUS could one day endanger peace and liberty on earth.

However, Eisenhower's warning fell on deaf ears of the US leaders that have followed him since—though one could argue that they merely symbolize nothing more than a figurehead under the thumb of the deep state.

In particular, during the tenure of the 40th POTUS Ronald Reagan (1981-1989), MICOTUS more than doubled its inertia even when no hot war was being fought.

In a speech delivered to Evangelicals at the height of the cold war in 1983, Reagan alluded to the former Soviet Union as the "Evil Empire"—in a reference to what he perceived as a lack of liberty for those living under the Eurasian Federation as well as its hunger for nuclear proliferation.

No one should have been fooled by Reagan's rhetoric back then nor should anyone today be foolish enough to buy into the absurdity that America has a monopoly over liberty.

If anything, MICOTUS jeopardizes little liberty that Americans have here at home and others across the globe.

Indeed, Reagan was using Soviet Union as a smokescreen to shield the very evil being minted under his own command.

Although Eisenhower's prophecy has been fully realized today, he would have rather wished that it did not as he finds himself rolling over in his grave.

I should declare that I was not in attendance at Eisenhower's farewell address—his dire warning rather remains a matter of historical record.

Nevertheless, on the basis of barbaric crimes committed against humanity over the past several decades, a neutral observer would be inclined to conclude that although NATO was conceived as North Atlantic Treaty Organization in 1949, it has today unequivocally morphed into North Atlantic Terrorist Organization—thanks to MICOTUS being its biggest sponsor and beneficiary.

While NATO might be driven by the conviction that it is too big to fail as it begins to salivate for a mouthwatering showdown to make a killing through the looming World War III, it is exactly such hubris that plants the downfall of giants.

Given that hegemonic wars are renowned for making and breaking of alliances, the odds of NATO becoming dismembered over the next decade or so in the midst of World War III or in the postbellum era are statistically high.

This could particularly bear fruition when it finally dawns up European nations that their dependence on Russia and China for the supply of precious commodities and dirt-cheap goods is far more important to the well-being of their masses than continuing to be a party to a military alliance that only benefits their master on the other side of the Atlantic.

One might argue that the Western values shared between Europe and America are far too important of a sociopolitical asset to drive a wedge between such a decades-old alliance.

Alas, money matters and blood batters.

Even two brothers would be willing to go to war when for instance they find themselves at loggerheads over the equitable division of an inherited property—their blood ties and shared values no longer count.

In fact, history has shown time and again that the odds of animosity rather than friendship becoming a default setting are directly proportional to the degree of shared cultural and consanguineous ties between two parties.

In other words, Europe and America ought to be enemies rather than friends given their close cultural and blood ties—their decades-old friendship is nothing more than an anomaly in the bigger scheme of things.

Admittedly, some of the worst wars and conflicts over the centuries have been waged between brotherly nations and often driven by their monarchs with a direct line of blood between them.

History is indeed not only oscillatory but also a laboratory full of knowledge and wisdom that we can only disregard at our own peril.

| 2.3 | GLOBAL RESET

Given that the world has been mired in a sociopolitical upheaval over the past quarter-of-a-century from living beyond means through institutional fraud run amok to the hilt to debilitating economic stagnation that continue to bloat by the day, only fools would think that such calamities will somehow disappear and a better tomorrow will emerge by itself.

Unfortunately, such a societal reboot does not occur spontaneously but rather it happens to be an endothermic process.

In a manner that an endothermic reaction requires the input of heat so as to lower the activation energy of the transition state to generate a product, a destructive mechanism with the potential to strike fear and chaos into the hearts and minds of people on an apocalyptic scale seems to be a prerequisite to rid our society of such a baggage of evils so as to make way for a fresh start.

Just as World War II (1939-1945) accomplished that goal some 84 years ago so will World War III over the next decade as utter fear and chaos engulf our society and, in doing so, purge humanity of mischief so as to enable it to come to its senses once more.

A brighter tomorrow is indeed on the cards but only after humanity has been handed due retribution for having gone bonkers over the past several decades.

Once a few cities have been nuked into the ground, hardly anyone would indeed be left with the urge to continue a reckless lifestyle of self-indulgence and hedonism nor would anyone dare to put up a Ponzi over the several decades that follow until people's memories of hard times begin to fade away once more.

It is noteworthy that fools have been debating World War III ad nauseam since the outbreak of 1962 Cuban Missile Crisis.

Alas, they are utterly ignorant of history in that the odds of a global conflict dwindle as human society walks past annus horribilis of oqual cycle as it did some 84 years earlier in 1944 but then they begin to swindle as it cycles back to that horrible year as is the case today with the next annus horribilis (2028) barely years away.

Simply put, the odds of a full-fledged global conflict breaking out ebb and flow in tandem with the progression of oqual cycle as exquisitely captured by the "apocalypse oquacycle".

Since the birth of Modern Age in 1451, the world has indeed borne testament to deadly conflicts and civil wars breaking out across the globe in the vicinity of annus horribilis each time the oqual cycle approached its closing stages.

With the next annus horribilis (2028) barely years away as the current oquannium (1955-2038) draws to a close, the world is once again teetering on the verge of navigating another hell-on-earth to which our civilization has become accustomed to in that it returns to our shores once every 84 years on average.

Today, there is indeed no going back as the sociopolitical upheaval that has been gathering momentum with the passing of each year since the outset of 21st century has already crossed the Rubicon.

The question is not whether such sociopolitical crisis will bring about World War III but whether it will make World War II (1939-1945) look tame by comparison.

While we are inching ever closer to our rendezvous with destiny just as we did some 84 years earlier during the 1940s, the end of the current oquannium is far from nigh as the looming global conflict could linger well deep into the 2030s.

Still, lessons from the past are aplenty as to what we can expect over the next decade or so.

A spate of perpetual conflicts—from America's decades-long self-destructive 9/11 Wars in Afghanistan (2001-2021) and Iraq (2003-2011) through civil wars in Syria (2011-date) and Libya (2011-date) to Russian-Ukrainian War (2022-date)—during the second half (1997-2038) of the current and seventh oquannium (1955-2038) has already laid the foundation for the outbreak of World War III in the near future so as to put an end to the ongoing societal madness with the arrival of a new dawn of hope and prosperity in about a decade or so.

A similar drama also unfolded during the second half (1913-1954) of the previous and sixth oquannium (1871-1954) beginning with the outbreak of World War I (1914-1918) that was then followed by a serious of other conflicts around the globe that would ultimately culminate with World War II (1939-1945) as the oqual cycle drew to a close and ushered in a new dawn across the globe during the 1950s.

Likewise, the second half (1829-1870) of the fifth oquannium (1787-1870) was also bedeviled by numerous conflicts beginning with the Second Seminole War (1835-

1842) followed by the Mexican-American War (1846-1848) and ending with the American Civil War (1861-1865) as the oqual cycle petered out and heralded a new dawn on American soil during the 1870s.

As the fifth oquannium (1787-1870) bid farewell, new dawns were also witnessed across much of the globe courtesy of conflicts such as the European Revolutions (1848-1849), the Crimean War (1853-1856) fought between Russia and the Ottoman Empire with the latter aided by European powers, and the 1857 Indian Mutiny against the British colonialists.

In particular, the European Revolutions (1848-1849) laid the foundations for the birth of modern-day nations such as Italy (1861) and Germany (1871) just as the sixth oquannium (1871-1954) kicked off.

Long story short, the looming World War III is not only unavoidable but it is also lurking on the horizon and daring to administer an antidote to neutralize humanity's excesses and imbalances amassed over the past several decades.

What could trigger the outbreak of World War III in earnest? Are there any parallels to draw from World War II?

TODAY'S SOCIOPOLITICAL LANDSCAPE BEARS STUNNING ECHOES OF THE SECOND HALF OF PREVIOUS OQUANNIUM

While World War II may have come to Europe in 1939 with Hitler's invasion of Poland, its roots can however be traced back to the early 1930s.

In 1931, driven by the greed for raw materials to feed what was then its growing empire, Imperial Japan intentionally detonated a dynamite near a Japanese-owned railway track in what was then known as "Manchuria" in northeastern China.

After leveling the charge against Chinese dissidents for the dynamite explosion and using it as a pretext, the Japanese military invaded Manchuria and established a colonial outpost.

The resulting occupation of a Chinese region by Japan marked the beginning of a perpetual period of hostilities and skirmishes between the two Asian neighbors that is viewed by some as the initial outbreak of World War II in 1931.

With Hitler coming to power in Nazi Germany in 1933, Japan not only found a perfect cheerleader to advance its colonial ambitions but World War II also quickly began to gain inertia across Eurasia.

By the time the World War II officially ended in 1945, more than 14 years had elapsed since the false-flag operation was staged in Manchuria by the Japanese military in 1931.

Today, the global crisis unfolding in plain sight bears many parallels to the onset of World War II.

In 2014, Russia annexed the Crimean peninsula in a manner reminiscent of Japanese occupation of Manchuria in 1931—the two events bifurcated by just under 84 years.

In 2017, Trump took the helm in America in an echo of Hitler's rise to power in Nazi Germany in 1933—the two events falling apart exactly 84 years.

While a deranged-and-wicked soul a la Hitler only emerges once in a millennium, Trump nevertheless shares many parallels with the Nazi madman in that he also upholds extremist ideologies from bigotry and xenophobia through populism and nationalism to his disdain for the rule-of-law.

In 2019, Modi not only stripped the UN-declared disputed territory of Indian-controlled Kashmir of its autonomy and statehood—that had been granted to it by the Indian Constitution since 1948—but also heavily remilitarized it so as to fully integrate it into India unilaterally without any regard for international law.

Such a deeply controversial move by Modi bore stunning echoes of Hitler's gambit to remilitarize the Rhineland in 1936—just a little over 84 years earlier—in utter violation of the 1919 Treaty of Versailles.

That treaty signed in the aftermath of World War I (1914-1918) required Deutschland to keep its military out of its Rhineland region—comprised of modern-day states of Rhineland-Palatinate, North Rhine-Westphalia, and Hesse in western Germany and bordering France, Luxembourg, Belgium, and Netherlands—so that it would act as a buffer zone and allay fears of another conflict breaking out.

In 1935, Hitler enacted the so-called "Nuremberg Laws"—a roster of deeply anti-Semitic laws that institutionalized discrimination and persecution of Jewish people, including the confiscation of their properties and stripping them of their civic rights as well as the right to German citizenship.

In 2019, Modi followed in the footsteps of Nazi madman and signed into the law the deeply anti-Muslim bill called the "Citizenship Act"—exactly 84 years later in an echo of Nuremberg Laws—that would grant Indian citizenship to migrants from the trio of Afghanistan-Bangladesh-and-Pakistan provided that they are non-Muslims.

A spitting image of his buddy Trump, India's abhormanic leader Rowdy Modi no doubt embraces an ultra-nationalist propaganda coupled with his extreme disdain and marginalization of India's 220M Muslims—who together would make up the seventh largest nation on the planet.

In the context of oqual cycle, 2023 marks the same timepoint in the current oquannium (1955-2038) as did 1939 exactly 84 years earlier in the previous oquannium (1871-1954) in a manner similar to the fact that the month of January bears many echoes of its predecessor from the previous year.

Accordingly, a scenario similar to what happened during the 1940s awaits us over the next decade or so.

Given that World War II did not begin-in-earnest until 1939, it seems that another global conflict is about to get underway once again.

Admittedly, a number of recognizable shoes from Putin's Greater Russia through Trump's Make America Great Again to Rowdy Modi's Hinduization of India have already fallen as they did some 84 years earlier prior to the onset of World War II.

If World War II began with Japan's invasion of Manchuria in 1931, then World War III began some 84 years later with Russia's invasion of Crimea in 2014.

If World War II began with Germany's invasion of Poland in 1939, then World War III has also begun some 84 years later with Russia's full-fledged invasion of Ukraine in 2022.

Admittedly, the echoes of 1939 have once again begun to reverberate with the 2022 Ukraine-Russia War showing no signs of abating.

Just as Nazi Germany and Soviet Union signed a pact to divide Poland between them in 1939, so did Russia and China some 84 years later in 2022 to go about their territorial business with a mutual understanding and cooperation in their attempt to reclaim what they believe to be their destiny in Ukraine and Taiwan, respectively.

With a 20/20 hindsight in a decade from now, the ongoing Ukraine-Russia conflict will come to be viewed as the start of World War III.

What could be the next shoe to fall so as to herald the beginning-in-earnest of World War III in a manner akin to Hitler's invasion of Poland in 1939?

PERSISTENT ECONOMIC STAGNATION SERVES AS A POTENT CATALYST FOR TRIGGERING GLOBAL CONFLICTS

History has shown time and again that a sustained economic stagnation serves as a budding ground for regional and global conflicts.

With a growing number of nations spearheaded by the likes of United States and European Union mired in mountains of debt and on the precipice of going underwater, the dire economic plight of the masses across much of the globe does not bode well over the foreseeable future.

Over the next several years leading up to annus horribilis (2028) of the current oquannium (1955-2038), such ongoing economic upheaval will likely plunge the world into a deep depression leaving billions across the globe without work and unable to put food on the table in an echo of what the world experienced during the 1930s.

That in turn could significantly destabilize the world with major powers not only blaming each other for the lingering catastrophe but also using their sticks, wherever they can, to advance their propaganda—driven in no small part by the greed and hunger for the control of world's finite resources.

With such a tinderbox rapidly bloating, all that will be missing is a spark (or an old-fashioned match) to put it on fire so as to mark the beginning of a full-fledged global conflict.

With dark clouds of depression thundering to burst and inundate even higher grounds, many world leaders will lose their head and engage in irrational decision-making as a last resort to avert their Titanic from sinking but with the potential to ignite a global conflict.

One such precedent is illustrated by the irrational invasion of too-big-to-be conquered USSR by Nazi Germany in 1941—a deeply asinine act that cost Hitler not only the war but also eroded any hope of minimizing the collateral fallout from what was up till then a regional conflict.

Had Hitler not invaded the USSR, that European showdown may not have turned into a full-fledged global conflict, much less come to be known as World War II (1939-1945).

Why did Hitler commit such a suicidal act?

Under an economic depression, even the best of minds begin to act like the rest of minds.

Although deeply misplaced, Hitler sensed insecurity and feared that Britain and Soviet Union were secretly hatching a gambit to attack Germany after it had conquered so much across Europe by 1941, from Poland to France, and refused to go cold turkey—or withdraw immediately from the occupied territories.

In actuality, not only was there a deep mistrust between Britain and Soviet Union but they were also far from being in bed with each other, much less planning to tie the knot.

Admittedly, a few years before, while Nazi Germany signed various strategic and economic pacts with the USSR in 1939—so as not to stick their nose into each other's territorial ambitions—Britain rejected the Soviet proposal for a tripartite military alliance with France.

In return, the USSR refused to not only cooperate with Britain as the war wore on by 1941 but had no interest whatsoever to intervene in the growing conflict largely orchestrated by Hitler up till that point.

Yet, the psychopathic mind of Hitler would not go to sleep at night but would rather be planning its own ruse to checkmate both the United Kingdom and the Soviet Union at their own game.

In particular, Hitler feared that while he would not be able to simultaneously take on United Kingdom and USSR on the western and eastern fronts respectively, his military was nevertheless powerful enough to quickly defeat the Soviets so as to put them out of the warring colosseum before taking on the mighty British in a one-on-one showdown come 1942—with France having already fallen to Nazi Germany in 1940.

Alas, the USSR would prove too big to be conquered.

What was planned to be a military excursion to be over in a couple of months in what came to be known as the "1941 Operation Barbarossa" ultimately bogged down the Nazi army for years in an alien land with not only frigid nights but also no boundaries to overpower.

Often times, the Nazi soldiers simply died of bitter cold and deadly hunger due to the lack of provision of sufficient supplies in the inhospitable wilderness and gargantuan landmass of USSR.

When they kept the cold and hunger at bay, Stalin's Red Army would lay a trap to their advancing ambitions.

To say that the mindless invasion of USSR by Nazi Germany amounted to an act of martial suicide would be something of a huge understatement.

Had Hitler not invaded the USSR, the world would have likely followed a very different trajectory—a diametric opposite of what it did—some 84 years ago.

It would also be reasonable to conclude that had the world not been under the spell of the Great Depression during the 1930s, not only Hitler's Soviet blunder but even World War II could have altogether been averted.

According to Murphy's law, anything that can go wrong will go wrong.

While that law remains deeply controversial, few doubt that its validity is best demonstrated during times of crisis and an economic depression that almost always befall humanity during oqual winters as the oqual cycle draws to a close.

Today, being in the midst of oqual winter (2018-2038) of the current oquannium (1955-2038), it indeed seems that anything that can go wrong is going wrong.

Yet, this is just the tip of the iceberg.

With NATO literally fighting Russia through a proxy war in that the Ukrainian resistance against the Siberian Tiger is largely fueled by an ever-growing military paraphernalia and tactical know-how arriving from the United States and European Union, it is only a matter of time before the ongoing Russia-Ukraine War tailspins into a wider global conflict.

Simply put, the decades-long provocation of Russia by NATO has now finally morphed into a direct conflict though it is till being kept under wraps from the scrutiny of the public at large.

Such a stupiditious move by NATO amounts to nothing short of a casus belli (or an act of war) with the ball now being in Russia's court though the Siberian Tiger is unlikely to retaliate back instinctively but rather at the time of its own choosing just when it sees an opening on the American front.

One such mouthwatering opening could arrive as early as 2024.

With Trump being the favorite to take on the ageing-and-inept clown currently occupying the White House in the 2024 US Presidential Election, the scene is indeed set for the American society to plunge into a civil war at a time that would be perfectly in line with what the oqual gods have in mind in that 2024 would be literally knocking on the door of bi-oquannial (2 x 84 years) ceremony in 2029 of the outbreak of American Civil War (1861-1865).

With neither Trump nor Biden likely to knock each other out in a decisive manner due to the fact that they would both be running on their partisan propaganda rather than what is best for America, the odds of the 2024 US Presidential Election producing no clear winner are therefore extremely high.

That Americans would be presented with a choice between two ageing devils to lead the nation is yet another sign of how low the country has hit.

Surely, America is not without its angels but such great souls have a clear heart not to even think about heading the mob rule, not to mention that their character would be assassinated by money in politics even before they were to face public scrutiny.

Indeed, no decent human being would ever run for a public office and those who do so are motivated by their propaganda rather than public service.

What will happen if there is no clear presidential winner in 2024?

With results likely to be too close to call in some states, even the election authorities may refuse to declare a winner, at least in a timely manner.

Even if they do declare an outright winner, there would be no respite for the American society at large.

If Biden is declared winner, Trump and his army would declare war on America.

If Trump wins, Biden's army will likely refuse to accept the outcome.

Either way, America is doomed come 2024 even in the absence of an outright civil war breaking out.

And it could get a lot worse given that the oqual winters are renowned for elevating Murphy's law to a divine status in that if anything can go wrong, it will definitely go wrong during such calamitous times.

Given that we are already in the midst of oqual winter (2018-2038) of the current oquannium (1955-2038), it would be perfectly in line with the unforgiving spell of oqual cycle to pull off the unthinkable twist beyond our wildest imaginations—Trump winning the 2024 US Presidential Election while he is locked up in prison after finally having been convicted for his criminal past.

How does this help Russia?

The monumental collapse of American society that once prided itself on democracy and freedom would be a godsend for not only Russia to finally square up against the NATO bully but China would also become emboldened to finally make a move to reunite with its long-lost soul Taiwan against the backdrop of United States fighting for its own survival at home and with little public support to become embroiled in fighting others' wars.

Not that America will step back by any stretch of the imagination but the low morale of US armed forces will only play into the hands of its enemies trying to undercut its global hegemony.

In fact, the Russia-Ukraine War has not only incentivized the Asian Giant to finally tie the knot with the Siberian Tiger but it is also a godsend for China in that it has enabled it to:

1) Gobble up precious Russian commodities for pennies-on-the-dollar to fire up its manufacturing engine like never before thanks to Western sanctions against the Siberian Tiger and driven by the urgency to rapidly expand its military paraphernalia with a global conflict lurking on the horizon;
2) Pursue closer military alliance with Russia in order to end American hegemony that looked like an impossible goal prior to the outbreak of Ukraine War; and
3) Exploit the Ukraine War as a smokescreen to launch its own invasion of Taiwan in its long-stated goal of reuniting the renegade island with the motherland.

With a common adversary and shared goals, the alliance between Russia and China will indeed hit new heights as they begin to cooperate on every front to kick America out of Asia through what will enter the annals of history as World War III.

AMERICA'S AILING MANUFACTURING WILL BECOME ITS ACHILLES' HEEL AS WORLD WAR III BREAKS OUT OVER THE NEXT DECADE

While the use of force to resolve the Taiwan issue might have been unthinkable at the outset of the 21st century, China's military paraphernalia today is not to be underestimated with the Chinese navy now being the largest in the world and rapidly dwarfing its US counterpart—a truly daunting feat that should not be lost on anyone given that the wars are won and lost at sea.

And when it comes to battling it out at sea, preponderance reigns supreme over all else in guaranteeing the triumph as attested by history time and again.

To say that a nation's military is only as good as the strength of its manufacturing would be a huge understatement.

Although there is no doubt that America's military arsenal is technically more advanced than that of the Chinese, technological superiority is however only one of many facets of the overall strength of a nation's armed forces.

While China may not match America in terms of its superiority, the Asian Giant nevertheless reigns supreme in its ability to quickly replace its bazookas and in relatively large numbers—the single most important factor in determining the outcome of a war in accordance with history.

In marked contrast, America's ability to replenish its ammunitions is only as good as its ailing manufacturing that has been in decline for decades thanks to its ever-growing dependence on the supply of dirt-cheap goods and services from other nations with China leading the charge.

Tellingly, America and NATO will likely run out of weapons to fight against the combined forces of China and Russia—which between them have everything that one needs to win a large-scale protracted war with the latter being not only the breadbasket but also an infinite reservoir of raw materials and the former renowned for its unparalleled production capacity.

Not only that but China will also choke its enemies as it prioritizes its manufacturing powerhouse to serve the needs of its armed forces fighting the war rather than feeding civilians across America and Europe to which the latter have become accustomed to and heavily dependent upon.

With the spigot of goods and services being turned off, America and Europe will likely plunge into an economic depression with few goods and services available to keep the masses quiet at home, not to mention that the cost of what little is available will go through the roof.

Inflation is indeed an inevitable outcome of global conflicts as the familiar supply chains and workhorses that have been taken for granted for decades are finally either cut off or diverted away.

With a rapidly bloating military at its disposal thanks to its unparalleled manufacturing prowess, China has indeed begun to not only saber-rattle in recent years but has also upped-the-ante on reunification with Taiwan by any means possible by 2030 or thereabout.

While America may have been buoyed when it came to defending the likes of Kuwait against the whipping boys of Iraq during the Gulf War (1990-1991), defending Taiwan will be a whole different ball game.

Not that America cannot play the hard ball but the potential for collateral damage of epic proportions will mean that cooler heads will prevail and an all-out war with China may fail to materialize in Asian waters.

Still, reunification of China with Taiwan bears the potential to mark the end of America's role in Asia to the delight of its eternal foes such as Iran and Russia.

History holds a glaring lesson for the waxing and waning of hegemons.

For example, it was the loss of Suez Canal to Egypt in 1956 that marked a watershed moment in the rapid disintegration of the empire upon which the sun once never set.

In the aftermath of the botched-and-bungled plan that came to known as the "1956 Suez Crisis", the British Empire was left to not only lick its wounds but it also lost its mojo forever.

Today, with the dark clouds of another global conflict hanging over its shoulders, America is poised to follow in the footsteps that the British Empire took in the bygone century.

Fearing the humiliation that the British Empire tasted in 1956 coupled with its prestige being tarnished forever, America will undoubtedly take some sort of stand against China in the event of an invasion of Taiwan even if that involves using its proxies scattered across large swathes of Asia.

Being China's archrival along with close military alliance with America, India may not only begin to confidently salivate but it may also be assured by the Pentagon of an opportunity of a lifetime to grab disputed lands and territories along its eastern border with the Asian Giant while the latter is preoccupied on its own eastern front to contain the fallout from the invasion of Taiwan.

They say that friends in need are friends indeed!

To prove that point, Pakistan's powerful and battle-hardened military will stand with China rather than stand back and could in turn attack India along its northwestern border, thereby not only saber-rattling to slice the Indian Kashmir but also marching-in-lockstep with the threat of tearing apart the Asian Diamond where it hurts most—in the breakaway regions with deep-rooted separatist movements such as Khalistan brewing in the Indian Punjab.

Such a cunning ploy used by Pakistan may not only outfox the Indian trickery but it will also foil and thwart India's land-grabbing plan crafted to divert Chinese hold on Taiwan on the other side of the conflict in the Chinese Sea.

The India-Pakistan confrontation bears the potential to shepherd the conflict from the Chinese Sea to the Arabian Sea at the mouth of the Persian Gulf—home to mortal enemies such as Iran and Saudi Arabia with the potential for something to misfire in the vicinity of the deadly war-prone Strait of Hormuz.

In particular, against the backdrop of the rapidly-expanding conflict in Asia, Iran will likely forge an alliance with Pakistan to further bolster the China-Russia axis and fancy its chances to kick what it perceives to be the American Devil out of what it sees as not only its Mecca but also Jerusalem.

Cheered on by a cacophony of "Death to America" by its people, the Iranian regime will feel that the time to write its destiny has finally arrived on its shores.

With Iran having entered the war, it may not be long before Israel joins America and NATO out of its own grievances against the Islamic Republic having threatened to wipe the Jewish State off the face of earth for decades.

While retaliating to an Iranian aggression or exploiting the mayhem, America will go ballistic and unleash its deadly firepower to take out the Ayatollahs that it has been trying to do so since 1979, thereby settling old scores.

Alas, America has a terrible record of settling old scores as is evident from the unethical-and-immoral war masterminded in the aftermath of 9/11 attacks to take out Iraq after failing to do so during the Gulf War (1990-1991) a decade earlier.

Importantly, America's intervention will also serve to castigate China directly and push it back—or at least let China know who the reigning champion is.

A direct confrontation with China will almost certainly draw the likes of Japan and South Korea into the conflict due to their own grievances with the Asian Giant with the potential for the conflict to spill over into other regions of the globe.

In particular, North Korea will align itself with the China-Russia axis and square up to neutralize any threat posed by South Korea and the US forces operating from the Korean peninsula.

Unlike its predecessor some 84 years earlier, the odds of World War III coming to America's doorstep are however extremely high given the long-range hypersonic missiles at the disposal of its enemies.

Not only that but World War III also bears the potential to turn nuclear.

Admittedly, the global conflict straddling the annus horribilis has always outshined its predecessor due to the emergence of ever more destructive killing machines over the course of oqual cycle.

Nor do world leaders shy away from using the most lethal weapon at their disposal as they lock horns to settle the contest for the control of the world and its resources.

Since the dawn of the current oquannium (1955-2038), global powers have hitherto funneled trillions-of-dollars toward developing a paraphernalia of nukes in order to gain a military edge over their rivals.

To believe that such apocalyptic weapons are only for the showroom would be to sweep history under the rug.

In the 16th century, the cannon took the honors for being the most deadly weapon.

In the 17th century, it was the musket that would prove more deadly than anything ever invented before.

In the 18th century, the rifle would replace the musket.

In the 19th century, the machine gun was introduced to kill on a scale like never before.

In the 20th century, the likes of bomber aircraft, the ballistic missile, and the nuclear bomb became flying ammunitions that would inflict deaths on a gargantuan scale.

In the 21st century, homo insapiens (or fools) are salivating at the prospect of testing each other's resolve with nukes (or missiles carrying nuclear warheads).

On the other side of the bedlam after the nuclear dust has settled in about a decade or so in the postbellum era, China will emerge as the most powerful nation through not only being reunified with Taiwan but also being crowned the world's new hegemon.

The Korean peninsula will also likely undergo reunification to the delight of the world community.

On the Indian peninsula, the Kashmir Valley will likely be handed over to Pakistan in exchange for calling an end to all disputes, thereby ushering in the beginning of a new dawn of friendship between the two consanguineous (or blood-tied) nations.

Russia will emerge as an even bigger giant through the annexation of new territories running along its southwestern border and a born-again global power a la Soviet Union with a huge geopolitical influence.

As for America, it will be left to lick its wounds as it packs its bags and curtails its military excursions in Asian waters to the foremost delight of American taxpayer.

An end to America's unchallenged hegemony would imply that it can finally begin to build its own infrastructure at home rather than continuing to squander its energy and resources at smashing up the world into pieces in a futile cycle.

Like much of the globe elsewhere, Americans would finally wake up to a new and brighter dawn even though USD would have lost the prestige of being the dominant world currency as it begins to be overshadowed by the rapidly-growing influence of CNY in international trade some time during the 2030s just in time for the arrival of a new oquannium in 2039.

Voilà Guerre Mondiale III.

All told, the World War III over the next decade or so will usher in a global reset in that the astronomical havoc unleashed upon our world will serve as a catalyst to create megatons of new jobs as well as replace the old-and-degenerate system with new technologies.

Many nations will undergo rebirth, or at least feel that they have been born again.

The borders of so many nations will be redrawn as territorial disputes are resolved for the most part though the Israel-Palestine conflict will likely linger on until the onset of the oqual winter (2102-2122) of the next oquannium (2039-2122).

World War III will also pave the way to reset the monetary system of most nations back to an organic state either through inflating away the mountains of debt or simply through bankruptcies, not to mention that most countries will also switch to a digital currency some time during the 2030s.

Notably, governments become emboldened to push through big agenda such as defaulting on debt and minting a new currency by leaps and bounds against the backdrop of a global conflict unfolding at their doorstep and being comforted by the fact that there would be little or no public backlash against new measures that would have otherwise been unthinkable in the antebellum era.

Every deed is indeed not only kosher but also halal during times of war!

Outside government agendas, the apocalyptic fear combined with the humongous cost of human life will serve as a wake-up call for hoi polloi to come to their senses, learn to live within their means once again, and begin to exercise humility once more at the expense of self-indulgence.

And so will marriage and family become the toast of the town once again as they rightfully reclaim their primal place at the front and center of human society as the current oquannium (1955-2038) bids farewell and the curtain is raised over a new one in about a decade or so.

3 | CULTURAL WAVES

Notwithstanding the impact of astronomical factors, the central premise of oqual cycle is that it is probabilistic rather than deterministic in that the severity of the fallout from our rendezvous with destiny seems to be largely governed by our own actions.

For example, the first half of oqual cycle is powered by the steady rise of a myriad of sociopolitical tailwinds such as morality, peace, collectivism, globalism, entrepreneurship, moderation, transparency, nonpartisanship, ethnic harmony, baby boom, economic well-being, and institutional trust.

On the other hand, the second half is essentially a mirror image of the first half in that it is marred by a plethora of sociopolitical headwinds such as immorality, conflict, individualism, populism, fraud, debt, corruption, partisanship, xenophobia, baby bust, wealth polarization, and institutional distrust.

Such antagonistic forces are essentially a manifestation of an interplay of goods and ills in our society.

Accordingly, one would expect cultural aspects of human society to waltz in lockstep with the progression of oqual cycle.

Today, most nations around the globe are indeed bedeviled by a plethora of cultural bugaboos from self-indulgence and overconsumption through tanking fertility and an aging population to add to rising immigration and a general loss of satisfaction with life.

Are such cultural dilemmas sticky and never going away such that we must adapt to a new normal?

Or perhaps we have been here before and what we are seeing today represents nothing more than a rendezvous with our past such that it too shall pass with the good old days returning to the front and center of our society once more.

You bet!

In fact, such cultural waves seemingly ebb and flow in sync with the progression of oqual cycle.

While violence in our society is beyond the scope of this maiden edition of the book, rudimentary analysis nevertheless suggests that it also ebbs and flows in tandem with the oqual cycle.

In particular, there has been a precipitous rise in mass shootings across America since the 1999 Columbine High School Massacre that not so coincidentally occurred almost in parallel with the onset of the second half (1997-2038) of current oquannium (1955-2038) so as to mark the beginning of violent times ahead just as the oqual cycle turned on its head.

Like other facets of human civilization, mass shootings will also peak around annus horribilis (2028) before they begin to peter out over several decades beginning with the arrival of the next oquannium (2039-2122).

In order to delve deeper into how cultural waves affect our society, let us divide our somewhat finger-licking discussion into the following topics:

        3.1 Demographic Trends
        3.2 Cultural Dysphoria
        3.3 Consumption Mania
        3.4 Institutional Fraud

| 3.1 | DEMOGRAPHIC TRENDS

Given that I attended primary school not only under the shadow of trees but also under the shadow of four older siblings in rural Pakistan during the 1970s, you might be quick to preempt how lucky I must have been.

Well, damned if you do, and damned if you do not.

In the first case, having four older siblings was hardly a cause for celebration as many of my classmates had twice as many brothers and sisters.

In the second scenario, being the little one not only came with a lot of perks and terks but it also propelled me to become the life of the party at home and away.

Admittedly, it was not just my neck-of-the-woods hustling and bustling with a torrent of toddlers as if they had just hatched out of eggs—as my mother would have me believe in the wake of my incessant curiosity of learning where the babies came from against the backdrop of an equally impressive battalion of hens wandering around every household—but the rather high fecundity (or fertility) on display was a hallmark of the then young nation of Pakistan which came into its own being in the aftermath of 1947 Indian Partition as the British Raj (1757-1947) came to a grinding halt after almost 200 years.

What caused such an unprecedented upsurge in the fertility rate among Pakistani women?

Was it due to girls gone wild in the wake of irrational exuberance of having realized their dream of a separate homeland?

Was it perhaps due to men gone child after being battle-hardened for years but, all of a sudden, no one else left to wrestle with?

Or was there more to it than meets the eye?

PAKISTAN'S BABY BOOM WAS ETCHED IN THE STARS

Given that the birth of Pakistan essentially coincided with the arrival of a new dawn of hope and prosperity as the current oquannium (1955-2038) kicked off barely after the honeymoon was over for what is today the fifth most-populous nation on earth, the unprecedented baby boom witnessed over many decades that followed should hardly be surprising.

In fact, during much of the first half (1955-1996) of the current oquannium (1955-2038), the fertility rate hovered around six babies per woman of childbearing age in Pakistan.

However, with the onset of the second half (1997-2038) of the current oquannium (1955-2038), the fertility rate among Pakistani women began to precipitously nosedive such that it is currently on track to fall below three babies per woman of reproductive age over the next decade or so.

Importantly, such a contrasting change of demographic fortunes with baby boom followed by baby bust across the two halves of the current oquannium is hardly unique to Pakistan but rather has been a hallmark of most other nations.

But, there is one important caveat to this rather simplistic picture that must be ironed out in order to fully appreciate how demographics of a nation oscillate with the oqual cycle.

In what is dubbed the "canonical model", population growth of a nation is envisioned to rise during the first half of oqual cycle and then pivot so as to reverse course during the second half as told by the demographic story of Pakistan over the course of the current oquannium.

However, due to atypical sociopolitical factors at play, this may not always be the case as the first half may well be underscored by an anemic population growth while the second half experiences a boom in what can be framed as the "non-canonical model".

For clarity, both of these antagonistic models have been incorporated into what is dubbed the "population oquacycle".

While the canonical model is expected to be the rule for most countries, the non-canonical model will likely prevail when a nation's demographics are unceremoniously perturbed by unusual circumstances as seems to be the case with Pakistan during the previous oquannium.

Although population data apropos the previous oquannium (1871-1954) for the region that comprises today's Pakistan must be taken with a grain of salt, a very similar demographic trend is however also at play vis-à-vis modern-day India.

This implies that population dynamics of both India and Pakistan over the previous oquannium must be taken at face value rather than overlooked.

Notably, what happens in India also happens in Bangladesh and vice versa.

Unsurprisingly then, the demographic trend of Bangladesh over the previous oquannium is also very much akin to that of India and Pakistan.

One can therefore logically conclude that the reasons for the trio of modern-day nations of India, Pakistan, and Bangladesh to have experienced a non-canonical demographic trend over the course of previous oquannium (1871-1954) must be identical—particularly given that all three nations were then three sides of the same triangle under the British colonial rule during much of that period.

How can one account for their non-canonical demographic trends?

Why did population growth of the three Indian nations during the second half (1913-1954) of previous oquannium (1871-1954) upstage that of the first half (1871-1912) at odds with the oqual theory?

The answer lies in the socioeconomic factors.

Admittedly, the first half (1871-1912) of previous oquannium was plagued by a spate of rolling droughts and famines epitomized by the likes of the Indian Great Famine (1876-1882) that stretched across much of what is modern-day India [16].

Top that up with the fact that the first half (1871-1912) of that oquannium also coincided with a long stretch of de-industrialization on the Indian peninsula beginning circa 1750.

What does de-industrialization mean?

WORLD WAR I WAS A GODSEND FOR INDIANS

In 1700, at the peak of Mughal Raj (1526-1857), India was a manufacturing powerhouse boasting the world's largest economy due primarily to the strength of its textile industry with trade links across the globe.

In 1757, Britain established itself as the dominant colonial power on the Indian peninsula in what would essentially mark the birth of British Raj (1757-1947)—with the Mughals retained as a symbolic figurehead up till 1857.

In doing so, Britain wasted no time in asserting its authority over the Indian economy through measures such as protectionist policies that would bar the import of Indian goods into Britain and across its vast empire all the while flooding the Indian markets with British goods.

In particular, powered by the 18th Century Industrial Revolution, Britain's machine-driven textile industry unleashed mass production of goods and services at a fraction of the cost of the Indian textile—which for its part would continue to be produced through the traditional handloom technology, thereby quickly losing its competitive edge.

To be sure, the Industrial Revolution marked the transition from an agrarian society largely powered by hand-driven technology to a machine-driven economy that first began in Britain circa 1750 and then quickly spread across much of the Western world as the 18th century closed out.

As for India, Britain's Industrial Revolution not only marked the death knell for the Indian textile industry but also put millions of people out of work and those who were lucky enough to survive the axe found themselves primarily working on the cotton and jute fields as the nation was reduced to a shadow of its glorious past with raw materials now becoming its primary export instead of more valuable textiles.

To add salt to wounds, Britain also refused to implement its proprietary machine-driven technology on Indian soil so as to maintain a competitive edge over handicrafts.

Simply put, India was not only de-industrialized by the British colonialists but the plundering of its bountiful resources from cotton and jute through silk and steel to spices and grains, and dare I mention my favorite tea, would bankrupt the Indian economy as the 18th century closed out with such economic stagnation continuing throughout the 19th century and into the early 20th century.

Importantly, the dire impact of British colonialism on Indians is further highlighted by the fact that the native population growth remained heavily suppressed throughout much of 18th and 19th centuries.

Given such a negative impact of socioeconomic factors on the Indian society, the lack of a discernible cyclical trend in baby boom followed by baby bust over the course of fifth (1787-1870) and sixth (1871-1954) oquannia should hardly be surprising.

In fact, Indian population grew at a turtle's pace of 0.4% annually from the outset of British Raj (1757) till the start of World War I (1914) over a span of 157 years, all the while the British population flourished at almost three-fold.

But, since then, the population on the Indian peninsula has been growing at a commanding pace of over 1.6% annually as it spiked from 310M in 1914 to over 1800M today in 2023.

Yet, many Western un-intellectuals today claim that the British Raj was far from being a doom and gloom for the Indian masses as Britain left the nation with vast networks of railroads.

Alas, such parochial minds fail to understand that the railway tracks largely connected seaports to resource-rich lands rather than traversing through the hinterlands to serve the needs of the masses.

Just because a thief leaves their footprints behind does not by any stretch of the imagination render their actions righteous.

How did Indian de-industrialization end?

As military hawks would tell you, wars are good for the economy as they usher in windfalls by leaps and bounds.

Indeed, wars not only trigger mass production of goods and services but also revitalize many rundown factories and even demand repurposing of non-profitable companies to serve the needs of soldiers instead of civilians.

However, the war is a double-edged sword in that it can make as well as break an economic engine due to its destructive nature.

Fortunately, the outbreak of World War I (1914-1918) would be a godsend for the Indian economy in that it would make rather than break India's back as Britain was left with no choice but to put Indian manufacturing industry into first gear so as to meet the humongous demands of that global conflict.

In particular, India would be required to supply anything and everything that it could from coal and steel through cement and textiles to food supplies and battalions of soldiers.

With such aggressive contracts of war to meet, there was no shortage of work as millions would benefit with the stagnant Indian economy having turned into a thriving one overnight in the midst of World War I.

In fact, the war economy not only saved many Indian industries—such as the then fledgling Tata Steel that had only come into being less than a decade earlier in 1907—from going underwater but also bloated their fortunes in that they would continue to hit home runs even after the demands of World War I had ceased.

In other words, World War I not only put an end to India's de-industrialization but also jumpstarted its re-industrialization with widespread economic opportunities for the masses that had not been witnessed in over 150 years since the beginning of the British colonial rule in 1757.

Long story short, the duo of a spate of rolling famines and the lack of employment opportunities for the masses due to de-industrialization policies of the British colonialists conspired to keep a lid on baby boom during the first half (1871-1912) of previous oquannium (1871-1954) at odds with the rather auspicious spell of oqual cycle.

However, the switch to war economy with the outbreak of World War I (1914-1918) almost in parallel with the onset of second half (1913-1954) of the previous oquannium (1871-1954) would herald a period of relative riches for the masses on the Indian peninsula through extensive employment opportunities and, when you are blessed with riches, you also turn off your switches as you channel your energy to what you are naturally good at—make babies and lots of them.

And make they did as the baby contagion spread like a wildfire across the Indian peninsula—thanks to our deeply-ingrained herd behavior which may have been beneficial in the jungles but it almost always plants our downfall in today's hi-tech world—all the while the Europeans were at loggerheads whose populations by comparison would plummet against the backdrop of a quartet of World War I (1914-1918), Influenza Pandemic (1918-1920), Great Depression (1929-1939), and World War II (1939-1945).

In a nutshell, a rather unusual set of socioeconomic factors likely accounts for the non-canonical trend observed in population growth of the three Indian nations in that it appears to have exploded rather than being pared back during the second half (1913-1954) of the previous oquannium (1871-1954).

That is a truly impressive feat given that the then pan-Indians were able to deliver such an unexpected baby boom in spite of having lost nearly 20M souls—or 6% of the then combined population of some 320M in 1920—to the 1918 Influenza Pandemic.

Importantly, such a baby boom would continue skyward well deep into the first half (1955-1996) of the current oquannium (1955-2038) after which it seems to have experienced a dramatic pullback with the onset of the second half (1997-2038).

Simply put, while the demographics of the trio of consanguineous (or blood-tied) nations experienced a non-canonical trend during the previous oquannium (1871-

1954), they have nevertheless seamlessly transitioned into a canonical one over the course of the current oquannium (1955-2038).

Notably, the baby boom during the first half (1955-1996) was largely powered by relatively prosperous times as fondly remembered through Jawaharlal Nehru Era (1947-1964) in India and Ayub Khan Era (1958-1969) in Pakistan.

However, in line with the ominous spell of the second half of oqual cycle, baby boom turned into baby bust beginning with the arrival of annus turnilis (1997) of the current oquannium (1955-2038).

Still, all three Indian nations have come a long way from their humble beginnings with the end of British Raj in 1947.

In 2023, India surpassed China to become the most-populous nation of the world with more than twice as many mouths as Europe or North America.

Mashallah!

While Indian men may naively argue that size does not matter, it surely does as babies power the economic engine of a nation by tempers and tantrums.

On that auspicious note, the current dip in fertility rate for all three Indian nations will likely reverse course with the arrival of the next oquannium (2039-2122) in over a decade though it will never emulate its unprecedented feat observed during the dawn (1955-1975) of the current cycle (1955-2038)—as witnessed firsthand during the 1970s though being duped into believing that I and other toddlers of my generation had all hatched out of eggs and, had it not been for Biology 101, I could well have ended up becoming a chicken farmer driven by the false perception that breeding and raising kids must be a piece of cake.

But, then, I sometimes wonder how in the world would humanity have learned about the oqual cycle.

In fact, that seems to be my true calling and, boy-oh-boy, I could not have imagined a life without scholarly activities as much as the illogical hens would have liked to have me in their corner given my selfless Vorgoan trait of putting the interests of others before my own.

Believe you me, if you want something done well, do it yourself.

But, if you want babies done well, have Virgo do it.

What about other nations beyond the Indian peninsula?

How do their demographics play out over the course of oqual cycle?

Located in the Indian Ocean less than 40 miles off the southern tip of India, let us make Sri Lanka our next stop before we sail onto my former hunting ground United Kingdom and then from there, we will round off the trip with a docking on the familiar shores of United States before we disembark and continue our journey further afield on another explosive aspect of our culture in the next section.

SRI LANKA'S BABY BUST TOO SHALL PASS

Being an isolated island with minimal perturbations from external factors such as migrations and wars, Sri Lanka serves as an excellent model for studying population dynamics—particularly given that we are trying to probe what happened over the past several centuries rather than decades.

Indeed, it seems that the World War I (1914-1918) delivered no windfall for the island nation of some 22M today as it bucked the rather auspicious demographic trend witnessed across the Indian peninsula in that its population growth followed an almost perfect canonical behavior in agreement with the oqual theory over the previous and sixth oquannium (1871-1954) with baby boom unfolding over the first half followed by baby bust over the second half.

Likewise, Sri Lanka also appears to have followed more or less canonical demographic trends over both the fifth (1787-1870) and the seventh (1955-2038) oquannia though in each case the baby boom and baby bust appear to be somewhat out of lockstep with the progression of oqual cycle.

This should be hardly surprising given that the oqual cycle is not set in stone in a manner akin to the annual cycle but rather its dynamics are highly fluid and malleable as they are largely dictated by our own actions in a probabilistic manner rather than being wholly deterministic—or rather they represent an interplay between celestial and sociopolitical factors.

Notably, Sri Lanka's baby boom during the first half (1955-1996) of the current oquannium (1955-2038) having peaked somewhat earlier than expected bears stunning echoes of its batsmen pioneering the art of taking the bowlers to task right from the get-go in limited-overs cricket during the 1990s but then often peaking too early to make most of their daring initiative.

One can only hope that Sri Lankan babies having already born into future do not follow in the footsteps of Jayasuriyas and Kaluwitharanas but rather make most of their head start as charting a successful life requires perseverance not slogging.

Importantly, the factors driving premature termination of baby boom during the first half (1955-1996) of the current oquannium (1955-2038) likely reside in the decades-long Sri Lankan Civil War (1983-2009) that is believed to have claimed around 100K lives, not to mention its negative impact on birth rate as well as positively affecting emigration out of the country.

Add to that the fact that Sri Lanka's ongoing baby bust (or rather population bust) during the second half (1997-2038) of current oquannium (1955-2038) is also in no small part driven by emigration due to a rising number of its nationals immigrating to greener pastures elsewhere around the globe in the wake of economic bedlam that has been brewing over the past decade or so.

In 2022, after decades of living beyond its means, the island nation defaulted on its national debt.

Today, many Sri Lankans helplessly wonder whether the ongoing economic meltdown is the new normal and whether they will once again be able to return to the good old days of baby boom.

Notwithstanding Sri Lanka having turned into Sorry Lanka, today's dire baby straits too shall nevertheless pass as the current oquannium (1955-2038) draws to a close over the next decade or so.

And close it will as Sri Lanka once again rises from the ashes with another strong and impressive bout of baby boom getting under way as early as 2030s but by no later than 2040s.

Adios Sri Lanka! Bienvenue au Royaume-Uni!

TRADITIONAL WIVES RESCUE THE BRITISH ARK FROM SINKING

While the rate of population growth may serve as a good proxy for differentiating between baby boom and baby bust for developing nations where net migration has little or no impact on their overall demographics, it is unlikely to be a good substitute for Western nations whose populations are heavily dependent upon an influx of immigrants.

Although one ought to be directly looking at the birth rate, long-term data for such a key demographic are however hard to come by.

Still, for what it is worth, Britain appears to have experienced more or less canonical demographic trends during the fifth (1787-1870) and sixth (1871-1954) oquannia across a span of roughly 150 years when it reigned supreme as the world's most dominant imperial power.

In particular, Britain first emerged as the dominant global power during the late 18th century at the expense of France.

And such a rise to global dominance coupled with economic prosperity sparked an impressive wave of baby boom at home with the outset of the first half (1787-1828) of fifth oquannium (1787-1870).

However, tumultuous times driven by endemic corruption among its ruling elite at home and abroad as epitomized by the 1857 Indian Mutiny severely hamstrung the second half (1829-1870) of fifth oquannium (1787-1870) such that it would be marked by baby bust on British shores in line with oqual theory.

A more or less similar demographic trend played out over the course of the sixth and previous oquannium (1871-1954).

In particular, the first half (1871-1912) of the previous oquannium (1871-1954) largely coincided with relatively prosperous times to have befallen not only blue bloods but Brits across all walks of life as underscored by the memorable Late Victorian Era (1870-1901) coupled with the British Empire hitting its zenith circa 1900—when the British Navy ruled the ocean waves, the British Pound ran the global trade, and the British wives were vying to hold their own with a rather high fertility rate as popularized by none other than their own Queen Victoria delivering an eye-popping nine royal-minted kids from her throne at a rate of one child every other year over a span of 17 years.

However, as forewarned by the ominous spell of oqual cycle as it turns on its head, all hell broke lose on European shores during the second half (1913-1954) of the previous oquannium (1871-1954) such that the hefty cost of two world wars both in economic terms and human life weighed heavily on Britain with the baby boom quickly dying up into baby bust as if it were in awe of free-fall under the pull of unforgiving gravity.

Such a dramatic change of fortunes would continue to spill over into the current and seventh oquannium (1955-2038) at odds with the oqual theory.

Although what was likely a short-lived baby bump at the interface of the previous (1871-1954) and the current (1955-2038) oquannia, it however quickly whittled away during much of the first half (1955-1996) of the current oqual cycle as if it had turned into baby bust before yielding to what appears to be baby boom during the second half (1997-2038) in a non-canonical fashion.

Why did British demographics experience such a non-canonical trend during the current oquannium (1955-2038) with baby bust (or population bust) followed by baby boom (or population boom) over the two halves, respectively?

The answer seems to lie in socioeconomic factors as well as post-colonial immigration to Britain.

Although Britain enjoyed a bout of relatively prosperous times like most other nations during the first half (1955-1996) of the current oquannium (1955-2038) as underscored by the Swinging Sixties, it however also continued to suffer economic woes more than its fair share after having been virtually bankrupted by the heavy cost of World War II (1939-1945) that would leave the nation with a debt burden of almost 250% of its economy.

In fact, Britain's debt drag would not fall below an acceptable level of 50% of the economy until the 1970s and, when it did, the nation would be stung by a duo of deadly stagflation and currency collapse sparked by massive budget deficits with the International Monetary Fund (IMF) coming to the rescue at the expense of tarnishing its prestige of being a global power upon which the sun once never set.

Understandably, such economic doldrums during the 1970s not only failed to generate the thrust necessary for a full-fledged baby boom to emerge but also turned the rather short-lived baby bump of the 1950s and 1960s into baby bust (or population bust) for the remainder of the first half (1955-1996) of the current oquannium (1955-2038).

Although Britain's fertility rate briefly flirted with three babies per woman of reproductive age during the 1960s, it would however quickly tumble below two in the face of self-inflicted economic wounds during the 1970s.

To add insult to fertility, Britain's population growth rate also plummeted to 0% during much of the 1970s—with the number of births and new immigrants arriving largely offset by more or less an equal number of deaths and emigrants leaving the country for greener pastures elsewhere.

For all its doom and gloom, the first half (1955-1996) of the current oquannium (1955-2038) however did engineer a new wave of fresh blood in the form of post-colonial immigration to Britain in droves.

In the wake of having lost nearly 4M people to death or injury during the two world wars (or roughly 8% of the then nation's population) in the midst of the second half (1913-1954) of the previous oquannium (1871-1954), Britain suffered a massive labor shortage—particularly for low-paid unskilled jobs in the then booming textile and steel industries.

To meet the shortfall out of desperation, Britain turned to its former colonies in the hope of recruiting young men in their Twenties and Thirties with a horse-like build, beaver-like industry, and weed-like adaptability so as to ensure that they would have no qualms working night shifts at odd hours under dirty and frigid conditions.

Such a Hail Mary move would hardly disappoint as there was no shortage of volunteers given that British wages would dwarf what colonial men could earn back home, not to mention that almost all of them were peasants ploughing the fields and breeding livestock to meet their daily sustenance.

Given more mouths than sprouts coupled with their centuries-old link to Britain, the three Indian nations would rise to the challenge once more to serve their former master and contribute a lion's share of their strongest men packing their bags and heading for greener pastures during the 1950s and 1960s with the immigrant tide having ebbed as the 1970s kicked off.

While other nations such as the Caribbean islands would also follow suit, there was perhaps no place like my hometown Mirpur that saw its male population dry up during those two decades with single mothers left behind to fend for themselves and their young offspring all by themselves—a scenario that my own mother endured during the 1970s for almost a decade on her own with five young kids to feed (with me being the little one), all the while my father worked in England.

It was not just my father but most of my first-and-second uncles as well as their first-and-second cousins who would also immigrate to England during the 1960s and 1970s.

One of the major drivers for exodus out of my hometown was the construction of the Mangla Dam during the 1960s that would submerge much of the low-lying fertile lands home to sprawling towns and villages in rural Mirpur.

The loss of their livelihoods left many Mirpuris destitute and desperate for a new life elsewhere with many moving to other cities in Pakistan as well as the Middle East but most chose to go to Vilayat (the Indianized name for England) for a few years so as to enrich themselves before returning back home to their traditional wives and bragging about their riches befitting of a good husband and father.

Alas, they never did.

That should have been hardly surprising given that migration is largely a one-way traffic wherein humans are always moving forward and never turn back.

Indeed, the very essence of human civilization, migration keeps nations in the remaking over and over again lest they turn stale beyond the pale.

What became of Mirpuri men who never returned home from Vilayat?

For a time, rumors abounded that the handsome and worksome Mirpuri men had not only saved Sheffield steel foundries and Bradford textile factories but that they had also fallen prey to White girls.

And few would dare not toast that mouthwatering gossip given the cliché the world over that men have got to do what they have got to do.

However, none of that had materialized.

Rather, it was their traditional wives that would join them later in Vilayat.

Whoever said that men are unfaithful must have never met Mirpuri men.

What happened to Mirpuri men pretty much happened to all men from India, Pakistan, Bangladesh, and the Caribbeans who had immigrated to England.

While the 1950s and 1960s largely witnessed an immigration tide of men to Britain, the 1970s and 1980s would see a wave of their traditional wives and young families joining them.

And this is where things get even juicier for Britain.

With the arrival of their families during the 1970s and 1980s, the immigrant men made Britain their home rather than a stepping stone as they had planned to do so when they first arrived.

However, their longing for their home countries never subsided for one moment, particularly for the immigrants from the three Indian nations with a very proud and rich culture that traces its roots to some of the earliest human civilizations such as Mohenjo-Daro—an ancient city excavated recently along the Indus River (running through the spine of modern-day Pakistan) with a highly-developed infrastructure that is believed to have paralleled the sophistication of the likes of Mesopotamia.

And so when the kids of such immigrants came of age during the 1980s and 1990s, their home countries became their first stop to shop for their potential partners in what is often referred to as "arranged marriage"—a popular tradition even today across the Indian peninsula where young men and women are not only brought together through family connections to tie the knot but often "arranged" by their parents or close relatives.

Importantly, fishing for marriage in familiar waters would continue to fuel a never-ending wave of immigrants to Britain from the Indian peninsula, not to mention that their rather high fertility rate would also serve to neutralize and turn population bust into population boom as the 1990s closed out almost in sync with the onset of the second half (1997-2038) of the current oquannium (1955-2038).

Simply put, Britain's population boom observed over the past couple of decades has largely been fueled by what are today called "Asian Britons"—British citizens of Asian descent with those from the trio of India-Pakistan-and-Bangladesh making up the lion's share among them.

The proof of my proclamation lies in British pudding.

In 1970, Asian Britons barely made up 1% of Brits and only a little more than 10% of British babies were delivered by foreign-born mothers.

In 2023, a little under 10% of Brits traced their roots to Asia and over 30% of British babies were delivered by foreign-born mothers.

Nevertheless, recent waves of immigrants fleeing persecution and other asylum seekers from across the globe have also likely contributed to an upsurge in British population growth over the past couple of decades.

To say that immigrants have saved the British ark from sinking would be a huge understatement.

Not only have they turned Britain into a culturally-rich society but without their enormous contributions, Britain would be a dying nation today.

With the overall British fertility rate having remained dangerously well below two babies per woman of reproductive age since the 1970s, one wonders where would Britain be now without the traditional wives.

Although Britain's population boom seen over the past quarter-of-a-century hardly gives chills due to the rather low fertility rate, better days lie ahead with the arrival of the next oquannium (2039-2122) in over a decade or so.

On the basis of the nation's current population dynamics, one can safely conclude that a bona-fide baby boom is on the horizon for Britannia as it is set to experience a canonical demographic trend over the course of the next oquannium (2039-2122) in line with the oqual theory.

While Britannia may never rule the waves again, its growing army of traditional wives will nevertheless come to be viewed as the envy of Europe in the not too distant future—a New Britain is already in the making and threatening once again to take the world by storm.

Watch out, India!

All told, Great Britain is undergoing a demographic metamorphosis into Global Britain at a supersonic velocity—the like of which has perhaps never been witnessed since the transition of Roman Albion into Anglo-Saxon Britain beginning in the 5th century.

As recently as 1970, Britain was 98% White.

In 2023, almost 15% of Brits are non-White and breeding like rabbits.

Before shifting gears, I should add that an economically-prosperous nation demands a fertility rate of roughly three babies per woman of reproductive age so as to not only hold the demographic line but also provide a little more juice to make sure that the population keeps ticking slightly upward to neutralize unexpected loss of life through natural disasters or otherwise—and to ensure that the old-young equilibrium forever remains tilted to the right.

On the other hand, countries with a fertility rate below two are essentially dying nations and heading for calamitous times ahead.

Examples of major nations fighting for their survival due to low fertility rate are South Korea (1.1), Japan (1.4), and Italia (1.5)—a baby boom is nevertheless on the cards for all three nations with the arrival of an auspicious spell of oqual cycle in about a decade or so after the dust from the looming World War III has settled.

What score does America get on its fertility card?

Vamos a ver! On va voir! Let us see!

FROM AMERICA'S BOOMERS TO ONE AND DONE

In the pantheon of nations with a long-standing history and culture stretching back millennia, America does not even register on the scale.

In fact, America is still in its infancy trying to figure out what it wants to be and where it wants to be in the bigger scheme of ancient civilizations.

Being an infant nation, America is therefore constantly being remade with a new wave of immigrants with the turn of each century.

In the 18th century, it was conceived as a commonwealth of Anglo-Saxons.

In the 19th century, it viewed itself as a White nation.

In the 20th century, it would redefine itself as a multiracial country.

In the 21st century, it is on course to becoming a multicultural society.

Today, for the first time ever in nation's 250-year history, second-generation Americans are beginning to take pride in their cultural and lingual heritage unlike earlier generations compelled to conform to Anglo-Saxon norms with English being their sole language lest one risked being ostracized as un-American.

Being multilingual is the new norm for the next generation of Americans.

That is a huge positive as we all know the benefits of being able to juggle more than one tongue as it not only adds an extra layer of plasticity to our brain cells but also helps us to connect better with the world at large.

Long story short, America has largely been in the making during the 18th and 19th centuries as it would not reach a relatively critical and stable mass until the arrival of 20th century.

In other words, having been in infancy for much of the last 300 years, it would be a big ask to expect US demographics to oscillate with alternating bouts of baby boom and baby bust in sync with the oqual cycle.

Add to that the fact that the never-ending influx of immigrants from all corners of the world and in relatively large numbers continues to skew America's population dynamics even today.

This would be particularly applicable to the previous oquannium (1871-1954), the first half (1871-1912) of which came hot on the heels of the American Civil War (1861-1865) followed by multiple waves of European immigrants that will continue into the 20th century until the enactment of the so-called 1924 Immigration Act.

A deeply racist policy, that 1924 act practically banned immigration from Asia and significantly reduced it from other parts of the world but Western Europe so as to weed out what the nation believed to be the "inferior stock" through the introduction of quotas for each nation based on its proportional representation among the citizens of the United States.

Thus, the precipitous drop in US population growth during the second half (1913-1954) of the previous oquannium (1871-1954) could well be attributed to a drop in immigration rather than necessarily due to baby bust—though it is very likely that the quartet of World War I (1914-1918), Influenza Pandemic (1918-1920), Great Depression (1929-1939), and World War II (1939-1945) must have negatively impacted the family structure and with it the birth rate on American soil as such calamities no doubt severely crippled much of the globe.

Notwithstanding such perturbations from external factors to internal population dynamics, the current oquannium (1955-2038) nevertheless appears to be broadly following a canonical demographic trend.

In particular, the so-called Boomers generation coincided with the beginning of the first half (1955-1996) of the current oquannium (1955-2038).

However, like Britain, such a baby bump was short-lived and did not continue deep into the first half of the current oquannium due primarily to the negative impact of Vietnam War (1965-1975) on the American society both in economic terms and sociopolitical harmony.

In particular, the heavy cost of Vietnam War spilled over into the US government running budget deficits which led to a loss of confidence in the greenback that would in turn spark a run on its gold reserves during the 1960s.

In 1971, under the watch of the 37th POTUS Richard Nixon, such an economic reality-check would subsequently lead to the abolishment of gold standard as America could no longer honor the redemption of dollar notes upon the request of none other than its closest European allies.

Then came the 1973 Oil Crisis—when the Organization of the Petroleum Exporting Countries (OPEC) spearheaded by Saudi Arabia declared an oil embargo against the United States and its allies in response to its support for Israel during the 1973 Arab-Israeli War.

As if that embargo had not taken its toll, America would be plunged into uncharted waters once more through the 1979 Oil Crisis—when Iran's oil production tanked in the wake of the 1979 Iranian Revolution, which led to the replacement of monarchy with what we know today as the Islamic Republic.

In the wake of that twin energy crisis during the 1970s, the price of crude oil spiked 1200% in nominal terms from $3/barrel in 1973 to $40/barrel in 1980.

When the cost of energy goes through the roof so does the cost of goods and services for all creatures great and small.

Unsurprisingly then, the economic well-being of the nation during the 1970s was heavily stifled through a deadly bout of stagflation—a combo of stagnant economy due to high unemployment coupled with inflation—followed by a spate of rolling recessions during the early 1980s.

The conventional wisdom has it that inflation dies out with the onset of a recession due to the fact that the rising unemployment cuts the consumer spending power which in turn reduces demand and, with that reduction in demand, the price of goods and services also drops to match the economic equilibrium.

That rule of thumb holds true both temporally and spatially except under the following four scenarios, which will lead to persistent inflation even in the midst of a recession, thereby producing stagflation:

1) **Money printing**—While excessive printing of money without any goods and services to go with it may not immediately lead to consumer price inflation due to the fact it may find solace in assets on Wall street rather than making its way to Main Street right away with a lag that could last many years, an increase in money supply against the backdrop of stagnant economic growth nevertheless bears the potential to skyrocket the price of goods and services.

2) **Currency collapse**—Recession develops in sync with devaluation (or collapse) of national currency due to excessive money printing or a debt default. The resulting plunge in purchasing power will inherently lead to an increase in the cost of goods and services being imported from other nations even if there is a reduction in demand as was the case with Weimer Germany during the 1920s and is also the case today across much of the developing world.

3) **Energy shock**—Recession coincides with a spike in energy prices, which could be triggered through the reduction of energy supply due to natural disasters, wars, or embargos as was the case during the 1970s oil crises. Since energy is the bedrock of everything we consume, the price of goods and services will continue to rise even if the demand tanks under this situation as of course was the case across much of the Western world during the 1970s. Given the potential of the ongoing Russia-Ukraine War to cause an energy shock, the 1970s stagflation could well make a comeback across much of the Western world during the 2020s.

4) **Supply-chain bottleneck**—Recession occurs in concert with a supply-chain bottleneck such that there is a disruption in the transport of goods and services due to embargos, wars, or natural disasters as was partly the case in the wake of the 2019 Coronavirus Pandemic. Nevertheless, the current bout of inflation that began in 2021 across the Western world is largely a product of overconsumption due to the financial system having been flooded with teradollars without any goods and services to have gone with it. Had the masses not been provided with cheap money, it is very unlikely that we would have had the inflation that we are facing today. On the contrary, we would have likely experienced a deflationary bout absent government intervention.

What is a recession you might ask.

In the wake of the economic rut faced by Americans during the late 1970s under the watch of the then sitting 39th POTUS Jimmy Carter, the then US Presidential nominee Ronald Reagan delivered a fitting note while addressing his supporters leading up to the 1980 US Presidential Election:

> "Recession is when your neighbor loses his job. Depression is when you lose yours. And recovery is when Jimmy Carter loses his."

Today, however, one could rephrase those remarks as:

> "Recession is when you get paid more for staying home rather than working a job. Depression is when you lose all of that windfall after getting sucked into a Ponzi. And recovery will only come after the systemic fraud in the society is purged through the looming World War III over the next decade or so."

Long story short, economic woes of the 1970s threw a spanner in the American baby production lines such that the baby bump of the 1950s and 1960s that created the Boomers cohort not only failed to materialize into a full-fledged baby boom but also uncharacteristically turned into baby bust before too long.

Even the ratification of the 1965 Immigration Act—that opened the door for millions of new immigrants from every corner of the world irrespective of what they looked like—failed to uplift the US population growth in a meaningful way.

With the onset of the second half (1997-2038) of the current oquannium (1955-2038), the US population growth would continue to disappoint and has hitherto remained bottled for the most part.

This should be hardly surprising given that more and more American families are opting to either go babyless or settle on just one and done.

And who could blame them given the financial cost of raising babies these days and all the troubles that follow as elegantly pointed out by my neighbors from hell who claimed to be raising not one but rather half-a-dozen babies.

However, upon closer interrogation, it turned out that the couple was actually talking about their puppies.

When grilled about their plans for adding human babies to their rather mutt-packed family, they countered:
> "Puppies are a much better investment. They require no 529 Plan (or college fund). They do no drugs. They never get arrested for misdemeanors. They do not get pregnant. We just cannot wrap our head around having kids nor do we understand why others put up with them given all the drama that follows."

Still, there is a plenty of cause for celebration for the infant nation given that America not only runs on the blood of immigrants but that it has always been powered by their babies.

America se mueve con la sangre de los inmigrantes!

Not only are immigrants not bothered by two and zoo but they are also eager to make it three and ski, and some even dial it up to four and store, while others go as far as five and drive.

With immigrants making up almost 15% of US population today, the scene is indeed set for a baby boom to get underway with the arrival of a new dawn of optimism and prosperity as the current oqaunnium (1955-2038) draws to a close in about a decade after the dust has settled on the ongoing sociopolitical bedlam.

And with the arrival of such a dawn, what has become the much-derided institution of marriage over the past couple of decades will also make a come back with widespread popularity as it rightfully reclaims its primal place in the society across the globe.

|3.2| CULTURAL DYSPHORIA

During my decade-long odyssey through England straddling across much of the 1980s and 1990s, I had become accustomed to the familiar "Merry Christmas" greetings as each calendar year drew to a close.

Not once did it ever occur to me that such a simple religious catchphrase that openly celebrated the Christian faith would somehow be perceived as being offensive by anyone, irrespective of their religious inclination.

In fact, the widespread popularity of "Merry Christmas" paraphernalia from greeting cards to personal items only served to reaffirm my own faith and the appreciation for others' religious proclivities.

However, after moving across the pond from London to New York to pursue my postdoctoral research barely a year after the arrival of annus turnilis (1997) of the current oquannium (1955-2038), I would immediately begin to notice that "Merry Christmas" somehow had begun to be sacrificed and demoted just as the new kid on the block "Happy Holidays" would take its place by leaps and bounds as the Noughties (2000s) marched along.

To add salt to wounds, public display of Christmas signs could invite complaints, protests, and even litigation by the far-left (or radical-left) groups who had declared war on religion with Christianity being in their crosshairs.

And if that salt sprinkled on open wounds was not bad enough for the Christian faithfuls, then the 2010 billboard—projected above the eastbound entrance to Lincoln Tunnel as one drove from New Jersey under the Hudson River into Midtown Manhattan—with the message "You know It's a myth: This season, celebrate reason!" printed next to a silhouetted nativity scene was nothing short of an open declaration of war on Christianity.

On a personal level, such a dramatic deviance unfolding on American soil was particularly troubling given that back in Britain, I had learned that United States was a deeply Christian nation relative to Europe.

Although somewhat baffled, I would simply sweep the whole fiasco of what would later come to be called the "War on Christmas" under the rug due to being preoccupied with advancing my scientific endeavors when working 60+ hours week-in week-out was a norm not that much has changed in my life since then nor in the lives of today's dedicated scientists, juniors and seniors alike.

It also helped that I found it a lot easier to work with the thermodynamics of protein society rather than trying to understand the theodynamics of human society.

However, a little over a decade later, that nagging curiosity re-entered my stratosphere such that I was left with no choice but to take the intruder by the horns once and forever.

SPIRITUALITY IS HARDWIRED INTO OUR DNA

Today, with the oqual cycle at my fingertips, I would revisit the War on Christmas that began nearly a quarter-of-a-century ago to make sense of it.

While the origins of "Happy Holidays" can be traced as far back as the early 19th century, the somewhat secular and bizarre greeting appears to have been first popularized during the 1840s in America—courtesy of media outlets such as the New York Herald and the New York Daily Tribune—with its popularity rising exponentially over the next couple of decades or so before it begins to taper off with the arrival of the previous and sixth oquannium (1871-1954).

But, with the onset of the second half (1913-1954) of previous oquannium, "Happy Holidays" begins to gain traction once more after World War I (1914-1918) rising precipitously during the 1930s and 1940s.

Aunque usted no lo crea!—Dare you believe it!

The widespread use of "Happy Holidays" once again began to be shelved just as the current oquannium (1955-2038) kicked off during the 1950s—and the secular greeting would by-and-large remain under the radar over the next several decades.

However, with the onset of the second half (1997-2038) of the current oquannium (1955-2038), "Happy Holidays" would once again emerge from the silos and steadily bloat over the next couple of decades into what today may be dubbed "foie gras" widely served in many big cities across America to the consternation of Christian faithfuls.

Like the production of foie gras, the unsuspecting masses have been gavaged (or force fed) with "Happy Holidays" by the radical left through their monopoly of mainstream media and institutions so much so that those having ditched "Merry Christmas" are hardly cognizant of the far-left propaganda.

Psychologists would argue that following the herd is an easier option as treading unchartered waters on your own requires megatons of mental power.

Long story short, the alternating troughs and crests observed in the popularity of a catchphrase as simple as "Happy Holidays" results from what psychologists call "cultural dysphoria"—though I would also label it "religious dysphoria" in the sense that culture and religion are essentially two facets of the same coin which are deeply intertwined and often inseparable from each other.

However, what psychologists do not know is that cultural (or religious) dysphoria seemingly ebbs and flows over the course of oqual cycle in a manner akin to other regressive forces that hold human society hostage during the second half as embodied in the "dysphoria oquacycle".

Put another way, people's affinity and antipathy toward their religion (or religious heritage) represent two opposing forces that are always in a tug of war with the former edging out the latter during the first half of oqual cycle, and vice versa.

No matter how much grudge many people hold against religion, they somehow cannot shake it off from their lives due to what I have dubbed the "euphoria-dysphoria equilibrium"—an intricate societal plank that seesaws from left to right in sync with the progression of oqual cycle.

Thus, people seem to gravitate toward their religion and traditional values during the first half of oqual cycle so as to push the euphoria-dysphoria equilibrium well over to the left.

And then with the onset of the second half, the euphoria-dysphoria equilibrium begins to shift to the right as has been the case over the past couple of decades across much of the globe.

Admittedly, even secular individuals who declare no faith or hold grudge against religious institutions often end up solemnizing almost every aspect of their lives from births through marriages to deaths as religious events.

To say that human civilization is very much dependent upon religion and faith would be a huge understatement.

If it was not due to faith, we would have perhaps never left the woods.

Faith fuels our civilization as it helps us to overcome the thermodynamic bottleneck in order to break through the glass ceiling so as to reach new heights.

In fact, religion is in our DNA and those who try to run away from it face the wrath of biology through being condemned to extinction.

Those who claim to celebrate reason rather than faith are in fact the ones missing the forest for the trees—brimming with ignorance and hubris may earn one a few plaudits but it also quite often plants their downfall.

According to the 2005 book titled "The God Gene" by American geneticist Dean Hamer [17], spirituality indeed appears to be hardwired into our DNA so much so that the lack of faith predisposes an individual to becoming extinct.

In other words, faith is hereditary in that the inheritance of the proverbial God gene predisposes individuals to spirituality.

While such a hypothesis is highly debatable, there is no doubt that spirituality confers an evolutionary advantage upon individuals by conjuring up a sense of belonging to a community as well as adding an eternal meaning to life.

In fact, not only faith but almost every aspect of our lives is hereditary from the very words that enable us to communicate to our eating and sleeping habits that have been passed onto us through generations.

Just because we may have smartphones that our grandparents did not in no way implies that our lives are wholly independent of our past and that we can redefine everything however we so wish.

That is exactly the self-destructive path that the radical left is pursuing today in their quest to blur the lines and claim that our cultural norms are nothing more than social constructs.

Apropos their abracadabra and mumbo-jumbo, there is no woman or man nor is there talent or lack thereof, everybody can be whatever they want to be, and the reasons why they cannot be what they want to be is due to societal oppression and prejudices.

If such hocus-pocus does not smell of a generation gone astray and being fast-tracked for extinction, then one does not even have one cent of scent.

Long story short, religion has been an integral part of our civilization for millennia not due to ignorance but rather the lack thereof led communities to self-destruct themselves as many are already on that fateful path once again today thanks but no thanks to cultural dysphoria.

To be sure, dysphoria is the direct antonym of euphoria.

On the one hand, cultural dysphoria is the general feeling of being discontent or confused about one's place in the society even though they are an integral part of it in one way or another.

On the other hand, cultural dysphoria may also express itself in one's desire to be the exact opposite of what they are, biologically or otherwise.

While retaining its original flavor, I have also extended the definition of cultural dysphoria to refer to the plight of individuals in the society in the wake of sociopolitical upheaval befalling humanity during the second half of oqual cycle and their desire to return to good old days rather than rise up to the challenge and deal with it as embodied in the motto: "When the going gets tough, the tough gets going!"

Admittedly, most people today are very dissatisfied with their lives against the backdrop of what seem to be never-ending upheavals coupled with greed and fraud having taken center stage in our society.

But, things did not use to be like this barely a few decades earlier as many openly share their nostalgia of those earlier times.

If we had a magic wand, almost everyone around the world would indeed be willing to travel back to the good old future of the second half of 20th century—that broadly coincided with the first half (1955-1996) of current oquannium (1955-2038)—at the expense of giving up many modern luxuries of the fledgling 21st century such as smartphones, social media, online shopping, and so forth.

This scenario is perhaps best illustrated by the plight of today's Pakistanis—who together make up the fifth most-populous nation (240M) after the quartet of India (1450M), China (1440M), America (340M), and Indonesia (280M).

PAKISTAN IS THE POSTERCHILD OF EVERYTHING THAT IS WRONG WITH OUR SOCIETY TODAY

In Pakistan, the ignominious leaders have been promising Naya (or New) Pakistan since the outset of 21st century but only for that ill-timed experiment to have backfired recently with a vengeance—thanks but no thanks to the dire spell of the second half (1997-2038) of the current oquannium (1955-2038).

In order to lure the electorate to their camp, every Pakistani leader over the past couple of decades has been upping the ante over their rivals to offer the masses ever more handouts through for example importing commodities and then cutting the price in half so as to deliver on their promises at the expense of pushing the nation into an ever-deepening debt hole.

Such a bureaucratic fraud with the potential to propel a nation toward bankruptcy is of course not unique to Pakistan but rather the modus operandi of almost every other democratic nation with America leading the charge.

Blame the leaders all you can but they have been doing exactly what anyone would have done to make life easier for hoi polloi lest they lose their vote and get booted out of the office.

Admittedly, it seems that like the parable of Pakistan, democracy has not only destroyed most nations that gave it refuge but that it has also ended up enslaving the very people it vowed to liberate.

Still, fools would argue that democracy has been hijacked by the elite and wealthy and that today's sociopolitical upheaval is a making of their lax policies running excesses and imbalances to the hilt.

To the contrary, running excesses and imbalances is the very essence of a democratic system for not doing so would mean that hardly anyone would show up at the polling station.

It is in human nature that when you can smell a free meal, you immediately stop fending for yourself.

Not only that but democracy also empowers the masses to sell their vote in exchange for free goodies and hoodies.

As a child growing up in rural Pakistan during much of the 1970s and 1980s, I vividly recall firsthand every single soul from old to young and even children barely out of their diapers working day and night, seven days a week, on their livelihoods from raising livestock through ploughing the fields to harvesting the crops.

It was humanity living in perfect harmony with Mother Nature with no obnoxious gases released into the atmosphere nor toxic waste generated and almost everything one needed to live a comfortable life was produced at home, not to mention that most people lived well into their 80s and had never seen a doctor in their entire life nor taken any medicine.

Fast forward to today, and most Pakistanis are not only suffering from a plethora of maladies like people elsewhere across much of the globe but they have also long parted company with their agrarian lifestyle comforted by the bogus promise of their leaders to provide them with notes in return for their votes.

Not only that but most have even forgotten the traditional skills necessary to fend for themselves should it ever become necessary.

"Why raise a cow when you can get the milk for free", many Pakistanis confide in me to justify as to why they have given up on a life of purpose.

Today, ordinary Pakistanis are indeed biting the bullet of their own making rather than their leaders being incompetent to run the nation's affairs.

Long story short, democracy has not only planted the spectacular downfall of Pakistan but also that of most other nations.

Admittedly, the fact is that democracy only exists on paper rather than in practice—a reality that the likes of China are fully aware of and, unlike the herd, the Chinese leaders have been super-smart to steer clear of such a deeply-flawed system that is more likely to break than make a nation.

It is indeed no coincidence that while China is flying with colors today, the herd across much of the globe is sinking like a stone even though they were assured that their Titanic built on democracy was unsinkable.

One could argue that while everyone has education, hardly anyone has the wisdom for if they did they would not be doing what everyone else is doing!

Such wisdom, albeit scarce, is nevertheless the cornerstone of every successful individual and nation alike.

As for the failed nation of Pakistan devoid of wisdom though with plenty of education, bankruptcy has predictably come home and it is now payback time for the unforgiving laws of nature spare no one.

With a debt default all but a mathematical certainty to add to a complete societal meltdown in the wake of deadly inflation, none knows what will become of Pakistan unless one pays heed to the subtle mechanics of oqual cycle.

Driven by the nostalgia of good old days, Pakistanis on both sides of the sociopolitical spectrum are now shamelessly demanding Purana (or Old) Pakistan when they ought to be moving forward rather than going back in time.

During my fledgling years, I would indeed witness firsthand a relatively prosperous Pakistan buttressed by a rather high moral compass coupled with a heightened sense of community during much of the 1970s and 1980s to even fonder memories of Pakistan during the 1950s and 1960s handed down to me by my parents and grandparents.

In those good old days, most Pakistanis held public-and-private institutions in a rather high esteem and their leaders commanded huge respect for their progressive agendas and good governance that largely kept the nation self-sufficient and debt-free.

To add icing on the cake, the Pakistani leaders would also get the red-carpet treatment while on state visits to the West.

Additionally, Pakistan used to be an economic posterchild for many Asian nations during much of the 1950s and 1960s and it would often act as a conduit to open up communication channels between its neighbors that had no diplomatic ties with Western nations and even parts of the Muslim world.

Admittedly, such relatively prosperous times during the 1950s and 1960s were shared by most nations in those good old days as fondly remembered through:

- Golden Age in America (1950-1970)
- Swinging Sixties in Britain (1960s)
- Les Trente Glorieuses (The Thirty Glorious Years) in France (1945-1975)
- Wirtschaftswunder (Economic Miracle) in Germany (1948-1975)
- Il Miracolo Economico (The Economic Miracle) in Italy (1948-1963)
- El Milagro Español (The Spanish Miracle) in Spain (1950-1975)
- Jukagaku Kogyoka (Economic Miracle) in Japan (1950-1975)
- Khrushchev Era in Russia (1953-1964)
- Nehru Era in India (1947-1964)
- Ayub Khan Era in Pakistan (1958-1969)

Today, when reminded of the Ayub Khan Era, most senior Pakistanis get chills as they eagerly take a trip down memory lane.

However, across their northeastern border, their Chinese friends not only bristle with rage but also get goose bumps.

Unfortunately, the Chinese Golden Age of the current oqual cycle was delayed due to the self-inflicted wound that would enter the annals of history as the Chinese Great Famine (1958-1962) thanks to Mao Zedong's ill-conceived policies that backfired with a vengeance.

Nevertheless, the hard work and unwavering conviction of les chinoise would be richly rewarded with far more than they had bargained for as the nation turned capitalist after its revolutionary leader Deng Xiaopeng signed an historic trade pact with the then 39th POTUS Jimmy Carter in 1979—with Pakistan providing the backchannel for such negotiations due to the then lack of direct diplomatic ties between China and United States.

Simply put, Chinese Golden Age would anomalously arrive almost half-a-turn later during oqual autumn (1997-2017) in lieu of oqual spring (1955-1975) as the current oquannium (1955-2038) nominally entered its second half in 1997—spring and autumn are essentially mirror images in meteorological terms and so are summer and winter.

While China's unprecedented economic prosperity over the past several decades oversaw more than half-a-billion of its people lifted out of poverty, it regrettably did not trickle across its northwestern border through the sky-high Karakoram Highway down into its all-weather friend Pakistan.

Today, one indeed finds a toxic enantiomer of what were once deeply-respected institutions and leaders in Pakistan who have either lost public trust, are ridiculed for their propagandas, or viewed as nothing more than Western lapdogs.

Importantly, most Pakistanis in those earlier times were renowned for close and extended familial ties in that they by-and-large lived in harmony with each other, would quickly pitch-in to divide the workload-and-agony of their relatives and neighbors in what was then a largely agrarian society, all the while cooperating to multiply the shared fruits-and-joys of their labor so as to ensure that everyone within their social orbit was being taken care of.

In fact, it used to be so rare to find close-knit families fighting over petty things—such family politics likely affected no more than about one in ten families during much of the second half of the 20th century.

Today, family politics runs deep in the blood of most Pakistanis so much so that it is rare to find a clan that is at peace with itself—with as many as nine out of ten families affected wherein not only siblings but even their offspring refuse to speak to each other in a meaningful way over minor issues that have been foolishly blown out of proportions through a positive feedback loop.

Add to that the fact that the very neighbors who would once act as your most-trusted cheerleaders in that they would not only have your back but also stick their neck out on your behalf not so long ago have steadily morphed over the past several decades into your worst antagonists who are now vying for every opportunity to harm you or, at the very minimum, they eagerly await a free dose of schadenfreude—the psychological quirk wherein people derive pleasure from the misfortunates of others.

Across their eastern border, their Indian brethren can perhaps relate to the dilemma facing Pakistanis as they themselves have encountered a diametric change of fortunes of their own over the past several decades as idiomatically expressed below:

> "Ek zamaana woh tha ke aulaad apne maayi baap ko apni jayidad samjhati thi; aur ek zamaana aaj hai ke santaan apne maata pitta ki jayidad ko apna samjhati hai!"—"In the good old days, the children would consider their parents to be their most valuable asset; today, the progeny appraises the property of their progenitors to be their most valuable real estate!"

> "Ek zamaana woh tha ke mushkil tha apna makaan banaana magar ahsaan tha kisi ke dil main apna ghar basaana; aur ek zamaana aaj hai ke ahsaan hai apna makaan banaana lekan mushkil hai kisi ke dil main apna ghar basaana!"—"In the good old days, the hardship encountered with building your house was offset by the ease with which one could chisel a place in a woman's heart; today, the ease with which one can build their house is counterbalanced by the adversity encountered in sculpting a place in a woman's heart!"

> "Ek zamaana woh tha ke ghar main lakshmi ke aane se sab kuch aa jaata tha; aur ek zamaana aaj hai ke ghar main lakshmi ke aane se sab kuch chalaa jaata hai"—"In the good old days, the marriage would bring so much good luck with it that it will turn a man's hut into his mansion; today, the marriage brings so much curse that it turns a man's mansion into a hut!"

> "Ek zamaana woh tha ke lakshmi lakshman ko raja samjhati thi taake woh khud rani ban sake; aur ek zamaana aaj hai ke lakshmi lakshman ko ghulaam samjhati hai bina soche ke woh khud ghulaam ban jaati hai!"—"In the good old days, the woman would consider her man to be her king so that she could also become a queen; today, the woman treats her man like a slave without even realizing that she becomes one too!"

> "Ek zamaana woh tha ke pattni patti ko parameshwar samjhati thi; aur ek zamaana aaj hai ke pattni sonay chandi ko apna parameshwar maanti hai!"—"In the good old days, the woman would consider her husband to be her gold; today, gold has become her means to an end!"

Tellingly, the familial and sociopolitical woes of Indians and Pakistanis are widely shared by people throughout the world as almost every nation from Afghanistan to Zimbabwe is not only scrambling to reverse the trend of the disintegration of moral values and the loss of sense-of-community but also finds itself teetering on the brink of bankruptcy due to having become addicted to an easy life through borrowing money in a reckless manner as if there would be no tomorrow.

While the likes of Zimbabwe and Venezuela have been in dire financial straits due to hyperinflation and debt-default since the outset of the 21st century, the fate of many other nations also appears to have been sealed as they begin to fall down one after the other like dominoes with the onset of the ominous oqual winter (2018-2038) of the current oquannium (1955-2038).

In 2020, the likes of Lebanon, Suriname, and Zambia went underwater after failing to meet their debt obligations.

In 2022, Sri Lanka joined the disgraceful chorus of nations unable to pay their debt.

Other nations such as Argentina, Belarus, Ecuador, Egypt, El Salvador, Ethiopia, Ghana, Kenya, Nigeria, Pakistan, Tunisia, and Ukraine are on course to face the debt music over the next couple of years or so.

And it is only a matter of time before many more nations will go belly up as the dire spell of oqual cycle leaves no stone unturned as it draws to a close.

Had such nations had the wisdom and knowledge of such a dire spell of oqual cycle, many would have surely averted their downfall through pursuing responsible fiscal and monetary policies rather than continuing to live beyond their financial means.

Those who fail to pay heed to the dire spell of oqual cycle do so at their own peril.

Indeed, while the lingering sociopolitical crisis of epic proportions across much of the globe will eventually end over the next decade, it is not going to end well.

As for Pakistanis, they need not return to Purana Pakistan but rather be patient as a bona fide Naya Pakistan is indeed waiting on the horizon but, unfortunately, it will not arrive soon enough for many as their ongoing pain-and-suffering will only continue to swell as the fallout from the current oquannium (1955-2038) reaches its crescendo over the next decade or so.

For now, Pakistanis must put up with the looming qiyamat (or day of reckoning) just as they did some 84 years earlier in the wake of the 1947 Indian Partition in a never-ending yet what remains an unbeknown story to them of "qiyamat se qiyamat tak!"—"from doomsday till doomsday!"

On the other side of qiyamat, Pakistan will once again rise from the ashes with the return of those good old days of the second half of the 20th century just as human civilization on the Indian peninsula and across much of the globe has done so every 84 years on average since the beginning of times.

Likewise, the familial woes of Indians and others around the globe are of course transitory and the good old days when marriage was concomitant with a deluge of blessings will once again return, and so will the days of baby boom, with the start of the next oquannium (2039-2122) in over a decade or so.

Would that also hold true for the Western nations?

In addition to cultural dysphoria, the Western world however has also been recently beset by a rapidly rising tide of gender dysphoria, the like of which it has never encountered before.

In a nutshell, gender dysphoria is a perception among a growing number of normal young adults (and even children) born with a perfect set of either male or female genitalia but who feel that they belong to the opposite gender rather than what has been carved out by their biology, including in particular the great lengths to which their anatomy and endocrinology have gone.

Surely, human body is not a gadget that can be repurposed at will.

Alas, the proponents of gender dysphoria would have you believe otherwise either due to their laughable folly or primarily being driven by the greed of making a killing through commercialization of distorting and lacerating otherwise perfectly normal human bodies with disturbing consequences for their subjects and the society-writ-large.

Such fools do not understand that neither masculinity nor femininity represent mutually-exclusive discrete quanta but rather a continuum (or spectrum) of overlapping male and female characteristics.

There is no such thing as an ideal man or woman to which every male or female must conform to.

For example, not all men are alpha males nor dominant creatures but rather many men tend to exhibit a varying degree of femininity which they should wholeheartedly embrace rather than seek surgery to become a fake woman.

Likewise, alpha females tend to be very dominant and self-confident as they not only send shivers down men's spine but they are also highly sought-after creatures due to their leadership qualities—they are nevertheless women and they ought to be very comfortable in their God-given identity rather than seek medical intervention to have their female genitalia plucked out in an effort to become a fake man.

Ditto for tomboys who should also embrace their womanhood as it is rather than try to fit a stereotypical hourglass who is afraid to step outside her abode without makeup or, even worse, consider becoming a fake man.

Nor should anyone hold a grudge against alpha males or alpha females for a society without strong men and strong women would be a no society at all—if that was not true, our biology would have long sent such dominant creatures packing into the annals of our evolution a la our distant cousins Neanderthals.

In fact, alpha males and alpha females are the movers and shakers of our civilization and without their ruthless-yet-selfless drive for the betterment of our society, all of us would be living today in a pothole.

Who are the proponents of gender dysphoria?

WOKEISM POSES THE BIGGEST THREAT TO THE SURVIVAL OF THE WESTERN SOCIETY

In what has been dubbed "Wokeism", the far-left (or radical-left) leaders and their entourage muddy the societal waters through a deeply-polarizing and disruptive ideology that claims to be aware of what it perceives to be sociopolitical prejudices, injustices, and inequalities endemic to human society as embodied in the so-called "critical race theory".

In other words, the Wokeists push the propaganda that the success or failure of an individual is due to inherent (or systemic) bias in the society and that such cultural anisotropy is highly skewed against minorities.

Well, geez, if a little goatherder from a poverty-stricken corner of the world can make it big, then anyone with half his talent can make it too in their own backyard provided that they channel their energy toward what matters in life rather than squander it on beating the bushes looking for reasons to lay the blame on the society for their failure.

Needless to say, the Wokeists set out to right the wrongs through their own perverted means and under their own intolerant terms without any input from those who disagree with them—particularly with regard to their push for the normalization and democratization of societal evils such as profanity, obscenity, theft, and destruction of historic landmarks.

Not only that but they want to impose their wicked religion upon the whole of humanity so as to not only have the masses condone their gobbledygook but to even do as they say and as they do.

The Wokeists often justify their nihilistic actions on the basis of societal injustices committed decades and centuries ago—rather than moving past our past, they are gung-ho on exploiting the past to advance their propaganda.

Anyone who challenges their perverted worldview or disagrees with what they believe gets called all sorts of epithets not to mention that they are also not shy of verbal and physical harassment—it is their way or the highway.

More specifically, the uncivilized and dangerous behavior of Wokeists drives a stake through the moral fabric of the society by challenging the millennia-old societal norms perfected by the laws of nature as illustrated below:

1) **Playing the victim card**—The Wokeists paint minorities as victims and White men as their oppressors instead of letting go of our past as what happened in earlier times must not be judged by today's moral standards. For one, such bigoted ideology is deeply patronizing toward minorities who rather ought to feel self-confident that there is nothing that they cannot achieve in life rather than being told that their misfortunes are due to their oppression by the society. For two, it is equally offensive to White men as they must not be held responsible for the actions of their ancestors, particularly when they were conducted according to the norms of their times.

2) **Promoting gender dysphoria**—Rather than emphasizing the role of math and science in school curriculum, the Wokeists push their preposterous hogwash of profanation of teaching material for young kids so as to indoctrinate them into believing that they are not what they are but rather what they feel in utter violation of biology. Such absurdity centered on gender dysphoria sets a dangerous precedent in that the human brain is very fluid and malleable in its ability to adapt to any caricature it is compelled to do so and, as such, it may not be long before many mentally-distorted individuals pretend that they are anthropomorphic cats or dogs rather than humans as they seek medical intervention to become what they feel rather than what they are. Their next stop could be to push for the legalization of a matrimonial union of sorts between human and beast not to mention that many adherents of such a phony religion are already practicing that. Gender dysphoria

represents nothing more than the tip of the hedonistic iceberg threatening to capsize the Western ark. No wonder then that many Westerners have already started jumping onto the unsinkable Noah's ark. All are welcome aboard. No ticket needed.

3) **Hierarchy equals discrimination**—The Wokeists preach the dangerous ideology that we are all equal in terms of our abilities even though nature designed us to be highly specialized in conducting certain tasks over others. Only a small fraction of us for instance would make bricklayers, builders, chefs, doctors, engineers, farmers, plumbers, professors, scientists, and so forth. If we are all equal, then why even have academic assessments to differentiate the brightest from the weakest. We might as well dole out an A grade to everyone though many universities are already doing that due to the "customer" demand for the top grade in exchange for top dollars. The Wokeist malarkey has even infected universities too by blurring the lines between meritocracy and mediocrity as the students rather than professors get to choose what they are being taught so that they can get the grade that they need rather than a grade that reflects their academic potential. Needless to say, a society without a hierarchy is no society at all.

4) **Reward without work**—The Wokeists promote the bogus view that everyone should be able to have everything irrespective of their contributions to the society through the provision of the so-called "universal basic income" with some even going as far as saying that everyone should even be paid the same salary. Such a preposterous view based on complaining rather than attaining not only makes socialism look like Shangrila but it stands to create a society where most individuals have no zest for life when they can live off the back of others. One's reward in the society ought to be directly proportional to their industry and only physically-challenged individuals ought to be provided for by the society out of compassion with everyone else required to fend for themselves.

5) **Preaching without action**—The Wokeists breed an army of vigilantes to fight against what they perceive to be societal injustices and environmental excesses without holding themselves accountable for their own actions. For example, a growing number of climate activists are the product of such a hypocrisy in that while they lecture others on the threat of global warming, they themselves continue to maintain an oversize carbon footprint rather than pare back their own addiction to consumption. Talking the talk is easy but walking the walk is not for the faint-hearted.

Many Americans wonder whether the Wokeist propaganda is an elitist plan to depopulate the nation and the world-writ-large.

Yet, others attribute it to the work of the devil.

In actuality, the unraveling of the Western society is best explained by my grandad's philosophy that a rewarding life is primarily defined by three things: "Roti, kapra, aur makaan!"—"Food, clothing, and shelter!"

He would continue: "Jab bandhe di khawaish inaan cheejaan thoon barr jaandi hai, te ohh shaitaan bann jaanda hai!"—"When a man's desire exceeds such basic necessities of life, he turns into a devil!"

Even today, my beloved grandad's deliberations would strike a chord across all cultures from East to West.

Not long ago, success in the Western world and across much of the globe was indeed dictated by being able to:
    1) put enough food on the table;
    2) have a cloak to cover the body; and
    3) afford a roof over the head.

Then came along all the luxuries and redefined what happiness meant.

Today, transgressions from self-indulgence to hedonistic pleasure are the new luxuries.

In other words, the unprecedented metastasis of Wokeism through the spine of Western society over the past decade is shocking but hardly surprising given that mischief befalls:
    1) Well-fed and pampered mouths such that they grow up thinking that everything falls from the sky and that even the wildest of their temptations have a solution unlike hungry mouths having naturally learned to curtail them;
    2) Offspring raised through helicopter parenting such that they will not only forever remain incapable of navigating societal waters on their own but also susceptible to being indoctrinated; and
    3) Self-indulgent souls devoid of zest for a productive and rewarding life such that their idle hands steadily morph into devil's tools to the detriment of the society.

In particular, the human brain is never satisfied no matter how much it is provided with as it is always on the hunt for new adventures, and quite often, such adventures lead to transgressions that leave a humble soul gasping for answers as to why people resort to such despicable behavior when they ought to be grateful for having been born into a society full of resources and ample opportunities, the like of which would be the envy of the bygone generations of our forefathers.

Long story short, it seems to me that the only thing the Wokeists are aware of is their own failures in life and, as such, they want others to fail too as it would somehow normalize their own poor state of affairs.

Not only are they destroying the Western society from within through their nihilistic practices run amok in virtually every school so as to convert young kids to Wokeism before they are even capable of rational thought but they are also rapidly exporting their evil and intolerant religion to every corner of the world.

It is as if the Wokeists are on a mission to remake the world in their own perverted image and, if they cannot do that, then there ought to be no world at all.

They know that they are going down but they want to take the rest of us down with them too.

Accordingly, the Wokeists represent nothing short of the modern-day equivalent of Gog and Magog who somehow seem to have been unshackled to divide and destroy humanity as we have known since the beginning of times.

But, destroy they will not as the magnificent biology has a few tricks up its own sleeve to guarantee the survival of those who refuse to fall prey to mischief and continue to honor the divine laws of nature.

Interestingly, today's rise in immorality and deviance is nothing new as it also plagued much of the Western society during much of the second half (1913-1954) of the previous oquannium (1871-1954).

During those earlier times, big cities across America and Europe witnessed not only an upsurge in the widespread circulation of salacious magazines-books-and-movies but also normalization and ubiquitization of stage nudity and erotic entertainment that were then increasingly at odds with family values and will forever continue to be so.

Just as the immorality wave largely petered out with the arrival of the current oquannium (1955-2038), so will today's Wokeism as the curtain is raised over the next oquannium (2039-2122) in over a decade or so.

In particular, the tide of cultural dysphoria will begin to ebb as its counterpart in euphoria begins to flow over the next decade or so on the other side of the bedlam.

And so will return the good old days of "Merry Christmas" as "Happy Holidays" heads for the burrows to go into its familiar multidecadal hibernation in the wake of religious euphoria rightfully reclaiming its place in the society.

In the meantime, we could preempt the rather slow spell of oqual cycle by being self-confident about our own identity and place in the society as well as not being coy of expressing our deep respect and appreciation of others' faiths.

With that, heck with "Happy Holidays" and the radical left as people of wisdom and knowledge ought to join hands to express their wishes through what they wish to say without mincing words as each calendar year draws to a close:

"Merry Christmas!"
"Happy Hanukkah!"
"Happy Kwanzaa!"
"Happy Yule!"

All told, the next tide of cultural dysphoria as expressed through greetings such as "Happy Holidays" and moral deviance (though it may no longer be called Wokeism) will begin to gain traction around annus turnilis (2081) and reach its peak around annus horribilis (2112) of the next oquannium (2039-2122).

Till then, stay healthy and wealthy!

|3.3| CONSUMPTION MANIA

In 1994, after having earned my baccalaureate in Biochemistry and being placed top of the class from the University of Manchester in England, I momentarily let my temptations get the best of me as I went on a rare shopping spree in order to pat myself on the back with the purchase of my first ever personal gadget—an unassuming Walkman to the tune of GB£40 (then equivalent to around US$60).

Far from being a splurge as some of my friends would allege given my minimalist lifestyle, that portable cassette player was by far the cheapest brand that I could find in my neck of woods at a time when online shopping had yet to be conceived with the internet having just taken off—although the World Wide Web became publicly available in 1991, it would be many years before it entered the mainstream not to mention that it was a primitive technology back then relative to what we know today.

Fast forward some 30 years, and today's portable music players can be had at less than half of what broke my bank three decades earlier even though the overall cost of living has at least tripled over the same timeframe.

So what gives?

TECHNOLOGY IS DEFLATIONARY

Rapid advances in technology reduce the cost of manufacturing through: 1) greater automation that leads to greater output and reduction in labor; and 2) improved efficiency that reduces the cost of energy per unit output.

Thus, what were once the exclusive domains of the wealthy steadily become democratized and affordable among the masses.

While the deflationary nature of technology may come to be ingenuously viewed as a bonanza from the perspective of self-gratifying consumers, it in fact spells trouble for the well-being of our planet and, dare I say, our own.

Admittedly, most people of my generation lived a rather frugal life through much of the 1980s and 1990s whether by choice or due to the lack of affordable technologies to the delight of environmental gods.

However, such organic culture centered on being content with needs rather than wants would turn on its head due to the rapid advances in both affordability and availability of consumer technology arriving almost in parallel with the onset of the second half (1997-2038) of the current oquannium (1955-2038).

Toward this demonic territory, two major breakthroughs struck our consumer culture almost in unison at lightning speed with the exaggerated threat of Y2K still hovering over our heads just as the 21st century rolled in.

First, in 2000, Google leveraged its monopoly of search engine to transform itself into a first-ever online advertising platform for retailers around the globe.

Second, in the same year, Amazon initiated its own quasi-monopoly of online marketplace to third-party merchants scattered across the planet.

Together, these two online giants not only significantly helped push the cost of merchandize down through free-market competition but also made it available to the masses with a click of a mouse.

For example, cell phones were as rare as diamonds as recently as the 1990s both in America and across Europe.

Barely a decade later, cell phones however became a-dime-a-dozen across much of the Western world, particularly with the introduction of 3G (or Third Generation) mobile technology in 2001—while 3G enabled data to be transmitted at a relatively fast network speed in the Mbps range with a significant reduction in latency, today's 5G is however capable of data transfer at Gbps.

What would be viewed as a boon for the consumers as championed by the capitalists would however soon turn out to be a baboon for the well-being of our precarious environment.

Indeed, our reckless overconsumption (or consumption mania) turned parabolic just as the second half (1997-2038) of the current oquannium (1955-2038) kicked off— thanks but no thanks to a quantum leap in the mass production of electronic goods from personal computers through smartphones to digital cameras coupled with democratization of online shopping.

Not only has such overconsumption been akin to a gunshot wound to the head having left our planet teetering on the brink of a mental collapse but it also appears to be the root cause of today's sociopolitical upheaval having befallen much of the globe—today's skyrocketing public and private debts for instance have largely been driven by our consumer culture having become accustomed to living beyond its means.

Add to that the fact that overconsumption has also led to the emergence of an ever-growing litany of new public health catastrophes from the narcissistic urge to keeping up appearances through keeping up with the Joneses to keeping up with Doctor Jones's appointments with practically no time left to do anything useful and productive in life.

As I have been professing throughout my life, overconsumption and health are mutually exclusive and inversely correlated.

On the same token, the internet is the smoking gun that proves that every form of technology is a double-edged sword in that it represents a trade off between its benefits versus harms to the health of our environment as well as our own.

How did we get here?

Why do people resort to overconsumption?

OVERCONSUMPTION IS A MEANS TO AN END

In today's society, overconsumption has become a means to an end—the belief that ultimate goal in life of being successful is obtained through one's ability to grandstand (or flaunt) their material possessions.

In other words, overconsumption has become a measure of one's status and place in the society rather than an individual solely being defined by their talent and industry.

While such consumer culture has been the mainstay of the wealthy and elite throughout modern times, its democratization among the masses however appears to oscillate in sync with the progression of oqual cycle.

Thus, overconsumption ebbs to reach a low in a lifetime during the first half of oqual cycle before it begins to flow to reach a high during the second half as embodied in the "overconsumption oquacycle".

Put another way, the consumer culture largely lies to the left of what I have dubbed "needs-wants equilibrium" during the first half of oqual cycle but then begins to steadily shift to the right with the onset of the second half.

Being in the midst of the second half (1997-2038) of the current oquannium (1955-2038), no one should therefore be aghast at today's consumption mania having gone bonkers from Alibaba to Zimbabwa.

In particular, today's consumers find solace in overconsumption at the first sign of a double or trouble thanks to banks willing to extend credit to anyone willing to go to bed with them in return for hefty profits.

For example, in the wake of the 2019 Coronavirus Pandemic with the luxury of hunkering down in their abodes or doing little or no work from home, consumers turned to online shopping to ratchet up their burden on the environment through overconsumption when they ought to have made sacrifices both for the sake of their own health as well as that of their planet.

In marked contrast, the first half (1955-1996) of the current oquannium (1955-2038) was largely driven by needs rather than wants with an unprecedented baby boom powering a rise in organic consumption rather than overconsumption as the world population more than doubled from 2700M in 1954 to 5800M in 1996 over a span of 42 years.

While Mother Earth does not mind being overpopulated as it has mechanisms in place in-and-of-itself—such as predator-prey and health-disease equilibria—in order to enforce a healthy population balance among all earthlings, it will not tolerate an iota of overconsumption.

That is due to the fact that every extra mouth participates in the so-called "carbon cycle"—every ounce of carbon consumed from Mother Earth is returned back to the atmosphere, so as to power photosynthesis in plants, during one's lifetime via respiration and upon their death via putrefaction (or decomposition).

Unlike such organic consumption, overconsumption largely powered by the combustion of fossil fuels is however detrimental to the health of what is our true alma mater (or nourishing mother) due to pollution of air and water, wrecking of rainforests, and pillaging the land of its resources.

For much of our civilized history stretching back millennia, Homo sapiens have indeed lived in more or less perfect harmony with their alma mater and, as a dessert to go with their free lunch, they would also be rewarded with a relatively disease-free life for their good table manners.

However, with the arrival of the so-called Industrial Revolution during the second half (1745-1786) of the fourth oquannium (1703-1786), that millennia-old harmony would come to an abrupt end in that it would lead to an unprecedented feeding frenzy on consumption by leaps and bounds for the first time ever in human history due to the mass production of goods and services ushered in by a litany of new and more efficient technologies from mechanized textile industry through chemical manufacturing to metal production.

Notably, the 18th Century Industrial Revolution is a notable period in our checkered history second only to the Neolithic Revolution that unfolded some 10 kiloyears ago when Homos sapiens first underwent a transition from being nomadic hunter-gatherers to permanent settlers as they adopted agriculture and began to domesticate animals.

Like its predecessor, the second half (1829-1870) of the fifth oquannium (1787-1870) also bore witness to a new wave of overconsumption against the backdrop of the rapid growth of a roster of new technologies such as the steam train and electrical telegraph that respectively revolutionized transportation and communication for the masses, albeit at a significant cost to the health of the environment.

Some 84 years later, overconsumption would make a familiar return to the front and center of Western society during the second half (1913-1954) of the previous and sixth oquannium (1871-1954) and, in many ways, it spectacularly served as a dress rehearsal for today's consumption mania.

In fact, today's bogus and immoral credit products such as BunPal (short for Buy Now Pay Later), issued by the likes of PayPal, fueling overconsumption among the downtrodden segments in the society are nothing new but essentially a reincarnation of their ancestors from the second half (1913-1954) of the previous oquannium (1871-1954).

For example, for the first time ever, retailers-en-masse began to sell big-ticket items to American consumers with only a small down payment with the remainder to be paid via monthly installments during the 1920s.

Such credit expansion to the masses unearthed a rising wave of feeding frenzy on a slew of products—from cars through electronics to clothing—to the wrath of Mother Nature.

In particular, it was during the 1920s that the likes of radios, phonographs, vacuum cleaners, washing machines, and refrigerators became democratized as overconsumption went through the roof like never before thanks once more to a quantum leap in mass production of such technologies of that bygone era.

In fact, buying on credit during the 1920s became so popular that even an average Joe and Jane not only started biting off more than they could chew but also began to trade stocks on margin—a practice of borrowing money from a bank (or broker) to buy shares of a publicly-traded company with the traded asset being held as a collateral—driven by the misguided belief that happy times will never end though that was the narrative that the masses were being fed by the money gurus in a reverse echo of today's financial culture engulfed in the flames of ubiquitous fraud run amok to the quartic power.

Alas, such self-indulgent and fake culture built on a house-of-cards was brought back to earth with the onset of Great Depression (1929-1939).

Some 84 years later, a similar reckoning awaits today's legion of fools munching on self-indulgence and being completely oblivious to the dire lessons of history.

Where do we go from here?

CAPITALISM IS AN AFFRONT TO MOTHER EARTH

While consumption in the form of basic necessities of life such as the trio of food-clothing-and-shelter has been part and parcel of Homo sapiens since the Neolithic Revolution some 10 kiloyears ago, today's consumer culture is however largely driven by wants rather than needs.

That should set off alarm bells because our wants today far exceed the ability of our planet to recycle its resources in a timely fashion so as to provide us with another round of feeding frenzy without being stressed to the point of falling sick.

In other words, our planet has no qualms about meeting our consumer needs but when such needs become excessive by orders of magnitude, it does not bode well for Mother Earth nor its inhabitants.

Today, it should therefore be hardly surprising that our despicable consumer culture has left our environment on the brink of collapse.

For example, the production of gigatons of toxic waste through overconsumption each year has heavily contaminated our ecosystems and food chains so much so that today it has become impossible to find an uncontaminated source of drinking water, much less that of healthy food anywhere on the planet.

That salmon that you think is good for your health, think again, as it is likely to be loaded with a spate of heavy metals that screw up our body's physiology in so many unremarkable and unthinkable ways by virtue of their ability to act as endocrine disruptors—they bear the potential to either mimic or disrupt the action of our endogenous steroid hormones such as estrogen and testosterone [18].

Add to that gigatons of toxic chemicals released into the environment each year through our reckless dependence on gas guzzlers from cars to planes and one can see why we as a human society are not only fighting for our survival but our hedonistic actions also do not bode well for an environment already on a tipping point with overconsumption threatening to wreak havoc on our livelihoods in the very near future.

The disingenuous and greedy capitalists often brag about the greatness of a capitalist society on the pretense that even the poorest of Americans are wealthier than most people outside the Western world.

Little such bigoted bots understand that the true wealth rests in the crests of material resources and in environmental well-being rather than in the heaps of paper notes, which can become worthless if printed en masse.

Indeed, if it were not for the United States monopoly over the world currency thanks to its powerful military with the impunity to bulldoze any nation that dare not honor such monetary hegemony, most Americans would starve to death in that they will no longer be able to pay for the manufactured goods imported from other nations with China heading that list of faithful servants.

Put another way, millions of Americans without a proper job can afford to eat like an emperor, dress like a king, and drive like a prince because their government can print the dollars at will while ordinary people in poorer nations are working off their back day-in day-out to meet their material demands in return for what are nothing more than junk pieces of paper.

If that is not exploitation of the weak and vulnerable through intimidation and subjugation, then there ain't such a thing as exploitation.

In fact, that is the practical definition of capitalism.

Not only capitalism and exploitation are essentially two sides of the same coin but they are also incompatible with the well-being of our planet.

Given that capitalism is primarily concerned with delivering huge profits in monetary terms for its stakeholders, an economy based on such an exploitative system will inherently be driven by mass production of goods and services even when they are not needed at the expense of the destruction and plundering of Mother Earth.

To add salt to its wounds, another dirty face of capitalism is that it indoctrinates the masses into believing that overconsumption is a means to an end.

As pointed out by Vance Packard in his 1960 book titled "The Waste Makers" [19], the capitalists go to great lengths with their design in order to engineer quick turnover of consumer products via the following mechanisms:

    1) **Functional Obsolescence**—wherein the design makes the product wear out quickly or become obsolete through for example being unable to be upgraded to a new part or software; and

    2) **Psychological Obsolescence**—wherein the design makes the product lose its fad even before it wears out such that it is no longer in trend and thus must be replaced by "weak" minds to fit in the crowd.

In his 1928 book titled "Propaganda" [20], American theorist Edward Bernays notes that capitalists are fully aware that mass production is only profitable when buttressed with ruthless advertising and propaganda so as to make demand the centerpiece of their golden goose:

> "Mass production is only profitable if its rhythm can be maintained—that is, if it can continue to sell its product in steady or increasing quantity. The result is that while, under the handicraft or small-unit system of production that was typical a century ago, demand created the supply, today supply must actively seek to create its corresponding demand. A single factory, potentially capable of supplying a whole continent with its particular product, cannot afford to wait until the public asks for its product; it must maintain constant touch, through advertising and propaganda, with the vast public in order to assure itself the continuous demand which alone will make its costly plant profitable."

In his 1931 book titled "Only yesterday" [21], American historian Frederick Allen reflects that capitalists are not afraid to use psychological tools such as indoctrination and intimidation to get the consumer hooked on anything and everything lest they risk becoming a pariah in their social orbit:

> "Business had learned as never before the immense importance to it of the ultimate consumer. Unless, he could be persuaded to buy and buy lavishly, the whole stream of six-cylinder cars, super-heterodynes, cigarettes, rouge compacts, and electric ice-boxes would be dammed at its outlet. The salesman and the advertising man held the key to this outlet. As competition increased, their methods became more strenuous. No longer

was it considered enough to recommend one's goods in modest and explicit terms and to place them on the counter in the hope that the ultimate consumer would make up his mind to purchase. The advertiser must plan elaborate national campaigns, consult with psychologists, and employ all the eloquence of poets to cajole, exhort, or intimidate the consumer into buying."

In his 1942 book titled "Capitalism, Socialism and Democracy" [22], Austro-American economist Joseph Schumpeter concludes that the capitalist engine is highly dynamic in that it is constantly on the hunt for introducing new technologies to consumers to make a killing at any cost:

> "Capitalism, then, is by nature a form or method of economic change and not only never is but never can be stationary. And this evolutionary character of the capitalist process is not merely due to the fact that economic life goes on in a social and natural environment which changes and by its change alters the data of economic action; this fact is important and these changes (wars, revolutions and so on) often condition industrial change, but they are not its prime movers. Nor is this evolutionary character due to a quasi-automatic increase in population and capital or to the vagaries of monetary systems of which exactly the same thing holds true. The fundamental impulse that sets and keeps the capitalist engine in motion comes from the new consumers' goods, the new methods of production or transportation, the new markets, the new forms of industrial organization that capitalist enterprise creates."

In the 1955 Journal of Retailing [23], American analyst Victor Lebow urges retailers to not only adopt product obsolescence but also indoctrinate consumers into believing that overconsumption is a means to an end and the holy grail of their ultimate place in society:

> "Our enormously productive economy demands that we make consumption our way of life, that we convert the buying and use of goods into rituals, that we seek our spiritual satisfactions, our ego satisfactions, in consumption. The measure of social status, of social acceptance, of prestige, is now to be found in our consumptive patterns. The very meaning and significance of our lives today expressed in consumptive terms. The greater the pressures upon the individual to conform to safe and accepted social standards, the more does he tend to express his aspirations and his individuality in terms of what he wears, drives, eats, his home, his car, his pattern of food serving, his hobbies. These commodities and services must be offered to the consumer with a special urgency. We

require not only forced-draft consumption, but expensive consumption as well. We need things consumed, burned up, worn out, replaced, and discarded at an ever-increasing pace. We need to have people eat, drink, dress, ride, live, with ever more complicated and, therefore, constantly more expensive consumption. The home-power tools and the whole do-it-yourself movement are excellent examples of expensive consumption."

Long story short, overconsumption driven by the capitalist propaganda lies at the heart of every societal problem today from our precarious health through relationships to being able to live a debt-free life without being enslaved.

Add to that the fact that capitalism is not only an affront to Mother Earth but it is also incompatible with a free and prosperous society.

In fact, the capitalist nations are built on a house of cards that will sooner or later collapse like their socialist counterparts before them.

In particular, neither capitalism nor socialism offers a viable solution to our societal problems that seemingly snowball into an 800-pound gorilla as the oqual cycle closes out.

This is due to the fact that both of these systems are essentially kleptocracies wherein the corrupt ruling elite enslaves the masses and exploits them to enrich themselves and their corporate cronies.

However, prior to the 18th Century Industrial Revolution that planted the seeds for the capitalist propaganda and overconsumption, humans for the most part lived in a perfect harmony with their alma mater in a relatively free and prosperous society with virtually no role of government in their lives.

In other words, every generation more or less lived in the footsteps of their forefathers with little or negligible change in technological improvements even over a span of centuries, thereby limiting their impact on the environment.

Contrast that with today's society where technology becomes obsolete by the day, if not by the hour, due to the capitalist drive to make profits at the expense of the destruction of the environment.

Such a feeding frenzy on technology-esque products unfolding at lightning speed is simply unsustainable in the long run.

Something has to break and, when it does, the society will pay a hefty price.

I should add that, during my childhood life in rural Pakistan (1971-1985), I experienced firsthand being part of a society not only living in a perfect harmony with their environment but where everyone was also raised to fend for themselves without any intervention from outside.

While that agrarian lifestyle may have deprived us of modern-day facilities such as electricity and running water, we nevertheless exercised so much freedom and spotless health—the envy of which sometimes makes me wonder whether it was worth transitioning to a capitalist lifestyle awash with lies, fraud, indoctrination, disease, and propaganda.

While I am not advocating for the return of humanity to an agrarian lifestyle by any stretch of the imagination, we can nevertheless kick the government out of our lives for human society would be much better off without being misled and exploited by kleptocrats.

Not only do government policies strip the masses of their ability to stand on their own feet so as to lead a life of dignity and respect but they also plunge them into a life of misery based on free handouts and social welfare.

In a nutshell, capitalism and environmental well-being are mutually exclusive.

Nor should anyone be surprised that it is primarily the capitalists who are championing the threat of global warming as a veneer to conceal their dirty practices so as to divert attention away from what amounts to nothing short of a Trojan horse for the environmental well-being.

And without the well-being of our planet, our lives will continue to be plunged into an ever-deepening canyon of sociopolitical chaos.

One indeed cannot have the cake and eat it too!

On a brighter note, today's consumption mania will crest around annus horribilis (2028) of the current oquannium (1955-2038) before it tapers off as the needs-wants equilibrium begins to shift to the left, particularly with the arrival of the next cycle (2039-2122) in over a decade or so.

One of the major drivers of such a pullback will be the horrible times befalling humanity over the next decade when survival will take precedence over feeding frenzy as the consumer economy turns into war economy.

As the saying goes, chickens ultimately come home to roost.

Today, we are indeed biting the bullet of our own making as we tread through dire sociopolitical straits in uncharted waters.

Our day of reckoning is inching ever closer for one cannot expect to reap roses after having planted thorns aplenty.

In 1758, at the dawn of Industrial Revolution and perhaps unaware of how it might come back to haunt humanity, Swedish naturalist Carl Linnaeus rather generously classified human beings as Homo sapiens (or prudent human).

Given that our bad table manners today would even leave hyenas in Serengeti and Masai Mara gasping for a breath of fresh air, the International Commission on Zoological Nomenclature perhaps ought to reconsider revoking that title and renaming us as Homo insapiens (or wicked human).

Should Homo insapiens be perceived to be politically incorrect, then perhaps other alternatives such as Homo destructivicus or even Homo consumericus would be just as befitting our disguised, albeit bona-fide social characteristics.

Still, all is not lost.

To rephrase an old saying, where there is a will there is a drill.

If good were to ever prevail over evil, then the following policies could be implemented to the delight of Mother Earth:

1) Penalize and revoke the license of corporations involved in the production of substandard goods that only create waste and hazard for the environment. Such a policy would serve as a double-whammy against overconsumption through not only reducing waste but also raising the cost of goods so as to discourage demand.

2) Promote awareness and benefits of living within one's means among the masses through social media and other channels in lieu of promoting the stigma of being left behind unless one keeps up with the Joneses.

3) Impose heavy taxes on social and business activities that contribute to waste and pollution such as driving and flying. The taxes raised from such measures could be used to clean up the environment.

4) Outlaw disposable (or single-use) products from cutlery through paper towels to shipping boxes.

5) Outlaw advertising that promotes demand for non-essential goods and services from electronics through cosmetics to globe-trotting.

6) Outlaw personal loans and revolving credit of all kinds other than what is absolutely essential such as a mortgage or a business loan. Consumers ought to put up or shut up for the sake of their own well-being.

While the implementation of such policies would constitute the first step toward restoring what little dignity remains of our planet, it would nevertheless drive a stake through the heart of capitalism.

And, you bet, capitalists will never let their golden goose die at least in the foreseeable future even if they themselves remain mortal.

While the capitalist propaganda will only get the Earth sicker, it cannot destroy it.

Rather, it is the Earth that has the potential to destroy humanity should it cross the red line.

Indeed, the longer the capitalist propaganda survives, the madder the Earth will get.

And, like a madman, the Earth could also do the unthinkable—unleash its own kryptonite in the form of once-in-a-millennium flood for instance that could sink humanity with no capitalist ark coming to the rescue.

It is therefore all the more important to not only take stock of our life now but also hop onto the unsinkable Noah's ark before it is too late.

|3.4| INSTITUTIONAL FRAUD

A couple of weeks leading up to my birth in 1971, my mother tells me that she had a premonition that it was going to be a boy.

How so?

According to her superstitious beliefs, the legend has it that the direction of the change in the price of gold leading up to labor can reveal the gender of the baby—a good news marked by a steady drop in the price of gold begets a girl while a bad news underscored by a steady rise regrets a boy.

And rise it did after the United States took the greenback off the gold standard barely weeks before I would arrive and, when I did, the bad news turned into a pandemonium with the price of yellow metal going through the sunroof just as my mother struggled to keep me waterproof.

No wonder the world has never been the same again ever since I set foot on earth some five decades ago.

Indeed, many pundits trace the roots of today's economic upheaval to 1971 when the dollar stopped being pegged to gold and sparked the beginning of today's era of fiat money—or paper currency whose value is solely derived from the trust in the government rather than from a tangible source such as gold.

However, fiat money per se is not an evil.

On the contrary, fiat money is a blessing-in-disguise in that it spares the earth from being wrecked due to gold mining—the demand for gold would skyrocket under a gold-denominated financial system such that nations would be at loggerheads for territorial control of far-flung polar regions and deeply-entrenched ocean beds driven by the greed to dig up the yellow metal, not to mention that they may even head for heavens in search of prospecting (or finding) gold where God had even forbidden not only Eve and Adam but also Sita and Ram.

Simply put, today's dire economic straits are largely a product of the abuse of fiat money primarily through printing—a vice that is akin to an addict being given an ever-increasing dose of heroin with deadly consequences.

Not only does printing reduce the value of money but it also fuels a rising wealth gap between the elite and the masses—particularly when the governments set about tearing apart regulatory oversights so as to help their cronies in the corporate world to capitalize on low-hanging fruit as the stage is set for them to get filthy rich at the expense of the working class.

While the first half of oqual cycle is under the thumb of extensive regulation so as to keep fraudulent activities at bay, widespread deregulation creeps in with the onset of the second half and the results are very predictable as we can see in plain sight today with one Ponzi after another falling apart.

In what I have dubbed the "fraud oquacycle", fraud in our society is oscillatory in that it ebbs and flows in sync with the oqual cycle.

While frauds occur throughout the course of oqual cycle, their frequency and intensity skyrocket during the second half.

For example, fraud has been on the rise since mid 1990s almost beginning in concurrence with the onset of the second half (1997-2038) of the current and seventh oquannium (1955-2038).

In fact, today's fraud drama has been playing out during the second half of every oqual cycle since the beginning of times.

Such a fraudulent culture has so far caused the popping of the 2000 Dotcom Bubble and the 2008 Financial Crisis.

With the gunk causing those two financial crises being allowed to metastasize rather than being flushed out of the system, another financial meltdown of epic proportions is already in the making today against the backdrop of rising costs of financing mountains of debt.

Since 2008, fraud has indeed been run amok to the hilt in the form of cryptos, non-fungible tokens (NFTs), special purpose acquisition companies (SPACs), and meme stocks—the stocks of virtually bankrupt and zombie companies heavily traded on the market and catapulted to the sky, merely due to their popularity on social media rather than their corporate fundamentals, only for them to come back crashing to earth and leaving fools holding the bag.

Such Ponzis not only propelled the stock markets but also the housing markets around the globe to become extremely frothy and bubblicious in 2021—a crash-of-a-lifetime is thus once again on the cards, and like the 1929 crash, it will also leave millions of fools-and-horses without clothes.

Regrettably, today's reckless behavior on the part of humanity is nothing short of signs of terrible times on the horizon threatening to upend the very fabric of society to which we have become accustomed to in our lives.

For example, the 1920s during the second half (1913-1954) of the previous and sixth oquannium (1871-1954) saw an exponential rise and spread of fraud—the widespread emergence of a paraphernalia of get-rich-quick and pump-and-dump schemes unleashed by the likes of fraudsters, swindlers, and con-artists whose concerted actions planted the seeds for the 1929 historic crash of the stock market that would subsequently lead to the Great Depression (1929-1939).

Some 84 years earlier, a similar story unfolded.

While the first half (1787-1828) of the fifth oquannium (1787-1870) saw the launch of railway transport across many parts of Europe and North America, the second half (1829-1870) provided an opportunity for the Ponzis to capitalize on its growing popularity across much of the Western world.

Notably, in what came to be known as the 1846 Railway Mania in the United Kingdom, fraudsters scammed millions of people of their life-savings through selling shares of bogus companies that would claim to build new railway lines even though they only existed on paper a la SPACs of today.

Such a fraudulent culture during the 19th century led to severe economic setbacks underscored by bank failures and evidenced by a series of financial crises such as the 1837 Panic, 1847 Panic, 1857 Panic, and 1866 Panic across much of the Western world.

Being in the midst of the second half (1997-2038) of the current oquannium (1955-2038), no one should therefore raise eyebrows that a similar drama of Ponzis is being played out once again in plain sight.

In disguise of the Oracle of Omaha Warren Buffett, only when the tide goes out does one get to see those who are skinny-dipping (or swimming naked).

As the oqual cycle draws to a close, the tide does indeed go out on such fraudsters and their accomplices leaving them humiliated and behind bars for good though this law is not applicable to big banks.

What are the causes of today's fraudulent culture?

ABOLISHMENT OF GOLD STANDARD OPENED UP THE FRAUD GATES AND LET THE GENIE OUT OF THE BOTTLE

The roots of today's fraudulent culture at almost every societal and institutional level can be traced all the way back to degoldification of the dollar under the watch of the then 37th POTUS Richard Nixon in 1971—when America literally defaulted on its golden currency as it could no longer honor the redemption of dollar notes upon the request of none other than its closest European allies and therefore was left with no choice but to take the greenback off the gold standard.

While such an ungodly move may come to be viewed as the straw that broke the financial system's back, it represented nothing more than the first step in a series of others that would follow leading up to annus turnilis (1997) of the current oquannium (1955-2038) just as human civilization was about to turn on its head and, together, they would set the stage for the socioeconomic bedlam that we find ourselves in today in line with the dire spell of the second half of oqual cycle.

After having been outlawed in 1934 in the wake of the 1929 Financial Crisis during the tenure of the then 32nd POTUS Franklin Roosevelt, the ban on stock buybacks was however lifted under the watch of the then 40th POTUS Ronald Reagan in 1982.

In doing away with such a regulatory oversight, Reagan ushered in an era of utter madness as the stock buybacks would enable the market to be manipulated once again for the benefit of the wealthy—such a wicked financial loophole represents nothing short of legalized fraud as discussed in detail in §5.4.

In the same year, Reagan also signed into law yet another deregulatory bill that would come to be called the "1982 Garn-St-Germain Depository Institutions Act"—a nefarious act that would not only remove the regulatory ceiling on the interest rate that the big banks could charge on commercial loans but it would also enable small banks (or thrift institutions primarily involved with making mortgage loans) to participate in such risky investments.

Against the backdrop of such a deregulatory framework, the bankers wasted no time in making not only highly speculative investments on real estate using customer deposits but also participated in fraudulent transactions through for example deliberately inflating asset prices.

However, sooner or later, fraud does fall apart.

And so when it did, it led to the intervention of US government and a massive taxpayer bailout of banks through what came to be known as the "1986 Savings and Loan (S&L) Crisis" that first came to light in 1986 but its aftershock would linger on until 1995.

Notably, the fraudulent culture that exacerbated the fallout from the 1986 S&L Crisis was epitomized by bankers such as Charles Keating whose dirty tricks were in no small part abetted by no other than the then little-known Wall Street economist Alan Greenspan in return for handsome monetary compensation.

With a direct line to the upper echelons in the US government and being a kingmaker to influence the appointments of hand-picked men in authoritative positions at what was then the Federal Home Loan Bank Board (FHLBB), Greenspan played a central role in removing regulatory constraints at FHLBB—an agency charged with setting the rules for mortgage loans issued by banking institutions as well as acting as a watchdog over their speculative and risky investments—thereby providing Keating with the much-needed lifeblood to perpetrate his fraud during the early 1980s.

While Keating headed to jail for his crimes, Greenspan's stock soared and spun on its head to land him in his boyhood dreamland.

Notwithstanding his hand in the 1986 S&L Crisis, one of the biggest heists up till then that would cost the US taxpayers more than $100B against the then backdrop of $1T annual tax revenue, Reagan would go onto appoint Greenspan of all banksters to head the Federal Reserve in 1987.

And with that master stroke, Reagan set America on the road to becoming a Wild West before he would leave office in 1989.

Indeed, barely months into Greenspan's tenure, much of the Western world would face Black Monday—an infamous day when major stock markets around the globe crashed by more than 20% in a single day on 1987/10/19.

An extremely rare crash that had never happened up till then nor has it ever happened since then in over 200 years of stock market history, the 1987 Black Monday could be described as a four-sigma event that on average happens once every hundred years or so.

However, barring the failure of so-called circuit breakers charged with halting transactional activity during the trading hours in the event of roughly a double-digit drop in the stock market, the 1987 Black Monday is unlikely to ever transpire again in our lifetime and perhaps never even over multiple lengths of human lifespan thanks to Greenspan.

Rather than letting the free market flush the gunk out of the stock market and the financial system in the aftermath of 1987 Black Monday, Greenspan would however develop a monetary vice that has come to called the "Fed put"—a reassurance provided to investors and bankers from the Federal Reserve (or Fed for short) to indulge in highly speculative and risky investments.

In the event that their reckless wager falls on its face as it often does, the Fed put will be put to action in a steadfast manner so as to come to the rescue through providing much-needed liquidity or a credit line.

In other words, the Fed will buy the junk assets from investors and bankers as if nothing had happened at the expense of ordinary US taxpayers.

No one should therefore be surprised as to why the masses today find themselves in dire financial straits given that they have been milked to the last drop by fraudulent government policies that have continued to ensure a constant flow of capital from the small wallets of the poor to the deep pockets of the wealthy over the past several decades.

Why would the Fed rescue investors and bankers at the expense of small fish?

The investors emboldened by the Fed put are often bed buddies and cronies of those working in the top ranks of US government—almost everyone running the US financial system today for example happens to be a product of Wall Street in one way or another and helping big banks get filthy rich is akin to an adult child returning the favors of their parents.

In fact, the success of Fed put to keep the markets afloat even in the face of bad investments significantly raised Greenspan's profile and his canny know-how deeply resonated with the ruling swamp so much so that he would remain at the helm of the Federal Reserve until 2006 with the blessings of the 41st, 42nd, and 43rd—the three US Presidents that followed Reagan.

Today, the Fed put has grown into an 800-pound gorilla such that market participants no longer pay heed to the fundaments of publicly-traded companies that they wish to invest in but rather to the monetary policies of the Federal Reserve.

Indeed, from buying junk assets (or bonds) through what is called "quantitative easing" coupled with suppression of interest rates irrespective of the demands of the free market, the Federal Reserve can pretty much make the stock market waltz in any direction it so wishes for the most part.

In fact, many investors today taking on ever more risk are driven by the misguided perception that with the Fed put having their back, the stock market could only go up, and should it dare drop, the Fed will come in to buoy it up right away.

Alas, such fools are either too young to pay heed to history or they must have poor memories given the dire fallout from the 2000 Dotcom Bubble and the 2008 Financial Crisis.

Did Fed's actions cause those two crises?

You bet! But, there is more to it than meets the eye!

BIG BANKS FUEL THE BUBBLE IN INTERNET STOCKS THROUGH THEIR FRAUDULENT PRACTICES

In order to up the ante on deregulation undertaken by Reagan a decade earlier coupled with Greenspan's trickery at his disposal, the 42nd POTUS Bill Clinton would bring aboard the American flagship two more banksters to deepen the bleeding of the US financial system.

In 1995, Clinton would appoint a former Goldman Sachs right-hand man Robert Rubin to head the Treasury Department.

In 1999, Rubin would be replaced by Larry Summers with even deeper ties to big banks from Goldman Sachs through JPMorgan Chase to Lehman Brothers.

Hold your breath, mesdames et messieurs!

Winters is yet to enter the foray!

Together with Greenspan, Rubin and Summers would positively cooperate during much of the 1990s to repeal the anti-fraud 1933 Glass-Steagall Act—a law enacted in the aftermath of the 1929 Financial Crisis that required commercial banks, dealing primarily with providing services to retail customers and small businesses, to steer clear of more riskier financial products such as corporate loans and insurance handled by investment banks lest there is a repeat of 1929.

Additionally, the 1933 Glass-Steagall Act also barred the merger of commercial banks with investment banks so as to prevent them from becoming financial monopolies with the potential to derail the financial system through the misguided motto: "Too big to fail!".

In 1999, under Clinton's watch, the concerted efforts of all three former Wall Street banksters would finally drill a nail through the silky-milky coffin of the 1933 Glass-Steagall Act.

In doing so, the trio would deliver a long sought-after windfall for their former Wall Street employers and donors alike and, for their part in the heist, they would be showered with kickbacks to the tune of megadollars.

With the pro-fraud 1999 Gramm-Leach-Bliley Act having now superseded the anti-fraud 1933 Glass-Steagall Act, the commercial banks a la their big cousins investment banks were finally unshackled to join forces and go on the hunt for every speculative investment big and small that bore stunning echoes of one of my favorite Punjabi proverbs:

> "Annay kutay harnaan de shikaari!" — "Blind dogs do not see the irony in making a vow to hunt down the deer!"

Good luck with that!

But, the luck would soon run out for the big banks with the popping of what came to be called the 2000 Dotcom Bubble.

Driven by greed and hubris against the backdrop of newly-approved deregulatory environment that they had never thought would ever become a reality, the big banks played an outsized role in orchestrating that financial crisis by virtue of their power to fuel a massive bubble in internet stocks through promotion and hyping-up the valuation of anyone who had the guts to add the dotcom suffix to their brand before going public through what is called "Initial Public Offering (IPO)" even though the bankers knew from the get-go that most IPOs would go bust before too long.

By 2002, such a fraudulent practice by the bankers would shave more than $5T off the stock market capitalization and leave millions destitute.

Yet, the Securities and Exchange Commission (SEC)—founded in 1934 in the aftermath of the 1929 Financial Crisis and charged with the authority to provide an oversight as well as rein in speculation and manipulation of the securities being exchanged on the stock market—would simply turn a blind eye to the fraudulent behavior of big banks in fueling the 2000 Dotcom Bubble.

And, sorry, no points for guessing why.

The head of SEC was no other than Wall Street's own former fraudigy Arthur Levitt who apparently saw nothing wrong with speculative and manipulative practices of big banks contributing to the 2000 Dotcom Bubble.

In Levitt's defense, however, filing charges against the big banks would have been akin to biting the hand that once used to feed him.

Ouch! That must surely hurt.

Alas, Levitt shared no empathy with the masses who got sucked into the fraud and ended up not only taking a bath but also losing their shirt and pants.

In addition to the big banks, the Fed under the tutelage of Greenspan also had a big hand in first nourishing the 2000 Dotcom Bubble and then pulling the plug.

In 1999, the Fed's lose monetary policy pumped gigadollars into the financial system such that the excess liquidity encouraged a feeding frenzy on internet stocks by investors and bankers alike.

In 2000, barely a year later, the Fed would rapidly hike the interest rates, thereby raising the cost of financing the speculative behavior in internet stocks and causing the bubble to pop.

Simply put, the Fed's actions are akin to a double-edged sword for the market in that the "Fed put" buoying up the stocks can also quickly turn into "Fed call" pricking them and bringing them down to earth.

What exactly are Fed put and Fed call?

The Fed's "put" and "call" are financial jargons borrowed from ultra-complex and ultra-risky derivative trading (or options trading).

These two instruments enable the Fed to manipulate the free market through both monetary liquidity and interest rates.

In terms of monetary liquidity:
   1) The "put" option implies that the Fed will purchase an asset from investors when it turns sour no matter what, thereby providing an insurance of sorts and injecting liquidity into the financial system; and
   2) The "call" option does the exact opposite in that the Fed will offload an asset back to investors thereby reducing liquidity in the financial system.

In terms of interest rates:
   1) The "put" option implies that the Fed will cut the interest rates to make financing cheaper for investors so as to enable them to take on even riskier investments; and
   2) The "call" option does the exact opposite in that the Fed will raise the interest rates, thereby hiking the cost of financing and causing many investors to pee in their pants as the reality that they may no longer be

able to meet their financial obligations due to being overleveraged (or overburdened with debt) dawns upon them.

While the Fed put pumps up financial assets creating a bubble, the Fed call pricks the bubble and lets the air out.

Importantly, there is no obligation on the part of the Fed to exercise the "put" option but it often does so to meet the expectations of investors and, in particular, its cronies on Wall Street—who are fervently led to believe that the Fed has their back and it does for the most part.

However, such a conviction can fall on its face when the Fed is left with no choice but to exercise the "call" option to curtail irrational exuberance threatening to upend the financial system.

With the two options at its disposal, the Fed's actions over the past several decades have essentially amounted to baiting the suckers into the fraud by advertising a free lunch for all through the "put" option and then quickly switching it with an expensive menu that no one could afford through the "call" option.

Such manipulation of the free market on the part of the Fed is evidence that the US financial system is rigged to the core that only benefits the wealthy and those with close ties to the ruling elite.

Indeed, after pricking the 2000 Dotcom Bubble with interest rate hikes, the Fed would quickly turn on its head and drop them dead.

By 2003, the interest rates would almost begin to flirt with zero.

It seems almost surreal not to have seen what would be coming next given the backdrop of historically low interest rates coupled with deregulations having turned the Wall Street into a financial Wild West.

Enter the 2008 Financial Crisis.

BIG BANKS BRING THE FINANCIAL SYSTEM DOWN TO ITS KNEES THROUGH THEIR FRAUDULENT BEHAVIOR

In the good old days during much of the first half (1955-1996) of the current oquannium (1955-2038), commercial banks that provided mortgage to potential homebuyers would have a skin in the game in that they would be lending their own money largely amassed through the deposits of retail customers and small businesses with a direct accountability should anything go wrong.

Accordingly, the commercial banks were incentivized to thoroughly vet the borrowers and only approve those with a worthy credit lest they risked losing their investment and going underwater.

However, against the backdrop of deregulatory windfall that would begin to engulf the US financial system during the 1990s particularly after the introduction of the pro-fraud 1999 Gramm-Leach-Bliley Act almost in parallel with the onset of the second half (1997-2038) of the current oquannium (1955-2038), the investment banks in conjunction with commercial banks began to create a new mortgage pig dubbed "collateral debt obligation (CDO)" such that all the risk would be passed onto investors all over the world with the big banks left to splurge on easy pickings with the sky being the limit for the potential for profits.

In a manner that a derivative derives its value from another function in calculus, the CDOs were essentially the derivative financial products in that their value was based on one or more underlying assets such as a property or vehicle.

Given that the apparent value of such financial derivatives can be easily manipulated either directly through overstating the price of the underlying assets or indirectly through perturbing the demand-supply equilibrium to the left, the CDOs were therefore equivalent to ultra-risky time bombs that were guaranteed to implode sooner or later.

Add to that the cunning marketing approach undertaken by big banks to prey upon unsuspecting investors through promoting CDOs as if they were a cousin of their fixed-income CDs (or certificate of deposits).

How exactly did CDOs operate?

In a nutshell, the CDOs during the late 1990s and early 2000s played out as follows:
1) The commercial banks would approve the mortgage for potential homeowners as they had always done so but with no skin in the game as they would immediately pass the loan onto investment banks for a handsome premium.
2) The investment banks would turn the mortgage into a high-yielding CDO pig with mouthwatering returns compared to government bonds against the backdrop of what were then historically-low interest rates thanks to the Fed.

3) After paying the rating agencies humongous kickbacks to ensure that they not only put extra lipstick but also mascara aplenty on the CDO pig so as to make it highly attractive and enticing with a AAA-rating before marrying it off to unsuspecting but greedy investors, typically through pension and retirement funds, in return for hefty management fees.

4) For their part, the investors would be left licking their fingers after being reassured that their gorgeous and voluptuous CDO pig was collateralized by tangible assets such as a property and that it would be as secure as a traditional wife.

5) As the homeowners made their monthly mortgage payments to the commercial bank from where they had applied for the loan, the funds collected would be funneled through the investment bank all the way back to the finger-licking investors.

Fingers they would indeed lick during much of the 1990s as CDOs were being streamlined to make them appear as a genuine financial product using credit-worthy homeowners as guinea pigs with little or no risk of default.

However, the honeymoon would not last long for the investors.

In order to make a killing on their golden goose that paid handsomely with zero risk to the big banks, the CDOs would begin to be democratized among the masses irrespective of their ability to make monthly mortgage payments as it would be the investors left holding the bag instead of the bankers should anything blow up.

How could such a daylight fraud have unfolded as it did?

Where were the federal regulators?

To help the big banks achieve their fraudulent pursuits, their own reliable quartet of Greenspan, Rubin, Summers, and Levitt would be called upon to make sure that there would be no regulatory oversight from the US government getting in their way of making a killing like never before.

And the faithful quartet would quickly oblige as it set about indoctrinating anyone and everyone within the relevant ranks of the US government that it was time that every American had a home no matter what their income.

Before too long, such propertyganda would come to be spearheaded by no other than the 43rd POTUS George Bush as he made doing the bidding on behalf of his Wall Street donors a cornerstone of his presidency.

In 2002, Bushito buttered unsuspecting Americans up as to why it was necessary that they all owned a home:

> "And part of economic security is owning your own home. Part of being a secure America is to encourage homeownership. So somebody can say, this is my home, welcome to my home. Now, we've got a problem here in America that we have to address. Too many American families, too many minorities do not own a home. There is a home ownership gap in America."

Yeah right, welcome to my home!

I cannot even afford to pay my bills, much less a down payment!

No problema! Pobrecito Bushito had a bonito solutionito!

In 2003, Bushito reasoned that being unable to make the down payment should never be the reason not to realize the American Dream:

> "One of the biggest hurdles to homeownership is getting money for a down payment. This administration has recognized that, and so today I'm honored to be here to sign a law that will help many low-income buyers to overcome that hurdle, and to achieve an important part of the American Dream."

With Bushito promoting their gambit, the big banks would unleash the full gamut of their fraudulent CDOs onto unsuspecting Americans with little or no credit history nor down payment through what came to be called the "subprime mortgage"—a truly shocking venture by Wall Street vultures given that many Americans were unable to make their ends meet, much less being in a position to make the hefty monthly mortgage payments.

Having been given free rein to operate however they wished, the bankers would soon turn CDOs into a second derivative financial product called "credit default swap (CDS)"—whereas the CDO derived its value from an underlying asset such as a property, the CDS did so from the CDO itself.

With CDS rigs sheltering risks multiples greater than CDO pigs, they would nevertheless become quite popular among greedy investors in that they could trade a CDS as an insurance on a CDO irrespective of whether they owned the latter product or not—thus a single CDO could have multiple investors buying a CDS on it in the hope that should it blow up, they would profit handsomely.

This scenario is akin to multiple parties buying insurance on a single home suspected of sitting on a sinkhole or in the path of a tornado—should the home disappear during the course of the insured period, all insuring parties would have a laugh but they would all cry if it survived.

And, lo siento mucho, I am really short on points so just one point for guessing who made up the bulk of investors buying the CDS rigs.

Being fully aware of the fact that their CDO pigs were a ticking time bomb, the big banks rushed to snap up CDS rigs as an insurance as soon as they could get their hands on them.

That is akin to a property owner selling their home sitting on a sinkhole, with tell-tale signs beginning to appear, to unsuspecting buyers at an inflated price without even disclosing the risks beforehand and then immediately buying a wager on the same house that it would not see the year out.

That is a gigafraud.

And so were CDO pigs and CDS rigs.

Powered by such golden gooses on steroids, the bankers in charge of issuing CDO pigs and CDS rigs to customers would be incentivized to roll out as many parcels as they could since their salaries and bonuses were directly linked to their performance.

As the demand for CDO pigs and CDS rigs skyrocketed in the wake of Bushganda, the shrinking home supply would send the property prices through the roof as they would double over the decade centered on 2000.

With home prices having gone parabolic, the bankers could not believe their luck as higher valuations led to higher salaries and bonuses with top performers taking decamillions home annually against the backdrop of a median salary in the decathousands.

With ever more to scavenge in what had truly become a Wild West, it seemed as if the vulture party would never end but it always does.

Since monthly mortgage payments on CDOs were linked to the prevailing interest rates in most cases through what is called the "adjustable rate mortgage (ARM)", it seems that perhaps nobody had figured out what would happen in the event that they went up.

And up they would go before too long.

Although the Fed had begun to raise interest rates in a meaningful way from around 2005 onward in order to rein in the spike in home prices, the bankers would nevertheless keep their foot on the gas paddle rather than prepare themselves for the storm ahead.

Perhaps, the bankers were convinced that with their own boy Greenspan still at the helm in the Federal Reserve, their subprime Titanic would be unsinkable.

However, sensing that the ageing Greenspan being on the verge of entering his ninth decade may not be able to handle the looming blizzard and with the trio of Rubin-Summers-and-Levitt having long left Washington after delivering the goods, the bankers quickly began to prepare for a hard landing and braced themselves for damage control through getting two key appointments before all hell would break lose.

In early 2006, under Bushito's watch, Ben Bernanke with close ties to Wall Street would replace Greenspan almost three decades senior to him at the Federal Reserve.

In mid 2006, also under Bushito's watch, Henry Paulsen who had served as CEO of Goldman Sachs since 1999 and had played a pioneering role in democratizing CDOs among the masses would take the helm at the Treasury Department.

You get the picture!

The man who had a hand in perpetrating the subprime fraud was now being appointed to head the US financial system just before the Ponzi would unfold.

With Bush having turned into push and push having come to shove in the face of home prices continuing to defy gravity, the Fed now helmed by Bernanke would keep hiking the interest rates well into 2007.

Before too long, the monthly mortgage payments would begin to bloat for the homeowners as they were a function of the interest rate through the ARM.

With many Americans already behind on their original commitments, the bloating payments would soon begin to cost the homeowners an ARM and a leg as many were left with no choice but to default on their mortgage.

As monthly mortgage payments started to dry up one after the other, the CDO pigs and CDS rigs also began to go up in smoke one after the other.

In 2008, the resulting panic on Wall Street would begin to crash the stock market sending the broader financial system into a tailspin with one bad news after another acting as a positive feedback loop to fuel a vicious cycle of pandemonium that would enter the annals of history as the 2008 Financial Crisis.

Did the big banks face the music for their white-collar crime or did they get away with the murder?

Ladies and gentlemen, if you are just tuning in from outside the United States, welcome to the fraud capital of the world where fraudsters are not only given free rein to make a killing at the expense of the masses but they also get a pat on the back for their heist.

BIG BANKS GET A SLAP ON THE WRIST BEFORE BEING GIVEN A PAT ON THE BACK TO KEEP UP THE DIRTY WORK

The blowup of subprime mortgage had a domino effect on the broader financial system in the wake of the 2008 Financial Crisis.

Not only had the big banks gambled on subprime mortgage but they had also been heavily betting on other financial products through derivative trading with borrowed money.

In the face of being overleveraged through such super-risky investments and unable to meet their financial obligations as the subprime mortgages began to go up in smoke, many banks such as Lehman Brothers without sympathizers in Washington would be forced to declare bankruptcy.

However, many others such as Goldman Sachs with their own boys Paulsen and Bernanke in charge of the nation's purse strings would be bailed out to the tune of $700B at the expense of US taxpayers.

As for homeowners, millions would lose their American Dream and their livelihoods thanks to being misled by no other than the man for whom many had voted to lead the nation's highest office not once but twice.

As the saying goes, one reaps what they plant!

And as America goes, the only bush one must trust is their own!

Millions of others lost much of their retirement savings and nest eggs thanks to nearly $8T having been wiped off the US stock market by the time the crisis hit a nadir in 2009.

Although Wall Street was the epicenter, the echoes of the 2008 Financial Crisis would nevertheless reverberate across much of the world due to the global financial system being closely inter-linked.

Leading up to the 2008 US Presidential Election against the backdrop of such global financial upheaval, the then US Presidential nominee Barack Obama made a covenant with his cacophonous supporters that he would rein in the greed on Wall Street but, in all sincerity, his powerful rhetoric merely served to hypnotize the masses in order to capitalize on the waning voter sentiment in the establishment as he must have damn well known that one cannot bite the hand that feeds them.

Indeed, after taking the helm in early 2009, Hussein would hasten and deepen the ties between Pennsylvania Avenue and Wall Street through new appointments and reappointments of even more Wall Street banksters who had brought the global financial system into disrepute barely a year earlier.

In fact, Obama's drama would turn Dalai Lama on his head when the Tibetan spiritual leader learned that not only Summers but also Winters, the men who had brought America down to its knees through crafting what was up till then the biggest heist in American history, were now being appointed as Barack's economic advisors.

In Semitic languages such as Hebrew and Arabic, Barack (also spelled Barak) literally means "blessing".

Alas, Obama's rise to power signaled the precipitous decline of Barack-a-Allah (or Allah's blessing) on America.

Indeed, the nation hit Barack-o-bottom against the backdrop of the pendulum of justice having swung too far to the wrong side before Obama would leave office eight years later in 2017.

For starters, hardly any CEO had their feet held to the fire.

Nor would there be any penalty for such fraudsters.

Notwithstanding the sheer magnitude of the fraud committed by big banks, not a single CEO of an American banking institution was ever put behind bars for having developed what were nothing short of weapons of financial destruction.

By contrast, the 1986 S&L Crisis led to imprisonment of more than 1000 bankers even though it was only a shadow of the 2008 Financial Crisis.

Such contrasting outcomes were due to the fact that while the legislative authorities are largely devoid of fraud during the first half of oqual cycle, they themselves become increasingly embroiled and compromised by the wealthy with the onset of the second half.

Admittedly, for the most part, the 1980s and 1990s oversaw relatively happy times when the public trust in institutions was respectable compared to today when the same institutions have become the butt of all jokes and have lost all credibility.

Had all culpable CEOs faced the music in lieu of being slapped on the wrist for their egregious role in precipitating the 2008 Financial Crisis, the resulting shockwaves would have served to dent further growth of fraudulent activities on Wall Street, not to mention that such punishment would have also served to deter the rise of new Ponzis.

Rather, the lack of accountability for banksters created a fertile ground for a new generation of wannabe-fraudsters who since then have planted an ever-growing list of Ponzis before hyping them up to the hilt so as to defraud millions time and again.

No one should therefore be aghast that today's fraudulent culture makes the 2008 Financial Crisis look like a stroll in the park just as the latter made the 1986 S&L Crisis look like a child's play.

In fact, since the repeal of the anti-fraud 1933 Glass-Steagall Act in 1999, the big banks have been caught defrauding customers, laundering money, and cooking their books time and again without any serious penalties as if they are above the rule of law, which they are for all intents and purposes.

Being close relatives of Uncle Sam, that should hardly raise eyebrows, much less eyelashes.

Given such enormity of financial wrongdoings, our day of reckoning over the next decade or so will be equally enormous and painful for all wrongs are eventually neutralized by the laws of nature as the pendulum of justice swings back to the right side.

In a nutshell, the most straightforward conclusion that one can draw from the subprime mortgage blowup is that the Wall Street bankers were playing Russian roulette with other people's money.

Not only were the CEOs fully complicit and privy to this fraud but, driven by greed and hubris, they were egging it on with full force.

In fact, the excesses and imbalances of Wall Street amounted to a crime of the highest degree in that their wager uprooted the lives of decamillions, sent millions into depression, and condemned thousands to suicide in the United States alone.

Still, prevention is better than cure.

And the Fed had the medicine to do exactly that but it terribly failed to do so.

In no uncertain terms, the Fed played a central role in creating an environment ideally suited for the subprime fraud to flourish during the Noughties (2000s).

Without the Fed being dragooned by Wall Street cronies to drop and keep the interest rates Barack-o-bottom in the years that followed the popping of the 2000 Dotcom Bubble, it would have been impossible for the bankers to have pulled off the subprime fraud in that the higher interest rates would have been to the development of CDOs what garlic and sunlight are to the survival of vampires.

Why do low interest rates fuel fraud?

By keeping the interest rates super low over the past quarter of a century coupled with pumping teradollars into the financial system, the Fed would not only increase money supply but also lower the cost of financing the debt such that even an average Raja and Rani became emboldened to set up zombie startups on dirt cheap money and then hype up their bogus technology to lure fools and horses into their fraud.

In marked contrast, under an environment of higher interest rates, only genuine and profitable enterprises can afford to finance their new operations through borrowed money, thereby keeping fraud at bay for all intents and purposes.

Given that they generate no cash flow and continue to borrow money or raise funds to finance their old debts in a vicious cycle, the zombie companies also suck resources away from genuine enterprises.

Indeed, low interest rates are detrimental to the financial health of genuine enterprises in that they are forced to spend heavily to ward off the hyped-up competition and threat from zombie companies rather than channeling their precious resources toward innovation and investment.

In fact, today's financial culture is multiples more fraudulent than what transpired nearly two decades ago.

Neither the Fed nor anyone else in Washington learned anything from the 2008 Financial Crisis.

Rather than flushing out the gunk from the financial system, Washington has been on a mission to breed it to new heights through ever more lax oversights under the watch of every clown elected to the nation's highest office since 2000.

One wonders how the likes of Bushito, Obamito, Trumpito, and Bidenito can even sleep at night knowing too well that POTUS is nothing more than a symbolic figurehead used as a cog (or pawn) by the wealthy to drive their capitalist machine (or chess) and that their actions amounted to nothing short of a treasonous act committed against America and its people.

As for Americans who voted to have such disgraceful souls head the nation, they have quite a lot of soul searching to do themselves.

Given that a nation's leaders are only as good as its people, one must not hastily put the leaders on trial but rather the electorate for their poor judgement and being a party to the crisis befalling them.

Long story short, the US financial system is nothing more than a house of cards that is set to implode some time between annus horribilis (2028) of the current oquannium (1955-2038) and annus mirabilis (2039) of the next cycle (2039-2122) so as to purge the society of fraud in order to acquiesce to a new dawn without the baggage.

And when the US financial system does finally implode over the next decade or so, it will send shockwaves throughout the global economy as it wipes off the savings and livelihoods of the masses with the wealthy and elite having the last laugh as always.

To say that the 2008 Financial Crisis was a dress rehearsal for what is lurking on the financial horizon would be a huge understatement.

In 2006, prior to his confirmation by no other than the US Senate to helm the Treasury Department, Bushito sheepishly vouched for the nomination of Paulsen:

> "I'm pleased to announce that I will nominate Henry Paulson to be the Secretary of the Treasury. The past eight years, Hank has served as Chairman and Chief Executive Officer of the Goldman Sachs Group. It's one of the most respected firms on Wall Street. He has a lifetime of business experience; he has an intimate knowledge of financial markets and an ability to explain economic issues in clear terms. He's earned a reputation for candor and integrity. And when he is confirmed by the Senate, he'll be a superb addition to my Cabinet."

Given that a bank that had orchestrated one of the biggest frauds in the nation's history was being eulogized as "respected" and its CEO as a man of "candor and integrity" by no other than a POTUS, the fraudulent culture on American soil had been officially democratized with the US government's seal of approval and it would come to haunt the nation over the decades that followed.

And haunt it did.

In 2008, subprime mortgage was one of only a handful of frauds being cooked.

Today, there is a fraud everywhere one looks as evidenced by one bogus company after another going belly up every other week or so, not to mention that almost every report from inflation to employment being released by the US government on the nation's health is fraudulent and misleading.

Add to that the likes of Ponzis such as cryptos, meme stocks, NFTs, and SPACs having been democratized among the masses.

Why is crypto a fraud?

CRYPTO IS THE GRANDMOTHER OF ALL PONZI SCHEMES

Throughout modern times, fraudsters have tried to privatize (or decentralize) the currency but to have never availed.

Nevertheless, they did fulfill their intended goal of defrauding millions of fools through their scams each time.

Alas, the fools never pay heed to history for bona-fide currency has been and will always remain an exclusive tool of the state (or government) due to the fact that it must satisfy the following four criteria:

        1) unique and only of its kind;
        2) tightly regulated by a central authority;
        3) guaranteed by the state; and
        4) backed by a powerful military.

Since a private enterprise vying to run its own currency lacks all of these four features, it is inherently running a scam not a currency.

Never in the history of human civilization, a purported currency that lacked even one of the above-noted characteristics has ever gained widespread traction.

Admittedly, if the US dollar had not been backed by the world's most powerful military, it would have never become the world's reserve currency thanks to the 1944 Bretton-Woods Agreement—and, if it ever did, it would have long been ditched by most nations in favor of other more amenable alternatives.

One only has to look at the dire plight of the Organization of the Petroleum Exporting Countries (OPEC) such as Iran, Iraq, Libya, and Venezuela to see that the proof of my proclamation lies in the oily pudding.

In 1971, after Nixon took the greenback off the gold standard, Uncle Sam held a gun to OPEC's head and twisted the arm of its de-facto leader Saudi Arabia to have the dollar petrolized so as to beef up its demand as it began to plummet in the face of having become nothing more than a worthless piece of paper.

In what since then came to be known as the "petrodollar", the OPEC nations have been compelled to trade their oil and gas exclusively in dollar.

Any nation that were to go astray against such a hegemonic decree was not only to earn the wrath of Uncle Sam but would also risk becoming razed to the ground and turned into a pariah state.

While the likes of Iran and Venezuela were somewhat fortunate to evade the full force of Uncle Sam's military mania after they proposed to trade oil with other nations in non-dollar currencies such as the Euro at the outset of 21st century, others such as Iraq and Libya were brutally crushed into pieces.

Although the US dollar may not be backed by the yellow metal, it is nevertheless guaranteed by a precious commodity—the misleading notion peddled by many goldbugs that the greenback is a worthless piece of paper is therefore ill-founded in that it is definitely a petrodollar if not orodollar.

Alas, the days of petrodollar are numbered as more and more oil-producing nations have begun to trade their commodity in non-dollar currencies today.

Additionally, most nations today are not only mired in unsustainable level of dollar-denominated debt but they are also heading for bankruptcy over the next decade or so—a feat that would further tank the demand for the greenback.

And then Uncle Sam's cunning ploy to weaponize the dollar through economic sanctions against nations that it sees as hostile to its hegemonic interests only serves to damage the global standing of the greenback as a reliable source of international currency.

Being deeply-overleveraged itself with an exponentially-bloating debt also complicates the spider's web from which America would find it increasingly difficult to untangle and save the dollar.

That spells trouble for the dollar to continue to be the king of the world beyond the current decade.

Notably, dollar hegemony officially began with the Bretton-Woods Agreement during annus horribilis (1944) of the previous oquannium (1871-1954).

In line with the recurring spell of oqual cycle, the dollar hegemony will likely end some time between annus horribilis (2028) of the current oquannium (1955-2038) and annus mirabilis (2039) of the next cycle (2139-2122).

For now though, oil-producing nations must walk a tightrope and continue to honor the petrodollar lest they run afoul of Uncle Sam and risk becoming Iraqestroyed.

Does blockchain technology not set crypto apart from other currencies?

The footprint (or sales pitch) and the blueprint (or source code) behind crypto as an alternative and superior form of currency is damning to begin with.

Unlike the state-backed currency (or fiat money), an average Jay with basic computing skills can mint and launch their own crypto from the comfort of their cubicle with the potential to become a millionaire overnight.

Surely, the money does not fall from the trees unless it is in the form of crypto.

It is therefore hardly surprising that since its fraudulent inception in 2008 in the midst of the Great Recession (2007-2009), crypto has today snowballed into more than 20K tokens worldwide with thousands of new tidbits launched every year.

If that does not smell fraud, then one has no sense of fraud.

While the crypto fraud has been fittingly outlawed in many countries, there are other nations who have on the contrary provided it with a much-needed lifeblood and legitimacy in a last-ditch effort to keep their heavily debt-laden ships from running aground.

Alas, no matter how much lipstick one puts on a pig, it will still be a pig.

Indeed, a vast majority of crypto tokens have already failed with many having skyrocketed to a market capitalization of gigadollars within months of having gone public before spectacularly crashing to zero and becoming worthless within days of flirting with the heavens.

Since no good is produced nor any service is exchanged, the exponential rise in the market value of a crypto token exclusively results via a zero-sum game—fools pump up the crypto value until there are no fools left when the big whales take their chips off the table after getting filthy-rich and, in doing so, trigger the crash leaving the fools not only holding the bag but also facing the music.

In spite of such a casino unfurled in plain sight time and again, the cryptocons have nevertheless continued to gaslight newer recruits so as to entangle them into their spider's web of sorts through injecting fears of inflationary nature of fiat money when the crypto itself represents the mother of all things inflationary.

Such scary tactics along with flattering language are a hallmark of a fraud that should immediately set off alarm bells.

Alas, fools are renowned to have ears with which they hear not, eyes with which they see not, and minds with which they think not.

Surprisingly, it is not just the younger generations who are yet to get their feet wet in the real world that make up today's fools but even accomplished individuals from seasoned pundits through university professors to Nobel laureates appear to have also succumbed to the cryptoscam.

To rephrase an old saying, a genius easily parts with their money!

History attests to the fact that not only are such geniuses immune from getting sucked into frauds but the success of many Ponzi schemes can often be traced to one or more genius having acted as a protagonist to add a layer of legitimacy to the scam from its very beginnings.

Perhaps, the most notable example of how geniuses can and often fall prey to herd mentality is lent by the misfortune befalling Isaac Newton (1643-1727).

In 1720, with an apple of experience behind him at the age of 77, Newton nevertheless got caught up in the then feeding frenzy in stocks and set about aggressively buying shares into the South Sea Company with his life-savings just as its stock turned parabolic defying gravity as it did only to come back crashing down to earth months later and, in doing so, leaving the greatest-of-all-greats to have ever set foot on earth all but destitute.

Pobrecito Newtonito—Poor Little Newton!

In the aftermath of having parted with his fortune, Newton is alleged to have said that while he could easily calculate the motion of planets, he was clueless on how to mathematically model the irrational behavior of the crowd.

While Newton's life undoubtedly left an indelible mark on human civilization for its mammoth contributions to our knowledge of the universe and how it shaped future generations of scientists, his death would also leave us with a clue after he took his last breath at the age of 84 in 1727.

Newton would perhaps have the last laugh when he learns via social media or through other backchannels that it took people back on earth almost three centuries to figure out that his remarkable journey of life spanned exactly one full turn of oqual cycle.

What a nature's fitting tribute to a uniquely-gifted genius for Newton lived neither a year less nor a year more than what appears to be our allotted time on earth.

Newton could also take heart from the fact that his South Sea debacle was perhaps not as mind-shattering as that of a recently-minted Nobel laureate.

While driving on his way back home with his wife after picking up the Nobel prize, the laureate pulls up at a gas station—then after refueling and paying his bill, he is somewhat taken aback as he returns to his vehicle and helplessly watches his wife being on cloud nine while she is being chatted up by a hippie standing outside the passenger side of the front window.

Being a laureate, he keeps his noble charm but as they drive off, his macho instincts kick in when all of a sudden he lets his heart-wrenching agony out: "Honey, who was that crackpot you were all smiles with?"

She chuckles patronizingly: "Darling, he was my high-school sweetheart before I married you."

While giggling, he consoles her: "Well, geez, you did not marry him lest you would have also ended up like that."

She counters acrimoniously: "What do you mean? Had I married him, he would have won the Nobel prize!"

Long story short, even Nobel laureates can sometimes miss the forest for the trees!

All told, those without a sixth sense should understand that investment products marketed by pundits, celebrities, and geniuses are inherently frauds by their very nature—it pays dearly to keep pockets off such Ponzi schemes and mitigate the temptation to become sucked into them due to greed, herd behavior, or confirmation bias.

On the contrary, genuine enterprises a la Microsoft, Apple, Amazon, and Google not only had rather humble beginnings but they were also spearheaded by none other than the likes of college dropouts and entrepreneurs little known beyond their neck-of-the-woods.

When it comes to investing, one should focus on the horse not the jockey!

When will crypto fraud fall on its face?

The 1720 South Sea Bubble along with the 1637 Tulip Mania have hitherto been ranked as two of the biggest Ponzi schemes ever unfurled on earth.

Today, however, the cryptoscam has unarguably and undoubtedly become the grandmother of all Ponzi schemes in that it is not only head-and-shoulders but also chest-and-waist above anything that humanity has ever witnessed thanks to the exponential marketing power of social media in that it can quickly magnify the capture radius of potential fools and their savings.

Notwithstanding such ominous warnings, cryptophiles continue to stick their head in the proverbial sand—which is perhaps not at all surprising given that when one surrounds themselves with like-minded individuals whose biased views reinforce your own, then it becomes increasingly difficult to untangle from what psychologists refer to as the "confirmation bias".

Consistent with this psychological trap, crypto lovers continue to naively argue that what makes crypto so special is that it is independent of state interference by virtue of its inherent ability to operate out of the blockchain network—a decentralized and unregulated computer infrastructure accessible to any interested party.

On the contrary, little such fools understand that the lack of a watchdog (or an oversight) for the decentralized finance (DeFi) courtesy of the blockchain network is in fact crypto's biggest Achilles' heel.

Admittedly, as hard as it is for an individual to trust their money with a state-regulated institution such as a bank, it is utterly mind-boggling how one can depend on a mysterious network of computers scattered across the globe running on a poorly-codified and bug-prone infrastructure that can be potentially exploited by unscrupulous actors without borders.

If such a cryptic scheme where no one can be traced for a misconduct does not smell fraud, then there ain't such a thing as a fraud.

It should therefore come as a no surprise that the cryptos are extremely prone to being hacked where one's nest egg can be potentially stolen with a few clicks.

Indeed, billions-of-dollars have hitherto been embezzled in a perpetual string of crypto heists before it even managed to hatch out of its shell.

And billions more have been scammed through a slew of crypto platforms having already gone belly up due to their fraudulent practices that amounted to nothing short of a daylight robbery.

To add salt to wounds, that is just the tip of the crypto iceberg as many more bogus companies are on course to declare bankruptcies over the next couple of years-or-so as the cryptomania comes crashing down to earth.

Yet, cryptomaniacs do not shy away from ingenuously proclaiming that the cryptos are already being used as a currency—the nerds fail to even understand what a currency really is.

Unlike fiat currencies such as the dollar that can be directly used to pay for goods and services, the cryptos represent nothing more than tokens that must first be converted to a fiat currency prior to conducting a monetary transaction.

The lack of a watchdog coupled with a mysterious network apart, the hypervolatile nature of cryptos also renders them practically useless as a form of currency—a feature not lost upon merchants and payment processors who although provide gateways to convert crypto tokens into a fiat currency, they have no intention of accepting them as a direct form of payment.

Even if one assumes that a crypto token manages to overcome hypervolatility so as to gain a widespread traction as a form of direct payment, it would still remain highly vulnerable to hacking and fraud due to the lack of an oversight not to mention that it would also run afoul of Uncle Sam as and when it poses a threat to the dollar—and we know what happens next.

Needless to say, the crypto represents nothing more than a speculative token attractive to fools who believe that they can buy it at a lower price and sell it at a much higher to greater fools so as to get rich quick and declare their financial independence without ever having done any useful or tangible work in their lives—little they realize that they are actually nothing more than pawns in the bigger scheme of things where the only winners are the big whales and the little sharks get mercilessly devoured.

For those with malicious intentions, crypto is merely a token to launder money so as to bypass the radar of a central authority.

Nobody is condoning that it is acceptable for a central authority to monitor every transaction that we engage in—but crypto is not the solution to the state's totalitarian and heavy-handed approach toward its citizens.

As much as we detest such intervention by the state, it is nevertheless being conducted with our knowledge unlike dancing with the crypto devil that is destined to leave one destitute, sooner or later.

Notwithstanding its fraudulent nature, the crypto cloud does have a silver lining in that it not only makes cryptophiles much-sought-after species on dating sites but cryptomania has also jumpstarted the switch to digital currency just as the internet democratized the electronic currency at the outset of 21st century.

Unlike the electronic currency that requires a bank to act as a mediator when being transferred between two parties, the digital currency will be delivered on-the-fly between two digital wallets under the direct control of a central authority such as the Federal Reserve of the United States or the People's Bank of China.

In other words, while the transfer of electronic currency involves a rather cumbersome bank-to-bank (B2B) transaction that can occasionally incur hefty fees, the digital currency will not only employ a free-and-direct peer-to-peer (P2P) instant exchange without the intermediacy of a third party but will also likely work across borders as if the globe was one large monotonous community without monetary barriers for individuals and traders alike.

With the era of digital currency having already arrived in many nations and on the horizon elsewhere, conventional banking norms such as ATMs, cash transactions, and even brick-and-mortar branches are set to become obsolete over the next couple of decades or so—one's smartphone (or phablet) will essentially become their mobile bank that will accompany them wherever they go and whenever they go.

Importantly, every digital transaction will be conducted over the radar of a central authority with the potential to make illegal practices such as tax evasion and money laundering a thing of the past.

And so will die out for the most part today's fraudulent culture as the curtain is raised over the next oquannium (2039-2122) in about a decade or so.

After several decades of relative calm underscored by trustworthy institutions during the 2040s through 2070s, the next wave of Ponzis will begin to gain inertia circa annus turnilis (2081) of the next oquannium (2039-2122) reaching a crescendo around annus horribilis (2112) before it once again begins to peter out.

4 | XENOPHOBIC WAVES

While economic prosperity is by-and-large enjoyed by everyone across all social strata during the first half of oqual cycle, an exact mirror image is observed during the second half in that it is marred by an anemic economic growth coupled with the prevalence of endemic corruption that together fuel a rising wealth gap such that the money begins to flow from the labor-intensive class of poor to the wealthy and elite.

Such wealth polarization not only leaves the masses in economic doldrums as the second half of oqual cycle chugs along but it also serves as a much-needed platform for right-wing extremists to vent their anger on the elite with the affluent segments of minorities being a prime target.

Next, such right-wing propaganda finds an increasing level of support among the masses due to their own grievances and resentments in the face of their dire economic straits.

Sensing such a political polarization, right-wing leaders and demagogues exploit the masses for their own political gain and are often catapulted to the highest office in the land during poor economic times, which almost always hit rock bottom during the second half of oqual cycle.

With the minorities portrayed as economic opportunists gung-ho on annoying the interests of the majority by far-right leaders, it is only a matter of time before such xenophobia turns into social unrest, ethnic uprisings, or even ethnic cleansings during the second half of oqual cycle.

That the onset of the second half of oqual cycle marks the beginning of challenging times ahead for the minorities is perhaps best illustrated by the expulsion of Jews from Spain that occurred almost in parallel with the onset of the second half (1493-1534) of the first oquannium (1451-1534) in what came to be called the "1492 Reconquista"—when Muslim rule over the Iberian peninsula finally ground to a halt after nearly 800 years and, when it did, the Jews also lost the freedom to practice their faith and those who refused to convert to Catholicism were forced to seek refuge elsewhere around the globe.

Admittedly, today's rising wave of xenophobia and communal violence across much of the globe bears stunning echoes of the second half (1913-1954) of the previous oquannium (1871-1954).

Those dreadful times bore witness to the outbreak of a spate of genocides that together accounted for the ethnic cleansing of decamillions across the globe including in particular the following:
- Armenian Genocide committed by the Ottomans (1915-1917)
- Ukrainian Genocide conducted by the Russians through the famine-driven Holodomor (1932-1933)
- Chinese Genocide masterminded by the Japanese (1937-1945)
- Holocaust perpetrated against European Jewry by Nazi Germany and its collaborators (1941-1945)
- Indocaust stemming from the genocide and forced migration during the Indian Partition (1946-1948)

Since the onset of the second half (1997-2038) of the current oquannium (1955-2038), genocides around the world have been unsurprisingly once again on the rise in an eerie echo of what transpired during much of the second half (1913-1954) of the previous oquannium (1871-1954).

Notable cases include the systematic killings of as many as:
- 70K Bambutis by the Congolese government (2002-2003)
- 500K Darfuris by the Sudanese government (2003-date)
- 10K Yazidis by the notorious ISIS outfit (2014-2019)
- 40K Rohingyas by the Burmese government (2017-date)

Still, these statistics do not truly capture the full extent of ongoing oppression and killing of minorities by state-sponsored actors around the world.

Notably, at least one million Uighurs have been allegedly interned (or detained) against their will so as to Sinicize them by the Chinese authorities since 2014—though the extent to which this constitutes persecution is debatable given that the Chinese authorities have dubbed it "re-education", and one must not be quick to pass judgement on the Chinese culture using the Western benchmarks.

In particular, only fools would buy into the propaganda of grossly-exaggerated plight of Uighurs as reported by the rather biased-and-hypocritical Western media.

While they turned a blind eye to the systematic killing and uprooting of millions in the wake of 9/11 Wars, the Western media were among the first to call out China whose crimes pale in comparison.

To add insult to injury, the Western media deliberately portrayed the heinous crimes committed during the decades-long 9/11 Wars as a price worth paying for "freedom and liberty" even though they themselves are being denied such basic human rights in their own backyard.

Simply put, the Western media continue to use the questionable plight of Uighurs as a veneer to masquerade the evil acts committed by their own governments in that they must do the bidding on their behalf in order to remain in business.

When one holds themselves sacrosanct, they are inherently going to overlook their own devilish acts, all the while pointing a finger at others.

The Western media indeed have much soul-searching to do rather than continue to make fool of themselves through peddling a misguided sense of justice for humanity.

Admittedly, a growing number of Westerners are turning to foreign media to get unbiased and unfiltered news on domestic and international affairs.

Long story short, the magnitude and intensity of xenophobia follows a sinusoidal wave that ebbs during the first half of oqual cycle in the midst of relatively prosperous times enjoyed by the masses but then it begins to flow during the second half when things begin to turn sour.

In particular, the world is going to witness the ongoing wave of xenophobia around the globe reach its zenith around annus horribilis (2028) of the current oquannium (1955-2038), before it cools off with the arrival of the next cycle in 2039.

It is noteworthy that while small-scale genocides occur throughout the course of oqual cycle, their magnitude and intensity exponentially ramp up as the 84-year rhythm reaches its climax during the oqual dusk.

Admittedly, it is no coincidence that two of the most atrocious genocides in recorded history in the form of the Holocaust and Indocaust reared their ugly head just as the previous oquannium (1871-1954) drew to a close.

How universal is such a wave of xenophobia?

To address that question, we will limit our discussion to the following three case studies with huge implications on our society:

        4.1 White Supremacy
        4.2 Global Anti-Semitism
        4.3 Hindu-Muslim Conflict

| 4.1 | WHITE SUPREMACY

At the outset of 2021, the insurrection on the US Capitol by an armed mob of far-right extremists to prevent the transfer of presidential power underscored decades of a precipitous rise in White supremacy across America.

Not only was such a rebellion planned to restore America's greatness as a nation wherein White power-and-privilege had once dominated over non-Whites for centuries but it was also driven to reaffirm the racial superiority of Whites over other races in all walks of life.

In blunt terms, the holy grail of White supremacists is to replace the US government with a separate nation-state for White people and use its military might to advance the socioeconomic interests of what they call the pure Aryan race through exploitation and subjugation of non-Whites around the globe that they believe to be inferior.

White supremacy is therefore essentially a reincarnation of centuries-old European colonialism in today's world.

Powered by their so-called Fourteen Words' mantra "We must secure the existence of our people and a future for White children", White supremacists subscribe to the following tenets:
- 1) Whites are genetically superior to other races;
- 2) White civilization is superior to other cultures;
- 3) White power and privilege should dominate over other people;
- 4) Whites should live in exclusive zones so as not to commingle with other people socially or otherwise; and
- 5) Whites are in danger of extinction due to being outnumbered by a rising tide of immigrants in their own backyard.

Paradoxically, White supremacists fear diversity and pluralism that they naively believe to be an elitist plan to destroy them.

Well, jeez, it somehow does not seem to dawn upon them that it should be the inferior non-Whites that ought to fear the superior White race not other way round.

White supremacists are also hostile to the media and the institutions which they perceive to be detrimental to the interests of the White race.

And they would like to roll back civil rights for non-Whites so that the sociopolitical power solely resides in the hands of White people.

Notably, White supremacy often expresses itself in the geopolitical sphere under the cloak of ideologies such as Nazism and fascism.

While the ever-rising threat of a dystopian society as viewed through the prism of White supremacy may have caught America by surprise, what perhaps no one realizes is that such a xenophobic ideology does not crop up randomly out of thin air but rather it seems to ebb and flow over the course of oqual cycle.

In other words, White supremacy rolls downhill over the course of the first half of oqual cycle but then begins to climb uphill almost in sync with the second half in what is dubbed the "White oquacycle".

Indeed, White supremacy has been on an ascendancy on American soil and across the globe since the bombing of a federal building in Oklahoma City in 1995—that fateful tragedy occurred almost in parallel with the start of the second half (1997-2038) of the current oquannium (1955-2038) and would mark the beginning of what is today a deeply divided nation along ethnic lines.

It is noteworthy that White supremacy is not only being bred on the fringes of American society but it also finds home in the upper echelons of the ruling elite whose foreign policies are often predicated on the deeply-racist assumption that Western civilization is inherently superior to other cultures in an echo of European colonialists who were driven by what they believed to be their God-given superiority to rule over other nations in the bygone centuries.

Like colonialism before it, the defunct ideology of American exceptionalism over other nations also has its roots in White preeminence.

In fact, the decades-long self-destructive 9/11 Wars were essentially a product of White supremacy with the goal to remake the world in America's image of what it considered to be good versus bad as if other nations were bereft of moral values and righteousness.

Ironically, today, it is America that needs to look to other nations for guidance in the face of what amounts to nothing short of a societal meltdown at home from both the far-left and the far-right.

On the far-left, a rising tide of Wokeism is threatening to ravage the moral fabric of the American society.

On the far-right, a growing threat of a civil war breaking out on American soil over the next decade or so would be shocking but hardly surprising by any stretch of the imagination given the sociopolitical upheaval that engulfs the nation today.

However, America has been here before many times during the second half of every oqual cycle in the nation's 250-year checkered history.

PROTECTION OF SLAVERY WAS A MAJOR DRIVING FORCE FOR THE AMERICAN INDEPENDENCE

The very birth of the nation in 1776, during what was then the dusk (1766-1786) of the fourth oquannium (1703-1786), was in fact the culmination of decades-long push by White colonists to be granted greater authority to exercise absolute domination over the Native tribes and the Black people as independence from Britain would hand them a free license to kill the former and exploit the latter like never before.

Notably, slavery was first introduced on American shores in 1619 by the British colonialists barely a decade after they established their first colonial settlement in 1607 in what is today a historic site of Jamestown in the state of Virginia.

However, as the 18th century entered its second half, Britain not only began to make amends with its tyrannical past of having been at the center of institutionalization of slavery across the Western world but it would also increasingly find itself at unease in the face of White colonists vying to take the exploitation of Blacks to new heights under the watch of its colonial rule.

In fact, the then rising British Empire and the most dominant colonial force at the time was being peppered from every corner of influence to rein in slavery as it was damaging its global standing.

It would therefore be a huge understatement to say that one of the major driving forces for White colonists to declare independence from Britain in 1776 was to protect their golden goose of slavery.

And why would anyone kill the goose that lays the golden egg.

In the Black people, the White owners had a perfect subordinate workforce that would deliver them riches due to their absolute bondage in that their slaves:

      1) were denied education;
      2) could not legally marry;
      3) could be traded and put on sale like a property;
      4) had no claim to their own children who could be likewise traded;

5) could be raped or even murdered with impunity by their owners;
6) could not own or inherit anything; and
7) could be worked to death and often were.

Signed in 1776, the US Declaration of Independence proclaims that "all men are created equal".

Alas, as powerful as that dictation might sound, it spectacularly laid bare the hypocrisy of founding fathers as either they must not have believed what they preached to others or they must have considered the Black people to be sub-humans who in their eyes failed to even qualify as "men".

Surely, the founding fathers could not have had a multiracial society in mind lest they would have called for the end of slavery and equality for all people of God not just White men at the time the US Constitution was ratified in 1787—which not so coincidentally also happens to be the year when the fifth oquannium (1787-1870) got underway in that the dawn of each oqual cycle is accompanied by a breath of fresh institutions at the expense of old ones.

In their defense, however, one could argue that the founding fathers' vision for America should not be judged by today's standards as what may seem preposterous to us now was often perfectly in line with the norms of earlier times across the globe—those times were bad, not necessarily the people, as our conduct from a position of authority is often dictated by the times we live in.

In that sense, one could also argue the extent to which the centuries-old US Constitution is even relevant to our lives today.

Does one really need to own guns for their security in today's hi-tech world as opposed to living in the middle of nowhere in what was once an agrarian society?

Although stipulated in the 2nd Amendment ratified in 1791 a little over a decade after the birth of the nation, the repeal of the right of Americans to bear arms would however throw a wrench in the works of White supremacists often camouflaged as mass shooters.

In fact, as enshrined in the US Constitution, the right to gun ownership is essentially a tentacle of White supremacy as it once practically armed the owners to kill anyone they perceived to be inferior to them or annoying their interests with impunity—a scenario that has little changed over the past two centuries.

Today, however, what America needs is not guns but rather the reintroduction of capital punishment handed out in an expeditious manner to deter serious and serial offenders so that the fear of being sent to the gallows or chair solves the root causes of a lawless society that we have become.

Till then, those in favor of gun ownership are fully justified.

We must first fix the land of the lawless before we take guns away from people.

While the criminals are too often being allowed to walk free under the veneer of human rights, the victims are denied such rights as they are served injustice time and again making mockery of the rule of law.

What a terrible sign of the terrible times.

America has hit so low that it would do itself a big favor by taking a leaf out of other nations' playbooks to address the lawlessness that it has been breeding for decades at the expense of the rule of law.

For example, an individual undertaking a heinous crime such as mass shooting should be treated as a monster who has renounced humanity and bears the potential to pose serious threat to the society at large.

Rather than elevating such a mass shooter to the status of a celebrity garnering huge media attention and fanfare, they ought to be put to death immediately without a trial not only to serve immediate justice to the victims and their families but also to deter and inject fear into wannabee shooters.

To put icing on the cake, fear is free.

Not only does fear serve as the most powerful weapon to address lawlessness, it also does not cost the taxpayers a dime.

Las mejores cosas de la vida son gratis!—The best things in life are free!

AMERICAN CIVIL WAR MARKED THE ZENITH OF YET ANOTHER RISING WAVE OF WHITE SUPREMACY

In the aftermath of American Independence War (1775-1783), the then fledgling nation would however be showered with rather prosperous times thanks to the introduction of the Market Economy during the 1790s such that the scourge of White supremacy would take a back seat for the decades that followed.

However, such relatively happy times do not last forever thanks to the dire spell of the second half of oqual cycle.

Indeed, White supremacy would reemerge from the silos almost in parallel with the onset of the second half (1829-1870) of the fifth oquannium (1787-1870).

While the new wave of White supremacy began to exert its might as early as 1816 through what came to be called the First Seminole War (1816-1819), it did not begin-in-earnest until the outbreak of the Second Seminole War (1835-1842).

Notably, the First Seminole War (1816-1819) was triggered when the US military invaded what was then the Spanish Florida on the pretext that the Native tribe of Seminoles was complicit in helping to free the Black slaves from their White owners, and in going to war, Spain was forced to cede the Sunshine State to America through what came to be called the 1819 Adams-Onis Treaty.

In actuality, the annexation of Florida was driven by the urge to expand the footprint of White supremacy in order to broaden the subjugation of Natives-and-Blacks-alike through territorial control.

However, the Seminoles refused to accept White rule over what they considered to be their homeland for centuries and millennia.

The resulting standoff would usher in the Second Seminole War (1835-1842) during which the US military upped the ante as it went about relocating Seminoles out of Florida to federal territories in the American Southwest specifically earmarked for the Native tribes—such a barbaric act was in no small part achieved through conducting genocide on a large scale in order to cleanse Florida of virtually all Seminoles so as to turn the Sunshine State into an exclusive zone for White settlers.

That might seem like White supremacy running amok on steroids but it was only a harbinger of things to come.

Next, the Mexicans would become the whipping boys of White supremacy through what came to be called the Mexican-American War (1846-1848)—a bloody armed conflict during which the United States annexed from Mexico what is today much of American Southwest from Texas to California and, in doing so, literally laid the groundwork for the massive territory to be whitewashed through prioritizing White settlements at the expense of ravaging the livelihoods of Native tribes and driving them into all but extinction.

However, just as America's territorial ambitions were all but complete, cracks would soon begin to appear among Whites over the inhumane treatment of Black people, particularly with regard to the expansion of slavery into newly conquered territories in the American West.

While much of the American North espoused the idea of emancipation of slaves, the American South felt that this was a nothing-burger due to what it believed to be the superiority of Whites over Blacks.

And the political stakes of the American South would be further boosted through the intervention of the US Supreme Court.

In 1857, the US Supreme Court ruled that the Black people were not entitled to citizenship because they hailed from an inferior race and therefore they could not be granted the same privilege as White people.

In 1860, Abraham Lincoln was propelled to the nation's highest office as the 16th POTUS even though he failed to win in any one of more than a dozen slave states in the American South.

Being vehemently opposed to slavery, Lincoln's victory appeared to be the final nail in the Union's coffin as it not only irked the slave states but also sparked the secession of South Carolina a little more than a month after the 1860 election.

In 1861, another six slave states—namely Mississippi, Florida, Alabama, Georgia, Louisiana, and Texas in the order of their secession—would join South Carolina and, together, they would form the Confederate States of America as the nation erupted into what arguably remains the bloodiest conflict on American soil in what is called the American Civil War (1861-1865).

Although four more slave states—namely Virginia, Arkansas, North Carolina, and Tennessee—joined the Confederacy soon after the outbreak of civil war in 1861, the Union army turbocharged by black soldiers in relatively large numbers would ultimately emerge victorious and keep the nation united as we know it today.

While he made no secret of his opposition to slavery, Lincoln was no saint either as he had his own reservations about the coexistence of Black people within what he believed to be a White nation as he summoned Black leaders to the White House in the midst of the civil war in 1862 and asserted:

> "You and we are different races. We have between us a broader difference than exists between almost any other two races. Whether it is right or wrong I need not discuss, but this physical difference is a great disadvantage to us both, as I think your race suffer very greatly, many of them by living among us, while ours suffer from your presence. In a word we suffer on each side. If this is admitted, it affords a reason at least why we should be separated."

Simply put, the Black leaders would be told that they had nothing in common with the Whites, their coexistence was mutually detrimental to the interests of both races, that the plans could be worked out to ship the Blacks back to Africa once they were freed from the shackles of their owners, and that they could also be a part of the plan to colonize parts of Africa, Central America, and the Caribbeans.

The Black leaders would be stunned and flabbergasted as the weight of what they were being told would finally sink in—that they could be removed from the country where their ancestors had first disembarked almost 250 years earlier long before the arrival of most Europeans and that the war for which the Black men had signed up with a renewed hope for their liberty was after all not being fought to emancipate them but to preserve the Union.

Although the Black leaders would tell Lincoln that they would consider his offer out of their humility in the face of a presidential decree, they knew in their heart that America was their home and that their people would refuse to live or die anywhere other than where they had been born and the nation that they had built by the sweat of their brow.

Indeed, the faith of Black people in America was further vindicated when Lincoln issued the 1863 Emancipation Proclamation in the midst of the ongoing civil war to abolish slavery, thereby setting millions of enslaved people free.

In the aftermath of the American Civil War (1861-1865) and powered by the 19th Century Civil Rights Movement (1865-1896), the Blacks would finally walk free and immediately begin to look to the future rather than past as they enthusiastically engaged in rebuilding a ravaged nation through what came to be called the Reconstruction Era (1865-1877)—a period during which the Blacks would be integrated into the larger society through granting them civil rights on par with the Whites courtesy of the US Congress ratifying three key amendments to the US Constitution as outlined below:

1) In 1865, the 13th Amendment outlawed slavery and bondage;

2) In 1868, the 14th Amendment guaranteed citizenship to anyone born or naturalized in the United States as well as granting every individual equality before law; and

3) In 1870, the 15th Amendment bestowed upon every man the right to vote irrespective of their race, religion, or color—the enfranchisement of women however would not follow until half-a-century later in 1920 with the ratification of the 19th Amendment.

In spite of such a tectonic shift in the US Constitution, the Black people were far from being out of the woods yet as the American Civil War (1861-1865) was essentially the culmination of a rising wave of White supremacy rather than an end to their suffering as enslaved people.

While the slave-loving Confederates had been handily beaten by the greater good that lay in the American society, the spirits of White supremacy would nevertheless be kept alive through the birth of the Ku Klux Klan just as the civil war petered out.

Founded by Confederate veterans in the Tennessean city of Pulaski in 1865 shortly after the civil war ended, the Ku Klux Klan would rapidly metastasize from being a benign fraternity into a malignant force that would terrorize Black communities as it seeped across much of the American South over the next decade or so.

In particular, using the tools of violence and intimidation, the Klan would provide a fierce resistance to US government's policies directed at promoting the civil rights of Black people during the Reconstruction Era (1865-1877).

Although no longer enslaved, the Black people would continue to be marginalized and ostracized in that they would not truly break free of the shackles of slavery for another century thanks to the intervention of the US Supreme Court in 1896 that in a landmark ruling upheld racial segregation as constitutional on the pretense of "separate but equal".

In doing so, the US Supreme Court further planted the seeds for the incessant institutional discrimination of Blacks from the denial of equal-employment opportunities to their disenfranchisement at the state and local level.

Additionally, the Black people would face beating and lynching by White supremacists with impunity in what then still remained an apartheid nation even after slavery had been outlawed.

Notwithstanding their relegation to the lowest rung of society and being treated as nothing more than third-class citizens, the Black people were nevertheless "free" and would enjoy much greater liberty than they had ever been granted in the antebellum era (or before the civil war) as the previous oquannium (1871-1954) kicked off in line with the promise of a relatively prosperous dawn.

This was further aided by a relative decline in the fortunes of White supremacy.

While Ku Klux Klan's fierce opposition to civil rights for the Black people continued to strike a chord even among some abolitionists, White supremacy would nevertheless begin to experience a long-and-sustained period of decline during much of the first half (1871-1912) of the previous oquannium (1871-1954) due to two majors factors:

1) From the declaration of martial law in Klan-dominated areas to the use of military force to suppress its members across what were once the slave states in the American South, the heavy-handed approach deployed by the US government served as an antidote to keep White supremacy in check; and

2) Powered by the relatively prosperous times in what came to be called the American Glided Age (1870-1900), the support for the Klan by-and-large began to wane among the White masses even though many of them continued to view civil rights for Blacks as an encroachment on their sociopolitical interests.

Alas, Ku Klux Klan had only been driven into dormancy rather than having been put to the sword.

IMMIGRATION SPARKS ANOTHER WAVE OF WHITE SUPREMACY

In line with the recurring spell of oqual cycle, the Ku Klux Klan would be supplied with a new wave of lifeblood just as the grisly second half (1913-1954) of the previous oquannium (1871-1954) emerged.

With an upsurge in immigrants arriving from Eastern Europe and other parts of the world during the first quarter of the 20th century, the Klan once again began to command a huge following among White supremacists who feared anyone who did not look like them as they upped the attacks against new immigrants and also began to target the Blacks with a heightened resolve.

Such a rise in White supremacy was not only limited to those on the fringes of society but it also had allies in the US Congress that for its part would go onto enact the so-called 1924 Immigration Act—a deeply racist policy that practically banned immigration from Asia and significantly reduced it from other parts of the world but Western Europe so as to weed out what it believed to be the "inferior stock" through the introduction of quotas for each nation based on its proportional representation among the citizens of the United States.

Notably, the 1924 Immigration Act was less about Making America Great Again (MAGA) but more about Making America White Again (MAWA)—a familiar theme that returns to the front-and-center of White supremacists' conscience during the second half of every oqual cycle as is also the case today.

Thanks to the Great Depression (1929-1939), White supremacy became even more apparent as the Blacks were the first to be shown the door and last to be offered employment in what is sometimes recounted as "Last Hired, First Fired".

Even donning the military uniform did not spare the Blacks.

Although the Black men would fight with gallantry in both World War I (1914-1918) and World War II (1939-1945), many of them would be beaten and lynched upon their return home from the European coliseum—where the much bigger wave of White supremacy in the form of Nazism and fascism had made its counterpart on American shores look like a small ripple by comparison.

Interestingly, the demographic cohort born during the first quarter of the 20th century on American soil has come to be called the "Greatest Generation" due to the fact that not only did it bear the brunt of the fallout from the Great Depression (1929-1939) but many among that generation also fought in World War II (1939-1945) in one way or another.

Yet, it somehow seems to have lost upon American historians that while the Greatest Generation may have fought for the freedom overseas, it not only did nothing to defend the liberty of millions of Black people here at home but was also in no small part complicit in suppressing their civil rights.

Nevertheless, White supremacy would begin to taper off as the previous oquannium (1871-1954) drew to a close.

With the arrival of the current oquannium (1955-2038), a new dawn of relative ethnic harmony began to knock on the door.

Additionally, it would also open the door to right the wrong as the victims began to push back and neutralize the excesses of White supremacy gone bonkers.

Indeed, the Blacks and other minorities could finally breathe a sigh of relief as their sociopolitical status took a turn for the better courtesy of the 20th Century Civil Rights Movement (1954-1968) that would finally drive a stake through racist policies such as institutional discrimination and racial segregation—the latter required the separation of people on the basis of their race in almost every walk of life from schools and playgrounds through transportation and restrooms to restaurants and housing until as recently as the 1960s.

Named after deeply-racist theatrical shows dubbed "Jim Crow" that were being performed by White entertainers who earned their living through stereotyping and imitating the Black slaves via abhorrent acts such as blackface though to the delight of their White audience during much of the 19th century, those so-called "Jim Crow Laws" had been kept alive at the state and local level due to the intervention of the US Supreme Court in 1896 even though they had been outlawed nearly a century earlier via the ratification of the 13th (1865), 14th (1868), and 15th (1870) Amendments by the US Congress.

Thanks to the 20th Century Civil Rights Movement (1954-1968) spearheaded by Martin Luther King, the Jim Crow Laws would be finally outlawed through the ratification of the 1964 Civil Rights Act—a brainchild of the 35th POTUS John Kennedy who was assassinated before he could sign the act into law but it was nevertheless approved by his successor the 36th POTUS Lyndon Johnson.

A momentous masterstroke in the then nation's 188-year history, the 1964 Civil Rights Act banned racial segregation as well as discrimination based on race, ethnicity, color, religion, and gender.

That was followed by the 1965 Immigration Act that essentially reversed the racist immigration quotas stipulated in the 1924 Immigration Act almost half a turn of oqual cycle earlier and, in doing so, it opened the door for millions of new immigrants from every corner of the world irrespective of what they looked like.

Liberties are rarely achieved without making sacrifices and the 20th Century Civil Rights Movement (1954-1968) would demand more than a fair share of its own.

In 1963, the lives of four Black girls were cut short after the Ku Klux Klan bombed the 16th Street Baptist Church in Birmingham, Alabama.

In 1964, three Black men involved in the Civil Rights Movement were murdered by the Ku Klux Klan in Neshoba County, Mississippi.

In 1968, the talismanic leader Martin Luther King would himself pay the price with his own blood for his dream of America as a promised land for all people as he was assassinated in Memphis, Tennessee.

In all, the 20th Century Civil Rights Movement would claim 41 martyrs as per the inscription on the Civil Rights Memorial in Montgomery, Alabama.

Notwithstanding such setbacks, the Black people were propelled by their newly-granted civil rights as they would finally come home and walk with their head held high in the nation that they had built on their backs for centuries.

With White supremacy having been muzzled due to little support for its propaganda among the White masses against the backdrop of relatively prosperous times during much of the second half of the 20th century, the Blacks and other minorities would become increasingly integrated into the mainstream society as they set about making astounding contributions in every walk of life from arts through sciences to sports so much so that many pundits even began to wonder whether America was finally on a path to becoming a melting pot—wherein one's race and color would become a thing of the past so as to produce a culturally-diverse nation with a shared goal of reaching the idyllic land of nirvana.

Alas, they all forgot to pay heed to history as the dire spell of the second half of oqual cycle was yet to unleash its scourge on America once more.

A NEW WAVE OF WHITE SUPREMACY IS RAPIDLY GAINING INERTIA

While White supremacy had by-and-large stayed under the radar during much of the first half (1955-1996) of the current oquannium (1955-2038), it would begin to rear its ugly head once more almost in parallel with the onset of the second half (1997-2038) with the bombing of a federal building in Oklahoma City in 1995 by White supremacists that killed 168 people.

Since the outset of the 21st century, White supremacy has experienced an explosive resurgence once again thanks in large part to social media but also fueled by a tanking economic well-being with many among the White masses falling prey to the propaganda that the minorities are to be blamed for their rising socioeconomic misfortunes.

In particular, such a rising wave of White supremacy has been fueled by the following quintet of isms:

1) **Warism**—In 2001, what began as short and brief 9/11 Wars would turn into decades-long conflicts that would serve as a springboard for the radicalization of a growing number of veterans returning home and then joining the ranks of far-right militias with the goal of toppling the federal government and making America White again; the 2021 insurrection on US Capitol was in no small part spearheaded by White extremists and anti-government militias such as the Oath Keepers, Proud Boys, and Three Percenters—with many of them now facing trials for sedition and violent uprising against the US government.

2) **Obamaism**—In 2008, the shared anathema of the election of Barack Obama as the first non-White US President is believed to have been a wakeup call for a loosely-connected network of an array of far-right and

White-nationalist movements to coalesce into a united front under the umbrella of what came to be known as the "Alt-Right".

3) **Blimism**—In 2013, the birth of the Black Lives Matter (or BLiM) movement in response to police brutality and violence against Black people telegraphed the racial stereotyping and poor treatment of Blacks to the front-and-center of American conscience; in doing so, it has however also energized White supremacists to counter Blimism with an ever-growing legion of new recruits.

4) **Wokeism**—In 2014, an offshoot of BLiM called "Woke" emerged on the pretense of being abreast or aware of systemic injustice in the society but quickly became bastardized into a morally-disruptive cult that continues to serve as a fodder for the rapid growth of White supremacy, not to mention that it has also irked a big chunk of mainstream conservatives across all racial groups.

5) **Immigrationism**—The rapid explosion in immigrants from a paltry 5% of the US population in 1965 to almost 15% today in 2023 has been steadily adding further gasoline to the White fire as it continues to find new targets through the recruitment of disgruntled young White men more than ever before; it should be noted that everyone living in the United States is considered an "immigrant" unless they are either native-born nationals or naturalized citizens.

Admittedly, the fact that America is undergoing a demographic transformation by leaps and bounds is not lost on White supremacists.

As recently as 1950, the non-Hispanic Whites made up almost 90% of America.

Today, in 2023, the non-Hispanic Whites barely make up 60% of the nation.

By 2050, the non-Hispanic Whites are projected to become a plurality for the first time ever in what would then be the nation's 274-year history.

Understandably, such stats add further gasoline on the raging fire that White supremacy has turned into over the past couple of decades.

Add to that the fact that a growing number of media platforms have also begun to increasingly serve as a mouthpiece for White supremacy among mainstream conservative sociopolitical circles.

Although the Ku Klux Klan with over 150-year of history under its belt has also come out from the shadows with a vengeance, White supremacy today has largely been superseded by the Alt-Right on American soil.

Once operating primarily in cyberspace as a fringe far-right ideology, the Alt-Right began to gain traction after Barack Obama was elected as the first non-White US President in 2008.

However, the Alt-Right would not come to prominence until 2016 when it is believed to have played a central role in mobilizing support among the far-right as it helped to propel Donald Trump to the nation's highest office against all odds.

As the saying goes, you scratch my back and I will scratch yours.

Nowhere is that adage more relevant than what appears to have been a mutually-beneficial relationship struck between Trump and Alt-Right—which seems to have continued ever since in a marriage of convenience.

It should therefore be hardly surprising that during Trump's tenure (2017-2021), the support for the Alt-Right online and its tentacles on the ground grew exponentially for which, you guessed it, Donald claimed credit even though he would have us believe that there was no quid pro quo.

Few would doubt that Trump's presidency helped elevate Alt-Right to new heights from where it began to infiltrate into the ranks of conservative and right-leaning politics with huge ramifications for a nation already teetering on the precipice of a societal collapse.

Notably, the Alt-Right and its entourage have become increasingly active online and offline promoting in particular anti-Semitism, Islamophobia, and Negrophobia through posting racist flyers and organizing protests such as the 2017 Unite The Right Rally held in Charlottesville in the state of Virginia, and the 2017 March Against Sharia held in many cities across the United States.

In addition to its political activism, the Alt-Right also advances its propaganda through violence and intimidation.

In particular, the Alt-Right exerts a huge clout over the radicalization and indoctrination of young men online who then go onto carry out deadly attacks on the lives and properties of non-Whites in the real world.

Unsurprisingly, such racially-motivated attacks have been on the rise with an increasing frequency and intensity over the past decade or so in line with the dire spell of the second half of oqual cycle.

Over the recent past, some of the deadliest attacks conducted by White supremacists through bombings and/or gunfire include:

- **2022 Buffalo Shooting**—targeted Blacks in a supermarket killing 10 in Buffalo, New York, United States
- **2020 Hanau Shooting**—targeted Muslims in shisha bars killing 10 in Hanau, Hessen, Germany
- **2019 El Paso Shooting**—targeted Latinos in a Walmart superstore killing 23 in El Paso, Texas, United States
- **2019 Christchurch Shooting**—targeted Muslims at the Al-Noor Mosque killing 51 in Christchurch, Canterbury, New Zealand
- **2018 Pittsburg Shooting**—targeted Jews at the Tree of Life Synagogue killing 11 in Pittsburg, Pennsylvania, United States
- **2015 Charleston Shooting**—targeted Blacks in a church killing 9 in Charleston, South Carolina, United States
- **2012 Oak Creek Shooting**—targeted Sikhs at a gurudwara killing 8 in Oak Tree, Wisconsin, United States
- **2011 Norway Attacks**—targeted Whites believed to be promoting multiculturalism killing 8 in Oslo and 69 in Utøya

As demonstrated by the 2011 Norway attacks, it is important to note that White supremacists do not only target non-Whites but even Whites who subscribe to pluralism and refuse to buy into their bigoted propaganda.

While a number of counter organizations such as the Ctrl-Alt-Right and Delete-Alt-Right have recently taken root to push back on the Alt-right propaganda, it would however take more than just a keyboard to rein in White supremacy that has all but transformed America and the globe into a far cry from the relative ethnic harmony enjoyed by society-writ-large during much of the second half of the 20th century.

Being in the midst of the second half (1997-2038) of the current oquannium (1955-2038), the attacks engineered by White supremacists against minorities will continue to get more deadly around the globe over the next decade though they will likely crest around 2028, the next annus horribilis.

Notably, the threat of White supremacy triggering a civil war in the United States around 2028 cannot be ruled out—particularly with Donald Trump poised to make a come back in 2024 and with his presidency, or lack thereof, becoming a straw with the potential to break America's back.

Indeed, White supremacy has always had its advocates among the ruling elite and, in Trump, they have a perfect partner-in-crime to make America White again—although an extremely unlikely possibility, should it bear fruition, one can be rest assured that, as always, Donald will claim credit.

On the brighter side, as the current oquannium draws to a close in 2038, White supremacy will begin to dwindle as it heads for the burrows and will largely die out during the 2040s and 2050s.

Finally, the next deadly tide of White supremacy will begin to emerge from the burrows around annus turnilis (2081) of the next oquannium (2039-2122), and will likely pose a serious threat again circa 2100 as the annus horribilis (2112) begins to inch ever closer to the day of reckoning.

|4.2| GLOBAL ANTI-SEMITISM

While attending high school in England during the late 1980s, I would learn for the first time about Holocaust (1941-1945) with the take-home message that such a barbaric act committed at the heart of European civilization merely belonged to our past and that we had long moved onto good times with all the wicked souls forever obliterated from our planet.

Unsurprisingly, even my history teachers back then would fail to make the point that learning from our past was important to make sure that it did not repeat, much less have the wisdom to argue that the human civilization treaded through good and bad times in a perpetual wave-like manner.

In fact, good and bad are not only part-and-parcel of our civilization but they are also intertwined so much so that they beget each other in a manner akin to the relationship between day and night.

Today, my history teachers would roll over in their graves when told that Holocaust was not just a random event but rather the apotheosis (or culmination) of anti-Semitism that had been brewing on European soil and across much of the globe for millennia.

Indeed, the global Jewry had not only faced deplorable discrimination for millennia but such anti-Semitic waves had surged during the second half of virtually every oqual cycle only to dwindle as it drew to a close as exquisitely captured by what is dubbed the "anti-Semitic oquacycle".

For example, prior to the Holocaust (1941-1945), the Jewish diaspora across the globe encountered a wave of rising discrimination during the second half (1745-1786) of the fourth oquannium (1703-1786) since the outset of Modern Age—when Jews were increasingly expelled from many cities, banned from others, and even faced large-scale massacres from Middle East through North Africa to Europe.

That dire plight of the Jewish people around the globe was further exacerbated by a series of revolutionary wars fought for the economic preeminence between the then great powers from the Seven Years War (1756-1763) between Britain and France through the Anglo-Bengal War (1756-1765) between Britain and India to the American Independence War (1775-1783) between Britain and America.

Against the backdrop of such geopolitical mayhem around the globe, the 18th century anti-Semitic cloud nevertheless had a silver lining in that during the 1770s, it gave birth to Haskalah—an intellectual movement founded by European Jews to promote Jewish identity and cultural advancement among the Jewish masses across the globe, including the revival of the Hebrew language, all the while becoming assimilated into the larger civic life dominated by gentiles.

Guided by Haskalah, anti-Semitism would significantly subside during the first half (1787-1828) of the fifth oquannium (1787-1870).

However, the anti-Semitic wave would begin to rear its ugly head once more with the arrival of the second half (1829-1870) of the fifth oquannium (1787-1870)—when perpetual persecution and massacre of Jews on a large scale across North Africa, Middle East, and Europe would not only reach a fever pitch but Samuel Bierfield would also become the first Jew to be lynched on American soil in 1868.

Notably, such an upsurge in anti-Semitism would unfold against the backdrop of a spate of revolutionary wars breaking out across the globe from the Crimean War (1853-1856) fought between Russia and the Ottoman Empire with the latter aided by European powers through the 1857 Indian Mutiny against the British colonialists to the American Civil War (1861-1865).

Indeed, such global conflicts that peak during the oqual winters do not bear good omens for the well-being of the minorities.

Perhaps, the best way to demonstrate that the anti-Semitic wave of the 19th century reached its zenith during the second half (1829-1870) of the fifth oquannium (1787-1870) was summed up by none other than the then Pope Pius IX in regards to his views vis-à-vis the Jewish community of Rome after it lodged protests in response to the conversion of a young Jewish boy to Catholicism in 1871: "Of these dogs, there are too many of them at present in Rome, and we hear them howling in the streets, and they are disturbing us in all places."

Against the backdrop of such despicable treatment of Jews, the Jewish think-tank began to lay the foundation of Zionism from around mid-19th century at the expense of Haskalah founded some 84 years earlier—unlike Haskalah which promoted the integration of Jews within their larger communities, Zionism would espouse the nationalist ideology and the restoration of Eretz Yisrael (or Land of Israel) as a homeland for the Jewish people.

In his 1862 book titled "Rome and Jerusalem" and later translated into English in 1918 [24], German philosopher Moses Hess argued that the Jews were not a religious group but rather a separate nation and that the establishment of a Jewish state in Eretz Yisrael ought to be their central goal for it would serve as their spiritual and political center.

However, Zionism was largely kept under wraps for much of the second half of the 19th century due to the fear of backlash—and only after the anti-Semitic wave tapered off would it be formally launched by the Austro-Hungarian journalist Theodor Herzl in 1897, albeit with a bag of mixed reception.

Herzl must have wondered: "Damned if I had launched it earlier, damned for having done it now!"

Indeed, with the exception of Russian pogroms during the 1880s, the anti-Semitic wave by-and-large began to ebb during the first half (1871-1912) of the previous and sixth oquannium (1871-1954) with the result that Zionism failed to gain traction among the Jewish masses against the backdrop of relatively prosperous times befalling humanity across much of the globe—fondly dubbed as La Belle Époque in France (1870-1914), the Late Victorian Era in Britain (1870-1901), and the Gilded Age in America (1870-1900).

Although unable to communicate, each new oqual cycle would like to send out a rather cautionary note: "Oh people! Enjoy the good times for they are not going to last in perpetuity!"

Predictably, anti-Semitism began to surge once more at the end of World War I (1914-1918) just as the ugly second half (1913-1954) of the sixth oquannium (1871-1954) emerged.

In fact, anti-Semitism was largely confined to the fringes of right-wing European politics prior to World War I though anti-Semitic tropes continued to strike a chord among a sizeable portion of gentiles as they had always done so since the beginning of times.

JEWS TURNED INTO SCAPEGOATS FOR GERMANY'S DIRE ECONOMIC STRAITS

In the aftermath of World War I (1914-1918), the badly-wounded Germany attributed its humiliation to German Jews in that not only were they accused of stabbing-in-the-back and having acted as traitors but they were also scapegoated for Deutschland's financial woes—even though Jews served in disproportionately high numbers in the German military and fought with valor.

To add salt to their not-so-proverbial wounds, things continued to roll downhill for German Jews after having been stereotyped as not only disloyal and outsiders but also being treated as second-class citizens in their own backyard for much of the 1920s under what was then Weimer Germany (1918-1933) that had emerged after the defeat of Imperial Germany (1871-1918) and the abdication of its emperor Kaiser Wilhelm II.

Notably, Weimer Germany was beset by a persistent bout of hyperinflation during the 1920s after Deutschland put its money printer to work in order to pay off its debts and the brunt of the cost of World War I (1914-1918) courtesy of what came to be called the 1919 Treaty of Versailles.

As if hyperinflation did not exacerbate the pain and agony of German Jews as they increasingly became punching bags for Germany's dire economic straits, they would be caught flat-footed once more with the onset of Great Depression (1929-1939) that plunged Deutschland into an even deeper crisis as if the laws of physics had been overturned one after the other—even with a quad of quantum brains of Albert Einstein, Werner Heisenberg, Max Planck, and Erwin Schrödinger at its disposal.

First was the humiliating defeat of Imperial Germany in World War I (1914-1918).

Then came the ugly and persistent ultra-hyperinflation that decimated Weimer Germany's currencies one after the other from the Goldmark (1871-1914) through the Papiermark (1914-1923) and Rentenmark (1923-1924) to the Reichsmark (1924-1948)—the more recognizable Deutschmark (1948-2002) was the predecessor to today's familiar Euro.

While the Reichsmark did temporarily steady the sinking German ship during the 1920s, it nevertheless failed to prevent it from running aground as the Great Depression (1929-1939) would finally seal the nation's fate.

And so it did with Adolf Hitler taking the helm in 1933 of what came to be called Nazi Germany (1933-1945).

Fueled by Hitler's deeply anti-Semitic and populist platform, the writing had been on the wall for years for German Jews though few thought that the worse was yet to come under Nazi Germany.

In 1935, Nazi Germany enacted the so-called "Nuremberg Laws"—a roster of deeply anti-Semitic laws that institutionalized (or legalized) discrimination and persecution of Jewish people, including the confiscation of their properties and stripping them of the right to German citizenship.

In expressing a rather belated solidarity with my Abrahamic cousins, I solemnly declare: "Ich bin Jude!"—"I am Jew!"

Long story short, the palpable bigotry and humiliation unleashed upon European Jews during the second half (1913-1954) of the previous oquannium (1871-1954) would subsequently culminate with the Holocaust (1941-1945)—a systematic extermination of some six million European Jews, or two out of every three, under the orders of Hitler.

Those shocking numbers hardly capture the full scale of horror as being killed with dignity and honor is one thing but being deceived through false promises such as "Arbeit Macht Frei"—or "Work Sets One Free"—to add to a perpetual humiliation through forced labor, hunger, abuse, rape, suffering, and being stripped naked prior to being tortured to a slow and painful death is beyond the pale of even the most devilish act imaginable.

In 1939, prior to the onset of World War II, almost 10M Jews lived in Europe.

In 2023, 84 years later, European Jewry accounts for a little more than 1M.

Over the same 84-year timespan, the world population has quadrupled from 2000M to 8000M—even when assuming the birth rate among European Jewry to be half that of the global average over the past 84 years, there ought to be at least 20M Jews calling Europe their home today.

Those abhorrent stats should leave Europeans with much soul-searching to do.

As the saying goes, the only thing necessary for the triumph of evil is for good people to do nothing.

Indeed, the Holocaust triumphed because so many:
1) Good Europeans turned their backs on their duty to protect their Jewish neighbors;
2) Mainstream journalists and media across both sides of the Atlantic sugarcoated the Nazi propaganda and downplayed the persecution of European Jews; and
3) Western leaders and their corporate cronies prioritized profits over prophets as they refused to answer the call of Jews-in-need.

While the Holocaust triggered a mass exodus of what little remained of European Jewry to every corner of the world, it was made all the more reprehensible due to the fact that there were few takers of overloaded ships crammed with Jewish refugees—running for their precious lives—as they would be turned away by country after country rather than being allowed to disembark.

Many ships laden with Jewish refugees such as the SS Patria and MV Struma, which were respectively sunk off the coast of Haifa in 1940 and Istanbul in 1942, would sink to the ocean floors in plain sight of disgraceful world leaders with the authority to avert such a seismic catastrophe befalling humanity in desperate need.

In 1903, a bronze plaque was mounted inside the pedestal atop which the Statue of Liberty stands off the southern tip of Manhattan with the following message:
> "Give me your tired, your poor. Your huddled masses yearning to breathe free. The wretched refuse of your teeming shore. Send these, the homeless, tempest-tost to me. I lift my lamp beside the golden door!"

Even though the Statue of Liberty would have failed to capture the dire quandary facing Jewish refugees fleeing Nazi persecution, it would have hardly mattered as America also by-and-large refused to open its doors to Jews when it would have made the biggest difference to those in desperate need.

While the Holocaust dwarfed the pain and suffering of non-European Jews, it is nonetheless important to point out that the massacre of Jewish people elsewhere also led to their mass exodus out of many parts of the world—particularly from the Muslim World stretching across much of the Middle East and North Africa—during the second half (1913-1954) of the previous oquannium (1871-1954).

In what I have dubbed the "Holocaust Curse", Europe may perhaps never recover from its ugly past as the extermination and exodus of its colorful-and-vibrant Jewish community has not only left it with a massive brain drain but also with a retrogressive economic terrain ever since that dreadful human catastrophe unfolded on its doorstep in plain sight some 84 years ago.

Indeed, Jewish people have always given back to their communities more than they have ever taken.

History attests to the fact that the ingenuity and creativity of Jewish people has supercharged every country that they have called home not to mention that it has also transformed ordinary nations into superpowers.

And whenever such nations parted with their Jewish communities, their economic fortunes often nosedived into a deep canyon with no signs of ever flying again.

After being briefed about the expulsion of Jews from Spain in 1492, the Ottoman Emperor Bayezid II is alleged to have said that only fools would believe that the

Spanish royals were wise for they have handed over their national treasure to him—referring to the fact that the emperor not only empathized with the dire plight facing the Spanish Jews but even ordered his navy to help them move to the lands under his control.

When did the deadly spell of the second half (1913-1954) of the previous oquannium (1871-1954) ease off on the European Jewry?

HOLOCAUST WAS A GIANT ANOMALY IN THE RECURRING ANTI-SEMITIC WAVE

Just as good things eventually come to an end so do bad.

With the arrival of the current oquannium (1955-2038) during the 1950s, a new dawn of hope and prosperity had indeed begun for the Jewish diaspora around the globe.

With the State of Israel having come into being in 1948, Jews would once again not only walk with their heads held aloft but they would also put their onerous past behind and begin to rebuild their communities across the globe with a new vigor.

Admittedly, anti-Semitism had all but been put to the sword during much of the second half of the 20th century with anti-Semitic wave having once again reached a nadir around 1990s.

Alas, the anti-Semitic wave would once again begin to rear its ugly head just as the 9/11 attacks struck America in 2001 so as to signal the onset-in-earnest of the second half (1997-2038) of the current oquannium (1955-2038).

In the aftermath of 9/11, gentiles around the globe and particularly the Muslim World—without an iota of evidence—would be quick to lay the blame on Israel and the wider Jewish diaspora for having masterminded the 9/11 attacks in their gambit to control the world.

Sure enough, the 9/11 attacks were undoubtedly used as a pretext by the so-called "American neoconservatives" to remake the world in America's image of enslaving the masses and putting profits before prophets.

If some of those architects behind such a cunning ploy happened to be of Jewish faith, then that in no way should have been generalized to imply the guilt of the wider Jewish community just as much as the 9/11 attacks allegedly conducted by Muslim fanatics had nothing to do with Muslims-at-large.

However, the damage had already been done and the image of Jews as one monotonous group of people with a shared goal had already been planted in the minds of the gentile fools unable to reason or think outside the box.

Unsurprisingly, just as the World War I had tarnished the image of Jews so did the 9/11 attacks as well as the decades-long unethical-illegal-and-perpetual wars in Afghanistan and Iraq that followed.

Admittedly, the upward trend in anti-Semitism since 9/11 is telling with attacks on Jewish people, synagogues, and their wider interests rapidly becoming a-dime-a-dozen—they are not only happening with an increasing frequency but often with an amplified intensity in an uncanny echo of what the Jewish diaspora has always experienced during the second half of every oqual cycle, albeit the status quo is in no way comparable to their dire predicament during the second half (1913-1954) of the previous oquannium (1871-1954).

In particular, the Holocaust can be viewed as a giant anomaly in the recurring anti-Semitic wave—one can only pray to the Almighty God that such a devilish act from our past has been forever cast adrift in the far-flung oceans to never return again.

Today, the Jewish people are seemingly under siege once again from their communities through college campuses to social media—where anti-Semitic tropes and conspiracies have become rife and taken a whole new meaning in the rapidly-emerging metaverse.

Back on American soil, some notable anti-Semitic attacks from the recent past include the:
- 2014 shooting at the Jewish Community Center in Overland Park, Kansas
- 2018 shooting at the Tree of Life synagogue in Pittsburgh, Pennsylvania
- 2019 shooting at the Chabad of Poway synagogue in Poway, California
- 2022 hostage crisis at the Congregation Beth Israel synagogue in Colleyville, Texas

According to the Anti-Defamation League (ADL), which tracks anti-Semitic behavior across the United States, not only did 2021 register a record number of anti-Semitic incidents over the past four decades but hate crimes against the Jewish people have also been rapidly rising over the past decade or so.

To say that such a sharp upsurge in anti-Semitism serves as a canary-in-the-coalmine of what is lurking on the horizon for the human society as a whole would be to put it lightly.

Still, what goes up must come down.

After peaking around annus horribilis (2028) of the current oquannium (1955-2038), anti-Semitism will begin to precipitously dwindle during the 2030s and largely die out by 2040s in a manner akin to the 1950s.

The anti-Semitic wave will next begin to wax during the 2080s and intensify over the following decades peaking around annus horribilis (2112) of the next oquannium (2039-2122).

Why does the anti-Semitic wave ebb during the first half of oqual cycle only to flow during the second?

THE ECONOMIC WOES EXACERBATE ANTI-SEMITISM DURING THE SECOND HALF OF OQUAL CYCLE

It is an open secret that the Jewish community by-and-large has always been rather affluent relative to other ethnic groups.

In particular, the achievements and contributions of Jewish people to the wider society in every country that they have called home have not only been head-and-shoulders but also chest-and-waist above other groups since the beginning of times from the Roman Empire through the Ottomans to the British.

Today, the Jewish people continue to thrive with the same zest and spirit a la their ancestors who lived centuries and millennia ago in every corner of the world.

Why do the Jewish people punch well above their weight?

The Holy Quran explains [2:47 or 2:122]:

> "Ya-bani Israa-ee-lath-kuroo nihmati-yallatee an-hamtu alaikum wa annee fadhaltukum aa-lal-aalameen!"—"Oh Children of Israel! Remember my blessings that I bestowed upon you and I unequivocally preferred you across all the worlds!"

While God's word is final, a philosophical argument is nevertheless warranted.

Unlike their Christian and Muslim brethren who waste tons of their energy on fighting for territorial control, the Jewish culture is non-territorial and deeply-rooted in the rather fruitful pursuit of art and creativity—two essential ingredients for advancing knowledge and building wealth.

In other words, while Christianity and Islam are missionary religions with the urge to convert others to their faith by reason or sword if necessary, Judaism is a non-missionary faith with deep respect for everyone irrespective of their beliefs.

It is therefore no coincidence that while there are over 2000M Christians today with Muslims poised to overtake them by 2050, there are no more than 20M Jews worldwide even though they began their journey millennia before the other Abrahamic outfits would even emerge.

Notably, the restoration of the State of Israel as the promised land for Jews was somewhat of an aberration in the overall spirit of the Jewish culture.

Had it not been for the Holocaust to rear its ugly head during the 20th century, neither Zionism would have gained traction among the Jewish masses nor the State of Israel would have seen the light of day, at least in our times.

In fact, even today, orthodox adherents of the Jewish faith across the globe such as the Neturei Karta are vehemently opposed to the very existence of Israel in that they believe that Eretz Yisrael cannot be reclaimed by Jews until the arrival of the Judaic Messiah—a biblical figure who is to return to Earth at some point in future to once again lead the Jewish people back to the Land of Israel.

The Holy Quran proclaims [5:20 and 5:21]:

> "And remember when Moses said to his people:
>
> Oh my people! Remember Allah's favors upon you when He made prophets from among you, and made you kings, and gave you what He had never given to anyone in the world.
>
> Oh my people! Enter the Holy Land which has been ordained for you by Allah and do not turn back lest you become losers."

Well, there you go.

With all due empathy for the dire plight of Palestinians, the Quranic verdict for Eretz Yisrael as a homeland in perpetuity for the Jewish people is loud and clear.

And that is the least the Arab World should pay heed to.

Over the course of centuries and millennia, the Jewish people have been essentially driven out of every corner of the Middle East and North Africa (MENA) into what is today a rather small State of Israel.

While there is one Jew for every 50 Arabs across MENA today, the latter occupy a combined landmass that is 500-fold greater than the State of Israel.

Simply put, while the Arabs have ten-fold greater landmass per capita relative to their Jewish neighbors, they nevertheless remain gung-ho on their unwillingness to yield even an inch to their Abrahamic cousins.

One can only conclude that the blood rivalry runs much deeper than even the buried oceans of Uranus.

Still, the Jewish people can take heart from the fact that it is not the landmass but rather the landmark that counts in this world as well as in the afterlife with the Lord of Ram, Moses, Jesus, Muhammad, and others.

Although the Jewish diaspora comprises a paltry 0.25% of world population (or one soul out of every 400 is Jewish), it makes up almost a quarter of all the Nobel laureates ever awarded the prestigious prize, and a similar ratio is also etched among the wealthiest people in the world.

While many people scorn wealth, they often forget that money earned in a righteous way is a blessing-in-disguise for it not only brings prosperity to one's life but it can also be used to help others who are less fortunate as well as to build essential services for the wider community in one's own neck-of-the-woods.

Indeed, the Jewish culture is deeply motivated by the divine appetite to build and improve the moral, spiritual, and material well-being of their communities as embodied in the so-called "Tikkun Olam"—a central pillar of Judaic traditions.

Needless to say, philanthropy is virtually synonymous with the Jewish culture as one can bear testimony to that in every walk of life from schools through hospitals to community centers that serve the needs of all humanity.

Notwithstanding such impeccable Jewish contributions, the Jewish masses nevertheless end up bearing the brunt of the fallout from many societal ills.

For example, upon the collapse of a Ponzi scheme run by a Jewish individual, many gentiles are quick to stereotype the entire Jewish community even though Jews are not statistically any more likely than gentiles to engage in such unscrupulous activities.

Why the Jews are perceived to be so is due to the fact that they are disproportionately overrepresented among the elite and wealthy—and quite rightly so due to their ingenuity, creativity, and entrepreneurial prowess rather than having exploited the system more than any other wealthy individual.

Nevertheless, since it is only the wealthy that have the means to run genuine enterprises as well as bogus ones, the Jews are inherently going to be seen as bad guys even though the ratio of bad to good among Jews in the positions of power is the same as any other religious or ethnic group within that privileged demographic.

Indeed, no one has monopoly over good and bad for it transcends all cultures and societies in a proportional manner—after all, it is part-and-parcel of who we are.

Unfortunately, everyone pretends to be blind when the Jewish elite is punching well above its weight in the philanthropy arena but they all seem to have a 20/20 vision when it happens in the Ponzi schema.

That should hardly be surprising given that the human brain has naturally evolved to be more responsive to negative cues than positive ones in what psychologists refer to as the "negativity bias".

In what is called the "enthalpy-entropy compensation" in thermodynamics, an increase in enthalpy (or heat) is more or less balanced by a corresponding decrease in entropy (or disorder) such that there is no overall gain in free energy (or attraction) when two molecules encounter each other even under favorable conditions—such a compensatory effect acts as a bottleneck for the development of novel drugs harboring greater efficacy coupled with low toxicity.

In a similar manner, good and bad are akin to enthalpic and entropic forces in that they also suffer from the good-bad compensation—every ounce of additional good is apparently negated by a corresponding ounce of bad such that no matter how hard we try, we simply cannot shake off the bad from our society.

It is indeed a marriage of inconvenience between good and bad, albeit made in heavens—and, quite understandably, divorce is not an option.

How does the bad in our society fuel anti-Semitism?

The economic well-being of people across the globe deteriorates drastically during the second half of oqual cycle such that it leads to a rising economic gulf between the poor and the rich—with the Jewish people disproportionately overrepresented among the latter elite class of wealthy.

Although the wealthy Jews only account for a meager fraction of the Jewish diaspora-at-large, they all nevertheless get indiscriminately painted with the same brush across the full spectrum of their social strata when the daily struggles of most Jewish people are no different from those of the gentiles.

Admittedly, driven by their nationalist and populist propaganda, the right-wing extremists and demagogues exploit the rising wealth gap between the poor and the rich to gaslight (or manipulate) the masses into believing that their economic woes are in no small part due to the "wealthy" Jews.

Unsurprisingly, such misguided views set off a chain reaction that fuels anti-Semitism during the second half of oqual cycle that is otherwise relegated to the backburner for much of the first half when even the masses get to taste a good dose of economic prosperity and are therefore left with little grievances to blame others for what are overall happy times across the board.

Regrettably, it is the masses rather than the wealthy within the Jewish community that end up bearing the brunt of the cost of anti-Semitism as they increasingly become sacrificial lambs for right-wing fanatics and their entourage to vent their anger on.

Needless to say, the wealthy and influential Jews in the positions of power should be mindful of their actions as the fallout from their Russian roulette turns the ordinary Jewish people into punching bags, if not outright putting their safety in peril, at the hands of bigoted and racist minds in their community.

ISRAELI POLICIES FUEL ANTI-SEMITISM A LA WINDS FANNING WILDFIRE

Over the past couple of decades, there has been a growing public resentment in America against the ultra-powerful Israeli lobby that is perceived to literally own the US government as if it were a satellite state under the direct control of Israel.

In 1967, during the Six-Day War between Israel and Arab nations led by Egypt, the unarmed US Navy surveillance ship USS Liberty (AGTR-5) patrolling in the Mediterranean Sea off the northern coast of the Sinai Peninsula was intentionally and brutally attacked by a barrage of Israeli fighter jets and torpedo boats killing 34 and wounding another 171 members of the US military.

Why did Israel ferociously bite the hand that had generously spoon-fed it up till then and has continued to do so ever since it came into being in 1948?

Presumably either to keep the US surveillance at bay while Israeli forces moved ahead with their planned invasion of the Sinai Peninsula, or to create a pretext via staging a false-flag operation in order to lay the blame on Egypt such that it would become a target for the US military to unleash its firepower, thereby widening the conflict with the help of its all-weather ally.

How did America respond?

With the powerful Israeli lobby orchestrating every move of the US government, America's response was not only muted but rather its leadership from top-to-bottom under the then 36th POTUS Lyndon Johnson literally swept the whole botched-and-bungled operation under the rug out of fear of being booted out of office rather than holding Israel's hands, much more its feet, to the fire.

I should declare that I was in no way swimming in Mediterranean waters while the Israeli assault on a US Navy ship unfolded in 1967—rather, it is a matter of historical records corroborated by a large body of independent accounts, including intercepted messages and tapes, with no vested interests in either party.

However, I did witness firsthand the following theatrics from a more recent past.

In 2012, while the then 44th POTUS Barack Obama was campaigning for his reelection for a second term against Governor Mitt Romney, the then Israeli Premier Benjamin Netanyahu traveled to the US to literally campaign for the latter when it runs counter to political ethics for a foreign leader to interfere in internal affairs of another country, much more so for an Israeli leader to resort to such despicable tactics against a nation that is closely aligned with Israel.

Why did Netanyahu mock the sovereignty of not only America but what was then the sole superpower in the world?

Not only did Netanyahu share little political chemistry with Obama but the latter also opposed the then proposed Israeli settlements in East Jerusalem.

In doing so, Obama earned the wrath of the Israeli state that most people in the world perceive to be the one that calls the shots and pulls the levers of international politics.

Pobrecito Barackito!—Poor Little Barack!

Obama should have known better that the notion that the US President is the most powerful leader in the world holds as much water as the debunked ideology that printing money causes no inflation—a view unfortunately shared by mainstream media and their entourage of bogus economists, including many Nobel Laureates among them.

That should be hardly alarming given that the mainstream media are virtually synonymous with fake news in that their primary role has turned into doing the bidding on behalf of the government rather than telling it as it is and not being afraid of calling the spade a spade.

The proof of my proclamation lies in the media-terranean pudding.

No one should wonder why the 1967 Israeli blunder against the US Navy ship has never been covered by any news media on American soil.

Nor why a growing number of Americans are turning to foreign media to get unbiased and unfiltered news on domestic and international affairs.

After all, one can only put so much lipstick on a donkey as the laws of nature begin to neutralize the transgressions so as to revert everything back to the mean or quasi-equilibrium in thermodynamic terms.

Other than its heavy-handed approach toward Palestinians, many Americans also take issue with Israel being a juggernaut vis-à-vis its bullying of Iran.

While Israel has long been a nuke state, its vehement opposition to Iran becoming one is deeply troubling for the neutral-and-unbiased mind as such a hypocrisy has laid bare Israel's hidden propaganda of policing the world—what authority Israel or any other nuke state has to tell Iran what it can or cannot do.

Like Israel, Iran is also a proud civilization whose history stretches back millennia.

Like Israel, Iran's nuke program is also for self-defense purposes.

To claim that Iran would be more likely to deploy its nukes than any other nation in the event of a war would be deeply preposterous and insanely prejudicial.

Where does the State of Israel go from here?

Up till around the beginning of the Christian Era some 2000 years ago, the Jewish people were in a majority and ruled over much of what are modern-day Israel and Palestine through various kingdoms such as the Kingdom of Israel and the Kingdom of Judah.

Although Jews had been expelled from their homeland and forced to live in the wilderness by various powers well before the rise of Christianity, the expansion of Roman Empire across the Middle East during the 1st century marked the death knell for the Israelites as their exile and dispersion around the globe would reach a fever pitch in the aftermath of their kingdoms having fallen to the Romans.

Under the Roman Empire, the Jewish homeland would become heavily Christianized from around the 3rd century onward with the Jews becoming an increasingly smaller minority in what was once their own backyard.

In 0638, the Jewish homeland was conquered by the Rashidun Caliphate under whom it would quickly become Arabized and Islamized.

Over the next millennium or so, the Jewish homeland would exchange hands between various successive Islamic Empires such that it would become a majority-Muslim region around the 12th century.

In 1517, the Jewish homeland would fall to the Ottoman Empire and undergo further Islamization.

In 1917, during World War I (1914-1918), the Jewish homeland was conquered by the British Empire under what came to be called the "Mandate for Palestine".

In 1948, the modern-day State of Israel was restored as a homeland for the Jewish diaspora so as to lead them out of the wilderness after a hiatus of nearly two millennia, to serve as an antidote to anti-Semitism, and to make sure that the likes of utter evils such as the Holocaust would never see the light of day again.

In that sense, the security of Israel ought to be the responsibility of every decent nation on earth.

Yet, today's Israel has become a bully-on-steroids because its interests are predominantly aligned with bloating the coffers of its ruling elite and its wealthy stakeholders rather than ordinary Israelis whose daily struggles are no different from the masses elsewhere around the globe.

Today, like people in most countries, a growing number of Israeli citizens are becoming frustrated with being unable to cut through what has become an overarching red tape in their daily lives.

It seems to me that Israel has not only taken a leaf out of America's playbook but has also doubled-down on how to turn the government-of-the-people into an oppressive regime whose central goal is to control and enslave the masses so that they can be exploited for the benefit of the ruling elite and the wealthy.

It should therefore be hardly surprising that many young Israelis today are not only looking to emigrate elsewhere but a growing number of non-Israeli Jews are also fast becoming paranoid about their intricate relationship with Israel as it steadfastly marches toward crony capitalism in order to serve the top one percent at the expense of the masses.

Still, while Israel and Jews are anything but synonymous, they are unfortunately perceived to be as such by many gentiles around the globe.

Accordingly, the actions of the State of Israel and, in particular, the Israeli lobby matter a great deal as they bear the potential to turn public opinion against the Jewish diaspora-at-large.

To be clear, it is not just the State of Israel but virtually every state in the world is cruel in that its primary goal is to enslave and control the masses in order to exploit them to fill the coffers of the ruling elite.

In fact, the very ideology of a modern-day statehood is damning to begin with.

While the function of a state ought to be nothing more than a triad of securing the freedom and liberty of its citizens (through the police) to add to the defense against foreign interference (through the military) and to hold everyone accountable for their actions (through the judiciary), today's states cast a much wider net over the lives of ordinary people such that they not only steal from them but also leave them with no privacy over matters that are fundamentally of personal nature.

To say that the statehood is about serving the interests of a picominority of the ruling elite at the expense and exploitation of the masses would be something of a huge understatement.

Today, citizens in most countries do not even qualify as subjects but rather their fate is best captured as being nothing more than serfs who are trapped into a vicious cycle of debt from the day they are born till the day they die courtesy of the state propaganda—often sugar-coated as a must-have medicine before being rolled out through state-sponsored or corporate scams such as one must keep up with the Joneses, one must hand over a big chunk of their hard-earned income, one must pay for a worthless degree to become a qualified window cleaner, baby sitter, chef, driver, and what not.

It is therefore hardly surprising that most citizens of virtually every country not only feel trapped but also deeply resent their government because of its bureaucratic and barbaric policies that not only deprive them of their freedom and liberty but also steal the fruits hard-earned by the sweat of their brow.

Likewise, Israeli citizens are no different in that the actions of their government in no way express their complicity but rather a violation of what they stand for.

As for the non-Israeli Jewish diaspora around the globe, their affection for Israel is no greater than that of Irish Americans for Ireland, Indian Americans for India, or Chinese Americans for China.

No one in their right mind would point a finger at Indian Americans for the actions of India nor Chinese Americans for the deeds of China.

Accordingly, conflating the actions of Israeli government and Israeli lobby with the Jewish diaspora-at-large is hypocrisy at best and anti-Semitism at worst for the ordinary Jewish people around the globe are just as flabbergasted as anyone with the Israeli bureaucracy at home and abroad.

ISRAELI LOBBY SHOULD NOT BE ABOVE THE LAW

Today, Israeli lobby has grown into an ominous 800-pound gorilla on American soil with a spending power that would even dwarf the purchasing power of many nations-of-the-world.

It is therefore hardly surprising that anyone with the guts to criticize Israeli policies is not only ostracized but also labeled as anti-Semite even when many of such critical voices have the best interests of the Jewish people at heart.

For those with political ambitions, criticism of Israel amounts to nothing short of a political suicide as they will either be demonized if running for an office or booted out if they hold one.

It is noteworthy that inviting and welcoming external criticism has been a divine hallmark of the unprecedented success of the Jewish society for millennia.

As we all know too well, societies that suppress criticism are doomed to fail as they are unable to breed independent minds best suited for creativity and innovation—the two essential pillars of a prosperous society.

Ironically, blocking criticism of Israeli policies and choking the critics is not only at odds with Jewish values but one could even argue that it is the very actions of the Israeli lobby that constitute anti-Semitism.

Alas, the omnipotent Israeli lobby has come to view itself not only as sacrosanct but also as an invincible institution with nothing out of its grasp.

Yet, it is this very hubris that spells the downfall of the invincible in what ought to be psychologically referred to as the "Invincibility Curse".

In 1929, the Dow Jones had become so convinced that it could continue to forever defy gravity only to come crashing back to earth after taking a close shave with a loss of a whopping 89% by 1932—it would take the index 25 years (or exactly 9212 calendar days) before it would finally recover in 1954 and make a new high so as to put on a new suit-and-tie as it quickly masqueraded its dirty past just in time for the arrival of the current oquannium (1955-2038).

In 1941, Nazi Germany (1933-1945) naively believed that its military was so superior that it could easily invade and quickly conquer large swathes of what was then the Soviet Union through what came to be known as the "Operation Barbarossa" but it ended up being given a bloody nose such that it would shift the equilibrium of World War II (1939-1945) in favor of the Allies—had it not been for such an asinine act on the part of Nazi Germany as the previous oquannium (1871-1954) was preparing to bid farewell, the world could have followed a very different trajectory during the course of the current oquannium (1955-2038), perhaps the diametric opposite of what it did.

In 1941, taking a cue from Nazi Germany and driven by the conviction that it could knock America out before the Sleeping Giant would even have the chance to stand on its feet in the Pacific Ocean, Imperial Japan (1868-1945) ingenuously attacked the US Navy base at Hawaii's Pearl Harbor in order to make sure that its planned invasion of Southeast Asia would be made all the easier—not only did such a faux pas seal Japan's atomic fate but it also continues to haunt the island nation even today and perhaps will continue to do so forever in light of what appears to be the Russian occupation-in-perpetuity of Kuril islands.

In 1956, buoyed by victory over Nazi Germany in World War II (1939-1945), Britain dared to flex its muscles when it tried to regain control of the Suez Canal after it had been nationalized by Egypt in what came to be called the "Suez Canal Crisis"—not only was Vilayat left to lick its wounds but it also marked a watershed moment in the rapid disintegration of the empire upon which the sun once never set with the pound quickly plunging into a nosedive and forever losing its imperial luster while the then-fledgling Queen Elizabeth II (1952-2022) forever parting with her imperial mojo.

In 1971, driven by the euphoria of a rising military might on the back of relatively prosperous times in what was then West Pakistan during the 1960s, Pakistani leaders failed to address the urgent call and the dire economic plight of Eastern Pakistanis—not only would the nation go onto lose East Pakistan to become what is modern-day Bangladesh but its military would also suffer a humiliating defeat and forever become tarnished with the unwanted stigma of being complicit in the systematic and state-driven ethnic cleansing of millions of Bangladeshis.

In 1979, emboldened by what it believed to be its invincible gizmo of socialism, the Soviet Union (1922-1991) invaded Afghanistan in order to expand its orbit of communist propaganda in what turned out to be a decade-long purposeless war in an echo of America's Vietnam War (1955-1975)—such a mindless ploy not only left the Red Army demoralized but it also bankrupted the Eurasian Federation so much so that it began to collapse under its own weight even before its soldiers from the Pashtun homeland had fully returned home.

In 1984, after the euphoria of having emerged as a nuke state during the 1970s, India not only failed to properly address the needs of its diverse minorities but also became increasingly emboldened to use force as a means of suppression—in what came to be called the "Operation Blue Star", the attack on Sikhism's holiest site Golden Temple with tanks-and-artillery fire became the hill upon which not only the critical mass for a separate homeland of Khalistan for Sikhs would be reached but such a blunder has since continued to threaten the Indian union.

In 2001, using the 9/11 attacks as a veneer while brimming with the chutzpah of being the sole superpower destined for a utopian era waiting on the horizon with the promise of making its past look tame by comparison, the United States waged what would turn out to be decades-long wars in the Middle East in the name of liberty and freedom but with the hidden propaganda of changing the world order so as to extend the branches of its hegemonic tree farther than ever before—such a criminal gambit that would kill and uproot millions of innocent souls would not only backfire but would also come back to haunt America in that the embers of the decades-long self-destructive 9/11 Wars continue to rage to this day with the nation teetering on the brink of a looming bankruptcy with the US dollar edging ever closer to losing its global luster a la British pound in 1956 over the next decade or so coupled with social-and-moral decadence at home from soaring public debts through shrinking middle class to faltering infrastructure.

In what I call the "9/11 Curse", America literally dug its own grave in lieu of using the tragedy to undertake a big round of soul-searching so as to channel much-needed resources toward addressing what were then already becoming a growing plethora of domestic issues rather than funneling every dollar of US taxpayer overseas to smash the world into pieces with the sole intention of bloating the coffers of its ruling elite and the wealthy at the expense of the pain and suffering of the masses that we can all see in plain sight today.

And on a lighter note …

In 2004, the soccer giant Arsenal became "The Invincibles" when it not only won the English Premier League (EPL) title at a canter but also did so without losing a single game throughout what is perceived to be a long treacherous season, a feat never achieved before or since then in English Football—while the dire spell of the Billy Goat Curse on the Chicago Cubs lasted some 71 years, the Arsenal fans can only hope that the Invincibility Curse on the Gunners does not last as long as that of the cud-chewing ruminant given that their team has been a shadow of the heights it touched some two decades ago with that EPL title won being their last one and with no hope of winning another one anywhere in sight.

While that rundown constitutes nothing more than History 101, it should nevertheless serve as plenty of food-for-thought for the Israeli lobby for everything eventually reverts to the mean as no one is above the laws of nature—the transgressions inherently come pre-packed with a measured antidote such that one reaps as one plants.

Those laws are in no small part equally relevant to today's India.

|4.3| HINDU-MUSLIM CONFLICT

As recently as 2000, it seemed that Muslims felt at home in India and that the creation of Pakistan had been a blunder-of-the-century—with many Indian Muslims not only feeling so proud to be Indians back then but also poking fun at how retrograde my Pakistan was.

Not anymore.

Nearly a quarter-of-a-century later, many of those Indian Muslims confide in me that they could not have been more wrong back then, that they no longer feel safe in India, and that they wish their ancestors had left for Pakistan in 1947.

While I wholeheartedly empathize with them, I also remind them that what they are going through today is nothing more than a rendezvous with destiny that befalls humanity every 84 years when minorities around the globe bear the brunt of the fallout from the dire economic straits.

And that they must persevere for things will change for the better over the next decade or so when they will once again feel proud to be Indians.

For their part, they think that I am unable to share their agony and that my words are intended to be nothing more than a pun in that I am merely returning the favors a quarter-of-a-century later.

Well, I can only hope that they pay heed to the recurring spell of oqual cycle on our lives as it will not only transform their understanding of how they ought to view the society but also their own place within it.

Indeed, the ongoing marginalization of Indian Muslims by Hindu supremacists within their own backyard is nothing new but as old as the arrival of Islam on the Indian peninsula during the first millennium.

However, such Hindu-Muslim conflict is not random but rather it ebbs and flows across the two halves of oqual cycle as captured by what is dubbed the "Hindu-Muslim oquacycle".

In order to illustrate that point, I revisit the highs and lows in the perpetual Hindu-Muslim schism over the past 500 years.

MUGHAL RULE ALTERNATED BETWEEN BENEVOLENT AND MALEVOLENT EMPERORS ALMOST IN SYNC WITH THE TWO HALVES OF OQUAL CYCLE

The wave of Hindu-Muslim conflict has ebbed and flowed over the course of every oqual cycle ever since the Mughal era began in 1526—when a Mongolian prince named Babur invaded India from the north and brought with him a tornado of chaos when his soldiers went on a killing spree during what was then the dusk (1514-1534) of the first oquannium (1451-1534).

While the chaos continued well deep into the 1530s as the reign passed onto Babur's son Humayun in 1530, a period of relative peace would nevertheless ensue thereafter on the Indian peninsula during much of the first half (1535-1576) of the second oquannium (1535-1618) in parallel with the minority Muslim rule beginning to rapidly expand across large swathes of what was then a predominantly Hindu homeland.

In fact, Hindu-Muslim harmony reached its apex under the Mughal Emperor Akbar (1556-1605) during much of the second half of the 16th century.

Under Akbar's great vision, measured diplomacy, religious tolerance, and equality for his predominantly non-Muslim subjects—including the ultra-minority Sikhs and the ultra-majority Hindus—the Mughal Empire rapidly grew like a bamboo tree across much of the northern-and-central Indian peninsula, attracting alliances of regional kingdoms ruled by Muslims-and-Hindus-alike, as it underwent enormous expansion within a couple of decades.

In particular, Akbar's India experienced huge economic boom spearheaded by literary-and-technological innovations, social prosperity, and cultural harmony—the like of which have never been witnessed since on Indian soil.

Among so many of his great policies implemented during his distinguished reign of nearly 50 years (1556-1605), Akbar's abolishment in 1564 of Jizya—an old practice of levying a form of unfair taxation on non-Muslim subjects under Muslim rule—would no doubt stand out as a cardinal piece of his legacy.

Akbar also instituted a complete ban on cow slaughter out of respect for his predominantly Hindu subjects—a policy that would be upheld by his successors throughout the Mughal era (1526-1857).

The rather secular Akbar even experimented hybridizing Islam with other religions such as Hinduism so as to construct a new mystical faith modeled on Sufism that he dubbed "Deen-e-Ilahi"—or "Religion of My God"—in the hope that it would bring

Muslims-and-Hindus-alike closer together, alleviate deep-seated communal tensions between them, and unite humanity-writ-large within his vast empire.

However, with the arrival of the second half (1577-1618) of the second oquannium (1535-1618), troubles began to brew in Akbar's empire particularly with regard to the rebellious behavior of his eldest son and heir-apparent Jahangir—who not only attempted to revolt against his father but also began to show his true colors as a cruel maniac in that he would put to death anyone he did not like, or got annoyed by, and do so in the most inhumane manner possible.

With the death of Akbar in 1605, during the dusk (1598-1618) of the second oquannium (1535-1618), ethnic harmony however turned on its head as the reign was passed onto Jahangir.

While Akbar had carved out a large empire by the sweat of his brow, Jahangir would set about dismantling it with his reckless blow.

Simply put, Jahangir was a toxic enantiomer of his father—incompetent, often intoxicated, and inherently intolerant of the predominantly non-Muslim subjects under his reign.

In 1606, Emperor Jahangir would hastily order the execution of the fifth Sikh Guru Arjun on the account of heresy—after the Guru was accused of exploiting-and-corrupting the teachings of Islam and Hinduism as Sikhism rapidly began to take hold in Mughal India—though it was primarily driven by the Emperor's personal animosity toward the Guru.

The execution of their fifth Guru would forever turn Sikhs against the Mughal Empire—it would mark the beginning of Sikh quest to arm themselves for self-defense and for a future showdown with the Mughals for territorial control.

It was not only the ultra-minority Sikhs but even large segments of the ultra-majority Hindus that would also be alienated under Jahangir's reign with much of Mughal India left with a dose of soul-searching to do and in utter disarray vis-à-vis ethnic harmony.

Overall, Emperor Jahangir's reign (1605-1627) is remembered as a period of extreme trials-and-tribulations for Indians across all walks of life.

In 1627, upon Jahangir's death, Indians would finally be able to breathe a sigh of relief with the coronation of his son Shahjahan as his successor.

Under Emperor Shahjahan (1628-1658), a sustained period of relative peace and ethnic harmony would once again return to the Indian peninsula during much of the first half (1619-1660) of the third oquannium (1619-1702).

In spite of Islamization of India by abolishing many liberal practices and equal rights for his predominantly non-Muslim subjects first introduced by his grandfather Emperor Akbar circa mid-16th century, Emperor Shahjahan's reign leading up to mid-17th century would nevertheless usher in a long and sustained period of economic and social stability rather than be defined by his religious doctrine.

In particular, Shahjahan's reign is best remembered for spurring India to fully realize its cultural and artistic glory for he heralded the golden age of Mughal architecture that included the likes of Taj Mahal (India) and Shahjahan Mosque (Pakistan) among a multitude of other breathtaking monuments—the sight of which lets one travel back to the future.

In line with the dire spell of oqual cycle, ethnic harmony would nosedive once again just as the second half (1661-1702) of the third oquannium (1619-1702) arrived with the Mughal reign having been passed onto Emperor Shahjahan's son Aurangzeb in 1658.

After having his older brother—who was first-in-line-of-succession to his father's throne—executed through conspiracy and then ruthlessly having forced his father to abdicate, Aurangzeb's greed for absolute power should have served as a harbinger of despotic and tyrannical things to come for his subjects.

Being an orthodox Muslim, Emperor Aurangzeb ratcheted up the role that Islam would play during his reign relative to that of his father who himself was considered to be a very conservative ruler.

In fact, Aurangzeb would abandon pluralism altogether and go onto institutionalize Sharia—the Islamic code of conduct.

In doing so, Aurangzeb ushered in a number of cultural revolutions such as prohibition of alcohol, drugs, gambling, prostitution, and fornication.

Additionally, Aurangzeb outlawed sati—an old practice among many Hindus wherein a woman was compelled to sacrifice herself by sitting atop the funeral pyre upon the cremation of her dead husband.

To say that Aurangzeb's reign not only began with an iron-fist but that it would also put him in the eye-of-the-storm would be something of an understatement.

Admittedly, Aurangzeb's "my way or the highway" approach powered by his Islamic faith brought him in direct conflict with the predominantly non-Muslim Hindu-Sikh populace—many of whom would now put their differences aside and begin to unite to oppose the Mughal rule through carefully planted rebellions.

In doing so, the non-Muslims earned the wrath of Aurangzeb who in turn would go onto persecute them and double-down on his rage by ordering the large-scale destruction of Hindu and Sikh temples—presumably using the pretext that they provided shelter to the rebels opposing Mughal rule.

Additionally, regional kingdoms that refused to become subordinates (or vassals) so as to accept Aurangzeb's suzerainty were brutally crushed in order to expand the territorial orbit of Mughal Empire virtually across the whole of Indian peninsula.

Indeed, Aurangzeb's reign (1658-1707) is by-and-large derided by most Indian historians as it is believed to have forever set Hindu-Muslim schism alight in what was a crossing of the Rubicon—a turning point that presumably planted the seeds for a future partition of the Indian peninsula along religious lines.

In particular, Aurangzeb's death in 1707 significantly weakened the Mughal rule and created a power vacuum during much of the 18th century across the Indian peninsula with numerous rival powers from the ruling Mughals through the native Marathas and Sikhs to the British colonialists fighting for territorial control.

Accordingly, with a few brief periods of relative calm during the first half (1703-1744), much of the fourth oquannium (1703-1786) was mired in utter chaos and ethnic cleansings across all corners of the Indian peninsula.

BRITISH RAJ WAS ALSO GOVERNED BY A TALE OF TWO CONTRASTING HALVES ACROSS THE COURSE OF EACH OQUAL CYCLE

It was during the second half (1745-1786) of the fourth oquannium (1703-1786), when the British victory over the Mughals in the 1757 Battle of Plassey, at Hooghly River close to the Bay of Bengal, would lay the foundation for what would turn out to be nearly two centuries of British Raj (1757-1947), albeit beginning with the so-called "East India Company"—a British enterprise founded in 1600 to trade goods and services between East and West.

As the fourth oquannium (1703-1786) reached its crescendo against the backdrop of the American Independence War (1775-1783) unfolding on the Eastern coast of

North America, the British would emerge as a dominant colonial power on the Indian peninsula after having ousted their French, Dutch, and Portuguese rivals.

With the arrival of the first half (1787-1828) of the fifth oquannium (1787-1870), the Indian peninsula would once again breathe a sigh of ethnic relief and things would tamp down for the most part.

However, social unrest and ethnic violence on the Indian peninsula would once again rear their ugly head-and-shoulders with the arrival of the second half (1829-1870) of the fifth oquannium (1787-1870)—when the British Raj (1757-1947) would finally extend across every corner of the Indian peninsula with the Mughals being allowed to remain as a symbolic figurehead.

In doing so, the British suzerainty added gasoline to the resentment fire that had been gathering inertia among the native masses against the colonial master.

In particular, such a fire of humiliation would serve as a catalyst for Indians of all faiths to put their differences aside and unite against the British colonialists—the common adversary—in order to free themselves from being continued to be subjugated, oppressed, and enslaved in their own backyard.

In 1857, in the midst of the dusk (1850-1870) of the fifth oquannium (1787-1870), such flames of trepidation were set alight when Mangal Pandey—an Indian freedom fighter—was hanged by the British.

That execution not only triggered a series of rebellions and revolts against the British across much of the Indian peninsula but also put a final nail in the coffin of what little remained of the Mughal Empire (1526-1857).

In the aftermath of what came to be known as the 1857 Indian Mutiny, the British government took up the reins from the East India Company and put India under the direct rule of the British Crown during the then Queen Victoria's reign (1837-1901) through what came to be known as the 1858 Government of India Act.

With that British ordinance, perpetual humiliation and killing of Indians by the British colonialists would finally ease off as they were now not only being granted greater civil rights but they could also lay claim to being direct subjects of the Queen rather than having been treated as little more than slaves by the East India Company.

However, such a honeymoon period would not last beyond the first half (1871-1912) of the previous and sixth oquannium (1871-1954) in line with the dire spell of oqual cycle.

With the onset of World War I (1914-1918) almost in parallel with the beginning of the second half (1913-1954) of the sixth oquannium (1871-1954), the writing was on the wall for the end of relatively happy times that Indians had taken for granted over the past half-a-century-or-so.

With more than a million Indians asked to fight for the freedom of Europeans while they themselves were being denied the same liberties in their own backyard, the shameful hypocrisy of the British colonialists could not have been better exposed by anything other than World War I.

Nevertheless, Indian leaders led by their stalwart Mahatma Gandhi whole-heartedly supported the British during World War I out of misguided belief that their loyalty would be rewarded with independence and the end of colonial rule.

Rather, in the aftermath of World War I (1914-1918) in which as many as 100K Indian soldiers perished fighting for the British across the globe, the Indians at home would be compensated with what came to be called the "1919 Jallianwala Bagh Massacre"—wherein the British troops fired multiple rounds of live ammunition on a large crowd of unarmed Indians who had gathered in Amritsar in modern-day Indian state of Punjab to protest against a spate of perpetual wartime oppressive measures and the arrest of their civil-rights leaders.

What made that massacre all the more disturbing was the fact that the Jallianwala Bagh (or Jallianwala Park) was closed off on three sides with unscalable walls (or buildings) with a shared entrance and exit located on only one side—the bigoted British commander called to the scene took advantage of such a topographical setting and ordered his troops to block off the only exit before having them indiscriminately shoot at the crowd until they had exhausted all of the ammunition at their disposal.

Unable to flee from what had essentially turned into an inescapable coliseum, thousands of Indians were brutally and inhumanely put to death or left with debilitating scars, physical and psychological, for the rest of their lives.

That brutal attack on the very conscience of Indian society stung Gandhi into action one last time after he unloaded his own secret weapon of "Satyagraha" or "True Path"—a nonviolent movement that professed civil disobedience and noncooperation with the British colonialists across all walks of Indian life.

With Satyagraha at his disposal, the British were found wanting on all fronts as Gandhi had turned into their worst kryptonite.

That Satyagraha had indeed jump-started the final march toward independence was further highlighted with the execution in 1931 of Bhagat Singh—a revolutionary hero who took up militancy to fight for freedom against the British colonialists.

Although Bhagat Singh's militant approach was at odds with Satyagraha, he nevertheless played a leading role in awakening the conscience of Indians by becoming "Shaheed-e-Azam!"—"Great Martyr!"

Additionally, Bhagat Singh became a megaphone to express the sentiments of the voiceless masses after he coined the powerful Urindi catchphrase "Inquilab Zindabad!"—"Hail Revolution!"

While Gandhi had garnered an overwhelming support across all ethnic groups—including Hindus and Muslims alike—for his nonviolent movement to liberate India from the shackles of British slavery, fractures in his strategy would nevertheless begin to emerge before too long given the sheer complexity of India's multicultural makeup with each religious faction vying to hold its own.

In particular, the Muslim leader Jinnah was utterly opposed to Gandhi's political posturing as he believed that Satyagraha amounted to a form of anarchy that would be self-destructive in that the only way to secure independence was to engage with the British through constitutional means.

In 1939, such political polarization between the two Indian leaders would only intensify and take on a whole new meaning with the outbreak of World War II (1939-1945) with India once again in the line of fire to provide millions of soldiers and prioritize millions-of-tons of precious resources toward the war effort of its imperial master rather than for domestic consumption even though tens-of-millions of Indians would remain malnourished at home.

However, Gandhi must have held close to his heart the following motto: "Fool me once shame on you, fool me twice shame on me!"

Indeed, while Gandhi vehemently opposed the participation of India in World War II, his political nemesis Jinnah warmly cowed into British demands as he saw a golden opportunity to score political points.

And so he did as the British warmed up to Jinnah's divisive ideology of a separate homeland for Indian Muslims against a growing backdrop of ethnic uprisings and communal violence between Hindus and Muslims reaching a fever pitch and showing no signs of cresting.

In the aftermath of World War II (1939-1945), the badly-bruised British Empire would finally give into Indians' demand for independence but before playing one last gambit—dividing the Indian peninsula into what is modern-day India and what was then a bipartite Pakistan allegedly along religious lines but the reality could not have been farther than that in what came to be called the "1947 Indian Partition".

INDOCAUST UNDERSCORED THE DIRE SPELL OF THE SECOND HALF OF OQUAL CYCLE ON ETHNIC HARMONY

With the Hindu-Muslim uprisings having already reached the transition state, the 1947 Indian Partition would be unsurprisingly accompanied by Indocaust (1946-1948)—the large-scale genocide of at least 1M people and forced migration of another 10M during the partition of the Indian peninsula.

With the arrival of the first half (1955-1996) of the current oquannium (1955-2038), a new dawn of peace and prosperity would nevertheless emerge across both India and Pakistan in line with the promise of oqual cycle—though the latter would experience yet another partition of its own making with its eastern half breaking away and coming into its own being as Bangladesh in 1971.

That divorce along ethnic rather than religious lines was far from being amicable as it would trigger ethnic cleansing of millions of helpless Bangladeshis by Pakistani troops rather than due to inter-ethnic violence.

As if Pakistan had scored a penalty kick against India, the latter would hit back with a golden goal of its own in a little more than a decade later.

In 1984, in what is widely believed to be the "Sikh Genocide", tens-of-thousands of Sikhs in the Indian state of Punjab were systematically butchered by Hindu mobs to which the state authorities not only turned a blind eye but were also complicit to a large degree in the aftermath of the riots sparked by the assassination of the then Indian Premier Indira Gandhi by her Sikh bodyguards—the assassination itself was triggered after Indira Gandhi launched the "Operation Blue Star" to attack the Golden Temple, the Mecca of Sikhism, with tanks-and-artillery fire after it had been overtaken by a group of Sikh militants demanding greater autonomy for their homeland.

With the exception of the 1971 Bangladeshi Genocide and the 1984 Sikh Genocide, ethnic violence across the Indian peninsula by-and-large remained bottled during the first half (1955-1996) of the current oquannium (1955-2038)—thereby giving many a false sense of complacency that perhaps the bad times had forever been put to the sword.

Unbeknown to the masses of the dire spell of oqual cycle on a nation as ethnically diverse as India, the new wave of ethnic conflict of the current oquannium (1955-2038) would arrive somewhat earlier than anticipated with the onset of the second half (1997-2038).

In 1989, after it had enjoyed almost four decades of relative peace and ethnic harmony, the perpetual oppression of Kashmiri Muslims by the Indian government would boil over in the Indian-administered Kashmir.

Over three decades later, such an insurgency led by various Muslim separatist groups demanding a complete secession from India has not only reached a fever pitch but, in doing so, it has caused enormous collateral damage along the following two fronts:

1) Over 100K Kashmiri Muslims have hitherto been killed by the Indian security forces that are all but granted impunity from deploying a heavy-handed approach against unarmed civilians as they go about conducting extra-judicial killings on a gargantuan scale; and

2) Over 100K Kashmiri Pandits have been driven out of their millennia-old ancestral lands and hundreds killed by Muslim extremists.

What is deeply troubling about the Kashmiri conflict is the mass exodus of virtually the entire community of Pandits—a small minority of highly-distinguished Hindus who have garnered huge respect over the centuries for their art and creativity.

In particular, the peace-loving Pandits have been caught in the cross-fire between Kashmiri Muslims and the Indian state through no fault of their own—they have regrettably become the latest sacrificial lambs in the centuries-old Hindu-Muslim conflict.

Given that the Kashmiri Pandits are the ancestors of virtually all Kashmiris, one cannot imagine Kashmir without them.

Just as there is no Lahore without Sikhs and Hindus, there is no Kashmir without Pandits.

Regrettably, the echoes of humanity gone wild on the Indian peninsula some 76 years ago during the 1947 Indian Partition continue to reverberate across much of today's India and Pakistan though few seem to have learned anything from history.

Instead of paying homage to the dire fate of at least 1M mercilessly butchered to death and upward of 10M uprooted from their millennia-old homes, the 1947 Indian Partition is ingenuously celebrated by almost every Indian-and-Pakistani and their diaspora across the globe without any regard for the memories of those who perished in the bedlam—while multiple days are earmarked in the calendars of both nations to toast the end of the British colonial rule, not even a single night is eyemarked to commemorate the disproportionate price paid by at least a million souls who met a torturous death in lieu of much promised freedom.

To add salt to wounds, the school curricula of both nations have not only swept Indocaust under the rug as if it had never happened but what little accounts are made available to young generations are largely biased with each side portraying itself as the victim and painting the other as the aggressor—there is a plenty of room for finger-pointing but hardly any for hard truth.

Without young generations learning the hard truth about their brutal past, India and Pakistan will never hit a home run but rather continue to repeat such a cycle of madness at least once every 84 years.

Still, India is the first to extend an olive branch though with caveats aplenty.

In 2017, India erected the Partition Museum on its soil—the first ever of its kind devoted to the memories of over 10M people who either perished during the 1947 Indian Partition or were forced to become homeless simply because they happened to be on the wrong side of the despicable border callously inked by none other than the British.

For its part, Pakistan is yet to pitch in and recognize the utter evil committed on its side of the border some 76 years ago—that should sound alarm bells given that the oqual cycle has only begun to knock on Pakistan's door with its full force yet to be unleashed over the next decade or so.

In Pakistan, many locals proudly remind Indian visitors:
> "Jine Lahore ni vaikhya, ooh jamya hee ni!"—"One who has not been to Lahore is yet to be born!"

That dubious claim merits a befitting response:
> "Jithe apne Sardaar te Pandit nahi haa, ooh Lahore jinda hee nahi haa!"—"Without the hustle-and-bustle of its indigenous Hindu-and-Sikh children, Lahore is nothing but a dead city!"

Indeed, it does not occur to any Pakistani that today's predominantly Muslim Lahore is a shadow of its multicultural and multireligious past with millions of native Hindus and Sikhs wiped off its every street and corner in the most callous manner imaginable during the 1947 Indian Partition.

In 1947, prior to the partition, minorities made up more than 30% of Pakistan's demographics.

In 2023, 76 years later, minorities account for a little more than 3% among Pakistan's citizens.

That Pakistan suffered a massive brain drain during the partition is exquisitely summed up by its faltering economy heavily reliant on foreign imports rather than being able to produce and manufacture most of what it needs at home due to the lack of talent and skill.

To say that the Pakistanis could do with a dose of soul-searching would be to put it un-Pakistanly!

India has no room to rejoice either.

The very forces that fanned the flames of ethnic cleansing some 84 years ago across much of the then Jewel-in-the-Crown during the 1940s are once again at play with full force in today's India—if Indian leaders led by their ultra-nationalist Narendra Modi are not careful and refuse to tone down their divisive-and-inflammatory rhetoric and policies, India may end up experiencing yet another partition and thus having to deal with an unwanted sense of déjà vu as the dire spell of oqual cycle leaves no stone unturned as it reaches its climax.

Indeed, the Indian peninsula is yet to bear the brunt of the ethnic fallout from the second half (1997-2038) of the current oquannium (1955-2038)—with the seeds of ethnic conflict planted some 84 years ago already beginning to bloom.

Can history guide us as to what is in store for the minorities on the Indian peninsula as the current oquannium draws to a close?

INDIAN MUSLIMS ARE ONCE AGAIN AT THE CROSSROADS AND IN THE LINE OF FIRE

While the second half (1913-1954) of the previous oquannium (1871-1954) was largely marred by Hindu-Muslim discord on the Indian peninsula, the second half (1997-2038) of the current oquannium (1955-2038) has already witnessed ethnic conflict developing on multiple fronts from Hindu-Muslim conflicts through Hindu-Christian frictions to Hindu-Sikh hostilities.

In particular, over the past couple of decades, the Khalistan movement for a separate homeland for Indian Sikhs has not only garnered a huge following among the Sikh diaspora-at-large but it is also threatening to upend the Indian union made up of loosely-bonded ethnically-diverse groups, many of whom refuse to be Indianized or conform to Hindutva—the far-right ideology that calls for the interests of the majority Hindus to predominate over those of minorities.

More specifically, Hindutva represents a growing chorus of Hindu supremacists in a manner akin to the White supremacists.

Given that Hinduism is a catch-all umbrella term for a diverse array of religious philosophies and practices loosely stitched together, Hindutva is not only perceived as a threat by non-Hindus but it is also repudiated by large sections of Hindus in southern and eastern parts of India—or what constitutes India's Achilles' heel with secessionist movements having taken root and brewing aplenty.

This is all the more troubling given that Hinduism is arguably the most tolerant and peaceful religious doctrine on earth—had it not been, the likes of home-grown products such as Buddhism and Sikhism would have never gained a foothold on the Indian peninsula, much less foreign imports of Islam and Christianity.

Add to that the fact that Hinduism is also very accommodative in that it is open to blending in with new religious philosophies and even adopting them.

Since Islam first arrived on the northern shores of the Indian peninsula in 0712, Hinduism has undergone quite a bit of Middle-Easternization to its credit in that many words with Arabic-Persian roots are today in everyday usage.

Needless to say, India ought to bathe in its diverse ethnic and religious diversity rather than deride it—after all, what makes one Indian is not whether they go to a temple or mosque but the fact that they all share Indian values.

One could even argue that:
> Religion is temporary, tradition is permanent.
> Minorities are the goldmines that never run out of gold.
> Minorities are the keys to all things Goldilocks.
> The holy grail of a nation is the strength of its minorities not superiorities.

Yet, today's India has not only abandoned pluralism but even Hinduism as Indian leaders continue to play with the ethnic fire that bears the potential to balkanize the nation into many states.

Mahatma Gandhi must be rolling over in heavens every time he is being briefed about the dire plight facing his India today.

How did things turn sour for Indian minorities?

While Indian minorities had enjoyed a relatively harmonious time during much of the second half of the 20th century, their place in the Indian society began to be questioned with the rise of the right-wing Bharatiya Janata Party (or Indian People's Party) during the 1990s just as the first half (1955-1996) of the current oquannium (1955-2038) was readying to yield to its second.

Just as the 9/11 attacks signaled the beginning-in-earnest of hard times for minorities on American shores in 2001 so did the 2002 Gujarat Riots on Indian soil—the riots were triggered by a fire breaking out on a passenger train that killed 59 Hindu pilgrims in the Indian state of Gujarat.

Although the train fire was due to an accident, it was nevertheless blamed on Muslims by the state authorities—then under the stewardship of Narendra Modi—so as to create a pretext for provoking the far-right Hindutva groups to unleash a counter fire of revenge on what were perceived to be undesirable Muslims.

And so they did as Hindutva mobs went on a rampage for days causing not only widespread destruction of Muslim properties and raping Muslim women but also leaving as many as 1000 Muslims butchered to death.

According to an inside whistleblower, Modi ordered the state authorities not to intervene in the riots and rather let the Hindutva mobs vent their anger on Muslims.

In spite of his checkered past, Modi would nevertheless be rewarded for his deeply anti-Muslim and populist narrative as he would rise through the far-right ranks quickly and with flying colors over the next decade only to add further misery to the already bruised and demoralized Indian Muslims.

In 2014, things would turn on their head when the electorate catapulted the far-right parties to national power and Modi taking the helm became the Himalayas from which the ethnic harmony would nosedive into the Indian Ocean.

Since then the minorities, including in particular the Muslims, have not only been running for cover but they have also been made to feel like outsiders as if they are no longer welcome in India.

One can indeed understand a sense of despondency among today's Indian Muslims.

In 2019, the Indian electorate overwhelmingly returned Narendra Modi to the highest office in the land for another five years in a yet another sign of awful things to come for the minorities.

Barely months into his new tenure, Modi inked the so-called "2019 Citizenship Act"—exactly 84 years later in an eerie echo of the Nuremberg Laws enacted by Nazi Germany in 1935—that would grant Indian citizenship to migrants from the trio of Afghanistan-Bangladesh-and-Pakistan provided that they are non-Muslims.

While such a deeply anti-Muslim bill may sound like a godsend at first sight for non-Muslims afraid of being persecuted in the trio of aforementioned majority-Muslim nations, the hidden propaganda in the 2019 Citizenship Act lies in the fact that poor Indian Muslims—like poor Indians in general—do not carry any paperwork or legal documents to prove that they were born in India.

Without such documents, tens-of-millions of Indian Muslims remain vulnerable to not only being persecuted but also being deported to other countries with which they have no connection except for shared religious beliefs.

Simply put, the 2019 Citizenship Act essentially stipulates that no proof of birth is needed for the right to Indian Citizenship unless one is Muslim.

That is Islamophobia run amok to the hilt.

It is of course not only in India but Islamophobia has been on the rise since the onset of the second half (1997-2038) of the current oquannium (1955-2038) across much of the globe from Asia through Africa and Europe to the Americas in a manner similar to anti-Semitism and other forms of xenophobia.

With the current oquannium poised to end in 2038, Indian Muslims are far from being out of the woods yet—one can only hope that the Indocaust does not cast its ugly shadow on their precarious state of affairs over the next decade or so.

In particular, India's far-right leaders do not shy away from provoking their followers and reassuring them that the heavy-handed approach and marginalization of Indian Muslims is justified on the grounds that the Mughal Emperor Aurangzeb not only unleashed tyranny upon his non-Muslim subjects during the 17th century but that he also dared to wipe them off the map.

What the Indian leaders perhaps do not realize is that Aurangzeb was an absolutist, like other monarchs of his time, who was neither restrained by a constitution nor were there any checks and balances in the form of a legislature or religious authority to rein in the abuse of his power.

Today, Indian Muslims cannot therefore be held accountable for the actions of a tyrant who ruled India more than 300 years ago, no matter how barbaric.

India must look to the future not the past.

In disguise of the Russian icon Gary Kasparov, one can get quite far in democracy if they can convince the majority that they are the victims of the minority.

That is exactly what not only the Indian leaders but leaders around the globe have resorted to in the face of sociopolitical issues having turned into an insoluble maze—pitting the majority against the minority has become the only way to win votes rather than addressing real-life problems.

While Modi may have lost his Midas touch, his ultra-nationalist propaganda has nevertheless worked magic on his disciples with the urge for greed and money.

Indeed, against the backdrop of state-driven Islamophobia, a growing number of young-and-radical musicians desperate to find a niche in the rather competitive space are resorting to deeply offensive-and-threatening anti-Muslim lyrics such as:

> "Hindu ka hai Hindustan, Mullah jao Pakistan!"—"India is for Hindus, Muslims must go to Pakistan!"

In doing so, such far-right musicians see their bank accounts quickly bloat as their popularity on social media goes through the roof such that it serves as a positive feedback loop with the anti-Muslim music hitting new highs and rapidly becoming normalized among the masses with each new release of their audio or video.

Worse yet, mainstream journalists and other public figures spewing out anti-Muslim rhetoric night-in-night-out across hundreds of TV channels and media outlets on Indian soil has become a secret weapon to win top ratings with every channel trying to outdo its competitors through the innovative art of xenophobia and driven by the greed to earn a greater market share of the audience with the potential to make a killing on the back of others' misfortunes.

No longer is it uncommon for Indian Muslims to be portrayed as "termites" on mainstream media but even calls for Muslims to be lynched are patriotically beamed across many channels.

When challenged about such anti-Muslim propaganda, many Indian journalists are quick to point out that India has always been a sanctuary for Muslims and that it is Pakistan that remains a hell for minorities in its quest to reach ethnic purity.

While India can indeed lay claim to being a majority-Hindu nation with its minorities making up at least 20% among its demographics today, a little more than 3% of Pakistanis are non-Muslims—due to the fact that what once made up more than 30% of its people were systematically butchered and cleansed during the 1947 Indian Partition to which the then-fledgling state turned a blind eye.

Today, however, discrimination against minorities in Pakistan is by-and-large due to far-right Muslim extremists and bigots rather than driven by state actors a la situation in India.

In particular, over the past couple of decades, Pakistani state has been on a mission to restore gurudwaras and mandirs—which are respectively places of worship for the adherents of Sikhism and Hinduism—not only out of deep respect for its minorities but perhaps also as a step toward redemption for its sins committed against them during the 1947 Indian Partition.

Still, the Pakistani state can do little to prevent what nevertheless remains a pervasive disease among the Muslim masses who continue to view and treat the minorities like second-class citizens in their own backyard.

As for Indian journalists, it seems that pointing a finger at Pakistan's past is the best strategy to justify their propaganda—they are therefore hardly any smarter than their leaders whose anti-Muslim policies are predicated on the tyranny unleashed upon non-Muslims by a Mughal Emperor who died more than 300 years ago.

Why so many Indian journalists continue to use Pakistan as a yardstick to gauge the standing of their own nation is anyone's guess.

What is however not uncertain is that they in no small part have become the tail that wags the Indian dog.

Notably, the sheer banality and popularity of the xenophobic drama playing out on Indian airwaves has virtually destroyed unbiased journalism to the detriment of a nation that has long prided itself on secularism.

India is not only cutting off its nose to spite its face but it has also run out of arrows in the quiver as it finds itself between a rock and a hard place.

Indian chickens are surely coming home to roost in the not-too-distant future.

In fact, what was once a small group of Hindu supremacists on the fringes of Indian society has become democratized across much of today's India just as it was some

84 years ago during the 1930s though few seem to realize that it is a recurring wave that ebbs and flows over the course of oqual cycle.

Unsurprisingly, many Indian thinkers and philosophers argue that India has been forever transformed into a nationalist-and-fascist state with no future for minorities—they could not be more wrong though they will be willing to change their views once they become aware of the dire spell of the second half of oqual cycle on human society.

While better days lie ahead, Indian Muslims must nevertheless continue to tread water carefully for at least another decade.

This is particularly troubling given that India (220M Muslims) is home to the third largest Muslim community after Indonesia (240M Muslims) and Pakistan (230M Muslims).

While a relative minority in India, Indian Muslims would nevertheless constitute the seventh largest nation-of-the-world after India (1450M), China (1440M), America (340M), Indonesia (280M), Pakistan (240M), and Nigeria (230M).

The conventional wisdom has it that size matters in political matters but that does not seem to be applicable to the dire plight facing Indian Muslims.

Although Muslims make up 15% of India's demographics today, they are however severely under-represented in politics in that they constitute a little more than 5% of the Indian bicameral legislature made up of Rajya Sabha (Upper House) and Lok Sabha (Lower House).

Needless to say, Indian Muslims find solace in resorting to non-constitutional means in order to push back against their humiliation, scapegoating, and being turned into proverbial lambs in their own backyard.

For example, it is not uncommon for Indian Muslims to take to the streets to vent their anger in lieu of fighting back through constitutional means.

Unfortunately, such protests occasionally turn into riots as they are not only met by counter-protests by Hindutva sympathizers but also due to the heavy-handed approach unleashed upon them by the authorities.

And it does not end there.

Those arrested in the protests often face complete demolition of their homes on the predicate that they are illegal structures.

To the contrary, it is a very common practice in India to build a home without a permit if they were not already built decades and centuries before the building ordinances were even introduced into law by local authorities.

Rather than being grandfathered in (or exempted from new regulations), Muslim homes are often being grandmothered out (or wholly demolished).

Still, one can understand the demolition of illegal homes provided that such a move is not discriminatory against Muslims as it only adds gasoline to the ethnic fire rapidly spinning out of control.

On a brighter note, good old days for the minorities on Indian soil and across much of the world will return some time between annus horribilis (2028) of the current oquannium (1955-2038) and annus mirabilis (2039) of the next cycle (2039-2122) on the other side of the looming World War III.

5 | ECONOMIC WAVES

A corollary of oqual cycle is that the economic health of a nation rockets during the first half but turns anemic during the second.

This is due to the fact that, during the first half of oqual cycle, the overall economic well-being is powered by sociopolitical tailwinds such as morality, peace, collectivism, globalism, entrepreneurship, non-partisanship, baby boom, ethnic harmony, and institutional trust.

On the other hand, during the second half of oqual cycle, the economic well-being is plagued by sociopolitical headwinds such as immorality, debt, populism, corruption, xenophobia, partisanship, wealth gap, and dysfunctional governments.

Indeed, the economy is an intertwined facet of human civilization.

It should therefore be hardly surprising that our economic straits also exhibit an overall 84-year rhythm as they oscillate more or less in sync with the progression of oqual cycle.

For example, being in the midst of the second half (1997-2038) of the current oquannium (1955-2038), most nations around the globe not only find themselves in dire economic straits but they are also teetering on the brink of bankruptcy due to having become addicted to an easy life through borrowing money to the hilt as if there would be no tomorrow.

Additionally, a perpetual spate of deadly conflicts from the decades-long self-destructive 9/11 Wars in Afghanistan (2001-2021) and Iraq (2003-2011) through the Syrian Civil War (2011-date) to the Ukraine-Russia War (2022-date) have further served as an Achilles' heel for a sustained economic growth over the past couple of decades.

Add to that the fact that the implementation of barbaric measures and mandates in the wake of the 2019 Coronavirus Pandemic hamstrung the economic engine across the globe.

With so much printed money chasing fewer and fewer goods-and-services thanks to stay-home policies, the inflation fire raging across the globe today should hardly be surprising.

Yet, the fraudulent media and governments spearheaded by United States have continued to lay the blame on first supply-chain bottlenecks and then they found a scapegoat in the Ukraine-Russia War for the persistent inflation threatening to price the masses out of the free market.

Although inflation has ravaged societies-nations-and-empires-alike for millennia, we somehow never seem to learn from our past.

While the likes of Zimbabwe and Venezuela have been in dire financial straits due to hyperinflation and having defaulted on their debt obligations since the outset of the 21st century, the fate of many other nations also appears to have been sealed as they begin to fall like dominoes one after the other.

In 2020, the likes of Lebanon, Suriname, and Zambia went underwater after failing to meet their debt obligations.

In 2022, Sri Lanka joined the disgraceful chorus of nations unable to pay their debt.

Other nations such as Argentina, Belarus, Ecuador, Egypt, El Salvador, Ethiopia, Ghana, Kenya, Nigeria, Pakistan, Tunisia, and Ukraine are on course to face the debt music over the next couple of years or so.

And it is only a matter of time before many more nations will go belly up as the dire spell of oqual cycle leaves no stone unturned as it draws to a close.

In marked contrast, most nations across the globe enjoyed relatively prosperous times during much of the first half (1955-1996) of the current oquannium (1955-2038) as evidenced by fond memories of those eras such as:
- Golden Age in America (1950-1970)
- Swinging Sixties in Britain (1960s)
- Les Trente Glorieuses (The Thirty Glorious Years) in France (1945-1975)
- Wirtschaftswunder (Economic Miracle) in Germany (1948-1975)
- Il Miracolo Economico (The Economic Miracle) in Italy (1948-1963)
- El Milagro Español (The Spanish Miracle) in Spain (1950-1975)
- Jukagaku Kogyoka (Economic Miracle) in Japan (1950-1975)
- Khrushchev Era in Russia (1953-1964)
- Nehru Era in India (1947-1964)
- Ayub Khan Era in Pakistan (1958-1969)

Likewise, much of the fist half (1871-1912) of the previous oquannium (1871-1954) was also underscored by relatively good times befalling humanity across much of the globe as fondly remembered through:
- The Gilded Age in America (1870-1900)
- The Late Victorian Era in Britain (1870-1901)
- La Belle Époque (The Beautiful Epoch) in France (1870-1914)
- Gründerzeit (Founding Period) in Germany (1871-1900)

In line with the dire spell of oqual cycle, the economic growth of most nations across the globe however turned tepid during much of the second half (1913-1954) of the previous oquannium (1871-1954) as it was torpedoed by numerous catastrophes such as World War I (1914-1918), Influenza Pandemic (1918-1920), Chinese Civil War (1927-1949), Great Depression (1929-1939), World War II (1939-1945), and Indian Partition (1947).

Long story short, the economic prosperity of humanity waxes and wanes in sync with the progression of oqual cycle.

To demonstrate this phenomenon further at quantitative level using economic data from the United States as a proxy for the global economy, let us dissect our discussion under the following sections:

5.1 National Income
5.2 National Debt
5.3 Money Printing
5.4 Stock Market

| 5.1 | NATIONAL INCOME

Other than the revenue generated by selling off natural resources such as coal and oil, most nations typically generate what is called the "national income" through levying taxes on individuals and private corporations.

Defined as the market value of all goods and services exchanged within a country, the gross domestic product (GDP) is most frequently used as a monetary measure of the national income.

How does the national income vary over the course of oqual cycle?

In what is dubbed the "canonical model", the growth of a nation's income is envisioned to rise during the first half of oqual cycle and then pivot so as to reverse course during the second half.

However, due to atypical sociopolitical factors at play, this may not always be the case as the first half may well be underscored by an anemic growth while the economy experiences a boom during the second half in what can be viewed as the "non-canonical model".

For clarity, these antagonistic models have been incorporated into what is dubbed the "income oquacycle".

While the canonical model is expected to be the rule for most countries, the non-canonical model will likely be a hallmark of nations when their economies switch from being largely driven by domestic demands to becoming a global manufacturing powerhouse as was the case with the American economy during the previous oquannium (1871-1954) and now seems to be the trademark for the Chinese economy during the current oquannium (1955-2038).

Notably, there is a reason as to why the dawn (1871-1891) of the previous oquannium (1871-1954) in America has been dubbed the "Gilded Age"—the American economy was at best gold-plated rather than wholly golden.

Admittedly, while the skilled workforce made a killing on the then rapidly-expanding railroad economy, the fortunes of the unskilled masses and new immigrants arriving from Europe by-and-large remained gilded (or tainted).

In particular, the first half (1871-1912) of the previous oquannium (1871-1954) was hamstrung by the deep wounds inflicted upon the society during the American Civil War (1861-1865)—which would continue to weigh heavily against a sustained economic recovery during the decades that followed.

Additionally, the first half of the previous oquannium was punctuated with a slew of stubborn and deep recessions, which further torpedoed a sustained economic growth across all social strata.

In fact, the economic fortunes of Americans during the previous oquannium (1871-1954) in many ways paralleled the fate of Chinese during the current oquannium (1955-2038).

Thanks to Mao Zedong's ill-conceived policies that let the famine genie out of the bottle in what came to be called the Chinese Great Famine (1958-1962), the masses faced abject poverty during the dawn (1955-1975) of the current oquannium (1955-2038) in lieu of the rather prosperous times promised by the auspicious spell of oqual cycle.

This is due to the fact that wrong choices made by the leaders can easily derail what the rhythm of human civilization has in store for the masses.

Nevertheless, the hard work and unwavering conviction of les chinoise would be richly rewarded with far more than they had bargained for as the nation turned capitalist after its revolutionary leader Deng Xiaopeng signed an historic trade pact with the then 39th POTUS Jimmy Carter in 1979.

And capitalism would handsomely deliver the Chinese their rather belated Golden Age that would anomalously arrive almost half-a-turn later during oqual autumn (1997-2017) in lieu of oqual spring (1955-1975) as the current oquannium (1955-2038) entered its second half in 1997.

Simply put, the Chinese have enjoyed an unprecedented economic prosperity during the second half of the current oquannium in lieu of the first in a rather non-canonical fashion.

A similar non-canonical economic story unfolded for Americans during the previous oquannium (1871-1954) as elegantly captured through probing the long-term GDP growth rate—wherein the income growth during the second half (1913-1954) overshadowed that of the first half (1871-1912) at odds with the oqual theory.

However, such an anomaly can be accounted for by the rather unusual sociopolitical factors at play.

While the first half (1871-1912) was largely beset by slow recovery from the civil war coupled with a spate of deep recessions, the economic fortunes skyrocketed during the second half (1913-1954) thanks in no small part to a tectonic shift in manufacturing unleashed by the unprecedented demands of first World War I (1914-1918) and then World War II (1939-1945) just as America took up the baton from the British Empire for setting the new world order.

In sharp contrast, the US economic fortunes appear to have been mirrored and restored to a canonical model during the current oquannium (1955-2038) in line with the oqual theory.

Thus, during the first half (1955-1996) of the current oquannium (1955-2038), the US economy enjoyed a long and sustained economic growth that delivered riches across the board as captured by the American Golden Age (1950-1970) in line with the canonical spell of oqual cycle.

However, America's economic straits began to precipitously turn south almost in sync with the arrival of the second half (1997-2038) of the current oquannium (1955-2038) due in no small part to the self-inflicted hamstring in what came to be known as the decades-long self-destructive 9/11 Wars.

Regrettably, the embers of 9/11 Wars continue to burn to this day as the nation finds itself teetering on the brink of a looming bankruptcy coupled with social-and-moral disintegration at home from soaring public debts through shrinking middle class to faltering infrastructure as it increasingly flirts with turning into a banana republic of sorts.

With a seismic decline in manufacturing over the past 50 years at home, America has been literally reduced to printing money as its flagship product that is shamelessly being exported across the globe like a commodity.

Such a dire predicament of Americans is further highlighted by the fact that while median household income decupled from $3,500 in 1955 to $35,000 in 1996 over the course of the first half (1955-1996) of the current oquannium (1955-2038), it has hitherto only doubled to $70,000 since 1996 and is likely to no more than quadruple at best over the entire course of the second half (1997-2038).

Importantly, the contrasting tales of America's economy across the current (1955-2038) and the previous (1871-1954) oquannia—as exquisitely captured through the GDP growth rate—are a manifestation of the fact that while America was a rising power during the previous oquannium, it is a nation in decay as the current oquannium draws to a close.

In line with the spell of oqual cycle, American economy will continue to hit new lows for at least another decade before it reverses course and returns to a relatively organic state from around the 2040s in a manner akin to the 1950s.

Although China is set to take up the mantle from America as the new economic leader of the world over the next decade or so with the arrival of the next oqual cycle, the latter will nevertheless continue to be a major economic power though its best days long took a trip down memory lane.

|5.2| NATIONAL DEBT

Other than the revenue generated through the sale of natural resources, most nations typically fund their obligations through levying taxes on individuals and private corporations.

During the first half of oqual cycle, the income generated through such means usually suffices to serve the needs of the nation against the backdrop of a booming economy powered by a plethora of sociopolitical tailwinds.

During the second half of oqual cycle, the nation's monetary demands however outstrip its income against the backdrop of a tepid economy plagued by a barrage of sociopolitical headwinds .

Consistent with this argument is the fact that the US government rarely exercised budget deficits and often ran surpluses during the first half (1871-1912) of the previous oquannium (1871-1954)—and a similar story panned out during the first half (1955-1996) of the current oquannium (1955-2038).

In sharp contrast, the US government consistently ran deep budget deficits and rarely surpluses during the second half (1913-1954) of the previous oquannium (1871-1954)—and a similar story is already in the making during the second half (1997-2038) of the current oquannium (1955-2038).

In particular, the federal government ran a massive budget deficit for 16 years-in-a-row between 1931-1946 due to unprecedented expenditure on a roster of social-welfare programs such as the New Deal enacted to assuage the scourge of first the Great Depression (1929-1939) and then World War II (1939-1945)—with the budget deficit hitting a record 27% of the then nation's income of $200B in 1943.

Likewise, the federal government has been consistently running a budget deficit since 2002 which reached almost 15% of the then $20T economy in 2020 due to the mandated lockdowns that forced the shuttering of the economic engine in the wake of the outbreak of the Coronavirus Pandemic.

With more than a decade to go till the end of the current oquannium (1955-2038) and with World War III looming on the horizon, it is unlikely that the federal government will balance the budget in the foreseeable future.

On the contrary, the odds of the federal government surpassing the previous record of budget deficit, which reached 27% of GDP some 84 years earlier in 1943, are pretty high.

How do the governments finance the budget deficits?

In order to fuel the reckless spending that far exceeds the nation's income during the second half of oqual cycle, the governments usually borrow vast amounts of money from wealthy individuals, commercial banks, and foreign governments to meet such demands as embodied in the "debt oquacycle".

However, such debt financing is a cursed endeavor due to the interest paid on the bonds issued to the lenders as the cost of servicing the loan often turns into a self-perpetuating spiral of death if not kept in check.

While the annualized cost of servicing the debt averages at around 2% for wealthy nations such as the United States, it can run much higher for poor nations.

Even at a paltry 2% annualized interest, it becomes almost impossible to get out of the debt trap no matter how wealthy a nation is.

For example, the cost of servicing the US national (or federal) debt has averaged at around $500B-per-year over the past decade and it is expected to hit the $1T mark over the next decade.

Given that the US tax revenue averages around $4T-per-year, as much as a quarter of these earnings would soon be funneled toward servicing the nation's debt when such precious dollars could well have been used to fund productive programs such as investments in manufacturing and technological innovations.

Simply put, debt financing is an investment in past rather than future.

It must be avoided at all costs even if it means having the nation munch on grass and make other sacrifices.

After all, a worthy life is about making sacrifices rather than self-gratification.

However, leaders hungry for power must not pay heed to such an organic philosophy but rather they must raise the bar of who can spend more to make life easy for the masses in order to garner their votes.

Indeed, democracy destroys nations in that it is nothing more than a mob rule that promises the masses free handouts in return for their votes rather than what is best for the society as a whole.

It is no mere coincidence that the likes of China are rising fast while the fortunes of nations under the clutches of mob rule are evaporating by the hour.

It would therefore pay dearly for nations decimated by the false promise of democracy to think outside the box and look to China for a more organic economic model rather than continue to sink in sync with the herd.

Still, a manageable debt may sometimes be a necessary evil.

However, when debt burden exceeds a nation's income by more than 50%, it is a harbinger of dire economic straits waiting on the horizon.

On the other hand, when debt burden exceeds 100% of a nation's income, it becomes almost suicidal as it sets the country on a path to bankruptcy and a future of economic doldrums for generations to come.

With a debt burden inching ever closer to 250% of its income, Japan trumps all other countries as the most cursed nation in the world.

Coupled with the highest old-to-young ratio among all nations of the world, the Japanese face a future of absolute misery.

What grade does the United States get on its debt card?

In 2020, in the wake of the Coronavirus Pandemic, the ratio of US national debt to its income reached a record a little shy of 130%.

In 2023, three years later, that dreadful milestone seems to be quite comfortably sitting atop the summit of Mount Whitney that it even shied away from conquering during the bloody and costly World War II (1939-1945) some 84 years earlier—when it reached 120% of the then nation's income in 1946.

However, prior to the US becoming a global power at the outset of the 20th century just as cracks began to appear in the British Empire, things used to be a lot more rosier and cozier for Americans.

In 1829, just prior to the 7th POTUS Andrew Jackson took the helm, the federal debt stood at a little more than 5% of the then nation's income of $1B.

Driven by his religious conviction that the debt was ungodly and a curse upon the then country of a little over 12M people, Jackson made erasing the whole of nation's debt a cornerstone of what would become his unique legacy.

In 1835, after selling off large swathes of the federal land in the American West, Jackson would indeed fulfill his dream of paying off the country's debt in entirety—the only time ever in the nation's 250-year history that the federal debt stood at arithmetic zero.

However, unbeknown to Jackson the dire spell of oqual cycle, such a high moral ground was achieved in the midst of the second half (1829-1870) of the fifth oquannium (1787-1870)—the inauspicious period when the sociopolitical upheaval begins to rear its ugly head and, in doing so, sinks the economic prosperity just as the debt goes through the roof.

Indeed, barely after Jackson left office in 1837, the United States found itself fighting war after war on many fronts epitomized by first the Mexican-American War (1846-1848) and then culminating with the American Civil War (1861-1865) just as the fifth oquannium (1787-1870) drew to a close.

Such conflicts for territorial control are not only bloody but they are also costly even though they seem to be a necessary evil to revitalize human society once every 84 years on average.

And so they did as the United States not only annexed from Mexico what is today much of American Southwest from Texas to California but also kept the nation from becoming partitioned into two Americas at bay to the tune of having witnessed its debt balloon from 0% of nation's income in 1835 to almost 35% of the then $10B economy in 1870 just as the 18th POTUS Ulysses Grant was elected to the highest office in the land.

With the arrival of the sixth and previous oquannium (1871-1954), the US economy powered by a renewed vigor and rapidly sprawling network of railroads quickly began to outpace the nation's debt burden, which for a short period looked set to be heading to ground zero in an echo of 1835.

As the previous oquannium reached its midpoint in 1912, the US federal debt indeed dropped well below 10% of the then nation's income of $35B during the tenure of the then 27th POTUS William Taft.

However, the warmongering Woodrow Wilson taking the helm as the 28th POTUS in 1913 did not bear good omens particularly as the second half (1913-1954) of the previous oquannium (1871-1954) was yet to cast its ugly spell upon Americans and the world-writ-large.

And so it did without flinching as World War I (1914-1918) broke out almost in parallel with the onset of the second half of the previous oquannium.

With America now being a rising global power and with its own imperial ambitions of having a go at shepherding the world rapidly brewing, the opportunity to test its military might with what were then the big European boys headed by the British Empire in World War I was too good to forego.

However, such an expedition would once again send the US national debt through the roof as it would explode to almost 35% of the then nation's income of $80B in 1920 after all the dust had settled on the European coliseum of war.

During the 1920s in what came to be called the "Roaring Twenties", the rather boring and largely-speculative upsurge in economic fortunes would once again help to transiently rein in the national debt but the ugly spell of the second half of the previous oquannium in order to keep societal ills and transgressions in check was just getting started.

Admittedly, the unprecedented demands of the Great Depression (1929-1939) followed by World War II (1939-1945) would push the federal debt to what was then a record high of almost 120% of the then nation's income of $230B in 1946.

Importantly, the precipitous fall in the US national debt during the first half (1871-1912) of the previous oquannium (1871-1954) followed by its subsequent rise during the second half (1913-1954) has been superbly captured at a quantitative level.

A similar trend is also in the making for the current oquannium (1955-2038).

On the same token, quantitative analysis of debt-to-income ratio over the previous (1871-1954) and the current (1955-2038) oquannia suggests that this key economic benchmark drops over the first half of oqual cycle and then begins to head north over the course of the second half.

This striking observation further corroborates the notion that a nation enjoys a relative economic prosperity during the first half of oqual cycle but its fortunes begin to head south with the onset of the second half.

It is noteworthy that the US debt burden went through the roof as the previous oquannium (1871-1954) neared its end due in no small part to the socialist propaganda spearheaded by the then 32nd POTUS Franklin Roosevelt.

While many Americans today rue the status quo of United States having turned into a socialist state, the crux of the matter is that such a feat was single-handedly masterminded some 84 years ago by Roosevelt after he signed into law the Social Security Act in 1935.

Nevertheless, the rapid and sustained economic boom during much of the first half (1955-1996) of the current oquannium (1955-2038) helped to rein in the debt burden unfurled upon the nation during the closing stages of the previous oquannium (1871-1954).

Notably, the national debt would nosedive to just a tad above 30% of the then nation's income of $3T just as the tenure of the then 39th POTUS Jimmy Carter came to an abrupt end in 1981.

The 40th POTUS Ronald Reagan, Carter's successor, is often held in high regard in many corners across the nation but few Americans understand or have the guts to know that he was on the contrary nothing short of a devil-in-disguise.

In fact, Reagan was the first President since World War II who not only began to view debt as a blessing rather than a curse but he also upped the ante of dangerous brinkmanship against what was then the Soviet Union.

Over the course of Reagan's octannual term (1981-1989), the federal debt exploded exponentially from a little over 30% of nation's income to almost 50% with much of it funneled to bloat the US military.

This was particularly troubling given that such a lax approach to spending transpired during what were relatively good times of the first half (1955-1996) of the current oquannium (1955-2038) when neither a war nor a depression was being fought.

Still, many pundits are quick to draw parallels between today and the 1980s.

Alas, they are fools deprived of a logical approach to understanding the ups and downs of human civilization.

While much of the early 1980s was indeed marred by a double-dip recession and a deadly bout of inflation, those times were nevertheless relatively prosperous compared to the dire plight facing Americans today as summed up below:

1) Unlike the 1980s when the nation's debt was hardly a cause for concern, today's America is rapidly sinking under a sea of debt with either a bankruptcy on the cards or a collapse of the dollar looming on the horizon as it loses its global luster due to currency debasement driven by excessive money printing that began with the onset of the 2008 Great Recession and will likely continue as the country sails into the sunset;

2) Unlike the 1980s when the nation was by and large surrounded by high morals and a strong social cohesion at the expense of sociopolitical polarization, today's America is engulfed in the rapid disintegration of its

moral values coupled with a rising wave of deadly crime and social unrest threatening to push the country into a civil war a la 1860s; and

3) Unlike the 1980s when the nation was the sole superpower and still rising, today's America is an empire in rapid decline that has already started looking to its past rather than future for its glory.

Still, that does not exonerate Reagan for neither the soaring debt nor the rising military bode well for the long-term economic well-being of a country not to mention that their synergistic effect often bankrupts nations.

To say that Reagan set America on a course to becoming a banana republic would be something of an understatement.

Neither did his successor, the 41st POTUS George Bush, relent from pushing America further into harm's way as the federal debt kept outpacing the economic growth as it would flirt with 65% of the then nation's income of nearly $7T by the time he was booted out of the office in 1993.

For all his personal flaws and shortcomings, the 42nd POTUS Bill Clinton ought to go down in history as the last effective commander-in-chief of the American Empire as he fully understood the curse that a debt can unleash upon the economic well-being of a nation.

Under Clinton's octannual term (1993-2001), the federal debt was slashed from 65% to 55% of the then nation's economy of a tad over $10T in 2001.

With the 9/11 attacks that followed soon after Clinton's departure and a string of clowns taking the helm one after the other since then, America has been perilously pushed into deeper and deeper waters from where there is no escape with the federal debt precariously threatening to head for an even higher summit from the current level of around 130% of today's $25T economy.

How do nations overcome their debt burden?

A nation burdened with insurmountable debt, usually in excess of 100% of its income, has three options to redeem itself from the sinful undertaking:

1) Declare bankruptcy and refuse to pay creditors. Although the easiest option, it not only ruins a nation's global standing but also decimates its credit rating implying that there will be few lenders in future if at all and even if they would dare to do what no one else is willing to do, the cost of borrowing money for the bankrupt nation will go through the sky such that only the wickedest of leaders would pursue such a forbidden endeavor. Additionally, the bankrupt nation would also relinquish control

of any domestic and foreign assets, including infrastructure such as seaports and airports.

2) Make economy a priority such that it grows at a much faster rate than debt through heavy investment in manufacturing and entrepreneurship. However, such investment requires vast amounts of wherewithal (or capital) and, if the nation is already overleveraged, that would be a bridge too far. It is a catch-22 dilemma but nevertheless an a-priori solution that ought to be contemplated.

3) Print oceans of money to pay off at least some of the debt so as to bring it down to a more manageable level such that it can be outpaced by the future economic growth. Inflating away debt in such a manner is however only applicable to nations that have their loans denominated in their own currency such as the United States and European Union and, to a lesser extent, the likes of China and Russia. Even then, printing large sums of money not only invites inflation but it also risks increasing the cost of servicing the remaining debt as the currency becomes debased and devalued by leaps and bounds.

Long story short, prevention is always better than cure.

Good and responsible nations should never fall prey to the debt trap but rather exercise humility and learn to live within their means.

That is actually easier done than said but fools know not.

Alas, democracy is a bittersweet pill that rarely makes but often breaks nations.

For its part, using the veneer of World War III, America will most likely find refuge in its money printer to overcome its debt burden as it is unlikely to be overpowered by a potential economic boom even though the coming global conflict will provide ample opportunities to get the manufacturing engine kicking again.

In so printing its way out of much of its debt obligations, America will kiss goodbye to its currency retaining the status of the elephant in international trade with the CNY set to overtake the USD as the dominant global currency over the next decade or so just as the USD itself replaced the GBP some 84 years earlier as the previous oquannium (1871-1954) drew to a close.

It should be noted that the dominant global currency always belongs to the nation that has proven itself as the manufacturing powerhouse head and shoulders above all other countries.

Over the past couple of decades and over the foreseeable future, that title undoubtedly belongs to China.

Thus, CNY replacing USD as the dominant player in international trade over the next decade or so is nothing more than a rite of passage.

Still, USD will continue to be a major global currency though it will no longer be the king that it has been over the past century.

I should add that many goldbugs have been calling for the collapse of the dollar over the past decade or so.

Yet, nothing could be further from the truth as their anti-dollar tirade is due to their conflict-of-interest in that it represents nothing more than a sales pitch and fearmongering in order to draw the unsuspecting crowd to pump the price of the yellow metal to new heights.

All told, America's national debt will continue to skyrocket over the next decade or so before it pivots south via one way or another with the start of the next oqual cycle in 2039.

|5.3| MONEY PRINTING

While most nations balance their budgets during the first half of oqual cycle, the expenditure during the rather tumultuous-and-chaotic second half often far outstrips their income.

As noted earlier, such a budget deficit is usually met through "debt financing"—paying for certain needs through borrowing money from creditors.

However, the governments sometimes also opt to meet the budget deficit via an alternative tool called "monetary financing"—paying for certain obligations through printing money out of thin air.

How do governments print money?

In 1694, the British government created the Bank of England and authorized it to print money in the sum of just over £1M in order to pay the lenders from whom it had borrowed to finance what came to be known as the Nine Years War (1688-1697) with France—that tellingly broke out during what was then the dusk (1682-1702) of the third oquannium (1619-1702) mired in extreme sociopolitical upheavals across Europe.

In so doing, the Bank of England became the world's first central bank with exclusive possession of the British government's monetary balances and laid the pioneering groundwork to serve as a model for today's global financial system.

In today's digital age, money however does not need to be physically "printed" into paper notes.

Rather, a country's central bank is charged with the authority to control the flow and distribution of money within a nation.

The five largest central banks in the world are the US Federal Reserve (Fed), the European Central Bank (ECB), the People's Bank of China (PBOC), the Bank of Japan (BOJ), and the Bank of England (BOE).

Such central banks and others have the power to create new electronic money with a few keystrokes to meet the financial obligations of their governments.

Today, printing money is as simple as uttering the following oft-repeated Quranic command: "Kun faa-yaakun!"—"Be! There it is!"

To say that a central bank is nothing short of being the divine tridevi (or trinity) of Lakshmi-Parvati-and-Saraswati, the three-in-one goddess of money-power-and-respect in Hinduism, would be something of an understatement.

Still, printing money is anything but a godly act.

In particular, printing money without a corresponding basket of goods and services to go with it is an even bigger curse than borrowing money due to the fact that it not only bears the potential to price out the masses from the free market through inviting inflation but it also serves as the basis of ever-rising wealth gap between the elite and the masses-writ-large.

How does printing money make the wealthy wealthier and the poor poorer?

While governments print money all the time at a low basal level in line with a corresponding rise in goods and services, such a monetary vice usually skyrockets during the second half of oqual cycle as embodied in the "money oquacycle".

With the onset of the second half (1997-2038) of the current oquannium (1955-2038), the central banks around the world put their money printers at full throttle and began to flood the global financial system with ever-increasing injections of printed money.

In particular, such a money-printing binge was first triggered by the 2008 Great Recession and then further exacerbated by the 2019 Coronavirus Pandemic.

Since 2008, trillions of printed dollars and euros have been used to:
1) Feed big corporations in order to help them avoid bankruptcies;
2) Support small businesses so that they can keep their doors open; and
3) Dole out cash and stimulus checks to individuals so that they can stave off the financial stress unleashed by the calamities.

Today, however, the financial straits of small businesses and individuals remain as dire as ever even though they have been supplemented with multiple bouts of financial aid to the tune of trillions of dollars and euros over the past 15 years.

Where did these trillions go?

Because small businesses and individuals operate and live paycheck-to-paycheck, it does not matter how much money they are being provided with as it will be wholly expended as soon as it is in their hands.

However, such money does not simply evaporate into the stratosphere but rather it essentially amounts to a zero-sum game—the money expended by small businesses and individuals ultimately ends up in the coffers of big corporations whose fortunes bloat while the masses suffer due to their own absurdity in that living within their means would somehow make them lesser of a being.

The fact that printed money breeds inflation and reduces purchasing power further helps to expedite the transfer of wealth from the masses to the wealthy.

Simply put, money printing is a windfall for big corporations and the wealthy elite in that they are the ultimate beneficiaries of such an ungodly act committed by central banks.

That is precisely the reason why the wealth gap has significantly widened over the past 15 years, all the while the masses have been left high and dry even when they had been reassured by their leaders that the rising tide would lift all boats.

Yet, the crux of the matter is that while a rising tide of goods and services does indeed lift all boats, a rising tide of sheer money printing only serves to lift the big boats at the expense of sinking small ones.

The-powers-that-be are hardly ingenuous to be not aware of such an outcome with a mathematical certainty.

Rather, they are an integral part of crony capitalism—a political system wherein corporations thrive due to favorable government laws that allow them to exploit the masses for doing all the work in return for a little reward while concentrating all the profits among a small number of elites.

It should therefore be hardly surprising that the crony actions of the governments, particularly over the past couple of decades, have only served to bloat the fortunes of the wealthy elite while leaving the masses in dire financial straits.

However, the wealth gap between the elite and the masses was much narrower during the first half (1955-1996) of the current oquannium (1955-2038) due to a relatively booming economy that allowed the central banks to by-and-large sidestep the extravaganza of money printing.

Such a tale of contrasting fortunes across the two halves of the current oquannium (1955-2038) has been diligently captured at a quantitative level—a similar story also appears to have panned out during the previous oquannium (1871-1954).

Likewise, quantitative analysis of the ratio of printed money to national income over the previous (1871-1954) and the current (1955-2038) oquannia suggests that this key economic gauge drops over the first half of oqual cycle and then begins to head north over the course of the second half.

That this is so further corroborates the central premise of the oqual theory that a nation enjoys a relative economic prosperity during the first half of oqual cycle but its fortunes begin to dwindle with the onset of the second half.

When will the money printer be switched to a lower gear?

While the outstanding amount of money printed by the Fed seesawed around 6% of the nation's income from the outset of the current oquannium in 1955 till the outbreak of 2008 Great Recession, it rose to an all-time record high of 36% of $22T economy in 2021 in the wake of the outbreak of the Coronavirus Pandemic.

The prior record was set some 84 years earlier in 1940 during the previous oquannium (1871-1954) when money printed by the Fed reached 22% of the then nation's income of $100B in the wake of the Great Depression (1929-1939)—although it had teetered around 7% of the nation's income prior to the 1929 crash.

Today, the outstanding amount of money printed by the Fed as a ratio of the nation's income has barely budged from its all-time record high set in 2021.

However, in line with the recurring spell of oqual cycle, the Fed will take the foot off the money-printing paddle in the near future so as to allow the ratio of printed money to national income to head south under a clout of an economic boom as the current oquannium (2055-2038) draws to a close.

Like all other government lies and deceptions, the process of money printing is sugarcoated as "quantitative easing (QE)" with the assurance that the excess money being injected into circulation will be removed via "quantitative tightening (QT)" at some point in future when hard times are in the rearview mirror.

But, the central banks are ignorant of the fact that a perpetual bout of hard times is a hallmark of the second half of oqual cycle and that good times only arrive as it draws to a close.

Accordingly, money printing is practically an irreversible process in that QT is nothing more than a theoretical framework that has hitherto never been exercised-in-earnest by any central bank.

Rather, it seems that the excess money in circulation is neutralized through a rapid economic growth that arrives on our shores during the first half of oqual cycle, thereby enabling the central banks to keep a lid on the money printer just as the ratio of money in circulation to national income begins to drop.

In a manner that the national debt is inflated away through a rapid economic growth so is money in circulation shrunk away in a similar fashion.

Still, it is important to point out that there is no shortage of fools and horses in the upper echelons of US banking institutions who continue to argue that the trillions of dollars injected into the financial system in the wake of 2008 Financial Crisis was aptly justified but that further injections of QE in response to the outbreak of 2019 Coronavirus Pandemic were not warranted.

That bogus argument is like saying that it is okay to administer an individual with a daily injection of cocaine for one month but then it must be wholly withdrawn.

Monetary stimulus is never good under any conditions as it only makes the economy become addicted to cheap money, thereby not only fueling fraud to the hilt but also making it impossible to withdraw liquidity lest one crashes the financial system in a manner akin to weaning an addict off cocaine once they are hooked.

In particular, monetary stimulus serves as an antidote to flushing the gunk out of the financial system.

Indeed, one of the major roots of today's economic woes can be traced all the way back to the first injection of QE in 2008.

In the wake of 2008 Financial Crisis, fraudulent banks and institutions facing bankruptcy should have been allowed to go underwater rather being bailed out at the expense of the taxpayer.

As for the masses potentially being laid off and unable to find work, they should have been asked to rise to the challenge and make sacrifices in the face of what would likely have been an economic meltdown and a deep depression.

Importantly, such sacrifices would have helped to flush the fraud out of the financial system in lieu of being provided a lifeblood to support its exponential growth into an 800-pound gorilla that it has turned into today.

After all, a fulfilling life is about making sacrifices as it helps us to appreciate the joys of this world even more, not to mention that it used to be the modus operandi of America up till as recently as the arrival of the current oquannium (1955-2038).

A life without sacrifice is indeed no life at all!

Admittedly, it was against the back of such sacrifices that America rose to global preeminence some 84 years earlier.

Today, America's refusal to make sacrifices is exactly what has all but planted its downfall as a nation fearful of making sacrifices is all but doomed.

The QE chickens are indeed yet to come home to roost in that money printing not only serves to delay the day of reckoning but it also exacerbates the suffering as the looming financial crisis will prove to be far more deadly than what it would have been had the excesses and imbalances from the financial system been flushed out some 15 years ago.

|5.4| STOCK MARKET

Given the meteoric rise in the valuation of stocks on Wall Street over much of the past decade or so, it would be reasonable to argue that such a market bubble has been fueled by the excessive money supply due to the trillions of dollars printed by the US Federal Reserve.

However, there is more to it than meets the eye.

While a deluge of money may indeed serve as a sugar rush to boost the stocks over the short term, there appears to be however little or no positive correlation between money printing and an upsurge in the market in the long run over the multidecadal timescale.

For example, money printed by the US Federal Reserve increased by a little over 800% over the course of the first half (1955-1996) of the current oquannium (1955-2038), all the while the Dow Jones Industrial (DJI) rocketed by a staggering 1500%—the DJI outperformed the uptick in money supply by almost two-fold.

On the other hand, money printed by the US Federal Reserve has so far increased by 1800% over the course of the second half (1997-2038) of the current oquannium (1955-2038) yet the DJI has turtled ahead by no more than about 400% over the same timeframe—the DJI underperformed the upsurge in money supply by over four-fold.

That money printing has a little bearing on the long-term valuation of stocks is further corroborated by the relationship between money supply and stock market in major economies across Eurasia.

While money printing by the Bank of England (BOE), the Bank of Japan (BOJ), and the European Central Bank (ECB) has been more or less on par with that of the US Federal Reserve (Fed) over the past couple of decades, the Eurasian markets have nevertheless largely remained stagnant as noted below:

1) While London's FTSE-100 came within a touching distance of 7000 in 1999, it still continues to flutter around that milestone more than two decades later;

2) Europe's STOXX-600 all but reached 400 in 2000, yet it continues to hover around that mark more than two decades later; and

3) Although Tokyo's Nikkei-225 took off like a rocket during the 1980s reaching an altitude of close to 39000 in 1989, it is yet to surpass that record high set more than three decades earlier.

To say that there is a positive correlation between money supply and stock market is therefore a deeply flawed hypothesis.

It simply does not pass the smell test.

On the contrary, even if there is a positive correlation over a shorter window of time, it does not prove that a surge in the stock market is solely due to an increase in money supply.

Rather, it could be due to a mere coincidence as the basis of causality for an increase in the stock market may have its origins elsewhere.

Indeed, correlation does not necessarily imply causation and vice versa.

So what triggers irrational exuberance among the cheerleaders of the stock market whenever their auditory receptors pick up the slightest sound of the Fed's money printer going brrr?

Such fools are simply driven by their animal instincts in response to the monetary stimulus without contemplating any fallout from their actions in a manner that a dog starts salivating even when shown poisoned meat in a phenomenon that psychologists refer to as "Pavlovian response".

Just as poisoned meat will kill the dog, plowing money into stocks solely in response to a monetary stimulus rather than market fundamentals is not without its dire consequences either.

Over the past decade or so, the wind direction has been very favorable to the stock market but fools do not seem to realize that the wind can also change its direction and, when it does, it will be ugly.

So where does the printed money go?

Ironically, only a small fraction of the money printed by the Fed actually makes its way directly into the stock market.

Rather, the printed money largely serves to buy new as well as old (or long-dated) bonds, thereby driving down bond yields—or interest paid on bond investments.

As bond yields dip, the so-called bond holders (or vigilantes) flee the bond market in favor of the stock market due to a more favorable risk-to-reward ratio offered by the latter trade relative to the former.

Thus, printed money indirectly serves to funnel capital from the bond market into the stock market causing the latter to swell on nothing more than euphoria so as to not only psychologically calm the nerves of what are essentially "gamblers" but also egg them on to pour even their rainy-day funds into highly volatile and risky investments.

In other words, the sheer perception that the Fed is going to increase the money supply more than suffices to not only stop the bleeding but also turbocharge the stock market so as to provide it with much-needed tailwind to push it higher and higher until it does not.

Like the printed money, the stock market therefore essentially rides on thin air rather than corporate fundamentals under situations when the financial system has been inundated with a large excess of monetary liquidity.

Under such a scenario, Newton's third law of motion could be reworded as: "For every tailwind (or thrust), there is an equal and opposite headwind (or drag)!"

Simply put, the stock market solely hyperinflated by an increase in money supply is a recipe for a historic crash waiting on the horizon.

In order to fully comprehend the hyperinflation in stock market, one must also understand the difference between the stock valuation (or market value) and the actual worth (or book value) of a publicly-traded company (PTC)—also known as public limited company (PLC) in the United Kingdom.

Thus, while a company may be valued at $100B on paper in the stock market due to speculative trading by gamblers, it may not even garner $10B if it were to be sold off to a private entity.

It is indeed quite common for publicly-traded companies to lose as much as 90% of their market value during a severe stock market bust so as to realign them with their book value.

However, what goes up does not only revert back to mean sooner or later but sometimes even loses its shine forever.

In the context of stock market, one could even proclaim that many of today's darlings (or rising stars) are set to become tomorrow's has-beens (or fallen angels).

Think of the likes of Ford Motors (F), General Motors (GM), General Electric (GE), and ExxonMobil (XOM)—the blue-chips that once ruled the Wall Street during much of the second half of the 20th century are today even struggling to stay afloat on Main Street.

Simply put, when the price of a company's stock rises or drops, it only does so on paper—no money is created or destroyed as it is essentially a zero-sum game.

For example, the rise in the price of a company's stock is fueled by more shares being bought than sold—a drop in the price is conversely driven by more shares being sold than bought.

The money simply exchanges hands during these transactions—no goods or services are being created.

While the winners are rewarded through the sale of shares at a price higher than what they purchased them at, the losers are left to lick their wounds when they are forced to sell the shares at a price lower than what they had paid for them.

In what is called the "Greater Fool Theory", the fools buy shares in a company not because they understand the fundamentals, or believe that it will change the future, but rather because they speculate that they can sell the shares to greater fools at a higher price so as to richly profit from such a reckless adventure.

Together, such a herd of fools simply follows a speculative trend and jumps on the bandwagon due to herd mentality (or crowd psychology)—the power of herd mentality is such that it can drive the price of a stock beyond imagination until it does not.

Long story short, the gains of winners are exactly balanced by the losses of losers such that the stock market is nothing more than a game of casino primarily driven by speculative behavior rather than economic fundamentals.

But, unlike a casino, what happens on Wall Street often spills over onto Main Street.

A stock market crash can for instance upend an apparently strong economy and quickly trigger a recession with huge consequences for the economic well-being of the masses, even though most of them have never partaken in the stock casino.

Yet, it is those at the bottom rung of society who pay the biggest price for the reckless actions of the wealthy gamblers.

The fact that the stock market is essentially a zero-sum game is further corroborated by the observation that there is often a disconnect (or divergence) between Wall Street and Main Street.

Consistent with this notion, the overall return on stocks should be expected to dip during the first half of oqual cycle in the midst of an organic boom in economy when there is a little incentive for speculative behavior but rise during the second half just as the economy begins to head south due to fraudsters taking the helm and replacing organic products with phony ones as embodied in the "stock oquacycle".

Thus, the economic growth and stock market appear to be inversely correlated—they are mirror images of each other with the former excelling during the first half and the latter during the second.

Additionally, being a hallmark of the first half of oqual cycle, the rather high interest rates incentivize individuals to invest in bonds at the expense of the stock market due to a rather high risk-to-reward ratio in the latter trade.

In contrast, the interest rates tank during the second half of oqual cycle, thereby incentivizing individuals to flock to the stock market offering a lower risk-to-reward ratio rather than continue to trade bonds with rather paltry returns.

Admittedly, save for a brief feeding frenzy on the so-called Nifty Fifty during the 1960s and 1970s, the first half (1955-1996) of the current oquannium (1955-2038) was by-and-large a miserable time to be a stock gambler due to the fact that one could earn decent returns through trading bonds, thereby leaving little appetite for more riskier stocks.

However, this whole picture flipped upside down just as the second half (1997-2038) of the current oquannium (1955-2038) kicked off with the stock market becoming a much more attractive investment as most of us have witnessed firsthand over the past several decades from the dotcoms through the cryptos to meme stocks.

A similar tale of two opposite halves emerged during the previous oquannium (1871-1954) with stocks delivering scant returns during the first half (1871-1912) but stellar rewards during the second half (1913-1954).

That the overall return on stocks dips during the first half of oqual cycle but rises during the second half is also captured at a quantitative level for the previous (1871-1954) and the current (1955-2038) oquannia using the DJI as a proxy for the US stock market as a whole.

That this is so is further demonstrated through measuring the change in the ratio of DJI/GDP—which apparently serves as a more sensitive metric to gauge the behavior and valuation of the stock market.

Collectively, these data strongly argue that while it pays to be invested in bonds or other alternative assets during the first half of oqual cycle, the stock market is the sweet spot to be during the second half for those with the urge to get filthy rich and then brag about their riches.

It is indeed the second half of oqual cycle when fraudsters-and-gamblers-alike converge in droves on Wall Street and, in doing so, send stock prices through the roof defying gravity as they move higher and higher until the bubble is popped by a black swan.

If the stock market is nothing more than a casino, then how does a company benefit from becoming publicly-traded?

A company gets to raise funds for expanding its enterprise when it goes public—it issues shares to gamblers during its initial launch into the stock market in what has come to be referred to as the initial public offering (IPO).

However, driven by the motto "Fake it till you make it!", most companies that go public not only put a lipstick but also mascara on their filthy pig—their product is a huge hyperbole at best and an outright fraud at worst.

Beyond the IPO, a company can raise additional funds through issuing new shares to gamblers anytime it so desires though that risks causing its stock to plunge—as issuing new shares not only shifts the supply-demand equilibrium to the left but it can also trigger stock selloff by those without diamond hands.

An alternative mechanism through which a stock company raises funds is when it buys back its own shares at a reduced price during a market downturn for instance and then selling them later at a much higher price when the market heads north.

Importantly, stock buybacks also make a company more competitive as such a dirty trick unfurled by the executives shifts the supply-demand equation to the right, thereby inflating the stock price and luring evermore gamblers to come aboard and join in the buying frenzy though the fools know not that they are being trapped into a spider's web of sorts.

However, a company may sometimes buy back its own shares merely to stop the bleeding when its stock goes into a free fall due for instance to poor earnings or reports of a misconduct.

Alas, the ability of a company to artificially inflate its stock price and other fundamentals through stock buybacks without any increase in its productivity amounts to nothing short of being a legalized fraud.

Since executives usually own a big stake in their company, they therefore directly profit from stock buybacks—this tactic essentially serves as a backchannel through which executives conduct a heist in broad daylight atop being paid millions through their big fat paychecks and bonuses.

Would it not be better for a company to invest the funds in innovating and expanding its enterprise in a tangible way rather than using them to merely add aesthetics to its stock as well as enable the insiders-and-executives to richly profit from the spoils?

On the contrary, big companies are being incentivized to indulge in stock buybacks rather than invest their funds acquired through sales or borrowing into creating new goods and services.

Such a practice of stock buybacks thus blurs the lines between a genuine company and a gambling enterprise.

To say that the stock market largely amounts to a casino would be to put it lightly.

Unsurprisingly, when the despicable act of stock buybacks becomes synchronized between big companies, it can quickly inflate the whole stock market with a potential for hard landing with dire consequences for all.

Indeed, stock buybacks are believed to be one of the major contributors to at least two of the biggest stock bubbles ever witnessed in recent memory:
1) Between 1929-1932 in the midst of the Great Depression, the Dow Jones Industrial plummeted by a whopping 89%; and
2) Between 2000-2002 in the aftermath of the Dotcom Bubble, the Nasdaq Composite plunged by a colossal 78% as it threatened to eclipse the dubious fate of its more illustrious and less volatile cousin some 70 years earlier.

Given their potential for collusion, the stock buybacks were outlawed in 1934 in the aftermath of the 1929 Financial Crisis during the tenure of the then 32nd POTUS Franklin Roosevelt.

In 1982, some 50 years later, the ban on stock buybacks was however lifted so as to enable the stock market to be manipulated once again for the benefit of the wealthy during the tenure of the then 40th POTUS Ronald Reagan.

While Reagan's debt mania coupled with his anathema to regulatory checks-and-balances did temporarily lift the then sagging US economy during the 1980s, his impetuous actions however also planted the seeds for a culture of self-indulgence and reckless behavior that would begin to wreck the nation barely after he left the office in 1989.

Admittedly, one of the major drivers of the US stock market over the past decade or so has been the stock buybacks-on-steroids due to an increase in money supply courtesy of the Fed having printed trillions of dollars.

Coupled with a backdrop of practically near-zero interest rates since the 2008 Great Recession, the executives-and-gamblers-alike have therefore been incentivized to borrow dirt cheap money so as to pour them into the stock market in the hope of making a killing.

Such a speculative behavior has been further run amok to the nth degree in the form of cryptos, non-fungible tokens (NFTs), special purpose acquisition companies (SPACs), and meme stocks—the stocks of virtually bankrupt and zombie companies heavily traded on the market and catapulted to the sky, merely due to their popularity on social media rather than their corporate fundamentals, only for them to come back crashing to earth and leaving fools holding the bag.

In particular, the irrational exuberance of gamblers propelled the US stock market to become extremely frothy and bubblicious as 2021 drew to a close, a la its fate prior to the 1929 crash, as gauged by almost every metric available.

A once-in-a-lifetime crash is thus once again in the offing, and like the 1929 crash, it will also leave decamillions of fools-and-horses without clothes.

While doomers and gloomers have been calling for such an earth-shattering crash for decades, little they understand that it does not occur randomly but rather its odds dwindle as human society walks past annus horribilis of oqual cycle as it did some 84 years earlier in 1944 but then they begin to swindle as it cycles back to that horrible year as is the case today with the next annus horribilis (2028) barely years away.

Simply put, the odds of once-in-a-lifetime crash in the stock market (or other assets such as real estate) with the potential to wipe out the life-savings of decamillions ebb and flow in tandem with the progression of oqual cycle as exquisitely captured by the "crash oquacycle".

Notably, the 1929 crash uncharacteristically transpired earlier by about a decade than what might have been forecast by the oqual gods—a reminder that the oqual cycle is not set in stone but rather the exact timing of fallout from our excesses and imbalances is determined by an interplay between human behavior and astronomical factors.

With the annus horribilis (2028) of the current oquannium (1955-2038) barely years away, it seems that the stock-market bubble is likely on its last leg before it comes crashing down to earth in what would go down in the annals of history as once-in-a-lifetime crash on a scale comparable, if not greater, to the 1929 crash.

Admittedly, barely a week into 2022, the stock-market bubble seemingly began to pop one last time.

In 2023, more than a year after it hit what was a record high, the popping of the stock bubble bears the hallmarks of a crash that is just getting started and it will be a long-and-bumpy ride before it shows any signs of bottoming out.

Given that the world is teetering on the brink of World War III with so many dark clouds hanging over our head and shoulders, the stock market is indeed set to continue rolling downhill for many years to come though it will likely be interrupted by bear rallies every now and then.

Nevertheless, a new and powerful bull run will likely get underway on the other side of annus horribilis (2028) of the current oquannium (1955-2038) just as preparations get underway for the start of a new dawn of hope and prosperity.

It would therefore pay to build cash reserves now and beef up the dry powder so that it can be deployed when there is blood in the streets.

Still, it is important to remember that plowing money into the stock market is not an investment—it is speculation at best, Russian roulette at worst, and a casino for all intents and purposes.

Indeed, there is a reason as to why Warren Buffett has been dubbed the "Oracle of Omaha"—he is the most successful gambler of all time due to his investment prophecy rather than investment philosophy.

Had Buffet's big bet on the likes of Coca-Cola during the 1980s gone bust (and it should have given the exorbitant toxicity of that filthy beverage), none would have ever heard of him.

If you rather invest your money, then lend it directly to private and public companies when they issue bonds rather than merely gambling and betting on their market value through trading their stocks.

 CLIMATE WAVES

While growing up in Pakistan during the 1970s, my beloved grandmother would often share with us many memories of her prime years straddling the 1930s and 1940s in the midst of a tumultuous period of extreme trials-and-tribulations when a complete meltdown in ethnic harmony would trigger the bloody Indian Partition (1947) and mark the end of British Raj.

Among such a memorabilia, my grandmother would occasionally tell us that not only did she have to make-do with little resources due to crop failures as a result of droughts but that she also had to confront much hotter summers than what we had seen in our fledgling years.

While we deeply shared her agony back then, it would never occur to us that what she was talking about was in fact a recurring theme on our planet rather than just a random event.

Over the next several decades, the odyssey of my life would transcend several continents as it would take me from the heart of Asia to Europe and then to North America but I never forgot a single moment with my precious grandmother.

Today, it should therefore hardly come as a surprise that my photographic memory from almost 50 years earlier made me realize that the anecdotal accounts of my beji—as I used to call my grandmother with much affection—would resonate with numerous documented reports of the sweltering heat of the 1930s recorded over North America.

Although largely believed to be a man-made ecological disaster, Mother Nature had in fact also collaborated in no small part through unleashing heat waves and droughts to exacerbate the fallout from the so-called Dust Bowl—a decade-long intermittent period of dust storms that billowed over and choked much of North America in fits and starts during the 1930s.

In the dazzling light of such accounts of dire climate having befallen our planet some 84 years earlier, I immediately began to feel a sense of déjà vu in the footsteps of my grandmother.

Add to that the fact that after immigrating to England during the mid-1980s, I would wake up to piles of snow waiting outside on many winter mornings to my consternation just as my father would remind me how lucky I was compared to what he and my uncles had to endure during the 1960s and 1970s—when they were faced with having to shovel feet of snow on virtually every winter morning before they could drive to work as for instance underscored by the 1963 Big Freeze—the coldest winter spell witnessed on British shores in more than 200 years and that brought the nation to a virtual standstill for months.

Fast forward some 50 years, and heaps of snow waiting outside one's abode on winter mornings have become as rare as diamonds in England.

Such a dramatic shift in the English climate is indeed due to rising temperatures that have been witnessed across much of the globe over the past 50 years.

However, it seems that today's scorching heat felt by almost everyone across the globe did not just fall out of the sky but rather it bears parallels to the experiences of my grandmother some 84 years earlier in what was then British India and those who lived through the Dust Bowl in North America during the 1930s.

Of particular note here is the salient observation that the rather hot summers of today and the 1930s were interrupted by a period of decades-long relatively temperate climate.

Yet, climate scientists seem to sweep such an earth-shattering anecdote under the rug as they attribute the rising temperatures around the globe to an irreversible climate change that they have dubbed "global warming".

To be sure, the surface temperature of Earth has indeed risen by about 2°F since climate records began around 1850—with half of that upsurge having occurred over the past quarter-of-a-century alone.

While that may sound ominous, it gets much worse as politically-motivated climate scientists peddle the absurdity of global temperature rising by another 2°F by 2050.

However, such a dire forecast is predicated on the ridiculous assumption that the current climate trend must be irreversible in that the temperature could only continue to rise linearly as it has done so for at least the past 25 years, if not longer.

Yet, nature is inundated with so many phenomena that remind us time and again that what goes up must come down.

In fact, fluctuations in temperature are inevitable for a planet that is constantly in flux—only fools would expect the Earth's surface temperature to hold constant rather than oscillate over time.

Admittedly, the Earth is not only beholden to the sinusoidal oscillations of temperature over a day and a year, but it is well-documented that our planet experiences a barrage of climate cycles over millennia and megannia in a phenomenon loosely referred to as the "ice age"—with "megannia" being the plural form of "megannium" meaning a period of one million years.

In what is called the "Little Ice Age", the Earth experienced a sustained period of some 500 years roughly spanning from 1300-1850 during which the global temperature is believed to have dipped by several degrees [25].

With a rhythm of around a millennium, the Little Ice age was not only the most recent mini-ice age that ended less than 200 years ago but 1816 has also continued to garner attention in that it came to be remembered as the "Year Without a Summer".

In the wake of the 1815 Volcanic Eruption at Mount Tambora in Indonesia with the volcanic ash increasing the Earth's albedo (or its ability to block the incoming solar radiation) after being blasted into the atmosphere over the course of the year that followed, the global temperature remained depressed during the 1816 Summer with snow falling across many parts of Western Europe and North America—and presumably across many parts of Asia though I have been unable to track down any reliable historical records.

In light of the foregoing argument, it should therefore be hardly surprising that the Earth not only experiences climate cycles over millennia and megannia but also over shorter decadal and centennial timescales.

Long story short, the rising trend in global temperature witnessed over the past 50 years is in no uncertain terms due to the climate rhythm that oscillates in sync with the oqual cycle over a period of 84 years in a similar fashion to the sinusoidal oscillations of temperature over the course of a day or a year.

Notably, such an 84-year climate cycle could well be the missing link between Uranus and its impact on the affairs of earthlings as embodied in the oqual theory.

In particular, Uranus appears to exert a subtle control over human civilization by virtue of its ability to modulate the terrestrial climate in a sinusoidal fashion in sync with the oqual cycle in a manner akin to the annual climate cycle dictated by the orbiting of Earth around the Sun.

In fact, the unprecedented rise in global temperature witnessed over the past quarter-of-a-century is in no small part due to the Uranian spell on our planet and, as such, global warming is expected to not only plateau out but also head south as the current oqual cycle draws to a close over the next decade or so.

Likewise, the wrath of natural disasters from droughts through flooding to storms with an increasing frequency and intensity seen over the past quarter-of-a-century also seems to be largely due to the cyclical flux of our planet undergoing a self-cleansing process under the watchful eye of oqual cycle rather than a direct consequence of human activities.

Although the likes of earthquakes, tsunamis, volcanoes, and wildfires are beyond the scope of this maiden edition, a rudimentary analysis nonetheless reaches the same conclusion—that their frequency and intensity also ebb and flow in sync with the progression of oqual cycle.

While the drummed-up specter of global warming seems to be nothing more than a hyperbole hatched by devious actors around the globe in order to advance their propaganda, there appears to be nevertheless a seemingly upward trend in global temperature over the long run though far from being anywhere near as apocalyptic as that forecast by climate scientists.

Taken together, the terrestrial climate appears to oscillate over a period of 84 years in sync with the oqual cycle so as to produce a lower-order harmonic of the daily-and-annual temperature cycles.

To shed further light on this timely phenomenon, let us divide our ongoing discussion under the following sections:

    6.1 Temperature
    6.2 Droughts
    6.3 Floods
    6.4 Storms
    6.5 Climateganda

| 6.1 | TEMPERATURE

To test the hypothesis that the rising trend in global temperature witnessed over the past 50 years is due to the climate rhythm that marches in lockstep with the oqual cycle, I analyzed temperature data stretching at least as far back as the 1870s from a number of observatories scattered across the United Kingdom and publicly available courtesy of the Met Office [26].

While data from all of these observatories displayed remarkable climate oscillations over periods roughly spanning 84 years, the contrast was particularly notable for the data from the Stornoway station—located on an island off the northwestern coast of Scotland—presumably due to its remote location from urban centers such that the artificial temperature fluctuations due to what is called the "Urban Heat Island Effect" are minimized.

Needless to say, the temperature data from the Stornoway station are being used here as a proxy to probe how the global climate foxtrots with the oqual cycle.

Such analysis reveals that the daily-high temperature displays a remarkable wave-like behavior that has continued to oscillate in sync with the oqual cycle since 1871—a period that encompasses virtually all of sixth (1871-1954) and much of seventh (1955-2038) oquannia.

In particular, the daily-high temperature seemingly undergoes a steady drop over the first half (1871-1912) of previous and sixth oquannium (1871-1954) and then steadily rises during the second half (1913-1954) virtually in sync with the progression of the oqual rhythm.

A similar trend is observed for the current and seventh oquannium (1955-2038) with the daily-high temperature beginning to head south around 1955 and then turning north almost exactly at the midpoint in 1997.

Unsurprisingly, such an oscillatory trend over a period of around 84 years is also a hallmark of daily-low temperature as well as daily-mean temperature.

It is however noteworthy that there appears to be a slight uptick in the thermometer since 1871 as simulated by diagonal sinusoidal models.

In particular, such a rising trend in temperature is significantly more pronounced for the daily-lows relative to the daily-highs.

That the rise in daily-lows has outpaced the corresponding rise in daily-highs is evidence that the overall rise in global temperature since 1871 is largely due to the Earth getting less colder than more warmer.

This notion is further corroborated by the daily temperature differential that has displayed a precipitously falling sinusoidal trend since 1871 and is poised to continue to do so over the course of the next oqual cycle.

Importantly, the oscillatory behavior of temperature is exquisitely mirrored by a remarkably similar pattern in the number of air-frost days—the days on which the air temperature ≤ 0°C—though such a sinusoidal trend appears to be somewhat out of phase with the progression of oqual cycle.

Needless to say, the 84-year cyclical variation of temperature around the globe does not have to be perfectly synchronized with the oqual cycle due to an interplay between the local climate and astronomical factors.

Notwithstanding such anomalies, the data presented herein unequivocally suggest that the Earth apparently cools down during the first half of oqual cycle and then begins to warm up during the second half.

In other words, the Earth experiences what is called the "temperature oquacycle" over a period of 84 years that appears to be a lower-order harmonic of the daily and annual temperature cycles.

Of particular note is the observation that such multidecadal oscillation of global temperature produces a 42-year COOLING period in sync with the first half of oqual cycle followed by a 42-year WARMING spell during the second half.

However, the warming up during the second half outstrips the amplitude of the drop during the first half such that the Earth is overall heating up due to what appear to be astronomical factors rather than human activities.

In the context of our recent past, the Earth underwent a COOLING period during the first half (1955-1996) of the current oquannium (1955-2038) and it is currently experiencing a WARMING spell over the course of the second half (1997-2038).

Accordingly, a rising trend in global temperature is expected to continue over the next decade or so before it begins to head south just as the current oqual cycle bids farewell in about a decade or so.

Nevertheless, the Earth is overall getting warmer but it is a far cry from what the hyped-up climate forecasts have us believe.

Given that the Earth experienced the Little Ice Age between 1300-1850 [25], our planet undergoing the current bout of global warming should therefore be hardly surprising as it is not only trying to reclaim the warmer temperatures it once enjoyed but another mini-ice age likely awaits on the other side that should once again revert the global temperature to its long-term average.

It is noteworthy that the cyclical nature of global temperature over a multidecadal timescale has been well-documented for decades [27-30].

However, the data presented herein suggest that such a multidecadal temperature oscillation more or less occurs in lockstep with the progression of oqual cycle.

Taken together, it seems that the sharp uptick observed in global temperature over the past quarter-of-a-century is transitory rather than persistent due to the modulation of terrestrial climate by astronomical factors in a sinusoidal fashion such that it oscillates in lockstep with the oqual cycle.

How does one reconcile the fact that the ongoing global warming is due to astronomical factors rather than carbon dioxide (CO_2) emissions?

Although gigatons of CO_2 are being released into the atmosphere each year due to the combustion of fossil fuels, such emissions nevertheless pale in comparison to what is being discharged through natural processes such as cellular respiration by living organisms on land and in oceans.

In fact, much of CO_2 released into the atmosphere is immediately recycled back via carbon sinks such as topsoil, rainforests, rocks, and oceans.

It should therefore be hardly surprising that the atmospheric CO_2 levels have more or less remained constant over the millennial timescale.

Nevertheless, the atmospheric concentration of CO_2 has precipitously risen by 40% from around 300ppm in 1900 to 420ppm today—out of every million molecules of all gases that make up the atmosphere, 420 of those belong to CO_2 (or 420 parts per million).

While such an upsurge in the atmospheric level of CO_2 over the past century or so is significant, few have the wisdom to question whether it is beneficial or harmful to the planet and its inhabitants, plants and animals alike.

Rather, climate scientists assume a priori that the rising levels of atmospheric CO_2 must necessarily be harmful in that they are believed to correlate with a rise in global temperature due to their own intuition and biased views arising from their conflict of interest and further fueled by herd mentality and peer pressure.

Alas, correlation does not necessarily imply causation.

Even if one assumes that there is a correlation between a rise in global temperature and a rise in atmospheric CO_2, they are still left with establishing the causality (or solving the cause-effect equation)—rather than being the cause, the latter could well be the effect (or symptom).

This problem essentially amounts to the chicken-or-egg paradox—did the chicken lay the egg, or did the egg produce the chicken?

Simply put, the apparent rise in atmospheric CO_2 could well follow rather than precede a rise in global temperature—which itself could be due to one or more of the natural climate cycles known to occur over decades, centuries, millennia, and even megannia.

An overlay of multicentennial data indeed suggests that $\Delta[CO_2]$, or the annual rate of change in CO_2 emissions, has not only by-and-large oscillated in perfect harmony with the Central-England temperature (being used here as proxy for the global temperature) since around 1700 but that a rise in $\Delta[CO_2]$ also somewhat appears to lag the corresponding rise in the thermometer.

In other words, it is the rise in global temperature that begets a corresponding rise in $\Delta[CO_2]$ and a drop in the thermometer also leads to a drop in $\Delta[CO_2]$.

In particular, while the temperature over the past several decades has been rising, $\Delta[CO_2]$ has been experiencing a slump almost mirroring the trend in the thermometer over the same timeframe due to what appears to be a multidecadal lag between the cause (temperature rise) and effect (CO_2 rise).

That this is so lends unequivocal evidence that the greenhouse gas is unlikely to be the cause of the ongoing global warming in agreement with previous studies on Antarctic ice cores indicating that the rise in CO_2 lagged the rise in temperature by centuries [31-33].

This notion is further corroborated by the fact that there appears to be an overall negative correlation between global warming since around 1700 and CO_2 emissions as probed by Pearson's correlation coefficient.

Thus, although the global temperature has been on a rising trajectory since around 1700, the time-resolved Pearson's correlation coefficient displays an overall negative slope over the same timeframe.

It is noteworthy that there is a lack of discernible oscillatory trend that might be expected to move in lockstep with the progression of oqual cycle in the Central-England temperature.

This is due to the low-resolution and sometimes indirect measurement of temperature over Central England over the course of centuries, not to mention that such data do not refer to a well-defined location—as is the case with the temperature data from the Stornoway station discussed earlier—but rather represent an average over a much larger region.

Notwithstanding such drawbacks, the rather steep rise in Central-England temperature over the past 50 years is exquisitely paralleled, if not overshadowed, by an equally-impressive upsurge observed during the first half of the 18th century.

Such a burst of global warming observed during that earlier period roughly spanning 1700-1750 occurred well before the modern industrialization of our planet in the midst of the Little Ice Age that ended around 1850 [25].

Surely, that earlier global warming in our recent past must have been driven by astronomical factors rather than due to the combustion of fossil fuels concomitant with the release of CO_2 into the atmosphere.

Why anyone would therefore attribute the current trend in global warming to anthropogenic factors is anyone's guess.

Nevertheless, a neutral observer would conclude that the hyped-up threat of the current trend in global warming is due to either a knee-jerk reaction at best, or at worst, a propaganda engineered to exploit the masses and rally them to a new round of feeding frenzy on a roster of new technologies and consumer products fraudulently labelled as "environment-friendly".

In actuality, such bogus products from electric cars to solar panels represent a devil-in-disguise that will only plunge our planet into a deeper crisis in the decades and generations to come.

As a rule of thumb, no technology is good for the well-being of our environment—it is all about a trade off between the benefits versus the harms of a product.

Those looking for an "environment-friendly" technology should rather cut down on their toxic addiction to overconsumption as it will not only alleviate the suffering of the planet but also boost their own health and wealth.

|6.2| DROUGHTS

In light of the temperature oquacycle discussed earlier, one would assume that parts of the globe would be marred by dry spells during the second half of oqual cycle when the Earth begins to transiently heat up producing a multidecadal warmer period compared to the first half.

Notably, warmer temperatures promote evaporation of surface water—thereby drying out the soil in regions with low precipitation, causing vegetations to die out, and even making the topsoil becoming dislodged during high winds with the risk of turning the otherwise healthy land into a desert.

Consistent with this argument, the globe has indeed been caught in a quagmire of what seems to be a perpetual spell of severe droughts over the past couple of decades, the like of which we have rarely encountered in our lifetime.

Although many are quick to lay the blame on irreversible climate change for such a crisis, the crux of the matter is that this is most likely due to the Earth being in a cyclical flux and, as such, wetter days are just around the corner.

In particular, human civilization has encountered protracted but transitory dry spells a la ongoing droughts time and again as they appear to be a hallmark of the second half of oqual cycle.

This view is supported by the fact that the rainfall in the Scottish Northwest seemingly displays an 84-year cyclical rhythm though somewhat out of phase with the progression of oqual cycle.

It is notable that the rainfall steadily increases during the first half of oqual cycle and then reverses its course during the second half producing a quasi-sinusoidal pattern with a periodicity of around 84 years.

In the context of such cyclical variation observed in rainfall, the oqual cycle can be viewed as a perpetual tale of two halves—a "wet" period followed by a "dry" spell—with each lasting some 42 years.

Such an alternate spell of wet and dry periods over the course of oqual cycle suggests that the second half is much more likely to experience severe and extended bouts of drought in agreement with the spell of temperature oquacycle.

Consistent with this rationale, the drought conditions indeed tend to wane during the first half of oqual cycle and then wax during the second half as probed by the so-called Palmer Drought Index (PDI) for the American Southwest.

On the basis of broader PDI analysis, such a "drought oquacycle" alternating between an overall wet period followed by an overall dry spell occurring more or less in sync with the progression of oqual cycle also appears to hold true across other regions of the globe.

One should therefore be hardly surprised to learn that being in the midst of the second half (1997-2038) of the current oquannium (1955-2038), many parts of the world are either embroiled in once-in-a-lifetime drought or have already gone through a fair share of their own dry wrath of nature.

Lets us delve a little deeper into the second halves of the last three oquannia in order to further evaluate the generality of the drought oquacycle.

DROUGHTS HAVE HITHERTO BEEN A HALLMARK OF THE SECOND HALF (1997-2038) OF THE CURRENT AND SEVENTH OQUANNIUM (1955-2038)

Since drought is concomitant with crop failures, it often serves as a breeding ground for violent conflicts.

Indeed, one of the major triggers for the Syrian Civil War (2011-date) was what is believed to be the most severe drought ever recorded on Syrian soil between 2006-2011 with the water levels of rivers such as the Tigris and Euphrates having dropped dangerously low.

That Syrian drought at the outset of the second half of the current oquannium resulted in mass migration of people from rural areas to urban centers, thereby causing price inflation and sparking social unrest that continues to this day.

Elsewhere around the globe, the Australians have had to deal with their own prolonged dry spell called the Millennium Drought (2001-2009) in the recent past just as the second half of the current oquannium rang in.

Since 2019, much of Brazilian South has been gripped by a severe bout of drought with water level in Rio Paraná having dipped by as much as 30ft below average in some parts.

For the past couple of decades, much of the Indian North has also been experiencing drought-like conditions with groundwater in rapid decline coupled with repetitive bouts of low rainfall year after year such that many Indian scholars are increasingly concerned that they could well have their own Dust Bowl in the making—such a prophecy may well come to fruition as the current oqual cycle draws to a close over the next decade or so should the arable land continue to be overused against the backdrop of limited precipitation.

Across the Himalayas, China may have proved itself as the world's largest manufacturing powerhouse head-and-shoulders above all other nations but such an industrial feat has come with a huge price tag as the Asian Giant finds itself increasingly becoming dry and short of water supplies in order to continue marching toward its destiny of dethroning America and taking up the baton of global leadership.

For its part, America is hardly a stranger to droughts.

Since the outset of 21st century, the American Southwest has been under protracted drought conditions with Lake Mead, the nation's largest reservoir supplying water to 25M people and powering the hydroelectric turbines of the Hoover Dam, having dropped to one third of its full capacity in 2022.

Although what has been loosely-termed the American Megadrought (2000-date) is being attributed to irreversible climate change, the ongoing dry spell in the American Southwest is nevertheless transitory rather than persistent due to our planet being in a cyclical flux with wetter conditions poised to return across much of the globe in about a decade or so in line with the spell of oqual cycle.

PROTRACTED DRY SPELLS HAMSTRUNG THE SECOND HALF (1913-1954) OF THE PREVIOUS AND SIXTH OQUANNIUM (1871-1954)

Some 84 years before the ongoing American Megadrought, a far worse episode of a severe decade-long drought in the form of what came to be called the Dust Bowl befell North America during much of the 1930s in the midst of the second half of the previous and sixth oquannium.

What was arguably the worst ecological disaster in the nation's history, the Dust Bowl billowed over and choked much of North America.

Triggered by the conversion of mega-acres of arid grassland into arable land in the American Southwest coupled with deep-plowing resulting in the loss of protective grasses against the backdrop of a prolonged period of low rainfall, the dislodged topsoil quickly turned dry becoming vulnerable to being tossed up into the air and blown away by high winds for hundreds of miles.

The resulting dust storms powered by a severe bout of drought across much of the American Southwest would kill thousands of people and displace millions more as the Dust Bowl conspired to exacerbate the pain and suffering unleashed upon the nation by the Great Depression (1929-1939).

Across the other side of the globe, the Australians did not fare any better as they had to endure a catastrophe of their own in what since then has been referred to as the World War II Drought (1937-1945) during the second half of the previous oquannium.

Add to that the Northwest China Famine (1928-1930) sparked by one of the worst droughts of the second half of the previous oquannium as it led to widespread famine and claimed the lives of as many as 10M people.

While documented accounts are hard to come by, the Northern Indian peninsula being frequently prone to dry spells was also likely beset by severe droughts during the second half of the previous oquannium as per anecdotal accounts of my beloved grandmother.

Born in 1901, the year during which Queen Victoria (1837-1901) took her last breath, my grandmother once confided in us how she and everyone else around her had to occasionally make-do with the pakhra weed (caltrop) in lieu of more conventional grains such as the kanak (wheat) or the baajra (pearl millet) during her prime years just as the world around her was stifled by the Great Depression during the 1930s.

With a minimal dependence on moisture and taxonomically classified as Tribulus terrestris and commonly identified by various names that allude to the shape of its hooked bur (or fruit) such as caltrop or goat's head, the pakhra weed is a master of drought conditions and thrives on the driest of soils where all else fails.

The dire plight of my grandmother having to substitute the horrible pakhra for the much more palatable wheat and millet speaks volumes about what the dire nutritional straits many Indians must have encountered across much of the Northern Indian peninsula during the second half of the previous oquannium.

This is particularly notable given that my grandmother hailed from a relatively prosperous Rajput clan renowned for its land ownership and agricultural prowess — with Rajput being a portmanteau of raja (king) and putt (descendent).

One therefore wonders that if the mighty Rajputs were forced to survive on the pakhra weed, then the nutritional predicament facing ordinary Indians must have been multiples worse.

This school of thought is further corroborated by the 1943 Bengal Famine that claimed the lives of millions due to crop failures though that human tragedy is believed to be in no small part exacerbated by the British colonialists diverting food away in the most devious manner imaginable from Indian civilians to British soldiers fighting World War II (1939-1945).

Out of fear that snatching food from Indians in broad daylight could trigger social unrest and a dreadful rebellion, the notorious economist John Maynard Keynes working for the British Treasury devised a cunning plan to have the Bank of England (BOE) print huge sums of money such that it would price ordinary Indians out of the market through inflation leaving the British soldiers to gorge on the spoils without firing a shot.

Alas, what goes around comes around.

The sacks of printed money returned home in droves not long after the Vilayati colonial rule on Indian soil ended in 1947 and, soon thereafter, kick-started a deadly bout of inflation on British shores during the 1950s causing the pound to plunge against the dollar.

In 1861, at the outbreak of the American Civil War when the British Empire was rising fast, one GBP spiked to ten USD.

In 1939, prior to the outbreak of World War II, one GBP equaled five USD.

In 1950, after all the dust from World War II had settled with America having dethroned Britain for the global supremacy, one GBP barely garnered three USD.

In 2022, almost 84 years after GBP last held its own against USD, the pound hit all but parity with the dollar for the first time ever in history.

What a difference one round of oqual cycle makes—with GBP having lost 80% of its value against USD since 1939.

Two rounds of oqual cycle make an even bigger difference—with GBP having lost 90% of its value against USD since 1861.

No wonder then that even the poorest of Americans are now beginning to salivate at the prospect of their dream of meeting Blighty King becoming a reality as the fortunes of Dollar King continue to bloat.

But, before hitch-hiking across the pond to the other side of the Atlantic, they must first make amends with the ever-deepening American Megadrought (2000-date) threatening to overshadow the Dust Bowl of the 1930s befalling North America in the midst of the second half of the previous oquannium.

Although that is unlikely to pan out, such a calamity is nevertheless inevitable once every 84 years during the second half of oqual cycle.

PROLONGED DRY PERIODS CRIPPLED THE SECOND HALF (1829-1870) OF THE FIFTH OQUANNIUM (1787-1870)

Some 84 years prior to the Dust Bowl, the American Southwest was struck by an equally devastating prolonged dry period aptly named Civil War Drought during much of the 1850s and 1860s in the midst of the second half of the fifth oquannium.

In particular, the Civil War Drought is notable for not only weighing heavily on European immigrants heading from East to West looking for greener pastures but it also pushed the American bison to near-extinction as foraging opportunities became squeezed due to fierce competition between wild herbivores and domesticated animals.

Additionally, the crop failures for what was then a largely agrarian society only exacerbated the woes of Americans.

Needless to say, the Civil War Drought was a major trigger for its namesake conflict that all but sliced the nation into two.

In a magnitude comparable to the Civil War Drought, a protracted drought across much of Australian South during the 1850s and 1860s in the midst of the second half of the fifth oquannium has also been documented.

Likewise, a severe drought is believed to have befallen much of Europe during the 1840s leading to extensive famine and sparking a series of sociopolitical upheavals throughout the continent in what came to be collectively called the European Revolutions (1848-1849).

While Ireland's Great Famine (1845-1852) was caused by the potato blight, the Irish misery was exacerbated by widespread shortage of food across Europe due to the drought such that large quantities of food continued to be looted out of the country by England—the whole of Ireland then being a part of the United Kingdom and the Irish Republic only becoming independent in 1922.

In China, severe drought conditions during the 1850s and 1860s led to widespread famine and the outbreak of a large-scale civil war through rebellions such as the Taiping Rebellion (1850-1864) and the Nian Rebellion (1851-1868) that together significantly weakened the Qing Dynasty's grip on power just as the fifth oquannium drew to a close.

While there are no reliable data, I suspect that one of the major causes that fueled the 1857 Indian Mutiny against the British colonialists must have been the millions of undernourished mouths due to widespread drought and crop failures on the Indian peninsula during the second half of the fifth oquannium.

This view is supported by multiple bouts of famines across the Northern Indian peninsula during much of the second half (1829-1870) of the fifth oquannium.

Such hard times were additionally capped by Indian Great Famine (1876-1878) at the dawn of sixth oquannium (1871-1954), which is believed to have resulted in crop failures across much of the Indian South resulting in the death of as many as 10M people.

A RELATIVELY WET PERIOD IS WAITING ON THE HORIZON

Some of the most severe and protracted droughts that the world has experienced in recorded history have almost always occurred during the second half of oqual cycle.

This should be hardly surprising given that the Earth begins to heat up during the second half of oqual cycle, thereby favoring dry conditions.

Although the likelihood of severe droughts are multiples greater during the second half of oqual cycle, exceptions to this rule are nevertheless expected like any other natural phenomenon.

For example, one of the worst droughts to occur on Australian soil was the so-called Federation Drought (1895-1902) that reared its ugly head during the first half (1871-1912) of the previous oquannium (1871-1954).

Still, the ongoing bouts of drought around the globe are a hallmark of the second half of oqual cycle as we currently find in one rather than due to irreversible climate change.

Nevertheless, one must not disregard the fact that the quadrupling of global population coupled with ever more crowding of urban centers due to migration over the past century has put ever more stress on nature and its resources.

For the most part, the falling levels of water in rivers and lakes across the globe are transitory though they may not return to their prior highs anytime soon due to the overloaded demand placed upon them by our consumer culture.

All told, a relatively wet multidecadal period waiting on the horizon should put an end to our ongoing drought woes as the current oquannium draws to a close in about a decade or so.

|6.3| FLOODS

In light of the temperature oquacycle discussed earlier, one could argue that parts of the globe would be deluged by severe flooding during the second half of oqual cycle when the Earth begins to transiently heat up producing a multidecadal warmer period compared to the first half.

Notably, the relatively warmer temperatures trigger the melting of frozen water reservoirs such as the glaciers and ice caps causing rivers to overflow and inundate nearby communities.

Additionally, warmer temperatures produce warmer air which can hold more water vapor—thereby gaining the potential to unleash heavy and sustained rains which subsequently conspire with the melting of frozen water reservoirs to exacerbate flooding of inhabited areas.

In line with this school of thought, the globe has indeed been mired in what seems to be a perennial stretch of severe floods over the past couple of decades, the like of which we have rarely encountered in our lifetime.

Although many are quick to lay the blame on irreversible climate change for such a crisis, it seems that this is most likely due to the Earth being in a cyclical flux and, as such, relatively floodless days are just around the corner.

In particular, severe flooding appears to be a hallmark of the second half of oqual cycle in a manner akin to the recurring spell of droughts discussed earlier (see §6.2).

More specifically, the severity of flooding diminishes during the first half of oqual cycle but accelerates during the second half in what can be envisioned as the "flood oquacycle".

Since there is no quantitative barometer, one is therefore left with qualitative benchmarks such as the loss of life and property coupled with the extent of landmass becoming inundated to gauge the severity of such flooding.

On the basis of such a yardstick, let us take a qualitative look at the second halves of the last three oquannia in order to test the generality of the flood oquacycle.

It should however be noted that the flood oquacycle is primarily concerned with natural floods stemming from heavy rains and melting of frozen water reservoirs rather than due to storms, which are the subject of next section.

Likewise, man-made flood disasters resulting exclusively from dam failures, due to the bursting of their banks, are also not accounted for by the oqual cycle.

DEADLY FLOODS HAVE HITHERTO BEEN A HALLMARK OF THE SECOND HALF (1997-2038) OF THE CURRENT AND SEVENTH OQUANNIUM (1955-2038)

With a widespread radius and ravaging so many nations across much of Western Europe, the 2021 European Floods underpinned the extreme rage that Mother Nature is capable of unleashing upon humanity during the second half of oqual cycle.

Although United Kingdom is not particularly prone to flooding, it is nevertheless vulnerable to severe inundation during the second half of oqual cycle.

In what is known as the 2004 Boscastle Flood, the county of Cornwall in the British Southwest would witness a bout of extreme flooding described by the pundits as once-in-a-lifetime event though hardly surprising given that it occurred during the second half of the current and seventh oquannium.

However, the 2007 United Kingdom Floods would overshadow the severity of what was encountered three years earlier in Cornwall with rivers such as the Thames (London), the Cherwell (Oxford), and the Ock (Abingdon) bursting their banks and inundating much of Britain as if it were a scene out of a horror movie with the county of Gloucestershire becoming reduced to a temporal island due to the overflowing of the River Severn and the River Avon.

On the other side of the Atlantic, torrential rains in the mountainous regions led to deadly mudslides and flooded much of the coastal state of Vargas in the north of Venezuela in what is called the 1999 Vargas Mudslide—leaving decathousands dead and hectothousands homeless along with annihilation of much of the infrastructure and the livelihoods of local communities.

To Venezuela's north, severe flooding decimated many Caribbean nations including in particular the Hispaniola Island divided between modern-day Haiti and Dominican Republic in what are known as the 2004 Hispaniola Floods.

On the other side of the globe, the second half of the current oquannium has also kept the record keepers busy with new floods shattering centuries-old milestones.

While hardly a stranger to run-of-the-mill floods with the Himalayan glaciers capping its northern tip and the Indus River flowing through its spine on its way to meet the Arabian Sea, Pakistan is nevertheless prone to severe inundation during the second half of oqual cycle.

And so most living Pakistanis would get to taste their first rendezvous horribilis with inundation in the form of the 2010 Pakistan Floods that would go onto kill thousands, leave millions homeless, and cause enormous damage to crops.

Over a decade later, the nation would be met with an even more severe blow of nature called the 2022 Pakistan Floods that would inundate a third of the country's landmass and, in doing so, ravage properties and infrastructure on an unimaginable scale, leave decamillions homeless, and claim the lives of decathousands either through a direct hit or indirectly through the deadly water-borne diseases such as diarrhea, cholera, malaria, and dengue.

While one half of Pakistan attributes such flooding from hell to irreversible climate change, the other half believes that it is a taste of heavenly retribution being handed out to them due to their excesses and transgressions amassed over the past couple of decades.

In the context of oqual cycle, the latter half appears to be closer to the truth with the former acting rather like my goats that I trained to follow the herd while growing up in Pakistan during the 1980s.

Let us shift gears from Pakistan to what was once East Pakistan.

Being a flood-prone region due to the confluence of hundreds of rivers running through its heartland to reach the sacred waters of the Bay of Bengal coupled with being in the direct path of heavy monsoon rains, Bangladesh can be easily awarded the dubious title of the "Flood Nation of the World" as well as the much more prestigious one of the "Mecca of Rivers".

Unsurprisingly then, the Flood Nation would encounter its first deadly bout of what are called the 1998 Bangladesh Floods during the second half of the current oquannium—a calamity in which thousands were killed, millions were left homeless, and much of the nation's infrastructure and crops were ravaged.

The deadly floods would return to Bangladesh in 2004, and again in 2022, each time tearing apart much of the nation as if Yajuj and Majuj (or Gog and Magog) had returned to ravage the Mecca of Rivers.

Nevertheless, Bangladeshis can go to sleep rest assured that Yajuj and Majuj are safely locked behind a wall of mountain that they cannot breach until they become believers by uttering "Inshallah!"

Still, what happens in Bangladesh rarely stays in Bangladesh.

Due to being abutted by India on virtually all sides but its southern coastline, flooding in Bangladesh almost always spills over into India.

For its part, India is no stranger to its own direct rendezvous with inundation.

In what are called the 2013 North India Floods, much of Northern India would be battered by once-in-a-lifetime torrential rains and devastating floods that claimed the lives of thousands, destroyed crops and livelihoods of millions, and ravaged infrastructure on a large scale.

An equally-devastating bout of floods would return to India in 2019 affecting not only the north but much of the south of the country as well.

To India's east, the so-called 2011 Southeast Asian Floods disrupted the lives of decamillions on a scale never seen in a lifetime from Myanmar to Philippines to the tune of tremendous loss of life and property.

While floods have been part-and-parcel of Chinese civilization since the beginning of times, they have been particularly devastating during the second half of oqual cycle.

In the most recent episode, the Asian Giant was struck by the deadly 2010 China Floods during the second half of the current oquannium—that once-in-a-lifetime calamity claimed the lives of thousands, left decamillions homeless, damaged extensive infrastructure, and destroyed crops on a large scale.

The 2010 wave of severe inundation was particularly troubling given that China had already been struck by a comparable calamity a little more than a decade earlier almost in parallel with the beginning of the second half of the current oquannium through the so-called 1998 Yangtze Floods.

WIDESPREAD FLOODING WREAKED HAVOC DURING THE SECOND HALF (1913-1954) OF THE PREVIOUS AND SIXTH OQUANNIUM (1871-1954)

Some 84 years prior to the 2010 China Floods, the Asian Giant would be met by the so-called 1931 China Floods during the second half of the previous and sixth oquannium—that catastrophe is believed to be the deadliest flooding in recorded history as it claimed the lives of millions and decimated the livelihoods of decamillions more as it wreaked havoc on much of the then nation of some 500M people.

The Asian Giant would be struck again by once-in-a-lifetime natural disaster in the form of the 1935 Yangtze Floods that would claim the lives of hectothousands and displace millions in the midst of a decade marred by economic depression, severe famine, and civil war.

On the other side of the globe, the Central Americans would get to taste a once-in-a-lifetime inundation of their own in what came to be called the 1949 Eastern Guatemalan Floods—the like of which have not been witnessed since on the shores of Central America.

Back on Asian soil, Pakistan tasted its first ever rage of Mother Nature as an independent nation when heavy monsoon rains caused the River Ravi to overflow, thereby sparking severe inundation across much of Punjab and Sindh provinces in what came to be called the 1950 Pakistan Floods—a calamity from the second half of the previous oquannium only surpassed by the recent floods in 2010 and 2022 during the second half of the current oquannium.

To Pakistan's east, India would encounter an unforgettable calamity of its own remembered as the 1943 Madras Floods that resulted in widespread loss of life-and-property, and shook the Indian society to the core as it had barely recovered from the equally-devastating 1924 Kerala Floods.

It was not only in India that the bloody floods would test the resolve of the British colonialists but they would also come home with a vengeance during the second half of the previous oquannium.

In what is known as the 1928 Thames Flood, British icons such as the Westminster Hall and the London Underground would become severely inundated—the like of which the British capital has never experienced since.

As the previous oquannium (1871-1954) drew to a close, the British Southwest would be blasted by yet another rare inundation in the form of the 1952 Lynmouth Flood that caused substantial loss of life and property in the village of Lynmouth in the county of Devon.

DESTRUCTIVE FLOODS RAVAGED THE PLANET DURING THE SECOND HALF (1829-1870) OF THE FIFTH OQUANNIUM (1787-1870)

A little more than one full turn of oqual cycle earlier, United Kingdom would be severely deluged by the so-called 1852 Holmfirth Flood in the midst of the second half of the fifth oquannium—a calamity that resulted from the River Holme, located in the metropolitan county of West Yorkshire, bursting its bank after being pounded with days of torrential rain.

On the other side of the globe, the British dominion of Australia did not fare any better even though it is to flooding what sunlight is to a vampire.

In what came to be called the 1852 Gundagai Flood, heavy rains caused the Murrumbidgee River to burst its banks resulting in severe inundation of the town of Gundagai in New South Wales—the raging torrents swept whole homes in its path causing many residents to cling onto trees for days as they fought for their lives.

What has since then remained the deadliest inundation in Australia's recorded history, the 1852 Gundagai Flood literally turned the pueblo into a ghost town as it wiped out nearly half of the town's population of some 250 European settlers and swept away most of the properties.

And many of those who survived did so due to the heroics of Aboriginal men who used their canoes to launch multiple rescue missions in treacherous waters—that is all the more remarkable given that the Aborigines had been decimated by the introduction of infectious diseases such as smallpox and measles by Europeans.

To Australia's north, China is believed to have been deluged by what came to be called the 1851 Yellow River Floods during the second half of the fifth oquannium—a deadly disaster that resulted from the torrential rains causing the Yellow River to overflow and burst its banks, and in doing so, leading to destruction on a scale rarely witnessed up till then.

With no action taken by the government to avert the repeat of the disaster, the torrential rains would cause the Yellow River to burst its banks again in 1855, and then again in 1887, each time ravaging the nation like a monster from hell.

While it is likely that many other nations around the globe also bore the brunt of severe flooding due to heavy rains and the melting of frozen water reservoirs during the second half of the fifth oquannium, this view nevertheless remains speculative due to the lack of documented accounts.

A RELATIVELY FLOODLESS PERIOD IS WAITING ON THE HORIZON

The ongoing bouts of severe flooding around the globe are a hallmark of the second half of oqual cycle as we currently find in one rather than due to irreversible climate change.

Indeed, some of the deadliest floods that the world has experienced in recorded history have almost always occurred during the second half of oqual cycle.

This should be hardly surprising given that the Earth begins to heat up during the second half of oqual cycle, thereby triggering the melting of frozen water reservoirs causing rivers to overflow and inundate nearby communities.

Additionally, warmer temperatures during the second half of oqual cycle lead to rare but deadly bouts of torrential rains.

Needless to say, a synergistic cooperation between the melting of frozen waters and torrential rains is a perfect recipe for unleashing severe inundation during the second half of oqual cycle.

Still, severe flooding may also occur during the first half of oqual cycle though this is an exception to the rule.

In particular, nations prone to frequent flooding such as Bangladesh are unlikely to conform to the flood oquacycle.

Indeed, due to its precarious geographical location and being a gravitational well that pulls the waters of so many rivers beginning their journey upstream in far-flung mountains, Bangladesh gets torn apart by a deadly flood once every decade on average rather than once in a lifetime.

For example, over the course of the current oquannium (1955-2038), Bangladesh has been crippled time and again by deadly floods in 1974, 1987, 1988, 1993, 1998, 2004, and 2022.

Sadly, such a frequent cycle does not bode well for the economic well-being of Bangladesh in that the nation gets pummeled by a new bout of severe flooding before it has even had the chance to recover from the previous one.

While Bangladesh must continue to shower in uninvited waters, most other nations can look forward to a relatively floodless multidecadal period ahead as the current oquannium draws to a close in about a decade or so.

|6.4| STORMS

Storms arise due to the disturbance of the atmosphere with strong winds that are usually accompanied by heavy rainfall, thunder, lightning, or even snow.

Such storms release their energy through various forms such as tornadoes, cyclones, hurricanes, and typhoons.

When the core of the storm spins on its vertical axis forming a funnel-shaped column of wind moving forward, it is called a "tornado".

When the core of the storm spins around a central area with low atmospheric pressure as it moves forward, it is called a "cyclone".

Cyclones with a wind speed greater than 74mph are broadly categorized as "hurricanes" or "typhoons" depending on whether they form in the western hemisphere or eastern hemisphere, respectively.

In light of the temperature oquacycle discussed earlier, one could postulate that parts of the globe would become more vulnerable to being battered by storms during the second half of oqual cycle when the Earth begins to transiently heat up producing a multidecadal warmer period compared to the first half.

Since warmer temperatures promote evaporation of water, the storms traveling overhead gain inertia as they pull in water vapor from the warmer oceans below leading to the formation of more powerful winds and heavy rains—a toxic combination that does not bode well when such storms make a landfall in inhabited areas.

In agreement with this notion, the globe has indeed been mired in what seems to be a perennial stretch of deadly storms witnessed over the past couple of decades.

Although many are quick to lay the blame on irreversible climate change for such a crisis, it seems that this is most likely due to the Earth being in a cyclical flux and, as such, relatively calm days are just around the corner.

In particular, severe storms appear to be a hallmark of the second half of oqual cycle in a manner akin to the recurring spell of droughts and floods discussed earlier (see §6.2 and §6.3).

This view is supported by quantitative analysis of data on hurricanes recorded over the North Atlantic Ocean over the course of the sixth (1871-1954) and seventh (1955-2038) oquannia.

Notably, the hurricane frequency follows an 84-year oscillatory pattern more or less in lockstep with the progression of oqual cycle.

In other words, the number of hurricanes recorded during each calendar year drops over the first half of oqual cycle to reach a minimum and then begins to increase during the second half to hit a maximum.

A similar trend is also observed for the hurricane severity as probed by the so-called "accumulated cyclone energy".

Notably, the wave-like behavior of hurricane severity is somewhat out of phase with the oqual cycle, which is also the case with the oscillation of hurricane frequency.

Such a lag between the oscillation of frequency-and-severity of hurricanes recorded over the North Atlantic Ocean and the oqual cycle is most likely due to an interplay between the local climate and astronomical factors.

Notwithstanding such anomalies, it seems that the storm severity wanes during the first half of oqual cycle but waxes during the second half across the globe in what can be envisioned as the "storm oquacycle".

Being in the midst of the second half (1997-2038) of the current and seventh oquannium (1955-2038), no one should therefore be aghast at having been clobbered by a perpetual stream of destructive storms around the globe over the past couple of decades or so.

Making a landfall in the US state of Florida as it blew away infrastructure and wiped out whole communities, the 2022 Hurricane Ian was the latest reminder of the deadly spell of the second half of oqual cycle.

Barely a week earlier, the 2022 Hurricane Fiona became the deadliest storm to batter the Canadian East.

The 2021 Hurricane Ida smashed much of the US state of Louisiana after running amok through the Caribbean nations such as Jamaica and Cuba.

Being the most frequent target for hurricanes on the mainland US, the state of Florida in particular has been struck by a barrage of deadliest hurricanes over the course of the second half (1997-2038) of the current and seventh oquannium (1955-2038) such as:

- 2004 Hurricane Charley
- 2004 Hurricane Ivan
- 2004 Hurricane Jeanne
- 2005 Hurricane Dennis
- 2005 Hurricane Wilma
- 2017 Hurricane Irma
- 2018 Hurricane Michael
- 2022 Hurricane Ian

Likewise, Florida was also at the receiving end of some of the most devastating hurricanes to strike the mainland US during the second half (1913-1954) of the previous and sixth oquannium (1871-1954) such as:

- 1919 Florida Keys Hurricane
- 1926 Great Miami Hurricane
- 1928 Okeechobee Hurricane
- 1933 Treasure Coast Hurricane
- 1935 Labor Day Hurricane
- 1945 Homestead Hurricane
- 1947 Fort Lauderdale Hurricane

While Florida has also been a target for deadliest hurricanes during the first halves of the previous two oquannia according to historical records, the frequency and severity of such catastrophes has nevertheless appeared to significantly rise during the second halves.

In short, the contrasting plight of Florida over the two halves of oqual cycle is seemingly shared by virtually all regions across the globe that are prone to being struck by hurricanes.

|6.5| CLIMATEGANDA

Human body is an incredibly self-sufficient machine in that it has the ability to maintain a steady-state against an onslaught of daily internal-and-external physicochemical perturbations.

In what is technically referred to as "homeostasis", such a skillful mastery serves to regulate a plethora of conditions such as body temperature (thermoregulation), pressure (osmoregulation), pH (acidoregulation), and glucose (glucoregulation).

Add to that our body's ability to fight off microbial infections through a complex defense mechanism called "immunity".

Our body also possesses a highly-versatile built-in clinic with a wide-ranging expertise to provide medical care around the clock, perform complex internal and external surgeries, and even clean up all the waste at no charge to us.

To say that a healthy body heals, deals, and eats proper meals would be to put it earthly.

Like our body's homeostasis, our planet is hardly dependent upon doctors to ensure its well-being.

In what I call "geostasis", the Earth harbors a remarkable ability to regulate its physical conditions such as temperature and pressure as well as repair and cleanse itself by virtue of its ability to control and regulate its resources.

For example, the Earth's outer atmosphere not only filters out harmful radiation from the incoming sunlight but its magnetic field also wards off solar wind so as to prevent our planet from overheating.

Additionally, extra heat produced through human activities or geological processes is suppressed by oceans through the evaporation of water (H_2O) and vice versa such that the Earth maintains a relatively constant temperature until it transitions into a new natural climate cycle.

To say that the Earth has its own thermostat that cannot be altered by anyone other than astronomical factors would be to put it warmly.

Like our bodies, the Earth is also highly elastic-plastic-and-fantastic in that it harbors a remarkable ability to modulate its shape to mold around physical changes such as rising sea levels due to the melting of polar ice caps.

In the context of Newton's third law, it follows that for every inch in sea level rise, there is an equal and opposite rise in landmass somewhere on the planet such that the ratio of land-to-sea remains more or less constant over the millennial timescale.

Likewise, carbon exchange between the Earth and atmosphere is tightly regulated in what is called the "carbon cycle"—carbon travels back and forth between the atmosphere and the Earth in a perpetual cycle that began billions of years ago with the formation of our planet.

In fact, carbon sinks such as the topsoil, rainforests, rocks, and oceans act as buffers to regulate the atmospheric carbon dioxide (CO_2)—a transient rise in atmospheric CO_2 due to its release from the combustion of fossil fuels and volcanic eruptions is largely offset by the ability of carbon sinks to suck the plant staple out of the air and return it to a relatively steady-state.

In particular, rising levels of atmospheric CO_2 are met by an equally-measurable response from the oceans in that not only do they rise to the challenge and seamlessly absorb excess CO_2 but they also facilitate its reaction with calcium so as to form the insoluble calcium carbonate ($CaCO_3$).

After precipitating out of water, $CaCO_3$ serves as a building block for the synthesis of limestone on the ocean floor, and in doing so, it shifts the equilibrium away from the atmosphere so as to enable the ocean to mop up even more CO_2 until a new equilibrium is established in line with Le Chatelier's Principle to which many of us are introduced during our brush with elementary chemistry in high school.

Simply put, our planet is constantly in flux to ensure a relatively constant state of affairs for its diverse and colorful inhabitants.

Nevertheless, like our bodies, the Earth is also vulnerable to abuse.

Just as substance abuse and processed foods can wreck our health, so can our actions on the well-being of our planet.

Indeed, the biggest threat to the health of our planet comes from:
1) Pollution of air and water;
2) Poisoning of rivers and oceans;
3) Wrecking of rainforests; and
4) Overdraining the earth of its resources.

Yet, hardly anyone is talking about such pressing issues that not only imperil our precarious health but also bear the potential to turn our planet into a shipwreck.

What is everybody talking about then?

GLOBAL WARMING IS A DISTRACTION ENGINEERED TO DIVERT ATTENTION AWAY FROM ADDRESSING REAL-WORLD ISSUES

Global warming is not a recent phenomenon but rather it has been making rounds in scientific discourse for more more than two centuries.

In 1824, the French mathematician Joseph Fourier was the first to propose that the Earth's atmosphere may play a central role in attuning its surface temperature and, for his bold statement, he is often credited with the discovery of the so-called "Greenhouse Effect"—though it would not be referred to as such until the early 20th century (vide infra).

In 1838, the French physicist Claude Pouillet further added his weight to Fourier's Greenhouse Effect and even speculated that in addition to H_2O, CO_2 may also be a contributing factor.

In 1856, the American physicist Eunice Foote provided the first ever experimental evidence of the absorption of heat by CO_2—she would also hypothesize that the rising concentration of atmospheric CO_2 could change the Earth's surface temperature.

In 1859, the Irish physicist John Tyndall corroborated Foote's observations but also proposed that CO_2 and H_2O in the atmosphere not only absorbed infrared radiation but that they also radiated it back to the Earth's surface—thereby providing a complete physical basis for the first time ever of the Greenhouse Effect as we know it today.

In 1896, the Swedish chemist Svante Arrhenius claimed that the release of CO_2 into the atmosphere due to the combustion of fossil fuels was concomitant with a rise in global temperature—the notion that human activities could affect terrestrial climate was however perceived as being nothing more than a fodder for laughs at the time and, for all intents and purposes, it should have continued to be treated as such rather than being taken seriously for the real culprit behind our planetary woes today lies in overconsumption rather than fossil fuels.

In 1901, the Swedish meteorologist Nils Ekholm used the term "greenhouse" for the first time ever to refer to the ability of atmospheric CO_2 to act like a glass roof of a greenhouse such that it would allow sunlight through but trap the heat radiated back from the Earth's surface.

In 1907, the British physicist John Poynting would however take the honors for having coined the term "Greenhouse Effect" to formulate the principle of the trapping of infrared radiation by atmospheric H_2O and CO_2.

In 1938, on the back of what we now know was an expected but a transitory wave of rising temperatures in the midst of the second half (1913-1954) of the previous oquannium (1871-1954) due to the warming spell of oqual cycle on our planet as demonstrated earlier (see §6.1), the British engineer Guy Callendar suggested that the Earth was on a persistent path to getting warmer due to the release of CO_2 into the atmosphere.

The notion that CO_2 was the culprit behind such global warming was further picked up by the American meteorologist Charles Keeling during the 1950s.

In 1958, Keeling secured the funding from the US federal government to set up the so-called Mauna Loa Observatory in Hawaii in order to directly monitor and measure the levels of atmospheric CO_2.

Yet, unbeknown to Keeling the spell of oqual cycle on terrestrial climate, the global temperatures began to dip with the arrival of the first half (1955-1996) of the current oquannium (1955-2038) as for example underscored by the 1963 Big Freeze—the coldest winter spell witnessed on British shores in more than 200 years and that brought the nation to a virtual standstill for months.

What do you call it when the Earth starts cooling?

Global cooling, of course.

And, you bet, it was global cooling that began to upstage global warming during much of the 1960s and 1970s as it became the most pressing issue of those earlier times thanks to no shortage of propagandists on hand.

In fact, it would turn into a shouting match of sorts between those claiming that the melting of polar ice caps due to global warming would make the planet uninhabitable for future generations and others warning of a looming apocalyptic ice age due to global cooling.

With temperatures beginning to appreciably rise once more from around the 1990s almost in parallel with the onset of the second half (1997-2038) of the current oquannium (1955-2038), global warming would understandably win the day and become the hill upon which a new wave of climateganda (or climate propaganda) would rapidly gain inertia to plunge humanity into a state of delirium from which very few have managed to escape due to the contagion of crowd psychology.

Today, much of humanity has indeed been indoctrinated into believing that the looming threat of irreversible climate change (or global warming) is the most urgent call of our times.

Masses are being fooled into buying into the bogus view that such a catastrophe knocking on our door lies in anthropogenic factors—or human activities—primarily due to the release of gigatons of the so-called greenhouse gases such as CO_2 into the atmosphere each year as a result of our dependence on fossil fuels.

That they ought to be alarmed at such a reckless behavior with world leaders not only scrambling to overhaul and pare back the use of fossil fuels but many nations also vying to completely do away with them in the near future at the expense of renewable sources of energy such as sunlight and wind.

Alas, the actions of world leaders only exacerbate the suffering of the people and one would be naïve to believe that their newly-honed antics represent anything but a propaganda to sell new technologies disguised as "earth-friendly" even though they are the modern-day equivalent of a Trojan horse.

Just as their bogus policies from economy through education to health have left the masses teetering on the precipice of a societal meltdown, the climateganda will be equally devastating both for the planet and its inhabitants.

It is therefore hardly surprising that hoi polloi are being coaxed into believing that the human society is not only fighting for its survival but that their planet is on a tipping point with global warming threatening to wreak havoc on their livelihoods in the very near future.

Yet, the biggest threat to our planet is not from global warming as the Earth is perfectly capable of dealing with that on its own thanks to its innate geostatic mechanisms but rather from the hedonistic actions and the consumer culture of the masses that puts the health of our planet in peril and, by extension, our own.

To add gasoline to fire, a growing number of climate scientists have also joined the chorus of politicians to inject unwarranted fear into the minds and hearts of the people through making outlandish forecasts that all but have us inching ever closer to a doomsday scenario.

Unsurprisingly, such an engineered and coordinated propaganda serves as a fertile ground to attract scavengers-and-vultures alike gung-ho on capitalizing on such a doom-and-gloom as illustrated below via a sample of their utter Algorebage (or garbage) and fear-mongering having made rounds on mainstream media in the not-too-distant past:

> "Unless we act boldly and quickly to deal with the underlying causes of global warming, our world will undergo a string of terrible catastrophes!"
>
> "People are now suffering and dying from climate change!"
>
> "The Earth is in a death spiral. It will take radical action to save us!"
>
> "Collapse of civilization may have already begun!"
>
> "Our planet is fast approaching tipping points that will make climate chaos irreversible. We are on a highway to climate hell with our foot still on the accelerator!"
>
> "The world is going to end in 12 years if we don't address climate change!"
>
> "Around the year 2030, 10 years 252 days and 10 hours away from now, we will be in a position where we set off an irreversible chain reaction beyond human control, that will most likely lead to the end of our civilization as we know it."

Such an irresponsible and deliberate rhetoric suffices alone to paint global warming as nothing more than a hoax championed by lunatics who are more interested in changing their names to garner publicity rather than changing their lifestyles to genuinely alleviate the suffering of our planet.

Worse yet, such doomsday messages play into the minds of a rising wave of mentally-ill young adults who in turn adopt violent tactics that not only disrupt the vascular network necessary to maintain the blood supply to critical organs in the society but also put others' lives at risk.

Global warming as a cause for concern being championed by fools-and-horses, many of whom have barely broken free of their diapers (or nappies) rather than being in a position to understand the climate science, is a contrarian signal that the truth is the exact opposite.

Global warming as the most urgent call of our times being spearheaded by hypocrites who lead a lavish lifestyle with a carbon footprint as big as that of some cities should be equally alarming.

To say that such deranged souls have a political axe to grind rather than their genuine concern about saving the planet would be a huge understatement.

One can be rest assured that the real-world issues that affect humanity and our planet are constantly being swept under the rug rather than making rounds in the media.

As the saying goes—if you tell a lie big enough and keep repeating it, people will eventually come to believe it.

Not only does climateganda exquisitely fit that adage but it has also been doubled-down in that the lie is about an invisible phenomenon alleged to be occurring in the stratosphere bazillions of miles away from the ground so that the masses can be kept in the dark.

Not only that but any scholar who has the spine to question the climateganda quickly becomes ostracized from the academic community with no institution willing to hire them nor any publisher prepared to lend them a platform.

While climate change is inevitable and a natural consequence of the Earth's recycling and cleansing process, the hyped-up threat of global warming is nothing more than science fiction and a political weapon being used to distract humanity from paying heed to what is actually destroying our lives and the well-being of our planet from pollution of air-and-water through wrecking of rainforests to pillaging the land of its resources.

Does CO_2 not contribute to global warming?

CARBON DIOXIDE IS A FRIEND NOT A FOE

In elementary chemistry, we learn that there is an inverse relationship between the solubility of a gas in water and the ambient temperature—the higher the temperature, the lower the solubility, and vice versa.

Given that our oceans act as one of the major sinks for the storage of CO_2 due to it being sequestered by the deep-sea cold water as well as a breathtaking diversity of life such as phytoplankton and coral reef on the seabed, a rise in global temperature due to a natural climate cycle will be expected to unlock such oceanic carbon reservoirs and allow it to escape back into the atmosphere.

In addition to the release of CO_2 by oceans into the atmosphere, rising temperatures also facilitate its escape from other carbon sinks such as forests and the Earth's crust through wildfires and volcanic eruptions, respectively.

Add to that the fact that the rising temperatures also boost the release of CO_2 through an increase in respiratory activities at every level of life from soil organisms through plants to animals.

In fact, it is no coincidence that the world population has nearly octupled since the end of the Little Ice Age (1300-1850) from just over 1000M in 1850 to 8000M today—such an exponential increase has not only been powered by industrialization but perhaps more so by rising temperatures over the past 200 years.

Still, no one doubts that human activities contribute to a rise in atmospheric CO_2 but one cannot unequivocally argue that it is the cause of global warming.

To the contrary, such a rise in atmospheric CO_2 not only appears to be the effect rather than the cause of global warming as discussed earlier (see §6.1) but it also serves as a blessing-in-disguise.

Not long ago on a geological timescale, the levels of atmospheric CO_2 were something to be reckoned with and probably as high as two orders of magnitude greater than what they are now.

Today, the atmospheric level of CO_2 is closer to rock bottom that it has ever been in the long checkered history of our planet.

Thus, the truth would be closer to our atmosphere being in a carbon deficit rather than carbon surplus.

Not only do climate scientists have the whole picture upside down but they are also unlikely to admit their faux pas and change direction anytime soon.

Once one goes down the rabbit hole, they risk descending deeper into the wilderness rather than finding a way out.

How exactly are rising levels of CO_2 beneficial?

A rise in atmospheric CO_2 bears the potential to turn a desert into an oasis.

Admittedly, rising levels of atmospheric CO2 could bring about many benefits to our planet in that they act as a "fertilizer" or "supplement" with the potential to augment plant growth through turbocharging the Calvin Cycle—the main engine of photosynthesis.

In fact, many friends have confided in me that they believe that the plants have "ears" in that they seem to respond when being talked to.

This should be hardly surprising given that plants are essentially being blasted with a puff of CO2 as one breathes next to them—while the ambient air contains a paltry 420ppm of CO2, its concentration is two orders-of-magnitude higher at around 42,000ppm in the exhaled air.

Needless to say, I assured my friends that their observations were perfectly normal and that there was no need to see a psychiatrist, at least anytime soon.

Importantly, our planet has gotten a lot greener over the past century-or-so thanks to the rising levels of atmospheric CO2.

Yet, CO2 barely registers among the four major components of the dry air in the atmosphere, which in descending order are as follows:

- 78.08% Nitrogen
- 20.94% Oxygen
- 0.93% Argon
- 0.04% CO2
- 0.01% Trace gases (such as methane and nitrous oxide)

Nevertheless, the concentration of a compound is only relative as it holds no clues vis-à-vis its effect on a particular system.

Still, CO2 ranks only second to water vapor (or gaseous H2O) as being one of the two major components among the greenhouse gases with the likes of methane and nitrous oxide believed to be minor contributors to global warming.

Does CO2 not contribute to the Greenhouse Effect?

GREENHOUSE EFFECT IS TOO SIMPLISTIC A MODEL TO ACCOUNT FOR GLOBAL WARMING

The science upon which the notion that human activities cause global warming is predicated on a rather simplistic model as outlined below:

1) Human activities release greenhouse gases such as CO_2 into the air that in turn forms a blanket-like barrier in the troposphere, the lowest layer of the atmosphere;
2) Such a barrier does not impede the incoming sunlight due to the fact that its rather small wavelength (less than 1μm) does not interact with CO_2 molecules;
3) Upon collision with the Earth's surface, the sunlight loses energy in the form of heat and is therefore reflected back into the atmosphere as infrared radiation with a much larger wavelength (typically in the 1-1000μm range); and
4) Unlike the seamless entry of the sunlight reaching the Earth, much of the infrared light radiated back is absorbed by the blanket-like carbon layer in the troposphere, thereby trapping heat and warming the planet.

While this so-called "Greenhouse Effect" is the basis for our planet being much warmer than it would otherwise be due to the atmosphere acting as a blanket of sorts to trap the heat, the notion that the Earth's surface temperature can be perturbed by the release of anthropogenic greenhouse gases is largely supported by conjecture rather than hard facts.

In particular, the climate scientists envision the buildup of a carbon layer in the troposphere to be analogous to the rather thick glass roof of a greenhouse—such a preposterous assumption pours cold water over the notion that global warming is primarily the result of CO_2 emissions.

For example, unlike a greenhouse, the Earth's atmosphere has an infinite degrees of freedom—implying that such plasticity can easily counteract the effect of a perturbant such as CO_2 in line with Le Chatelier's Principle.

Nevertheless, a slightly deeper insight is warranted.

While it is clear that CO_2 absorbs strongly in the infrared region in a manner similar to H_2O and thus bears the potential to trap the infrared radiation reflected by the Earth's surface, the exact degree to which it contributes to global warming cannot be ascertained by even the most sophisticated tools at the disposal of climate scientists due to the complexity of so many factors contributing to atmosphere and climate.

That is indeed the very reason why the climate models can barely predict the weather a week in advance with a high degree of confidence, much less a month or year from now.

To argue that climate scientists have some secret tools at their disposal that can predict the climate 50 or 100 years from now is absurdity run amok to the quartic power.

To add salt to their wounds, the climate scientists always seem to masquerade the fact that 0.04% of CO_2 in the air pales in comparison to 4% H_2O, thereby making the latter a much more powerful greenhouse gas.

To say that water is the freon (or coolant) of our planet that helps to maintain the Earth's surface temperature in a relatively steady-state against a slew of natural and man-made activities would be a huge understatement.

Other than the fact that water vapor is the elephant in the room when it comes to trapping the infrared heat radiated by the Earth's surface courtesy of the Greenhouse Effect, a link between a rise in atmospheric CO_2 and its impact on global temperature is almost impossible to establish.

This is due to the complex relationship between changes in the surface temperature of Earth and its impact on clouds—which primarily consist of a mixture of water droplets and ice crystals trapped between dust particles suspended decathousands of feet up in the sky where the temperature is usually well below the freezing point of water.

Not only do clouds play a key role in keeping our planet cool by virtue of their ability to reflect the incoming sunlight back into the outer space but they also tend to warm it up through trapping the infrared heat radiated by the Earth's surface.

Accordingly, any mitigation or augmentation of clouds triggered for example by the warming of the planet—due to say a rise in atmospheric CO_2—will likely compensate or offset a rise in surface temperature via a negative feedback loop.

While the news that a rise in atmospheric CO_2 is unlikely to be the cause of a rise in global temperature may break Russian and Canadian hearts, it should nevertheless be a huge cause for celebration by those inhabiting desert regions such as Australia, North Africa, and Middle East—as rising levels of atmospheric CO_2 bear the potential to turn the deserts into oases.

Still, that should not imply that we go on a burning spree of fossil fuels as their production and utilization comes with a huge cost on at least four fronts:
- 1) Colliery (or coal mining) is an environmentally destructive pursuit that wrecks natural landscapes and causes widespread pollution even before coal is shipped to power stations and industries;
- 2) Fracking of subterranean rocks to extract oil and natural gas is equally destructive to environment and contaminates groundwater;

3) Oil drilling in the oceans impacts marine life and oil spillages wreak havoc on coastal communities; and

4) Combustion of fossil fuels causes air pollution and smog which are linked with a plethora of respiratory and cardiovascular ailments as well as many cancers.

Simply put, we should cut our dependence on fossil fuels due to their harmful effects on the well-being of our planet as well as our own lives rather than the fact that they contribute to global warming.

As discussed earlier (see §6.1), what appears to be a rising trend in global temperature due to the 84-year natural climate cycle oscillating in sync with the progression of oqual cycle is being used as a propaganda to scaremonger the unsuspecting masses so as to divert attention away from addressing the real impact of fossil fuels on our lives.

Is there a silver lining in our planet getting warmer?

Could global warming be a manifestation of Earth waging a war on us due to our reckless behavior that amounts to nothing short of ravaging the planet?

GLOBAL WARMING IS A BLESSING-IN-DISGUISE RATHER THAN A DEATH WARRANT

When we fall sick due to for example bacterial infection, our body's self-defense mechanism kicks in and responds by raising the temperature by as much as 5°F so as to put a brake on the microbial growth.

In doing so, such elevated temperature allows the body to recover lest it gets destroyed by what are often harmless parasites living in perfect harmony within our bodies and providing a useful service to us in a mutually-beneficial relationship called "symbiosis".

In a similar manner to microbial infection, the pollution of rivers and lakes coupled with destructive mining and deforestation driven by our consumption mania over the past century have made the Earth extremely sick, thereby triggering its innate self-defense mechanism to fight back through raising its temperature.

In other words, humans are essentially akin to microbes in a symbiotic relationship with the Earth being their host and, as such, wholly dependent on its provisions from air and water to nutrition.

When we begin to cause destruction of our host faster than its ability to repair itself in a manner akin to trillions of our own parasitic microbes living within our bodies, the Earth fights back with a vengeance a la our body's immune response to our own parasites when they begin to cause infection.

The point being that when we ravage the planet through our reckless addiction to consumption, the Earth wages a war against us through its own immunity.

Notably, the combustion of fossil fuels is only one of many ways in which we pollute our environment with overconsumption being the elephant in the room of factors contributing to the poor health of Earth.

One must therefore focus on reducing their overall consumption footprint rather than merely carbon footprint to stave off the malaise affecting our planet.

De-carbonization alone is nothing more than a propaganda as it diverts attention away from addressing de-consumption.

Long story short, the current bout of global warming that our planet is undergoing is likely a blessing-in-disguise in that it appears to be a natural flux designed to recycle and repair Earth's resources as well as put its inhabitants through a stress test such that the weaker earthlings are weeded out in a battle for the survival of the fittest through natural selection.

While the global temperatures will begin to tamp down as the next oquannium (2039-2122) rolls in over the next decade or so, it seems that the Earth is overall destined for a warmer climate in the long run in a sinusoidal manner rather than in a linear fashion as the bogus climate models claim.

Nevertheless, such global warming appears to be far from being a death warrant as it is likely to be a zero-sum game—wherein one's loss is another's gain.

While tropical and sub-tropical countries would be the biggest losers in the face of such global warming, nations with continental climate such as Canada and Russia stand to enormously benefit.

This is due to the fact that the ice caps in such nations would become exposed to sunlight for the first time in perhaps a millennium so as to not only provide new arable land for agriculture and trade but also compensate for the loss of tropical land becoming submerged under water or turning into a desert of sorts.

Additionally, forbidden regions such as Antarctica and Greenland could become the New Worlds and beacons of hope for people from all over the globe, particularly those escaping the brunt of the heat in the tropics.

Tellingly, the threat of global warming has been unnecessarily hyped up by:
1) Climate scientists who are primarily charged with looking into the impact of human activities on climate rather than natural causes—they therefore have the incentive to keep the poorly-defined connective tissue between climate and human activities alive and kicking lest they kill the goose that lays the golden egg;
2) Corrupt policymakers who stoke up interest in their propaganda through injecting fear so as to maintain a control over the masses and enact new laws favorable to their political interests;
3) Serial fraudsters who see an opportunity to make a killing on introducing new technologies to consumers using the cliché of environment-friendly renewable energy as a gimmick; and
4) Gullible fanatics who hold climate rallies and protests so as to be seen as good-doers, all the while continuing to lead a reckless lifestyle through maintaining an unnecessarily large carbon footprint.

Why technologies dubbed "environment-friendly", such as electric cars and solar panels, are anything but?

Are they just an enterprise driven by monetary greed?

CAPITALIST ECONOMY AND ENVIRONMENTAL WELL-BEING ARE MUTUALLY EXCLUSIVE

Due to the melting of polar ice caps and glaciers, large swathes of land in regions such as Greenland are becoming exposed and habitable for the first time in millennia.

While such regions have hitherto kept the destructive force of humanity at bay, they are now rapidly garnering the attention of billionaires.

Such fraudsters are targeting to ravage these new lands through financially backing mining companies that promise to dig up the hills and valleys in search of metals such as nickel and cobalt needed to power up electric vehicles.

That should set off alarm bells.

Not only are electric vehicles no more earth-friendly than their gasoline counterparts but mining itself is extremely harmful to the environment as it not only destroys natural habitats but also pollutes the planet.

In other words, the democratization of electric vehicles is largely driven by the greed of the wealthy rather than their genuine concern for the well-being of the planet and its inhabitants.

Little such fraudsters understand that the best defense against the destruction of our environment is cutting down on consumption not promoting it.

As the saying goes, what is good for the goose is good for gander—what is good for the wealthy is good for their stakeholders!

Indeed, the governments have been a party to the bogus electric revolution from the very beginning as they always are with every fraud since their actions are essentially a manifestation of the interests of the wealthy.

Yet, the real threat to our planet is not global warming but overconsumption that has made our planet so sick.

One should therefore be talking about reining in our reckless consumption mania that turned parabolic just as the second half (1997-2038) of the current oquannium (1955-2038) kicked off—thanks but no thanks to a quantum leap in the mass production of electronic goods from personal computers through smartphones to digital cameras.

We must therefore pare back our consumer-driven lifestyles for they are rapidly condemning our lonely planet to a future of misery.

No one in their right mind would disagree that pumping gigatons of toxic gases into atmosphere would be met with no consequences on our health and that of our environment in one way or another.

Likewise, pumping gigatons of toxic waste into our lakes and oceans annihilates our ecosystems upon which our well-being is so dependent.

Ditto for dumping gigatons of toxic waste on land for it not only adds to air pollution but, more importantly, toxic chemicals ultimately leach into nearby streams and rivers, thereby endangering our health through contamination of food chains—no one should be surprised that finding a reliable source of uncontaminated drinking water and healthy food has become next to impossible across most parts of the world today.

Notably, the burden of living with pollution largely created by Western nations often falls on poor countries.

In what is called "e-waste", millions-of-tons of old-and-obsolete electronic gadgets generated each year in Western nations are shipped to developing countries to be dumped there—the poor nations are thus not only made to face the brunt of fallout from the resulting pollution of such electronic waste but young children are also exploited to scour through such dangerous heaps of waste in order to recycle metals such as copper and gold.

Yet, rather than enacting policies to reduce our consumption and eliminate exploitation of the weak around the globe, the lawmakers do the exact opposite—they encourage grandmothering out (or replacing) an old technology with a new one through not only marketing it as an environment-friendly product but also providing tax credits to those who are willing to go to bed with them.

For example, electric cars have been hyped-up as a savior of our environment yet few understand that they likely pose greater risk to our livelihoods than their gasoline counterparts due to the fact that the rather inefficient batteries that power them up will have to be constantly disposed of onto landfills with the potential for the toxic chemicals to drain into nearby rivers and ultimately end up in our food chains—a typical battery in an electric car weighs around half-a-ton with deadly toxic metals such as lithium, nickel, manganese, and cobalt accounting for at least 10% of their weight.

Add to that conundrum the fact that most proponents of electric cars do not even realize that the power upon which they run does not fall from the sky but rather such electric devils-in-disguise merely shift pollution from one's neck-of-the-woods to the power station.

In fact, the real culprit in vehicular emissions is not carbon dioxide but rather nitrogen oxides which are largely responsible for air pollution, including smog.

While vehicular emissions are a major contributor to the total nitrogen oxides released into the atmosphere, the coal-fired power plants are not far behind—the electric cars that ultimately rely on such plants are therefore hardly any more environment-friendly than their gasoline counterparts.

Simply put, electric cars are wolves-in-sheep's-clothing that do not in any meaningful way reduce the carbon footprint that so many fools are trying to break free of so that they can lay claim to the ill-conceived view that their actions are no longer harmful to the environment.

Yet, an electric car only serves to exacerbate the pain and agony of our environment and hence our own lives—the only viable path to reducing our carbon footprint is to simply reduce our consumption rather than shift it from one bogus consumer product to another in the misguided belief that one's new lifestyle is more environment-friendly.

Donne-moi un break!

Like electric cars, solar panels are no guardian angels either in that their electronic components also stand to pose a huge risk to the environment at the end of their shelf life when they are dumped onto a landfill with the potential for carcinogens such as lead and cadmium to seep into nearby rivers and lakes.

To say that solar waste outweighs any benefits of solar energy would be to put it without mincing words.

Many pundits peddle the naivete that the only solution to the well-being of our planet is to create cleaner energy through scientific breakthroughs.

Yet, such fools fail to understand that every technological breakthrough inherently comes with a prepacked dose of undesirable secondary effects.

Never in our history have we ever created a perfect technology that is solely beneficial to us and our environment without any side effects, not to mention that such a hypothetical machine would violate the laws of physics.

The take-home message is that no technology is good for the well-being of the environment, and by extension, our own health.

Ni electric cars. Ni solar panels. Ni windmills. Not even nuclear fusion.

Yes, you heard that right.

Although it is not clear at this stage but to argue that nuclear fusion is unlike any other technology with zero waste products would be to violate the inviolable Newton's third law—the extraction of the rather scarce helium from natural gas to fuel fusion reactors could for instance offset its benefits.

One simply cannot have an action without an equal and opposite reaction!

Accordingly, the only way to protect our environment is through the old-fashioned way of being frugal and cutting down on consumption.

Rather than exploiting the hyped-up threat of global warming as a scaremongering tactic to advance their political propaganda, the policymakers ought to pass legislations that outlaw environment-unfriendly consumer products such as disposable (or single-use) plastics, papers, cardboards, and metals coupled with levying heavy taxation on toxic technologies such as driving and flying so as to encourage hoi polloi to adopt more environment-friendly lifestyles.

While such a move would undoubtedly destroy the capitalist economy, it would be a godsend for the well-being of our environment.

Driven by the propaganda of getting the masses hooked on unnecessary-and-toxic products as well as to keep them enslaved through indoctrinating them into adopting a lifestyle of living paycheck-to-paycheck, the capitalist economy and the environmental well-being are indeed mutually exclusive.

As much as the masses and their masters would like to have the cake and eat it too, that is simply not possible given the fact that their consumer-driven lifestyles will forever continue to wreck the planet unless capitalism is reined in so as to prioritize environmental health over detrimental wealth.

To say that it is primarily the capitalists fueling the climateganda would be to put it lightly though my French friends are somewhat more philosophical: "Le renard est dans le poulailler!"—"The fox is guarding the henhouse!"

One cannot indeed have the fox guard the henhouse and then reassure the poor chickens that their safety is the top priority.

What about the consensus view on global warming?

THE MAJORITY HAPPENS TO BE ALWAYS WRONG DUE TO HERD BEHAVIOR

Gullible fanatics defend the hyped-up threat of global warming by playing the consensus card—that there is a unanimous consensus among climate scientists that global warming is directly due to human activities.

Yet, history has time and again shown that sociopolitical causes driven by a consensus view have often plunged the human society into a turmoil due to the fact that they are often the product of conflict-of-interest, confirmation bias, and herd mentality (or crowd psychology) rather than hard facts.

The proof of my proclamation lies in the centuries-old pudding as illustrated below via a quartet of botched-and-bungled policies:

1) Up till as recently as the 18th century, the consensus among Western intellectuals of the bygone era was that the superiority of the White race justified the enslavement of the Blacks and the colonization of others—the results of such a bogus philosophy are all clear for us to see today as it not only left an indelible mark on our past but also destroyed so many indigenous societies and cultures and with them the loss of so much diversity on our planet.

2) In the late 19th century, in what came to be called "eugenics", the much-respected intellectuals of those times across the Western world spearheaded the propaganda of turning humanity into a super race through selective breeding of individuals adjudged to be "fit", all the while sterilizing others deemed "unfit"—not only would such a racist theory be abused for the genetic selection of the elite rather than biologically fit but it would also lead to the loss of genetic diversity through direct interference with natural selection as it came to a grinding halt before too long.

3) In the 20th century, the likes of nutritionists, physicians, media, and even the federal government in the United States were unanimous in declaring that the lipids (or fats) were our enemy number one and that they must be eliminated from our diet even when they were known to be the basic building blocks of life—not only did such a bogus ideology lead to a spike in health issues from obesity to diabetes among its disciples due to the lack of a balanced diet but the promoters of such a sham-and-scam also stayed mum on the toxicogenic effects of processed foods, the real culprits contributing to poor health; after the low-fat scam fell on its face, the consensus later moved onto the low-carb diet even though carbohydrates are the preferred fuel needed to power up a healthy body; today, the fools are once again being herded into the so-called protein-rich diet which is extremely unhealthy as it can send liver and kidneys into an overdrive with the increased risk of organ failure.

4) In the 21st century, in the wake of the 2019 Coronavirus Pandemic, epidemiologists the world-over reached a consensus that the best way to curb the pathogen was through the implementation of wholesale lockdowns and shuttering of the economic engine across the globe—not only did such a preposterous mandate send the society into a tailspin with the masses going into hiding and isolating themselves out of apprehension even when in desperate need of medical care or otherwise but the disproportionate fear injected into the society likely killed far more people than the coronavirus itself, not to mention that the

resulting chaos also decimated the economic engine as well as adding gasoline to the sociopolitical fire that has all but snowballed into a complete societal meltdown.

Why was a strategy as self-destructive as the lockdowns implemented?

Was there a malicious intention behind such mandates ordered across the globe?

The goatherder (or rather the philosopher) in me has this to say:
1) During hard times against the backdrop of a growing sociopolitical upheaval and, in particular, during oqual winters as was the case for the 2020 lockdowns that transpired at the outset of the oqual winter (2018-2038) of the current oquannium (1955-2038), those in charge of calling the societal shots often lose their head in that the every new step that they take to mend the wound actually happens to be the exact opposite of what they ought to have done. In lay terms, panicking during a troublesome situation only serves to exacerbate it. Simply put, our leaders might have had good intentions in implementing what they did but their ignorance of the dire spell of oqual cycle planted their downfall.
2) Not all of our leaders may be so innocent vis-à-vis the 2020 lockdowns in that those in the positions of power are far from being normal people conforming to the live-and-let-live doctrine but rather they are born to rule over others and, as a part of their authoritative psyche, they are often driven by the urge to control the sheep through injecting fear a la sheepdog. Such a despicable behavior on the part of our leaders may arise either due to their urge to test the waters to see how much power they can exercise over their sheep or due to the capitalist greed to introduce new draconian laws under the veneer of fear which otherwise may draw the ire of the public. Had it not been for a disproportionate amount of fear injected into the masses through the lockdowns, measures such as mandatory vaccination to add to the transition to conducting business and personal affairs online by leaps-and-bounds in the wake of the 2019 Coronavirus Pandemic would have undoubtedly failed to materialize.
3) With the cure being multiples worse than the pandemic itself and with an opportunity of a lifetime to make a killing on introducing new technologies and health measures, the capitalists with malicious intentions quickly jumped onto the political bandwagon and added their weight to a growing chorus of officials calling for the 2020 lockdowns. If this amounts to a sort of conspiracy behind the implementation of the lockdowns as many people are led to believe, then so be it. However, what is clear is that the wealth of capitalists has since bloated by trillions thanks to the lockdowns, all the while

the masses have been left in even deeper waters than they have ever been in their lives.

So what gives?

With a 20/20 hindsight of how a consensus view has often destroyed societies and nations, the popular belief that the ongoing global warming is irreversible and solely caused by anthropogenic factors will also come to be seen as a blunder of the millennium by as early as 2050 but by no later than 2100.

Not only that but we should be more concerned about our planet plunging into another mini-ice age over the next couple of centuries rather than getting roasted by heat.

In the meantime, let us cherish the fact that heat is a real treat for it powers our lives in contrast to cold that kills.

In summary, science is never settled nor is it based on consensus or preponderance, and as such:
1) The rise in global temperature witnessed over the past several decades is most likely due to an 84-year natural climate wave that will soon begin to plateau out before it heads south more or less in sync with the start of the next oqual cycle in 2039;
2) While human activities may have exacerbated the amplitude of such a climate wave, the major culprit appears to be overconsumption rather than the rise in atmospheric CO_2;
3) The apparent rise in atmospheric CO_2 witnessed over the past couple of centuries is most likely the effect (or symptom) rather than the cause of global warming;
4) Combustion of fossil fuels should be pared back because they cause environmental pollution rather than their impact on global warming; and
5) Demonization of fossil fuels amounts to nothing but a propaganda spearheaded by the wealthy to introduce new technologies dubbed "environment-friendly" even though they constitute nothing short of a Trojan horse with the potential to ratchet up the destruction of the planet like never before.

EPILOGUE

Since the outset of the current oquannium (1955-2038), a slew of imbalances and transgressions have once again become endemic to human society at every sociopolitical level.

To right the wrong, humans are therefore set for yet another rendezvous with destiny that arrives on our shores once every 84 years on average.

While such a meeting with destiny cannot be averted, how we deal with the fallout from the ongoing sociopolitical upheaval will determine our fate.

Bluntly put, how one approaches the looming crisis will determine how well one emerges on the other side of the bedlam.

Impulsive actions combined with egoism spell trouble, while thoughtful choices in conjunction with humility stand to assuage the wrath of the emerging crisis.

Thus, although the doctrine of oqual cycle may suggest that our lives are governed by determinism, it is ultimately our free will that in fact dictates the severity of the fallout from such a perennial rendezvous.

For example, no one doubts that our lives are to a large extent governed by the annual cycle.

One can predict with reasonable accuracy that the April showers will bring May flowers in spring, summer will be marred by humidity and hurricanes, crops will be harvested and leaves will fall in autumn, and frigid nights along with snowstorms will be a hallmark of winter.

On the same token, the recurring spell of oqual cycle on human civilization is also punctuated with a quartet of Uranian seasons from spring through summer and autumn to winter—with each season lasting a timespan of 21 years.

In a manner that we can forecast the terrestrial year ahead with some semblance of accuracy, the oqual cycle also equips us with breathtaking insights into what is in store for humanity over the coming decades.

Since the birth of Modern Age in 1451, human civilization has all but spanned seven full spells of oqual cycle.

Today, we are in the early stages of a long and dark 21-year winter (2018-2038) of the seventh oquannium (1955-2038) that is set to reach its crescendo and unleash the worst of its destructive rage upon our civilization as it marks its annus horribilis (2028) with our day of reckoning inching ever closer.

In particular, oqual winters are renowned for staging the collapse of old-and-degenerate sociopolitical orders so as to make way for a brighter dawn.

In 2023, we are more or less passing through the same constellation as we did exactly 84 years ago in 1939 in a manner akin to the fact that annual festivities bring a familiar atmosphere from one year to the next.

In other words, the ongoing oqual winter (2018-2038) is beginning to bear many echoes of the previous oqual winter (1934-1954).

How come have I never heard of the oqual winter?

Unlike the more familiar annual winter that an individual on average traverses dozens of times, the oqual winter comes only once in our lifetime and, even then, very few us have the logic to connect the dots.

For example, an individual born with the onset of the previous oqual winter (1934-1954) was not only too young but also shielded from having to experience the catastrophes that their parents had to endure from the Great Depression (1929-1939) through World War II (1939-1945) to Holocaust (1941-1945).

Today, being in the early stages of the ongoing oqual winter (2018-2038), that now-elderly-individual has virtually no firsthand memories of the previous oqual winter (1934-1954) in order to draw comparisons between the recurrence of two events roughly spaced apart by 84 years.

Still, many elderly people would tell you that they see many parallels between what they witnessed during their early childhood and what is unfolding today before their eyes.

In fact, I have been fortunate enough to personally talk to a number of octogenarians and nonagenarians—individuals who are aged 80-89 and 90-99 years, respectively.

They all confide in me that not only have they never seen anything like what they are experiencing today in their prolonged lives but that they always thought that they had already seen the worst—except of course that their memories of the previous oqual winter (1934-1954) have all but faded.

In order for humans to directly attest to the recurrence of hell-on-earth once every 84 years on average, they will have to live through at least a couple of full spells of oqual cycle disguised as tortoises with a lifespan long enough to meet such stringent criteria.

Alternatively, one could summon an elderly tortoise and they will indeed tell you that nothing could be closer to the truth than the dire spell of oqual cycle that they have to negotiate at least a couple of times in their adult lives.

To add icing on the cake, the anecdotes of tortoises come straight from the horse's mouth for they have no intention of pursuing a political career, much less running for the nation's highest office, or even tweaking climate models to help their cronies make a killing on introducing new consumer products under the guise of environment-friendly technology.

Long story short, what we have seen over the past several years since the onset of the current oqual winter (2018-2038) has hitherto amounted to nothing more than run-of-the-mill snowstorms with the once-in-a-lifetime blizzard yet to unleash its rage upon humanity.

In fact, comparisons between what humanity is going through today with what it did in the aftermath of 1929 Great Depression are far from being in short supply.

Just as that crisis-of-a-lifetime plunged the human society into a global conflict some 84 years earlier, we are once again heading into uncharted waters.

A global conflict is indeed all but obligatory to drive the final nail into the coffin of sociopolitical upheaval, that seemingly snowballs into an 800-pound gorilla as the oqual rhythm nears its end, in order to make way for a new dawn of optimism and prosperity.

Just as World War II (1939-1945) accomplished that goal some 84 years ago so will World War III over the next decade or so as utter fear and chaos engulf our society and, in doing so, purge humanity of mischief so as to enable it to come to its senses once more.

While we have been kicking the can down the road since at least the outset of 21st century, the cul-de-sac (or dead end) is inching ever closer as we are destined to reach there some time between annus horribilis (2028) of the current oquannium (1955-2038) and annus mirabilis (2039) of the next cycle (2039-2122).

All told, the oqual cycle lends a powerful model for not only making sense of the ongoing sociopolitical trials-and-tribulations of our own times but it also helps us navigate our future with rational wisdom in lieu of blissful ignorance.

Those who ignore the spell of oqual cycle will be doing so at their own peril.

In fact, groundbreaking discoveries are always met with skepticism at first and the oqual cycle being disregarded by the trawler and its entourage of seagulls is inevitable until it becomes widely accepted with the passage of time in a stunning echo of humanity's perpetual failure to pay heed to dire lessons of history.

For example, the notion that the Earth orbits the Sun was first proposed by Copernicus in 1515 but this so-called heliocentric view of our world would draw the ire of the clergy and continued to be mocked by fools and horses over the course of the next couple of centuries during which many who dared to subscribe to such a doctrine were either vilified or charred to death.

Even the likes of Galileo, Kepler, and Newton would be reprimanded for subscribing to what was then believed to be a heretic view at odds with religion during much of the 16th and 17th centuries, and it was not until 1758 that the church finally dropped its opposition to heliocentrism and only then it would go mainstream.

Just as the heliocentric model of our world stood the test of time so will the theory of oqual cycle though none of us alive today will unfortunately be around to celebrate its homecoming-in-earnest.

In closing, the oqual cycle forecasts the following prophecies to come to fruition some time during the decade beginning with annus horribilis (2028) of the current oquannium (1955-2038) and ending with annus mirabilis (2039) of the next cycle (2039-2122) so as to herald the true spirit of a global reset:

1) **Stock Market**—Having been inflated by cheap money for more than a decade, the stock-market bubble will pop and wipe off the life-savings of decamillions in America in an echo of the 1929 crash and making the 2008 financial meltdown look like a dress rehearsal. This is necessary to purge the gunk and fraud out of the financial system that has been gathering momentum over the past several decades in order to lend humanity a fresh start on its economic front with the arrival of a new oqual cycle. The European markets will likely fare much better given that money printing had little impact on their valuations as they have largely continued to remain depressed rather than having bloated a la their counterparts on the other side of the Atlantic.

2) **Real Estate**—Having been inflated by cheap money for more than a decade, the real-estate bubble across much of the globe will come down crashing so as to bring the property values in line with the earning power of an average household. In particular, the rather bloated valuation of commercial properties will bear the brunt of the wrath of oqual cycle as it draws to a close. In the wake of the 2019 Coronavirus Pandemic, the tectonic shift to conducting personal and business affairs online in lieu of office will also eat into the demand for commercial real estate, thereby further exacerbating the pain for real-estate moguls.

3) **Bank Failures**—Due to being overleveraged with mountains of debt coupled with their fraudulent practices, thousands of zombie companies will go belly up and, in doing so, they will also put thousands of their stakeholders such as lenders and banks underwater. The mainstream propaganda continues to indoctrinate the masses that the banks are well-capitalized and that the

financial system is sound and resilient. Nothing could be further from the truth. In fact, the very argument that the banks are well-capitalized is an oxymoron in that money loaned out to businesses and consumers at any given time is multiples greater than a bank's actual worth of deposits courtesy of the so-called fractional-reserve banking. During good times, such exorbitant lending is not an issue as a booming economy pays for itself. However, during hard times as is the case across much of the globe today, most borrowers are overleveraged to the hilt, not to mention that many startups that have borrowed billions from banks only exist on paper with nothing to show for except bogus products that will never see the light of day. Once such fraudulent companies go up in smoke as they are poised to do so over the next decade due to the dire spell of oqual cycle as it nears its end, they will take what are being portrayed as sound-and-resilient banking institutions down with them too. With a number of banks having already gone belly up this year, the bank failures are not only just getting started but they will also make the fall of banking dominoes one after another during the Great Depression (1929-1939) look like a child's play. Notably, it was not the subprime mortgage per se that precipitated the 2008 Financial Crisis but rather the big banks were brought down to their knees due to being overleveraged through uber-risky and ultra-speculative derivative trading. Today, such derivative trading on the part of big banks is multiples greater and, as such, their looming failures will likely dwarf what transpired some 15 years ago. In the context of the dire spell of oqual cycle, the 2008 Financial Crisis was a dress rehearsal for what is lurking on the horizon as we inch ever closer to our day of reckoning.

4) **Social Security**—Failed socialist experiments such as America's Social Security Administration (1935) and UK National Assistance Act (1948) that vowed to take care of people from the cradle to the grave beginning almost in parallel with the arrival of the current oquannium (1955-2038) will practically become defunct and worthless in that they will be inflated away and the handouts furnished to recipients will barely pay for peanuts, much less everyday cost of living. With the welfare paychecks being handed out to people across much of the Western world having already significantly fallen behind the cost of living due to soaring inflation over the past decade or so, one can already smell the beginning of the end of social security as we have known it in our lifetime.

5) **Reserve Currency**—The USD will lose its monopoly of being the global reserve currency and make way for CNY (or CNY-in-disguise of another currency) to emerge as the new dominant player in international trade. This is hardly a brainer given that the major global currency almost always belongs to the

nation that has proven itself as the manufacturing powerhouse head-and-shoulders above its competitors as the oqual cycle draws to a close. Nevertheless, USD will remain a major player in international trade though in the shadow of CNY in a manner akin to what happened to GBP after it was dethroned by the dollar thanks to the 1944 Bretton-Woods Agreement. With the dollar no longer being the king, the standard of living in America will precipitously decline in an echo of the plight of the British after the pound lost its global luster some 84 years ago.

6) **Chinese Hegemony**—China will undergo reunification with Taiwan as it knocks America off the perch to become the new hegemon and tiktoks the new world order centered around its national interests. As China's star rises and that of America dims with each passing year, it is hard to see how such a reunification central to Chinese hegemony can be averted, particularly in light of the fact that the territorial disputes are at the center of the mayhem trigged by the oqual cycle as it reaches its crescendo. Nevertheless, United States will continue to be a major global power in a manner akin to the fact that the British influence on global affairs did not merely evaporate from the planet after Britain was dethroned some 84 years ago. Just as the legacy of the British Empire left an indelible mark on human civilization so will American imprint continue to thrive for at least generations to come across the globe.

7) **Global Warming**—The climate propaganda will largely die out as environmental focus will shift from global warming to dealing with the true culprit of overconsumption putting the health of our planet in peril. Given that the root cause of our environment teetering on the precipice of a mental collapse is the pollution caused by overconsumption rather than fossil fuels, truth rather than propaganda will ultimately prevail with the beginning of a new dawn. The rather auspicious spell of the first half (2039-2080) of the next oquannium (2039-2122) will also ensure that societal evils such as fraud and propaganda are locked up for the most part for at least several decades though they will slowly begin to re-emerge from the silos with the onset of the second half (2081-2122).

LITERATURE

1. Modelski G (1987). Long Cycles in World Politics. Palgrave Macmillan (London, England, UK).

2. Strauss W and Howe N (1997). The Fourth Turning: An American prophecy. Broadway Books (New York, New York, USA).

3. Turchin P (2016). Ages of Discord: A Structural-Demographic Analysis of American History. Beresta Books (Chaplin, Connecticut, USA).

4. Spengler O (1918). The Decline of the West. Allen & Unwin (London, England, UK).

5. Toynbee AJ (1934). A Study of History: Volumes I-XII (1934-1961). Oxford University Press (Oxford, England, UK).

6. National Aeronautics and Space Administration (2023). Space Missions: Voyager 2. https://solarsystem.nasa.gov/missions/voyager-2/in-depth.

7. Kent DV, Olsen PE, Rasmussen C, Lepre C, Mundil R, Irmis RB, Gehrels GE, Giesler D, Geissman JW, and Parker WG (2018). Empirical evidence for stability of the 405-kiloyear Jupiter-Venus eccentricity cycle over hundreds of millions of years. Proceedings of the National Academy of Sciences of the United States of America **115**, 6153-6158.

8. Killion N (2008). Life Cycles. AuthorHouse (Bloomington, Indiana, USA).

9. Strauss W and Howe N (1991). Generations: The History of America's Future. William Morrow and Company (New York, New York, USA).

10. Dalio R (2021). Principles for Dealing with the Changing World Order: Why Nations Succeed or Fail. Avid Reader Press (New York, New York, USA).

11. Kennan GF (1997). A Fateful Error. The New York Times. https://nytimes.com/1997/02/05/opinion/a-fateful-error.html.

12. Friedman TL (1998). Foreign Affairs: Now a Word From X. The New York Times. https://nytimes.com/1998/05/02/opinion/foreign-affairs-now-a-word-from-x.html.

13. Putin V (2007). The 43rd Munich Security Conference. https://russialist.org/transcript-putin-speech-and-the-following-discussion-at-the-munich-conference-on-security-policy/.

14. Tyler PE (2000). Putin Declares He Will Shun Confrontation And Isolation. The New York Times. https://nytimes.com/2000/03/06/world/putin-declares-he-will-shun-confrontation-and-isolation.html.

15. BBC Breakfast With Frost Interview: Vladimir Putin (2000). http://news.bbc.co.uk/hi/english/static/audio_video/programmes/breakfast_with_frost/transcripts/putin5.mar.txt.

16. Mishra V, Tiwari AD, Aadhar S, Shah R, Xiao M, Pai DS, and Lettenmaier D (2019). Drought and Famine in India, 1870-2016. Geophysical Research Letters **46**, 2075-2083.

17. Hamer DH (2005). The God Gene: How Faith Is Hardwired into Our Genes. Anchor Books (New York, New York, USA).

18. Farooq A (2015). Structural and Functional Diversity of Estrogen Receptor Ligands. Curr Top Med Chem **15**, 1372-1384.

19. Packard V (1960). The Waste Makers. Ig Publishing (Brooklyn, New York, USA).

20. Bernays E (1928). Propaganda. Ig Publishing (Brooklyn, New York, USA).

21. Allen FL (1931). Only Yesterday: An Informal History of the 1920s. Harper & Row (New York, New York, USA).

22. Schumpeter JA (1942). Capitalism, Socialism, and Democracy. Harper Perennial (New York, New York, USA).

23. Journal of Retailing (1955). http://ablemesh.co.uk/PDFs/journal-of-retailing1955.pdf.

24. Hess M (1862). Rome and Jerusalem: A study in Jewish Nationalism (English Translation by Meyer Waxman in 1918). Bloch Publishing Company (New York, New York, USA).

25. Fagan B (2019). The Little Ice Age: How Climate Made History 1300-1850. Basic Books (New York, New York, USA).

26. Met Office (2023). United Kingdom's National Weather Service: Historic Station Data. https://metoffice.gov.uk/research/climate/maps-and-data/historic-station-data.

27. Folland CK, Parker DE, and Kates FE (1984). Worldwide Marine Temperature-Fluctuations 1856-1981. Nature **310**, 670-673.

28. Schlesinger ME and Ramankutty N (1994). An Oscillation in the Global Climate System of Period 65-70 Years. Nature **367**, 723-726.

29. Mazzarella A and Scafetta N (2012). Evidences for a quasi 60-year North Atlantic Oscillation since 1700 and its meaning for global climate change. Theoretical and Applied Climatology **107**, 599-609.

30. Gervais F (2016). Anthropogenic CO2 warming challenged by 60-year cycle. Earth Science Reviews **155**, 129-135.

31. Monnin E, Indermuhle A, Dallenbach A, Fluckiger J, Stauffer B, Stocker TF, Raynaud D, and Barnola JM (2001). Atmospheric CO2 concentrations over the last glacial termination. Science **291**, 112-114.

32. Caillon N, Severinghaus JP, Jouzel J, Barnola JM, Kang JC, and Lipenkov VY (2003). Timing of atmospheric CO2 and Antarctic temperature changes across termination III. Science **299**, 1728-1731.

33. Pedro JB, Rasmussen SO, and van Ommen TD (2012). Tightened constraints on the time-lag between Antarctic temperature and CO2 during the last deglaciation. Climate of the Past **8**, 1213-1221.

The author is Associate Professor in the Department of Biochemistry at the University of Miami Miller School of Medicine in South Florida.

Although a biophysicist by trade with close to 100 scientific publications, Professor Farooq is best characterized as a polymath whose working knowledge transcends fields as diverse as astronomy, economy, climatology, psychology, sociology, geopolitics, linguistics, history, and religion.

Amjad Farooq

Powered by such polymathy coupled with a fearless mind renowned for pulling no punches, this book presents what is nothing short of being a Rosetta stone of human civilization to add to a breath of fresh air and candor rarely on display in today's society mired in sociopolitical upheaval.

A once-in-a-millennium book and straight from the horse's mouth, The Oqual Cycle brings about a paradigm shift in how we view the world and our own place within it and, as such, it is a must-read for everyone irrespective of their national, ethnic, political, and religious affiliation.

Human civilization waxes and wanes over a period of 84 years

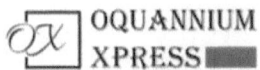
OQUANNIUM XPRESS

www.ingramcontent.com/pod-product-compliance
Lightning Source LLC
Chambersburg PA
CBHW022047160426
43198CB00008B/148